MYTHOLOGY OF THE PEOPLE OF SIKKIM

MYTHOLOGY OF THE PEOPLE OF SIKKIM

Jash Raj Subba

GYAN

NEW DELHI-110002

Mythology of the People of Sikkim

ISBN: 978-81-212-1023-2

First Published in 2009, Reprint 2017 in India by
Gyan Publishing House,
5, Ansari Road, Darya Ganj,
New Delhi-110002
Phones : 011-47034999, 9811692060
E-mail: books@gyanbooks.com
Website: www.gyanboks.com

Lasser Type Setting by: Quick Media, Delhi
Printed at : G. Print Process, Delhi

CONTENTS

PREFACE

Sikkim is a multi-racial, multilingual, multicultural, secular and democratic state of India. While studying religion and mythology of different races of Sikkim, we find different belief systems in different stages of development. Some of them are on the verge of assimilation with other developed religions, others are at the stages of extinction; and thus it is very difficult to segregate their original belief systems. No human society has yet been found in which some mythological motifs have not been rehearsed in liturgies, interpreted by seers, poets, theologians, or philosophers; presented in art; magnified in song; and ecstatically experienced in life-empowering visions.

Mythology is a miscellaneous collection of old tales and legends which embraces all of what we now call religion, science and philosophy (natural, moral and metaphysical). It asks fundamental questions – how the world began, how it will end, where humans fit in and how they can influence it, and how individuals and communities should interact. Since the questions are the same, we see common threads running through the mythologies described in this book: heavens above and nether worlds below; the critical importance of the sun, the moon and the stars; gods, heroes and monsters creating, transforming and destroying successions of nascent worlds; the sacred significance of the landscape itself, and of particular elements within it. An honest comparison of religion and mythology of the people of the world immediately reveals that all have been built from one fund of mythological motifs, variously selected, organized, interpreted, and ritualized, according to local needs, but revered by every people on earth. A fascinating psychological, as well as historical problem is thus presented.

Man, apparently, cannot remain him-self in the universe without belief in some arrangement of the general inheritance of myth. In fact, the fullness of his life would even seem to stand in a direct ratio to the depth and range not of his rational thought but of his local mythology.

The present 14 (fourteen) Himalayan tribes/races of Sikkim have been influenced by the two major oriental mythologies of Buddhism and Hinduism, and one occidental mythology of Christianity. After the first visit of *Guru Rimpoche* from *Banares* to *Dakar Tashiding,* West Sikkim on the way to Tibet during the 8th century; after migration of Tibetans with *Rigzin Godemchen* (1337-1408) at *Tashiding* area of Sikkim; after migration of more and more *Tibetans* from the north after the blood brotherhood treaty of *Khe-Bumsa* and *Thekong-Tek* during 1275 A.D.; and especially after the establishment of the Himalayan Kingdom—"The Greater Sikkim" in 1642 A.D.; and declaring Buddhism as a kingdom's official religion through the tripartite treaty of "*Lho-Mon-Tsong-Sum*" in 1666 A.D. (corrected date); Buddhism has tremendously influenced the belief systems of the *Lepchas* and the *Tsongs* (*Limboos*) the indigenous people of Sikkim. The early adoptees of Hinduism- the *Khasas* from the West on the other hand, have strongly influenced the other races/tribes of the entire Himalayan region after "the Greater Nepal Unification Process" started in 1760 A.D. (Stiller, Ludwig F. 1968). They eventually migrated to Sikkim after 1774 A.D. onwards mainly in the Western, Southern and Eastern Districts of Sikkim (Subba, J.R. 2008a). After the treaty of *Titalyia* in 1817 A.D., Sikkim came under British protectorate. Church of Scotland missionaries from Kalimpong, West Bengal started sending the *Lepcha* Christian adoptees, trained for conversion of their fellow *Lepchas* of Sikkim after 1880s (Subba, J.R. 2008a). Thus most of the indigenous people especially the *Lepchas* were converted to Christianity.

Amongst the most affected tribes or races are the *Khasas, Newars, Sunuwars, Bhujels, Thami, Majhis, Mangars,* and some

Gurungs. The tribes who adopted Buddhism leaving aside their *Bonism* long back are the *Bhutias, Tamangs, Sherpas,* and some sections of *Gurungs* and *Newars*. Partly affected by Christianity are the *Lepchas, Khambu-Rais* and *Yakhas* (Subba, J.R. 2008a; 143-157).

There are many lesser-known religions, belief systems popularly known as animist mainly by the westerners and the elite people in Sikkim. These are the ancient belief systems of different 14 (fourteen) hill tribes or races of Sikkim, namely: *Lhopo (Bhutia), Lepcha (Rong), Limboo (Tsong), Khambu-Rai, Yakha, Magar, Gurung, Sunuwar, Tamang, Sherpa, Thami, Majhi, Newar* and *Khasa* (Higher *Khasas – Bahun* and *Chettri;* Lower *Khasas - Kami, Damai* and *Sarki*) inhabiting Sikkim today. Many of these hill tribes or races have adopted many well developed religions of the world with insignificant traces of their own belief systems infused in these adopted religions now. The main aim of this work is an attempt to collect the valuable information of these lesser known "Belief Systems" or "Religions" and "Mythologies" of the different ethnic people of Sikkim for the first time for further research and development.

The first part of the book deals with the overview of the mythology of the people of Sikkim. It deals with the basic elements of mythology of the ancient myths, initiation of boys and girls, roles of shamans, reincarnation, myths and mythological functions, difference in myths and fairy tales, religion and mythology, love and marriage, transcendence, journey inward, mythology of sacrifice and bliss, mythology of eternity, mythology of death and afterlife, living beyond boundaries, the sky/*Akashik* field or *Lokas* or *Dens,* creative leaps etc. In brief, it elucidates the basics of mythological interpretations pertaining to the people of Sikkim.

The second part illustrates the overview of well developed religions and mythologies adopted by the people of Sikkim in brief namely Hinduism, Buddhism, Jainism and Sikhism in oriental mythologies, and Christianity and Islam in occidental mythologies. Plenty of literature is available on these mythologies and thus I have not dealt in detail on these mythologies. I have provided the salient features of these well developed religions and mythologies for better understanding of the subject.

The third part describes the lesser known oriental religions and mythologies of the people of the hill tribes or races of Sikkim in brief. Most of these lesser known belief systems or developing religions are in oral traditions. Systematic recording, documentation, understanding of these oral traditions, belief systems, religions and mythologies are lacking. Hence, the literature on these subjects are scanty except in the case of *Yumaism* of the Limboo tribes. I have tried my level best to collect, compile and edite the available information and have presented this work for further development in future. These lesser known oriental religions and mythologies of the people of Sikkim are:

1. *Yumaism* or *Yuma Samyo* (*Samyo* = religion) of *Tsongs/ Limboos* and *Yakhas*,
2. Animism or *Ninnammism* of the *Kirant Khambu-Rais* and *Yakhas*,
3. Animism or *Munism* and *Bongthism* of the *Lepchas*,
4. Animism of the *Mangars*,
5. Animism of the *Sunuwars*, and
6. Animism of the *Thamis*.

It is the first attempt made to study systematically both the oriental and occidental belief systems, religions and mythologies of the people of Sikkim. It is interesting to know the basic concepts underlying the belief systems, religions, gods and goddesses, origin of the universe, origin of life and destiny, afterlife and the mythologies of the people. Myths are the spiritual instructions of our ancestors. It unearths how our ancestors perceived the mysteries of God, origin of the universe, origin of life and destiny, afterlife; and tried to pass on what they experienced to the future generations in their own archaic ways.

Jash Raj Subba

ACKNOWLEDGEMENTS

I acknowledge my profound sense of gratitude to all the learned scholars, whose work I have consulted and referred to in this book. This study could not have been possible without the works of numerous scholars from whose works (as recorded in the reference), I have derived heavily, which enabled me to produce this comprehensive review on various religions and mythologies.

I acknowledge my thanks to my wife and daughters for their constant interest and cooperation.

Jash Raj Subba

PART-I

1

MYTHOLOGY OF THE PEOPLE OF SIKKIM—AN OVERVIEW

Sikkim, the 8th North-Eastern and the 22nd State of India is a state of diversity in the climate ranging from nearly tropical, sub-tropical, temperate, and alpine to snow-clad mountainous landscape; rich in both biodiversity and culture. The unexplored native peoples' lesser-known mythologies, as diverse as these landscapes; indigenous as well as influenced by the advanced mythology of the people who made inroad to this mountainous areas from outside; are briefly described in this work. The native peoples' legends reflect ways of life based variously on hunting and gathering, agriculture and fishing. Humans entered in this part of mountainous Sikkim Himalayas in antiquity as nomads (band socio-anthropological stage) during the Archaic Period of human migration (c. 38,000 – 2,500 B.C.) as hunters and gatherers in seasonal rounds. About 10,000 years ago, some woman folk of these people had discovered how to domesticate some of the wild plants they gathered and rear some of the wild animals around them. Tending these involved settling in one place also. The mountainous environment being harsh, remote, impenetrable and infertile to support the increasing populations, the inhabitants continued hunting and gathering, fishing, along with agriculture in small plots near their camps or villages or tend animals for a long, long time. With the increase of population societies were evolved, cultures evolved steadily from nomad groups, natural spirituality focused on earth and sky evolved belief systems as well as religions evolved in due course of time (Diamond, J. 1997; Subba, J.R. 2008a).

Yet each of these diverse cultures and social groups had one thing in common: the need for a mythology to explain not only the vastness and power of the cosmos and the wonders of nature, but also the mysteries of the human mind, with its desires, its fears and its capacities for good and evil, creation and destruction, and selfishness and altruism. The need of mythology was felt necessary probably not at the socio-anthropological category stage of *"Band"* but when the bands developed into a *"Tribal"* stages of human evolution due to increase of population and settlement of the people for agriculture. The need of mythology might have further intensified with more and more dependence on agriculture and limited availability of hunting animals and wild plants for food. This has lead to offering the newly harvested crops to the gods and goddesses for bumper harvest in the next season. Thus, the rituals evolved, myths evolved, belief system evolved, religions evolved and developed the mythology of the people of Sikkim in the process of evolution of modern society in its own primitive ways.

No human society has yet been found in which some mythological motifs have not been rehearsed in liturgies, interpreted by seers, poets, theologians, or philosophers; presented in art; magnified in song; and ecstatically experienced in life-empowering visions. Every people have received its own seal and sign of supernatural designation, communicated to its heroes and daily proved in the lives and experience of its folk. And though many who bow with closed eyes in the sanctuaries of their own tradition rationally scrutinize and disqualify the sacraments of others. However, an honest comparison immediately reveals that all have been built from one fund of mythological motifs, variously selected organized, interpreted, and ritualized, according to local needs, but revered by every people on earth. A fascinating psychological, as well as historical problem is thus presented. Man, apparently, cannot remain him-self in the universe without belief in some arrangement of the general inheritance of myth. In fact, the fullness of his life would even seem to stand in a direct ratio to the depth and range not of his rational thought but of his local mythology.

Mythology is not just a miscellaneous collection of old tales and legends. It embraces all of what we now call religion, science and philosophy (natural, moral and metaphysical). It asks fundamental questions – how the world began, how it will end, where humans fit in and how they can influence it, and how individuals and communities should interact. Since the questions are the same, we see common threads running through the mythologies described here: heavens above and nether worlds below; the critical importance of the sun, the moon and the stars; gods, heroes and monsters creating, transforming and destroying successions of nascent worlds; the sacred significance of the landscape itself, and of particular elements within it.

Even so, answers to these questions vary with the societies in general and in Sikkim particular that ask them, depending on their habitat landscapes, ways of livelihood and thinking, influence from their neighborhood etc. People of all cultures define the world as they experience it, so their mythologies must account for what they see. Every part of a landscape of the Himalayas has the potential for spiritual identity. This is often literal: high mountain peaks or places are close to the sky and the remote gods; big stone or huge rocks or a big tree or dense forest, big lakes or snowy glacier lakes or caves provide entry into the earth and hidden spiritual forces. All material things have spiritual potential – from egg-yoke to blood bubble sacrificed during their religious rituals. This mythological age is not lost in the deep past defined by science, for aboriginal concepts of time are both linear and cylindrical: linear as the steps and stages of a human life, and cylindrical as the generations that renew all life and the earth itself. This endless spiral means that the past never recedes into the distance; even the time of creation is only just beyond the reach of the myth-chanter. The mythological narratives of a culture are thus an eternal present, renewing social identity with every telling. These mythologies are in practice in every society in Sikkim, participated through religious rituals even today whether it is a *Lepcha, Limboo, Khambu-Rai, Sunuwar, Lhopo, Gurung, Tamang, Mangar,* or *Khasa* society.

A human life is so brief that the face of the earth seems absolute and unchanging. No living being has seen the billions of years of tectonic shifts, overwhelming seas and ice ages that have scarred the land, so the idea of a decaying world is almost unimaginable. Someone with superhuman power must have made the rivers, as we might trace a line in the sand. And someone must have given us the gifts of nature that we use to sustain our lives. In aboriginal thought, the time when powerful beings transformed creation's dark, empty lands into the familiar, sheltering earth is only just out of reach of memory. Life at that time was fluid. Those first ancestors shifted and changed form at will between humans, animals and objects as they carried out their formative tasks – bringing daylight and fire, hewing out the shape of the land and creating the stuff of cultural life.

The *Akasha*, the sky, *Tangsang Den* or the atmospheric layer around the Mother Earth must be the realm of gods and goddesses. The horizons may be the meeting place to the gods and goddesses by the mortal human beings – as it is believed in *Ninnammism* of *Khambu-Rais* and in *Limboos*. Beyond the horizons in the west, the evil powers such as *Sogha* or *Sugut* may reside; beyond the horizons in the East, the gods and goddesses may reside; beyond the horizons in the south, the terrifying demons may reside; while beyond the horizons in the north, boon bestowing powerful gods and goddesses may reside as in the believe system of *Yuma* religion. Well beyond the reach of even the highest mountains, the greatest powers reside there – light and darkness, the changing seasons, furious storms and life-giving rains; and it is the source of many creations. Some remote creators used the dark cosmos as a staging ground for their work, but in most narratives the sky (*Akasha/Lokas/Tangsang Den*) was a world with its own physical and social dimensions, not an airless void. Many mythologies divide this into several layers and their supernatural gods and goddesses rule these layers as seen in *Yumaism* (nine layers above the earth inclusive and nine layers inside the earth = 18 layers or *Dens*); as in the case of *Maya* mythology (13 layers above the earth and 7 layers inside the earth = 20 layers) etc. In many mythologies the earth has to be created for the living beings or especially for the human beings as in the case of *Yumaism*, for instance. The heavens may also be a final resting place for supernatural beings, Gods, Goddesses, departed souls – forefathers etc. The sky is crucial to cultural identity, because it defines the land and sets the rhythm of the world. The cycles of the sun, the moon and the stars evoke a sense of time, marking the passage of human lives. As a measure of space and time, the sky therefore unites the mythical and the actual in an eternal flow of darkness and light.

The heroic events of creation and transformation do not depend only on the recollection of ancient myths or traditions. They live on in the shape of the land itself: every towering mountains or twist in a river records the acts of the culture heroes who changed the earth as they lived on it, as in the *Lepcha* myths for instance. In some places, the marks of creation are still fresh. Since aboriginal people like *Lepchas* and *Limboos* and many others of this part of the Himalaya intertwine oral tradition and geography in their way, they still have a spiritual hold on their lost lands, a bond that they can verify and renew as long as those lands exist. The *Lepchas* believe that their progenitors were created by the God (*Rum*) out of the untrodden snow of Mount *Pundim* (Mt. Pandim) one of the five important peaks of Kanchenjunga. Similarly, the *Limboos* believe that their progenitors were created by the creator God (*Sigera Yabhundin Mang Porokmi Wambhami Mang*) out of the biomass of bamboo ash, fowl's excreta and rainwater at Mount Jannu (Mt. *Phoktanglungma Pembenlungma/ Kumbhakarna*) one of the five important peaks of Mt. Kanchanjunga. The aboriginal tribes *Lepchas* and *Limboos* believe that the earth is infused with spiritual energy. When supernatural beings shaped the lands during the age of transformation, all material things had the potential to live as humans and animals do. Because of this legacy, aboriginal thinkers see the earth as a living spiritual realm where supernatural beings still reside. Every territory of the land, the mountain peaks, rivers, streams, springs, trees, rocks and stones, forests, lakes, glaciers, has its special places of spirit dwellings of deities, divinities and retinue of divinities. High mountains and prominent rock formations, caves and crevices, waterfalls and springs are all spirit dwellings. Whether the earthly spirits live, ever watchful, above the land or are hidden away to be suddenly encountered on a path or waterway, they always remain powerful, even dangerous, in their abodes.

Monsters exist in every mythology to give shape and meaning to the unknown, the dangerous and the unwanted. Many mythologies like the *Lepcha* and *Limboo* myths describe how, when the earth was a still young, terrible creature raged across the land, threatening the fragile harmony of human and animal beings in the world. By the act of destroying these monsters, supernatural beings created the heroic, defined the limits of good and evil, and established supernatural power as an overwhelming force. But, while cosmic beasts disappeared, other dangerous creatures retreated only to the margins of the world, lurking just beyond familiar horizons, in the darkness or deep under water. Some of these are fearsome apparitions and the stuff of nightmare: bodiless heads or hideously deformed animals. These positive or negative acts are acknowledgement of life's dark side resolves the fundamental contradiction of nature – that it is at one time both a nurturing and a destructive force. Yet humans must always face the tension between appropriate and inappropriate thoughts and actions, reflecting the vagaries of a natural world that both sustains life and takes it. Mirroring this reality, transformers and cultural heroes were quixotically human, with the same lusts, desires and foibles as the people they would create. The *Lepchas* believe that their lord *Tamsangthing* arrived at *Tarkaol Tam-E-Tam* from *Pundim Chu* (i.e. river originating from mount Pandim) to deliver the *Lepchas* from the clutches of the demon king - *Laso Mun Panu*. He rejuvenated their moral strength and gave them supernatural powers to protect thyself through *Munism* and *Bongthingism* (*Pademism*). Similarly, the *Limboos* believe that their Demi-God *Sodhung Lepmumang* (*progenitor/father*) sent various types of *Phedangmas* (nine types) to protect the *Limboo* forefathers from the evil spirits and conduct offering of newly harvested crops to gods and goddesses for bumper harvest in the next season.

Death is not absolute in a world where nothing is inanimate, and time does not retreat endlessly into extinction; people withdrew from bodily existence, just as the culture-heroes did after the age of transformation. Those supernatural beings were responsible for the fact of death, usually because of some heroic failing. The path of the dead may lead into an underworld, into a remote land beyond the horizon, or into the sky. Most cultures hope that it will be a place of physical and spiritual ease. The indigenous belief systems or religions of the people of Sikkim believe that the soul never dies after one's physical death. The soul invariably originated from the center of origin some where in the *Akashic* field and entered in the physical body on earth. The soul is the property of ancestor deity or God or Goddess residing in the *Akashic* field. Thus, the soul of the deceased individual has to go or reached or accompany soul journey by the religious shaman priests to the *Akashic* field and handover it to the ancestor deity or indirectly to the Almighty God or Goddess, as in the case of *Yumaism* or *Munism*, for instance.

With migration of people in Sikkim from all the directions with the adopted developed mythologies of Buddhism (8th or 13th century onwards), Hinduism (1774 A.D. onwards), Christianity (1880 A.D. onwards), Jainism (1900 A.D. onwards), Islam and Sikhism (1975 A.D. onwards) etc., the hill tribes/races no longer intertwined only with their own earth and sky. The natives of the land listened and learned – sometimes avidly, but more often helplessly – about a single god or trinity gods and a morality fashioned on a distant continent. In some places they were also prey to conflicting ideas, as missionaries of different faiths competed for converts. Some groups resisted by creating new narratives to counter the new mythological teachings. Some adopted, embraced within their mythologies. Others attempted to avoid the total loss of their mythologies by appropriating (Subba, J.R. 2008a:143-157).

For example: during my study period, I met an old *Lepcha* gentleman at *Mangan*, North Sikkim. While discussing about the origin and destination of souls of the deceased, the *Lepcha* gentleman expressed his feelings about it. "I am supposed to leave this world shortly now, but frankly speaking I am totally confused about my destination. In the beginning I was a believer in *Munism* and my destination was *Rumlyang* (ancestor's world). Now, most of the people in the society have adopted Buddhism, and they talk about six worlds. I am confused which world I am supposed to leave. I do not know my destination as yet. Further, a good chunk of my society, are Christians now, and they talk about the spiritual body and soul leaving for heaven only after second coming of Jesus. I am confused what will happen if Jesus fails to come again. Thus, I am totally confused about my destination in my old age now." Similarly, I met an old gentleman who retired from Sikkim Government long back. While discussing about the origin and destination of soul he also found himself in utter confusion. He said "During my early ages I was a believer of so many faiths. I never bothered about my own belief system. I was Hindu during October at the time of *Dushehra-Diwali* festival and Christian during December for

Christmas celebration. I never thought about the origin and destination of soul after my demise. But now after my retirement, I started thinking about my destination. I am confused about my destination. I do not know where I am leaving after my death. This has been a very painful period for me now. I do not know about my destination as per my society's belief system. We never bothered for its study which was so essential".

In the mountains of Sikkim the voices of the gods spoke from the wind and thunder, and the spirit of God flowed in every mountain streams, tributaries of Teesta and Rangit, *Hee Khola, Keng Khola*, other streams and the whole state bloomed from the main five peaks of Kanchendzonga to the point where the Teesta and Rangit meet and joins the Brahmaputra River (*Tusroti Umroti* in *Limboo*) as a sacred place, the realm of mythic imagination. The modern men have yet to strip off the state of its mystery, a housecleaning of belief and still continue to nourish our imaginations. We are all seeking a meaning of life, an experience of being alive, so that our life experiences on the purely physical plane will have resonance within our own innermost being and reality, so that we actually feel the rapture/ecstasy of being alive. We are so engaged in doing things to achieve purposes of outer value that we forget that the inner value, the rapture that associated with being alive.

In the modern world, we dropped the literature of the magnificent human heritage we have in our great tradition of Plato, Confucius, the Buddha, Goethe, Guru Rimpoche, *Phedangmas, Muns* and *Bongthings, Mangpas, Dhami/Jhankri* and others who speak of the eternal values that have to do with the centering of our lives from the modern education curriculum. Now, a whole tradition of oriental and occidental mythological information has been lost in part or whole in the modern societies of the world. It used to be that these mythical stories were in the minds of people. These bits of information from ancient times, which have to do with the themes that have supported human life, built civilizations, and informed religions over the millennia, have to do with deep inner problems, inner mysteries, inner thresholds of passage, and if you don't know what the guide-signs are along the way, you have to work it out yourself. But once their subject catches you, there is such a feeling, from one or another of these traditions, of information of a deep, rich, life-vivifying sort that you don't want to give it up (Campbell. Joseph 1959; 1962; 1964; 1968; 1988; Jones, D. M. and Molyneaux, B.L. 2001: 10-249; Subba, J.R. 2005a; Chopra, Deepak. 2006).

Ancient Myths

The ancient myths were designed to harmonize the mind and the body. The mind can ramble off (move without any aim) in strange ways and want things that the body does not want. The myths and rites were means of putting the mind in accord with the body and the way of life in accord with the way that nature dictates. The ancient myths live in us as Archetype Memories – as certified by the famous psychologist Jung, C. G. (1875-1961). The stages of human development are the same today as they were in the ancient times. As a child, you are brought up in a world of discipline, of obedience, and you are dependent on others. All this has to be transcended when you come to maturity, so that you can live not in dependency but with self-responsible authority. If you cannot cross that threshold, you have the basis for neuroses. Then, comes the one after you have gained your world, the crisis of dismissal, disengagement, and ultimately death. That is the ultimate disengagement. So myth has to serve both aims, that of inducting the young person into the life of his world – that is the function of the folk idea, then disengaging him. The folk idea unsells the elementary idea, which guides you to your own inward life.

The tradition in Sikkim as in any one place of India, for instance, of actually changing your whole way of dress, even changing your name, as you pass from one stage to another. When one retires from a job, as I am today, he knows that he had to create a new way of life, and he changes his manner of thinking about his life, just in terms of that notion, moving out of the sphere of achievement into the sphere of enjoyment and appreciation and relaxing to the wonder of it all. The Buddhist incarnate Rimpuchies of Sikkim have a very good tradition of writing their life experiences before they descend from this physical world. This serves the Buddhist societies to remain ever updated the spiritual experiences of this physical consciousness. Similarly, many retiree of the Sikkim Governments have also started writing their memoirs, Sri K. B. Limboo, Ex-Minister SPWD in 2000; Sri K. C. Pradhan in 2008, for instance.

In *Yuma* religion of Sikkim, 18 (eighteen) stages of life are recognized. Each stage is well defined right from the day of conception in the mother's womb to the death of the individual and each stage of life has to pass on a series of life-styles; observe a series of live rituals. Death is no problem at all. The problem is in middle life, when the body has reached its climax of power and begins to decline as I am today, is to identify yourself not with the body, which is falling away, but with the consciousness of which it is a vehicle. This is something one has to learn from myths. What am I? Am I just a body that carries the consciousness (soul), or am I the consciousness (soul) of which the body is a vehicle? One of the psychological problems in growing old is the fear of death. But this body is a vehicle of consciousness, and if you can identify with the consciousness, you can watch the body go like an old car. There goes the fender, there goes the tire, one thing after another, but its' predictable. And then, gradually, the whole thing drops off, and consciousness rejoins consciousness. It is no longer in this particular environment. So these myths have to say about growing old.

In *Yuma* religion, while conducting the rituals of "*Sam Samma*", "*Samchamma*" and "*Sitongsing khema*", the *Phedangma* repeatedly addresses to the soul of the dead in the myth that "You have done nothing wrong, this is the way of life and death. One who comes to this physical consciousness with the body in the temporal world has to go like this only. Now you are shading your physical consciousness or the body here in this temporal world and leaving with the spiritual consciousness and joining your origin or your forefathers at *Sangram Pedang Den* in the village of your ancestors. This is for the last time you are being fed by your family members and close relatives in this physical word. Now onwards, they will not be able to feed you. You will not be dinning together now onwards. They will not be with you; you have to travel with us in the soul journey in the *Akashic* field to *Sam Yukna Den*. Please take the food, drinks etc. offered by your family members, relatives etc. now. After this you will be leaving etc. etc...."

The earliest evidence of anything like mythological thinking is associated with graves. They suggest that men and women saw life, and then they didn't see it, so they wondered about it. The grave burials with their weapons and sacrifices to ensure, a continued life, these certainly suggest that there was a person who was alive and warm before you who is now lying there, cold, and beginning to rot. Something was there, that is not here. Where is it now? The modern man evolved about 50,000 years ago. The humans discovered death when they were first humans, because they died. Now, animals have the experience of watching their companions dying. But, as far as we know, they have no further thoughts about it. And there is no evidence that humans thought about death in a significant way until the Neanderthal period (between 130,000 and 40,000 years ago), when weapons and animal sacrifices occur with burials (Subba, J.R. 2008b: 23-26). In the absence of any physical anthropological study in Sikkim so far, we have no evidence of ancient thought about death by humans in Sikkim as yet. However, every society has their own system of burial in the specific places preserved in many places even today. For instance, burial places like *Yeebung* of the *Limboos*, is very prominent, burial place of the *Lepchas, Khambu-Rais* around their households etc. except crematory systems of *Khasas* and Buddhists. These burial places of Sikkim could be explored through physical anthropological study in the days to come for more and more information.

Burials always involve the idea of the continued life beyond the visible one, of a plane of being that is behind the visible plane, and that is somehow supportive of the visible one to which we have to relate. That is the basic theme of all mythology - that there is an invisible plane supporting the visible one. This idea of invisible support is connected with one's society, too. Society was there before you, it will be there after you are gone, and you are a member of it. The myths that link you to your social group, the tribal/racial myths, affirm that you are an organ of the larger organism. Society itself is an organ of a larger organism, which is the landscape, the world in which the tribe moves. The main theme in ritual is the linking of the individual to a longer morphological structure than that of his/her own physical body. The mystery of death balances the theme of the mystery of life. It is the same mystery in its two aspects. The next theme is the relationship of this to the animal world, which dies and lives again.

Man lives by killing, and there is a sense of guilt connected with that. Burial, suggest that my friend has died, and he survives. The animals that I have killed must also survive. Early hunters usually had a kind of animal divinity – the technical name would be the animal master (*Pung Sam* in *Yuma* religion, *Pong-rum* in *Lepcha* and so on), the animal who is the master animal. The *Limboo* hunter offers the hunted viscera, ear tips, toe tips etc. to the master spirit of the animals after the prey is killed, and prays for good future hunting. If it is not done, he will not be successful for hunting in future. Others believe that if the preyed is left overnight as such, the animal master comes at night and make it alive and take away. If the animal master is pleased, it sends the flocks to be killed, Lepcha's *Pong-rum* worship, for instance. Thus, the basic hunting myth is of a kind of covenant between the animal world and the human world. The animal gives its life willingly, with the understanding that its life transcends its physical entity and will be returned to the soil or to the mother through some ritual of restoration. So in the early hunting societies there grew up between human beings and animals a bonding that required one to be consumed by the other. *Yuma* religion believes that every living being (plants and animals) was created for the survival of the human beings by the creator god *Sigera Yabhundin Mang Porokmi Wambhami Mang*. That is the way of life is. Man is a hunter, and the hunter is a beast of prey. In the myths, the beast of prey and the animal that is preyed upon play two significant roles. They represent two aspects of life – the aggressive killing, conquering, creating aspects of life, and the one that is the matter or you might say the subject matter. Hunting and killing is not simply slaughter, it is a ritual act, as eating is when you say grace between meals. A ritual act is recognition of your dependency on the voluntary giving of this food to you by the animal that has given its life. The hunt is a ritual and a ritual expresses a spiritual reality. The early myths help the psyche to participate without a sense of guilt or fright in the necessary act of life. The myths constantly refer to the dynamic in one way or the other – the hunt, the hunter, the hunted, and the animal as friend, as a messenger from God. Guilt is wiped out by the myth. killing the animal is not a personal act. You are performing the work of nature.

The animal has powers that the human doesn't have. For example, the *Phedangma* shaman priests in *Yuma* religion invariably have some animal spirits known as *Sam Sire* as their master spirits to perform the various shamanic functions of divination, control and healing of sickness, etc.

The Eastern relationship to animals is in contrast to the Western relationship to animals, where the Westerns see animals as a lower form of life. In the Bible the Westerns are told that we are the matters. The aboriginal *Lepchas* and *Limboos* of Sikkim believe that, "In the beginning of all things, wisdom and knowledge were with the animals. God did not speak directly to man. He sent certain animals to tell mankind that he showed himself through the beast. And that from them, and from the star and the Sun and the Mon, man should learn." The *Lepchas* believe that the God sent the birds to tell the humans when to sow the crop seeds brought from the God's land for cultivation.

Any worship place say a "*Mangkhim*" in *Yum* religion, a *Gompa* of Buddhists, a *Mandhir* of Hindus, a *Samkhalung* of Khambu-Rais is a landscape of the soul. When you walk into it, you move into a world of spiritual images. It is the mother womb of your spiritual life. All the forms around are significant of spiritual value. The imagery is in anthropomorphic form. The spiritual message is of a relationship of time to eternal powers that is somehow to be expressed in that place.

Initiation of Boys and Girls

The ancient caves speculate that they had to do with the initiation of boys into the hunt. Boys had to learn not only to hunt but how to respect the animals, and what rituals to perform, and how in their own lives no longer to be little boys but to be men. Those hunts you see were very, very dangerous. These caves are the original men's rite sanctuaries where the boys became no longer their mother's sons but their father's sons. Most of the figures in the ancient caves are male. We don't know exactly what happened to the female in this period because there is very little evidence to tell us.

But in primary cultures today the girl becomes a woman with her first menstruation. It happens to her. Nature does it to her. And so she has undergone the transformation, and what is her initiation? Typically it is to sit in a little hut for a certain number of days in the case of Hinduism (*Khasas* and *Newars*), and realize what she is. She is now a woman. A woman is a vehicle of life. Life has overtaken her. Woman is what it is all about – the giving of birth and giving of nourishment. She is identical with the earth goddess in her powers, and she has got to realize that about herself. The boy does not have a happening of this kind, so he has to be turned into a man and voluntarily become a servant of something greater than himself. In the ancient world human beings helped their sons for this transformation through the art of hunting.

So far as the mythology of the people of Sikkim is concerned there are myths in *Yumaism* of the *Limbboos*, *Ninnammism* of *Khambu-Rais*, *Munism* of *Lepchas*, explaining how nature initiates the girls for motherhood in nature. There is a beautiful myths of *Mujina Kheyongnama, Thosulungma Phiyamlungma, Yosulungma Mukkumlungma, Sisari Phandarima, Sadilli Dillihangma* etc. in *Yumaism*, how the girl-child was transformed into motherhood in nature, psychological feelings and desire of sex for reproduction, psychological feelings of the pregnant women, child nourishment etc. The myths also explain how the boys have no such transformation mechanism in nature and has to be taught by their mothers and elders for livelihood and attaining adulthood. *Mujina Kheyongnama* – the mother taught her son *Susuwangba Lalawengba* to become a bread earner or adult hunter known as *Sawa Yukphung Kemba*. Similarly, in the myth of *Munism* of *Lepchas*, how *Itpomu* and her husband *Komsithing* teach their son *Tarbong-bo* to become an adult and get married to the young girl who loved. Similarly, in the myth of *Khambu-Rais* how *Nakchong Susuli* was trained in bow-arrow and sward fighting by *Paruhang*; and *Lekpa* was trained for fighting by *Sumnima*. In the present world, it is the observance of the rituals where the young boys are encouraged to participate in the life rituals and ask them killing of sacrificial animals. In the process, the young boys are slowly helped in the transformation of boyhood to manhood, and also prepared for bread earning role for the family.

Then there is the motif of procuring food. The relationship of woman to the nature of the outer world is there. The women have to take into account the problem of the transformation of children into adults. That transformation is a fundamental concern throughout the ritual life of people. The people respond to the environment but the myth must be kept alive. The people who can keep it alive are artists of one kind or another. The function of the artist is the mythologization of the environment and the world. In the case of Sikkim, the religious shaman priests of different ethnic groups retained and kept alive the myths and mythology to this day.

The Woman is Life and the Man is the Servant of Life

The woman is life, and the man is the servant of life. The Woman has to produce life and nourish. She nourishes the growing fetus in the womb for ten months; nourish through breast-feeding and foods after the birth. She provides continuity of life generation after generation. The man is just a servant to the producer of life. Provide service through copulation; feed the family including her wife by hunting and gathering or cultivation or through other means of bread earning. The man is just like pollen of a flower. He goes on pollinating flower after flower that is it. He provides service to the female that is all. This is evident from the myth of *Sutchhuru Suhangpheba* (later as *Sodhung Lepmuhang*), who stays away from the family of *Sawa Yethangs* some where in the *Akashic* field *"Muringla Kharingla Tembhe"* in *Yumaism*. It is the mother *"Tetlara Lahadongna"* who looks after the sons on earth *"Sagarek Nugarek Tembhe"*. Similarly, *Komsithing* left for the *Akashic* field and the mother *"Itpomu"* who has to look after their progenies in *Munism* of *Lepchas*. In *Ninnammism* of *Khambu-Rais*, the father *Paruhang* stays away in the *Akashic* field and the mother *Sumnima* has to look after their progenies on earth. Thus, the man is always on the pollen-path looking for copulation or spread of pollens on the female flowers. They just provide service to the females. It is the mother, who has to look after her progeny, nourish them, trained them and gives them life on earth.

Shamans in Mythology

Shamans perform most of the rituals through ecstasy. In ecstasy one man or woman shaman suddenly experiences what we might call a possession. It is described as a flash, a kind of thunderbolt or lightening bolt, which passes from the pelvic area right up the spine into the head. And the one whose psychological experience, this traumatic experience, this ecstasy, would become the interpreter for others of things not seen. He or she would become the interpreter of the heritage of mythological life, for example, Black Elk, *Phedangma* in *Yuma* religion, *Mun* and *Bongthing* in animist *Lepchas*, *Mangpa* or *Bijuwa* of *Ninnammism* etc. The deities, who have been encountered powers, call them "*Sam Sire*" or "departed soul or consciousness of the dead" or "nature divinities" are retained throughout their lifetime. The connection is maintained, not broken. And these men or women then become the spiritual advisors and gift-givers to their people. So far as Sikkim is concerned, the religious shaman priests of different communities are the reservoirs of ancient myths, rituals and guides of the society. They are also the mediums for transfer of these oral traditions from generation to generations.

Myth and Mythology

The dictionary definition of a myth would be stories about gods. So then you have to ask the next question: What is God? A god is a personification of a motivating power or a value system that functions in human life and in the universe; the powers of your own body and of nature. *Myth* is an idea, and *Mythology* is the vehicle of that idea. The myths are metaphorical of spiritual potentiality in the human beings, and the same powers that animate our life animate the life of the world. But also there are myths and gods that have to do with specific societies or the patron deities of the society. In other words, there are two totally different orders of mythology. There is a mythology that relates you to your nature and to the natural world, of which you are a part, and it is called *Natural Mythology*. And there is the mythology that is strictly sociological, linking you to a particular society, and it is called *Social Mythology*. You are not simply a natural man; you are a member of a particular group or society. The nature-oriented mythology would be of an earth-cultivating people. The social-oriented system is of a nomadic people who are moving around, so you learn that is where your center is, in that group or society.

Myths are stories of our search through the ages for truth, for meaning, for significance. We all need to tell our story and to understand own story. We all need to understand death and to cope with death and we all need help in our passages from birth to life and then to death. We need for life to signify, to touch the eternal to understand the mysteries, to find out who we are. If you read your own religion, you tend to interpret your own religion in terms of facts, but if you read the other ones, you begin to get the message of the symbols. Myth helps you to put your mind in touch with this experience of being alive. It tells you what the experience is.

The mythological stories are the stories about the *wisdom of life.* What we are learning in our schools is not the wisdom of life. We are learning technologies and we are getting information. Mythology teaches you what is behind literature and the arts, it teaches you about your own life. It is a great, exciting, life-nourishing subject. Mythology has a great deal to do with the stages of life, the initiation ceremonies (womb worship, child naming etc.), as you move from childhood to adult responsibilities, from the unmarried state into the married state (marriage). All of these rituals are mythological rites. They have to do with your recognition of the new role that you are in, the process of throwing off the old one and carrying out in the new, and entering into a responsible profession.

Myth is essentially a cultural construct, a common religious or secular understanding of the world that binds individuals and communities together. Ideas such as rebirth, heaven and hell, angels and demons, fate and freewill, sin, Satan and salvation are religious myths. Ideas such as sovereignty, nation state, human rights, women's rights and animal rights are secular myths. Religious or secular, all myths make profound sense to one group of people. Mythology constitutes stories, symbols and rituals that make a myth tangible. The myth stories, symbols and rituals are essentially languages that are heard, seen and performed. Together they constitute the truths of a culture. From myth *come beliefs,* from *mythology customs.* Myth conditions thoughts and feelings. Mythology influences behaviours and communications. Myth and mythology thus have a profound influence on culture.

Many experts have defined myth and mythology in various ways. Myth is the foundation of life, the timeless scheme, the pious formula into which life flows when it reproduces its traits out of the unconscious. Many ethnologist, archaeologist, or historian would observe, the myths of the differing civilizations have sensibly varied throughout the centuries and broad reaches of mankind's residence in the world, indeed to search a degree that the "virtue" of one mythology has often been the "vice" of another, and the heaven of one the other's hell. The secret cause of all suffering is mortality itself, which is the prime condition of life. It cannot be denied if life is to be affirmed. Human suffering is a principal theme of classic mythology. The only true wisdom lives far from mankind, out in the great loneliness, and can be reached only through suffering. Privation and suffering alone open the mind that is hidden to others (Campbell, J. 1988:3-36).

Mythology is the song, as the *Phedangmas* or *Mangpas* sing the oral traditions of myth during religious rituals. It is the song of the imagination, inspired by the energies of the body. The main motifs of the myths are the same, and they have always been the same. If you find your own mythology, the key is with what society has grown up in a certain society you associate or belong to. Every mythology has grown up in a certain society in a bounded field. Then they come into collision and relationship, and they amalgamate, and you get a more complex mythology as we experience in Sikkim today.

Mythology in the modern opinion may be irrelevant to the human condition today. The mythological stuff is that the remnants of all that "gods and stuff" line the walls of our interior system of belief, like shards of broken pottery in an archaeological site, often found on the soils at *Daramdin*, West Sikkim. But as we are organic beings, there is energy in all that stuff. Rituals evoke it. It is not to identify oneself with any of the figures or powers experienced. The Indian *Yogi*, striving for release, identifies himself with the Light and never returns. But no one with a will to the service of others would permit himself such an escape. The ultimate aim of the quest must be neither release nor ecstasy for oneself, but the wisdom and the power to serve others as it is understood from the lives of the religious shaman priests of *Limboos, Lepchas, Khambu-Rais* etc. of Sikkim.

While talking to people about belief, they reveal the radiance of their own discovery. They reveal a joy for learning and living, to know the best that is known and thought in the world, and by in its turn making this known, to create a current of true and fresh ideas. Mythology is an interior road map of experience, drawn by people who have traveled it. It is the song of the universe, the music of the spheres, music we dance to even when we cannot name the tune. We are hearing its refrains whether we listen to the myths (*Mundhums*) of *Yumaism* or of *Khambu-Rai, Mukudum* of *Sunuwar* or *Munthem* of *Lepchas*. This grand and cacophonous chorus began when our primal ancestors told stories to themselves about the animals that they killed for food and about the supernatural world to which the animals seemed to go when they died. Out there somewhere, beyond the visible plain of existence, was the animal master (*Pong-sam* or *Pong-rum* etc.), who held over human beings the power of life and death; if he failed to send the beasts back to be sacrificed again, the hunter and their kin would starve. Thus early societies learned *"the essence of life is that it lives by killing and eating;"* that is the great mystery that the myths have to deal with. The hunt became a ritual of sacrifice, and the hunter in turn performed acts of atonement to the departed spirits of the animals, hopping to coax them into returning to be sacrificed again. The beasts were seen as envoys from that other world, a magical, wonderful accord growing between the hunter and the hunted since 2.5 million with invention of stone tools by our ancestors (*Homo habilis*), as if they were locked in a mystical, timeless cycle of death, burial, and resurrection (Subba, J.R. 2008b). Their art, the painting on cave walls, *Mundhums* of *Yumaism* or *Ninnammism* or *Munthem* of *Munism* and fairy tales gave form to the impulse we now call religion.

As these primal folk turned from hunting-gathering to domestication and planting, about 10,000 years ago by the modern thinking man evolved about 50,000 years ago, the stories they told to interpret the mysteries of life changed, too. Now the seed became the magic symbol of the endless cycle. The plant died, and was buried, and its seed was born again. This symbol was seized upon by the world's great religions as the revelation of eternal truth, that from death comes life, or as "From sacrifice, to bliss" (Subba, J.R. 2008b).

As Jesus said, "unless a grain of wheat falls into the earth and dies, it remains alone; but if dies, it bears much fruit." In the *Quoran* "Do you think that you shall enter the Garden of Bliss without such trials as came to those who passed away before you?" Once a troubled woman who came to the Indian saint saying, "O Master, I do not find that I love God." And the saint asked, Is there nothing, then, that you are?" To this she answered, "My little nephew." And he said to her, "There are your love and service to God, in your love and service to that child."

The images of God are many, calling them, "the masks of eternity" that both come and reveal "the face of Glory." God assumes such different masks in different cultures, yet comparable stories can be found in these divergent traditions, stories of creation, of virgin births, incarnations, death and resurrection, second coming, and judgment days. Truth is one; the sages call it by many names." All our names and images for God are masks signifying the ultimate reality there by definition transcend languages and art. A myth is a mask of God, too – a metaphor for what lies behind the mystic traditions differ; they are in accord in calling us to a deeper awareness of the very act of living itself. Freud and Jung both the famous psychologists felt that myth is grounded in the unconscious (Campbell, Joseph 1959; 1962; 1964; 1968; 1988: 3-36).

Rituals are Enactments of Myths

Ritual is group participation in the most hideous act, which is the act of life-namely killing and eating another living thing. We do it together, and this is the way life is. Myth relates directly to ceremony and tribal ritual and *the absence of myth can mean the end of ritual. A ritual is the enactment of a myth.* By participating in a ritual, you are participating in a myth. The early elementary culture comes out of an elite experience, the shamans (*Phedangmas* in *Yuma* religion, *Mun* and *Bongthing* in *Lepchas*, and *Dhami* or *Jhankri* of *Khasas*, *Mangba* or *Bijuwa* shamans of *Ninnamnism*), the experience of people particularly gifted, whose ears are open to the song of the universe. The shaman is a person male or female, who in his late childhood or early youth has an overwhelming psychological experience or enlightens soul of the dead (spiritual conscious), visits and stays throughout his or her lifetime that turns him totally inward. It is a kind of schizophrenic crackup. The whole unconscious opens up, and the shaman falls into it. This shaman experience has been described many, many times. It occurs all the way from Siberia right through the Americas to Tierra del Fuego. And the trance dance ecstasy is part of it. In every society, these shaman priests (Buddhist *lamas, Bahun* priests, *Phedangma* or *Bijuwa* or *Mun* etc.) conduct the ritual enactments of myths of their societies in their own way.

Fairy Tales

Fairy tales are told for entertainment, and have got to be distinguished between the myths that have to do with the serious matter of living life in terms of the order of society and of nature, and stories with some of those same motifs that are told for entertainment. Fairy tales are for children. A fairy tale is child's myth. These are proper myths for proper times of life. As you grow older, you need a sturdier mythology. There are truths for older age and truths for children. For instance, the Indian philosophy of *Maya*, the idea of life as a dream or bubble is difficult to understand by the young boys and girls. When the young boys and girls grow older, and everyone they have known and originally lived for has passed away, and the world itself is passing, the *Maya* myth comes in. But, for young people, the world is something yet to be met and dealt with and loved and learned from and fought with, and so, another mythology.

Mythical Stories

The Myths are the spiritual instructions of our forefathers. The mythical stories are not entertainment stories or folk-tales; because they can be told only at certain times of the year and under certain conditions. There are two orders of myths. The great myths, of the Bible or of *Mundhum* of *Yuma* religion or *Ninnammism*, or *Munthem* of *Lepchas*, or *Mukudum* of *Sunuwars*, for example, are the myths of the Churches, or of the sacred *Mundhum* (oral traditions) rituals. They explain the rites by which the people are living in harmony with themselves and each other and with the universe. Each time they tell the stories of universe creation. The understanding of these stories as allegorical (symbolic representation) is normal. The first humans who told the story of the creation had some intuitive awareness of the allegorical nature of these stories.

Folk Tales Vs Myths

There is a fine saying in India with respect to these two orders of myth, the folk idea (folk-tales) and the elementary idea (myths). The folk idea is called *desi,* which means "provincial", having to do with your society. That is for young people. The myth comes from the imagination, and it leads back to it. The society teaches you what the myths are, and then it disengages you so that in your meditations you can follow the path right in. Civilizations are grounded on myth.

Transcendent and Evil

Transcendent is a technical, philosophical term, translated in two different ways. In Christian theology, it refers to God as being beyond or outside the field of nature. That is materialistic way of talking about the transcendent, because God is thought of as a kind of spiritual fact existing somewhere out there. Living yourself is participating in the evil, or you are not alive. Whatever you do is evil for somebody. This is one of the ironies of the whole creation. Since, nature does not provide human beings an automatic form of survival; since he has to support his life by eating other's lives, that man's desire to live is evil, that man's life, as such, is evil. Life exists till you eat lives. You die when you stop eating lives.

Religion

Religion is a kind of sacred womb. It is designated to bring this extremely complicated thing, which is a human being, to maturity, which means to be self-motivating, self-acting. An old Zen philosopher said "God against man. Man against God. Man against nature. Nature against man and Nature against God. God against Nature – very funny religion". In the religious system of the Near East, you identify with the good and fight against the evil. According to Campbell, J. (1988) the Biblical tradition of Judaism, Christianity, and Islam all speak with derogation of the so-called nature religions. The shift from a nature religion to a sociological religion makes it difficult for the Westerners to link back to nature. But actually all of those cultural symbols are perfectly susceptible to interpretation in terms of the psychological and cosmological systems, if you chose to look at them that way. Every religion is true one way or another. It is true when understood metaphorically. But when it gets struck to its own metaphors, interpreting them as facts, then you are in trouble. A metaphor is an image that suggests something else. For example, Jesus ascended to heaven. Astronomy and physics have simply eliminated that as a literal, physical possibility. But if you read "Jesus ascended to heaven" in terms of metaphoric connotation, you see that he has gone inward, not into outer space but into inward space, to the place from which all being comes, into the consciousness that is the source of all things, the kingdom of heaven within. The images are outward, but their reflection is inward. The point is that we should ascend with him by going inward. It is a metaphor of returning to the source, alpha and omega, of leaving the fixation the body behind and going to the body's dynamic source.

Similarly, in *Yuma* religion *"Sam Sama", "Sam Chomma" and "Sitongsing"* rituals means participation in helping the departing soul of the dead by *Phedangma* priest for returning to the source. It is a metaphor again, the soul-complex of the dead leaving the physical body behind on earth and the soul or spiritual consciousness going to the body's dynamic source – to Goddess. The role of the *Phedangma* is to assist the soul of the dead in the process of journey to the source - *"Sangram Paydang Den"*. Reading the words in terms of prose is the denotation while reading the words in terms of poetry is the metaphor or connotation. Poetry gets to the unseen reality, beyond even the concept of reality, that which transcends all thought. The myth puts you there all the time, give you a line to connect with that mystery which you are. That is the reason why each and every Oral Tradition (*Mundhum*) of *Yuma* religion or *Ninnammism, Mukudum* of *Sunuwars, Munthem* of *Mun* is in poetry. "Art is a mirror held up to nature", said Shakespeare. The nature is your nature, and all of these wonderful poetic images of mythology or the oral traditions are referring to something in you. A novelist said, "Seat of the soul is there where the inner and outer worlds meet".

We must understand that each religion is a kind of software that has its own set of signal and will work. If a person is really involved in a religion and really building his life on it, he better stay with software that he has got. But a chap who likes to play with the software. Well, he probably will never have an experience comparable to that of a saint. Some of the greatest saints borrowed from anywhere they could, and constructed new software. That is what is called development of a religion. You can see it in the Bible. In the beginning God was simply the most powerful god among many. He is just a local tribal god. And then in the sixth century when the Jews were in Babylon, the notion of a world savior came in, and the biblical divinity moved into a new dimension. You can keep an old tradition going only by renewing it in terms of current circumstances. In the period of the Old Testament, the world was a little three-layer cake, consisting of a few hundred miles around the Near Eastern centers. No one had ever heard of the Aztecs, or even of the Chinese in the West. When the world changes, then the religion has to be transformed.

Reincarnation

The metaphor in Christianity that corresponds to reincarnation is purgatory. If one dies with such a fixation on the things of this world that one's spirit is not ready to behold the beatific vision, then one has to undergo purgation, one has to be purged clean of one's limitations. The limitations are what are called sins. Sin is simply a limiting factor that limits your consciousness and fixes in an inappropriate condition. In the oriental metaphor, if you die in that condition, you come back again to have more experience that will clarify, until you are released from these fixations. The reincarnating monad is the principal hero of oriental myth. The monad puts on various personalities, life after life. Reincarnation suggests that you are more than you think you are. There are dimensions of your being and a potential for realization and consciousness that are not included in your concept of yourself. Your life is much deeper and broader than you conceive it to be here. What you are living is but a fractional inkling of what is really within you, what gives you life, breadth, and depth. But you can live in terms of that depth. And when you can experience it, you suddenly see that all the religions are talking of that.

Mythological Heroes and Heroines

There are many stories of the hero in mythology. The mythological heroes or heroines have found or done something beyond the normal range of achievements and experiences. A hero or heroine is some one who has given his or her life to something bigger than oneself. There are two types of deed performed by the heroes. One is the physical deed in which the hero performs a courageous act in battle or saves a life. Lord *Tamsangthing* of *Lepchas* who rescues the *Lepchas* from the clutches of the demon *Laso Moong Pano*, for instance. The other kind is the spiritual deed, in which the hero learns to experiences the supernormal range of human spiritual life and then comes back with a message, Christ, Buddha or *Sodhung Lepmuhang* for instance. The usual hero adventure begins with someone from whom something has been taken, or who feels there is something lacking in the normal experiences available or permitted to the members of the society. These persons then take off on a series of adventures beyond the ordinary, either to recover what has been lost or to discover some life giving elixir. It is usually a cycle, on going and on returning.

Even if we happen not to be heroes in the ground sense to take the heroic journey inside ourselves spiritually and psychologically, for instance, a child is compelled to give up its childhood and become an adult, to die. This is a fundamental psychological transformation that everyone has to under go. We are in childhood in a condition of dependency under someone's protection and supervision for some early years; you are in no way a self-responsible, free agent, but an obedient dependent, expecting and receiving punishments and rewards. To evolve out of this position of psychological immaturity to the courage of self-responsibility and assurance requires heroic transformation. Everyone is a hero in birth, where he undergoes a tremendous psychological as well as physical transformation, from a condition of a little water creature living in a realm of amniotic fluid into an air-breathing mammal which ultimately will be standing. That is an enormous transformation, and had it been consciously undertaken, it would have been, indeed, a heroic act. And there was a heroic act on the mother's part, as well, who had brought this all about.

The male usually has the more conspicuous role, just because of the conditions of life. He is out there in the world, and the woman is in the home. In the myth of *Susuwengba Lalawenba*, we see how his mother – *Muji-na Kheyongna-ma* trains her son for the outside world to become a *Sawa Yukphung Kem-ba*. Also among the Aztecs and *Yumaism*, and *Ninnammism* for example, who had a number of heavens to which people's souls would be assigned according to the conditions of their death, the heaven or hell for warriors killed in battle was the same for mothers who died in childbirth. Similarly, the heaven and hell differs depending on the age and condition of the deceased child. Thus, giving birth as well as growing of child is definitely a heroic deed, in that it is giving over of oneself to the life of another (Subba, J.R.1999; 2005a; 2005b).

Mythology of Love and Marriage

According to Campbell, J. (1988), "the twelfth century love begins with the Troubadours, the nobility of province and then later other parts of France and Europe. The troubadours and their transformation of the idea of love got mixed up in religious life in a very complicated way. The troubadours were very much interested in the psychology of love. And they are the first ones in the West who really thought of love the way we do now, as a person-to-person relationship. Before that, love was simply Eros, the god who excites you to sexual desire. This is not the experience of falling in love the way the troubadours understood it. Eros is much more impersonal than falling in love. The experience of Eros is a kind of seizure. During that time, people did not know about Amour. Amour is something personal that the troubadours recognized. The troubadours recognized Amour as the highest spiritual experience, purely personal ideal. The kind of seizure (= taking sudden hold) that comes from the meeting of the eyes, as they say in the troubadour tradition is a person-to-person experience. That is completely contrary to everything the Church stood for. It is a personal, individual experience. So the courage to love became the courage to affirm one's own experience against tradition – the tradition of the Church in the West. And this accent on the individual gave faith in his experience and not simply mouth terms handed down to him by others. It stresses the validity of the individual's experience of what humanity is, what life is, what values are, against the monolithic system..."

In his opinion "Love is the impulse of life. It comes from the heart. The heart is the organ of opening up to somebody else. That is the human quality as opposed to the animal qualities, which have to do with self-interest. This is a romantic love as opposed to lust, or passion, or a general religious sentiment. Eros and Agape are impersonal loves. Eros is a biological urge. It is the zeal of the organs for each other. The personal factor does not matter. *Agape,* is love thy neighbour as thyself, spiritual love. It does not matter who the neighbour is. It is compassion, heart opening but not individuated as *Amour* is. The usual marriage in traditional cultures in India was arranged for by the families or by marriage brokers. It was not a person-to-person decision at all. In the Middle Ages, that was the kind of marriage that was sanctified by the Church in the West. And so the troubadour idea of real person-to-person amour was very dangerous. Because it was spiritual adultery as the marriages were all arranged by society, the love that came from the meeting of the eyes was of a higher spiritual value.

The individuals making a love must have a gentle heart, capable of love, not simply of lust. Amour is the path; through the meeting of the eyes love attains the heart. For the eyes are the scouts of the heart. So, love not love in general, it is love for that one woman or that one man. Today, we are living in two worlds, one in our own world, and the other in the world outside that has been given to us by the society. And the problem is to achieve a harmonious relationship between the two. An individual come into this society, so he has got to live in terms of this society. It's ridiculous not to live in terms of this society because, unless he does, he will not be living. But he mustn't allow this society to dictate him how he should live. One has to build up one's own system that may violate the expectations of the society, and sometimes society doesn't accept that. But the task of life is to live within the field provided by the society that is really supporting you.

One has to recognize that in domestic life there grows up a love relationship between the husband and wife even when they are put together in an arranged marriage. In other words, in arranged marriages of this kind, there is a lot of love. There is family love, a rich love life on that level. But you don't get this other thing, of the seizure that comes in recognizing your soul's counterpart in the other person. And that's what the troubadours stood for, and that has become the ideal in our lives today. This may be the reason the younger society of Sikkim today prefer love marriage to arrange marriage.

But marriage is marriage, and it is not a love affair. A love affair is a totally different thing. A marriage is a commitment to that which you are. That person is literally your other half. And you and the other are one. A love affair isn't that. That is a relationship for pleasure, and when it gets to be unpleasurable, it's off. But a marriage is a life commitment, and a life commitment means the prime concern of your life. If marriage is not the prime concern, you're not married.

In some marriages, romance does last. In others, it doesn't. But the problem, you see, the big word in this troubadour tradition, is "loyalty". Not cheating, not defecting, through whatever trials or suffering, you remain true. In marriage, every day you love, and every day you forgive. It is ongoing sacrament – love and forgiveness. The real word for marriage is "ordeal", in its proper sense. That is the submission of the individual to something superior to itself. The real life of a marriage or of a true love affair is in the relationship, which is where you are, too. Like the yin/yang symbol, here I am. And here she is, and here we are. Now when I have to make a sacrifice, I'm not sacrificing to her, I'm sacrificing to the relationship. Resentment against the other one is wrongly placed. Life is in the relationship that is where your life now is. That is what a marriage is, whereas, in a love affair, you have two lives in a more or less successful relationship to each other for a certain length of time, as long as it seems agreeable. Marriage is the symbolic recognition of our identity, two aspects of the same being.

What is marriage? The myth tells you what it is. It is the reunion of the separated duad. Originally you were one. You are now two in the world, but the recognition of the spiritual identity is what marriage is. It is different from a love affair. It has nothing to do with that. It is another mythological plane of experience. When people get married because they think it is a long-time love affair, they will be divorced very soon, because all love affairs end in disappointment. But marriage is recognition of a spiritual identity. If we live a proper life, if our minds are on the right qualities in regarding the person of the opposite sex, we will find our proper male or female counterpart. But if certain sensuous interests distract us, we will marry the wrong person. By marrying the right person, we reconstruct that image of the incarnate God, and that is what marriage is.

Marriage is a relationship when you make a sacrifice in marriage; you are sacrificing not to each other but to unity in a relationship. The Chinese image of the Tao, with the dark and light interacting – that is the relationship of *yang* and *yin*, male and female, which is what a marriage is. And that is what you have become when you have married. You are no longer this one alone; your identity is in a relationship. Marriage is not a simple love affair, it is an ordeal, and the ordeal is the sacrifice of ego to a relationship in which two have become one. It is, in a sense, doing one's own thing, but the one is not just you, it is the two together as one. And that is a purely mythological image signifying the sacrifice of the visible entity for a transcendent good. Marriage is not just a social arrangement, but it is a spiritual exercise. It is primarily a spiritual exercise, and the society is supposed to help us have the realization (Campbell, J. 1988).

In the *Limboo* community 15 (fifteen) types of marriages are in practice (Subba, J.R. 1999:411-451). However, psychologically only three types of marriages has been described in the myths of *Yumaism*. The various myths sang by the well-versed *Phedangmas, Sambas* and *Tumyanghangs* are:

(a) Myths of *Suchchhuru Suhangpheba* and *Tetlara Lahadongna* – incestuous relationship between brother and sister;

(b) Myths of *Pajoi Tentumyangba* and *Lupliadenhangma* – a marriage union outside the kinship complying with incest taboo;

(a) Myth of *Samba Sutlung Phungba* (*Wayoading Khokling Sakpa*) and *Sekngayang Pheknqayangma* (*Selliyong Phetliyonghangma*) – a marriage union based on parent's consent in the Society.

These stories describe the psychology of love and marriage of various eons relate the development of marriage institution and narratives are full of pathos, eroticism, heroism, humor, serenity, affection, amazement, and abhorrence.

Mythology of Journey Inward

The dream is an inexhaustible source of spiritual information about you. Myth differs from dream because a dream is a personal experience of that deep, dark ground that is the support of our conscious lives, and a myth is the society's dream. The myth is the public dream and the dream is the private myth. If your private myth, your dream, happens to coincide with that of the society, you are in good accord with your ground. If it is not, you have got an adventure in the dark forest ahead of you.

One of the main problems of mythology is reconciling the mind to the brutal precondition of all life, which lives by the killing and eating of lives. You are alive as long as you are killing and eating other lives. Once you stop this you are no more. As per *Yuma* religion, *your temporal origin is Biogenesis* and has to sustain your temporal life on bios or by eating lives. God has created you that way and has to live on killing and eating lives. You don't kid yourself by eating only vegetables, either, for they, too, are alive. *So the essence of life is this eating of yourself!* Life lives on lives, and the reconciliation of the human mind and sensibilities to that fundamental fact is one of the functions of some those very brutal rites to which the ritual consists chiefly of killing, in imitation, as it were, of that first, primordial crime, out of which arose this temporal world, in which we all participate. The reconciliation of mind to the conditions of life is fundamental to all creation stories. They are very like each other in this respect.

The dreams come from imagination. The imagination is grounded in the energy of the organs of the body, and these are the same in all human beings. Since imagination comes from out of one biological ground, it is bound to produce certain themes. Dreams are dreams. There are certain characteristics of dreams that can be enumerated, no matter who is dreaming them. Jung speaks of two orders of dream, the *personal dream* and the *archetypal dream* or the dream of mythic dimension. You can interpret a personal dream by association, figuring out what it is talking about in your own life, or in relation to your own personal problem. But every now and then a dream comes up that is pure myth, that carries a mythic theme, or that is said, for example, to come from the Christ/*Yuma*/ Buddha/*Maheswar* within.

Mythology of Sacrifice and Bliss

The sanctification of the landscape is a fundamental function of mythology. The mountainous geography of Sikkim Himalaya has done a great deal to shape our culture and our idea of religion. The gods of mountainous Sikkim is not the gods of the plains or the gods of the rain forest. When you are out in the plains or desert with one sky and one world, then you might have one deity, but in a jungle or in the mountainous Himalayas where there is no horizon and you never see anything more than ten or thousand yards away from you, you don't have that idea anymore. Thus, their mountainous geography, mountain streams/rivers, trees, jungles etc. shapes their image of divinity, and then they project it out and call it god. This is the reason why the mountain peoples of Sikkim have a number of gods and goddesses; in *Yumaism, Ninnammism, and Munism* etc. for instance.

The idea of god is always culturally conditioned. And even when a missionary brings what he thinks is God, his God, that God is transformed in terms of what the people are able to think of as a divinity. Society is always patriarchal. Goddess religions like *Yuma* religion emerged because the women played such a dominant role in the planting and harvesting activities and domestication of wild plants and animals of those early societies in the Himalayas where the wild resources was rich. At that moment, the women were the most important members of the society as the men were busy in hunting and gathering or on the pollen-path of copulation and reproduction as visualized from the myth of *Sutchhuru Suhangpheba* and *Tetlara Lahadongna* of *Yumaism*. Because of the women's activity of domestication of wild plants and animals, the hunting gathering life style of the early man slowly transformed into settled agriculture and thus moves over into the woman. The women were the important members in the cultivation and domestication family at the villages. They started offering their Gods and Goddesses whatever they could produce from the field or from rearing of animals for better harvest or rearing in the years to come. This tradition slowly gave rise to ceremonies of offering newly harvested crops and sacrificing domestic animals to the deities and divinities in the indigenous tribes of Sikkim (Subba, J.R. 2008b).

Since her magic of giving birth and nourishment, as the earth does, her magic supports the magic of the earth. In the early tradition, she is the first planter. Men were reluctant to adopt settled agriculture and were busy in hunting-gathering activities for a long, long time in the society. It is only later, when the plough is invented in the high culture systems that the male takes over the agricultural lead again. And then the simulation of coitus, with the plough ploughing the earth, becomes a dominant myth figure. Because of these differing approaches to myth are what we mean by the "way of the animal powers", "the way of the seeded earth", "the way of the celestial lights", and "the way of man's of the Himalayan region". These have to do with the symbolic system through which the normal human condition of the time is symbolized and organized and given knowledge of itself.

The values of these differing approaches will be a result of the conditions that govern life. For instance, the hunter is always directed outward to the animal. His life depends on the relationship to the animals. His mythology is outward turned. But the planting mythology, which has to do with the cultivation of the plant, the planting of seed, the death of the seed/seedling etc. and the coming of the new plant, is more inward turned. With the hunters, the animals inspired the mythology. When man wanted to gain power and knowledge, he would go into the forest and fast and prey, and an animal would come and teach him. With the planters, the plant world is the teacher. The plant world is identical in its life sequences with the life of man. So you see, there is an inward relationship there.

When the human beings changed their life-style from hunting and gathering to settled agriculture, there was a drastic and total transformation, not just of the myths but the psyche itself. This has happened slowly to different people with the beginning of settle agriculture, i.e. Southwest Asia (8,500 B.C), China (7,500 B.C), Mesoamerica (3,500 B.C), Andes and Amazonia (3,500 B.C.), Eastern United States (2,500 B.C.), Sahel (5,000 B.C.), Western Europe (6,000-3,500 B.C.), India (7,000 B.C.), Egypt (6,000 B.C.), and in the tribal societies of Sikkim only during the last decade of nineteenth century (1890s). To a hunter, an animal is a total entity; he is within a skin. When you kill animal, he is dead, that is the end of it. In agriculture, there is no such thing as a self-contained individual in the vegetal world. You cut a plant, and another sprout comes. Pruning is helpful to a plant. The whole thing is just a continuing inbeingness. Out of rot of the plants come new plants. If you cut off the limb of a plant, another one comes. Tear of the limb of an animal, and unless it is a certain kind of lizard, it does not grow again. So in the planting culture, there is a sense of death as not death somehow, that death is required for new life. When you have a planting culture, there is a fostering of the plant that is going to be eaten.

The practice of divination and the observance of ceremonies, family and tribal, are the two outstanding features of the ancient civilization of the Himalayas. They represent the contrasting ideals of individualistic and of social development. *Yumaism* believes that the creator god created two human idols one male and other female and put vital air in the creation of human beings. *Ninnammism* believes that the great self-existence, *Ninnamma,* produced finite existence, *Tayaripchi*. The finite evolved the two essential elements of nature *Paruhang* (male) in the sky and *Sunmima* (female) on the earth. *Munism* believes that *Rum* created *Foodong Theeng* (male) and *Najong nyue* (female) from the un-trodden snow of Kingchunjunga. Taoism believes that the great self-existence, *wu chi,* produced finite existence, *t'ai chi*. the finite evolved the two essential elements of nature, *Yang* and *Yin,* which may be translated as the male and female principles, or as positive and negative, or as light and darkness. Chu Hsi's account says that first was the self-existent and then the finite. The finite moved and there was *Yang* (light or the male principle); the finite rested and there was *Yin* (darkness or the female principle). In other words the sexual principle as known in propagation of animal life was predicated of nature as manifested in the finite; but there was no attempt to describe the infinite self-existent in terms of human forms or human experience. This primordial cause was unknowable and unexplainable. Worship of nature among the ancient Sikkimese people was common. The domestic ceremonies are the hearth, the portal, the house, and departure on journey. These ceremonies all originated among the early inhabitants of Sikkim. Worship of the god of hearth is universal.

The people's propensity to tell stories and to use mythologically their own ideas in oral tradition (*Mundhum, Mukudum* or *Munthem*) about natural and social phenomena added much mythic material to that found in the official records. The people of Sikkim are multilingual, multiethnic and secular since sixth or seventh century onwards. Hence, some of it, no doubt, was introduced by their neighbouring people or land mostly from *Bon* or *Pon* religion and *Mahayana* Buddhism from North and, Hinduism from West and Christianity from the south and was therefore adapted to the original traditions of the races. We shall not make any positive assertions about the "racial character" or "innate inclination" of the people as manifested in their native ideas or imagery. Yet no one can deny that different people show clearly different mental and spiritual traits in viewing their own life and in reacting toward their environment. The natural features and climate of the land inhabited by a people no doubt have a great influence upon their myth-making activity.

Nature seems to have favoured the mountain people by presenting to them her most soothing and charming aspects. The state exhibits nearly all stages of geological formation, and the climate ranges from the semi-tropical heat of the southern slopes to the severe winter of the north. Though small, the landscape of the state is richly diversified by mountains and streams, forest and culture. The myths and stories of all the fourteen hill tribes/ races identified in the State are not so well connected and systematized except the people who adopted Hinduism, Buddhism, Jainism, Sikhism, Islam and Christianity. There is certain cycle of cosmological ideas, but the links are often missing and many single stories remain quite dissociated.

Nature is inhabited by an infinite host of these deities and spirits, and human life is always closely associated with their thoughts and actions. Therefore the indigenous religions of Sikkim are combinations of nature-worship and ancestor-cult, and in most cases the nature-myth is inseparable from the story connecting the ancestral deity and from his worship, because the curiosity to know the origins of things works as strongly toward the physical world as toward one's own individual and social life. It is also evident that the more developed religions have limited myths to support the rituals e.g. Hinduism, Christianity, Islam, Jainism, Sikhism etc.. On the contrary, the ancient or lesser developed belief systems or religions have plenty of myths to support the rituals (*Yumaism, Ninnammism, Munism,* etc.).

Mythology of Eternity

Eternity is in love with the productions of time, says the poet Blake. The source of temporal life is eternity. Eternity pours itself into the world. It is a basic mythic idea of the god who becomes many in us. In Hinduism, the god who lives in me is called the "inhabitant" of the body. To identify that divine, immortal aspect of yourself is to identify yourself with divinity. Eternity is beyond all categories of thought. The ultimate mystery of being is beyond all categories of thought. And myth is that field of reference to what is absolutely transcendent. In religions the god or creator is the mother, the whole world is her body. The division of life into sexes was a late division. Biologically, the amoeba is not male and female. That is why it is absurd to speak God as of either this sex or that sex. The divine power is antecedent to sexual separation. Everything in the field of time and space is dual. The Garden of Eden is a metaphor for that innocence that is innocent of time, innocent of opposites, and that is the prime center out of which consciousness then becomes aware of the changes. Archetypes are elementary ideas, what could be called "ground" ideas. These ideas, Jung (1875-1961) spoke of as archetypes of the unconscious. "Archetype" is the better term because "elementary ideas" suggests headwork. Archetype of the unconscious means it comes from below. The difference between the Jungian archetypes of the unconscious and Freud's complexes is that the archetypes of the unconscious are manifestations of the organs of the body and their powers. Archetypes are biologically grounded, whereas the Freudian unconscious is a collection of repressed traumatic experiences from the individual's lifetime. The Freudian unconscious is a personal unconscious, and it is biographical. The Jungian archetypes of the unconscious are biological. The biographical is secondary to that. All over the world and at different times of human history, these archetypes, or elementary ideas, have appeared in different costumes. The differences in the costumes are the results of environment and historical conditions. It is these differences that the anthropologist is most concerned to identify and compare (Campbell, J. 1988; Hyde, Maggie and McGuinness 1993).

The god is the vehicle of its energy : And the force or quality of the energy that is involved or represented determines the character and function of the god. There are gods of violence, there are gods of compassion, and there are gods that are simply the protectors of kings or nations in their war campaigns. These are all personifications of the energies in play. But the ultimate source of the energies remains a mystery. Thus, a continuous war among principalities exists as it is in life itself. Even in our minds, when it comes to making a decision, there will be a war. In acting in relationship to other people, for example, there may be four or five possibilities. The influence of the dominant divinity in my mind will be what determines my decision. If my guiding divinity is brutal, my decision will be brutal, as well. One has to have faith or have experience of the wonder of life. One has to have experience of love; experience of hatred, malice, and wanting to punch this guy in the jaw. From the point of view of symbolic imaging, those are different forces operating in one's mind. One may think of them, wonder, love, hatred, as inspired by different divinities. One may think of them as metaphors for the impulses that move and guide him.

Energies come from our own life, from the energies of your own body. The different organs in the body, including your head, are in conflict with each other. And your life comes from the ultimate energy that is the life of the universe. But there must be somebody generating that energy; the ultimate mystery be impersonal God or gods; known by thousands of names throughout the world. They are all over the place. There is a tendency in the occidental mythology to anthropomorphize and accent the humanity of the gods, the personifications: Yahweh, for example, as either a god of wrath, of justice and punishment, or as a favoring god who is the support of your life, as we read, for example, in the Psalms. But in the oriental mythology, the Gods are much more elemental, much less human and much more like the powers of nature. In *Yuma* religion the God is in female form, both *Tagera Ningwaphuma* (Deity) and her daughter *Yuma Sammang* (divinity), whereas other deities (*Mangs*), divinities (*Sammangs*) and retinue of divinities (*Sammang Chyangs*) may be in masculine or feminine spirit form. Similarly, in many other oriental thinking, the divine power principally is in female form (*Durga, Kali, Saraswati, Luxmi, Parbati, Ninnamma* etc.) or masculine form (*Brahma, Vishnu, Maheswar, Paruhang,* etc.). But in the

Western thinking, God is in masculine form; for instance, God, and the son of the God (Christ) in Christianity. The idea is that you cannot imagine what you cannot personify. Plato said, "Thoughts are immortal and divine." That is what meditation is. Meditation means constantly thinking on a certain theme. It can be on any level. Meditation may be both physical and spiritual. For example, meditation on money is a perfectly good meditation. And bringing up a family is a very important meditation. There is an alone meditation in the church, or temple or *mangkhim*. So prayer is actually a meditation relating to and on a mystery. There is a form of meditation you are taught in Roman Catholicism where you recite the rosary, the same prayer, over and over and over again. That pulls the mind in. In Sanskrit, this is called *japa*, "repetition of the holy name -*Mantra*." It blocks other interests out and allows you to concentrate on one thing, and then, depending on your own powers of imagination, to experience the profundity sense of this mystery.

God is the god we have only imagined, but one has to break past one's image of God to get through to the connoted (signified in addition to the primary meaning) illumination (spiritual enlightenment). The psychologist Jung has a relevant saying: "Religion is a defense against the experience of God." The mystery has been reduced to set of concepts and ideas, and emphasizing these concepts and ideas and ideas can short-circuit the transcendent (going beyond material universe), connoted experience. An intense experience of mystery is what one has to regard as the ultimate religious experience. One has to go past the imagined image of Jesus or *Kali* or *Luxmi*. Such image of one's god becomes a final obstruction, one's ultimate barrier. You hold on to your own ideology, your own little manner of thinking, and when a large experience of God approaches, an experience greater than you are prepared to receive, you take flight from it by clinging to the image in your mind. This is known as preserving your faith. You know the idea of the ascent (act of rising) of the spirit through the different centers or archetypal stages of experience. One begins with the elementary animal experiences of hunger and greed, and then of sexual zeal, and on to physical mastery of one kind or another. These are all empowering stages of experience. But then, when the center of the heart is touched, and a sense of compassion awakened with another person or creature, and you realize that you and that other are in some sense creatures of the one life in being, a whole new stage of life in the spirit opens out. This opening of the heart to the world is what is symbolized mythologically as the virgin birth. It signifies the birth of a spiritual life in what was formerly an elementary human animal living for the merely physical aims of health, progeny, power, and a little fun. But now we come to something else. For to experience this sense of compassion, accord, or even identity with another, or with some ego-transcending principle that has become lodged in your mind as a good to be revered and served, is the beginning, once and for all, of the properly religious way of life and experience; and this may then lead to a life-consuming quest for a full experience of that one Being of beings of which all temporal forms are the reflections.

Now, this ultimate ground of all being can be experienced in two senses, one as with form and the other as without and beyond form. When you experience your god as with form, there is your envisioning mind, and there is the god. There is a subject (cause to undergo or experience something), and there is an object (some visible and tangible thing). But the ultimate mystical goal is to be united with one's god. With that, duality is transcended and forms disappear. There is nobody there, no god, no you. Your mind, going past all concepts, has dissolved in identification with the ground of your own being, because that to which the metaphorical image of your god refers is the ultimate mystery of your own being, which is the mystery of the being of the world as well. The heart of the Christian faith is that God was in Christ, that all the elemental forces are embodied themselves in a human being who reconciled mankind to God. This is the basic Gnostic and Buddhist idea. Jesus was a historical person who realized in himself that he and what he called the Father were one, and he lived out of that knowledge of the Christhood of his nature. Similarly, the heart of the *Yuma Samyo* faith is in *Tageraningwaphuma* or *Yuma* spiritual Goddess that all the elemental forces are embodied themselves in a spiritual Goddess *Tageraningwaphuma* (*Yuma*) and her daughter *Yuma Sammang*. The Almighty Goddess *Tageraningwaphuma* and Her daughter spiritual Goddess *Yuma Sammang* (divinity – daughter or incarnation or soul-form of *Tagera Ningwaphuma*) was one with same knowledge and source of energy as believed by Christians in the "Christ" and "Father".

The geography of the psyche is metaphorical language, but you can say that some people are "living on the level of the sex organs," and that is all they are living for. As per Sigmund Freud's philosophy, that is the meaning of life. Secondly, the Adlerian philosophy is "the will to power," that all of life is centered on obstructions and overcoming the obstructions. That is a perfectly good life, and those are forms of divinity also. But they are on the animal level. Thirdly, philosophy of life involves giving oneself to others one way or another. This is the one that is symbolized in the opening of the heart. Our source of life is the recognition of our life in the other, of the one life in the two of us. God or Goddess is a physical or spiritual image for that one life. *Yumaism* recognizes in the spiritual Grandmother (*Yuma*) image of that life. Hinduism recognizes in the trinity physical God and Goddess images of those lives. Christianity recognizes the spiritual image of God. We ask ourselves where this one life comes from, and people who think everything has to have been made by somebody will think, "Well, God made it." So God or Goddess is the source of all this. The word "religion" means *religio*, linking back. If we say it is the one life in both of us, then my separate life has been linked to the one life, *religio*, linked back. This has become symbolized in the images of religion, which represent that connecting link.

Jung, the famous psychologist, says that one of the most powerful religious symbols is the circle. He says that the circle is one of the great primordial images of mankind and that, is considering the symbol of the circle, we are analyzing the self. The whole world is circle. All of these circular images reflect the psyche, so there may be some relationship between these architectural designs and the actual structuring of our spiritual functions. We have inherited this from *Sumerian* mythology. We have inherited the circle with the four cardinal points and three hundred and sixty degrees. The official Sumerian year was three hundred and sixty days with five holy days that don't count, which are outside of time and in which they had ceremonies relating their society to heavens. Now we are losing this sense of the circle in relation to time, because we have digital time, where you just have time buzzing by. The circle, on the other hand, represents totality. Everything within the circle is one thing, which is encircled, enframed. That would be the spatial aspect. But the temporal aspect of the circle is that you leave, go somewhere, and always come back. God is the alpha and the omega, the source and the end. The circle suggests immediately a completed totality, whether in time or in space. No beginning, no end.

Jung speaks of the circle as a *mandala. Mandala* is the Sanskrit word for circle, but a circle that is coordinated or symbolically designed so that it has the meaning of a cosmic order. When composing *mondalas*, you are trying to coordinate your personal circle with the universal circle. In a very elaborate Buddhist *mandala*, for example, you have the deity in the center as the power source, the illumination source. The peripheral images would be manifestations or aspects of the deity's radiance. In working out a *mandala* for yourself, you draw a circle and then think of the different impulse systems and value systems in your life. Then you compose them and try to find out where your circle is. Making a *mandala* is a discipline for pulling all those scattered aspects of your life together, for finding a center and ordering yourself to it. You try to coordinate your circle with the universal circle. In *Yumaism*, the primary function of any rituals is encircling the Altar. It may be a *Yagrangsing, Tongsing, Sitongsing, Nehangma, Mekkamma, A-akwanama* in *Hangsitlang* (main pillar) of a newly built house etc. rituals. The Shaman priests always try to coordinate your circle with the universal circle or the center of your origin. The altars are the *mandalas* for coordination of your circle with the universal circle. Among the *Navaho* Indians, healing ceremonies are conducted through sand paintings, which are mostly *mandalas* on the ground. The person who is to be treated moves into the *mandala* as a way of moving into the mythological context that he will be identifying with; he identifies himself with the symbolized power. This idea of sand painting with *mandalas*, and their use for meditation purposes, appears also in Buddhism. The Buddhist monks practice sand painting, drawing cosmic images to represent the forces of the spiritual powers that operate in our lives. There is some effort, apparently, to try to center one's life with the center of the universe by way of mythological imagery. The image helps you to identify with the symbolized force. The images of myth are reflections of the spiritual potentialities of every one of us. Through contemplating these we evoke their powers in our own lives. When a scripture talks about man are made in God's image, it is talking about certain qualities that every human being possesses, no matter what that person's religion or culture or geography or heritage. God would be the ultimate elementary idea of Man. And we are all made in the image of God or Goddess. That is the ultimate archetype of man.

According to Chopra, D. (2006: 197-236), when all images have disappeared at the subtle-level, the dying person arrives at eternity. Eternity is the source of the soul. We cannot see eternity when we are alive, as it extends in all directions around us. At the end of the journey there are no loved ones, no physical destination, no memories of the material plane. Even the Buddhist phrase *"Clear Light"* is only a metaphor, since eternity is neither light nor clear. As you get closer to eternity, you won't experience being dead or alive. You won't be male or female. You are back to your source. This stage is known as *Moksha,* or liberation. Eternity gives you more freedom than the mind can conceive. The account of eternity, now famous in NDE (Near Death Experience) literature, comes from an artist named Mellen Thomas Benedict, who died of a brain tumor in 1982. That he could be dead for an hour and a half, only to return to life. Benedict's journey practically provides an encyclopedia of the afterlife. He found himself out of body, aware that his corpse was lying in bed. His perception was greatly expanded, he could see over, around, and under his house, and he sensed that he was enveloped in darkness, but soon a brilliant light became evident. He moved towards it, aware that if he entered the light, he would be dead. At this point Benedict made a startling decision. He asked the experience to stop, and it did. Benedict called a halt so that he could talk to the light. As he did so, it continually changed shapes, sometimes resembling Jesus or Buddha, other times turning a complex pattern like a *mandala* or archetypal images and signs, as he puts it. The light told him (or, to be precise, transferred information to his mind) that a dying person is given a "feedback loop" of images that fits their own belief system: Christian images are seen by Christians, Buddhist images by

Buddhists. Being a loop, the dying person can enter into the experience and shape it, as Benedict found himself doing. (The light explained that he was a rare case: most people proceed ahead without question).

Benedict saw so many shifting images, may have to do with his immersion in world religions and spiritual traditions after he was diagnosed with cancer. Next Benedict became aware that what he was actually seeing was the Higher Self matrix, which he describes as a "*mandala* of human souls; that is, a cosmic pattern of consciousness". He realized that each person has a Higher Self that serves as an oversoul and also as a conduit back to the source. Gazing at the matrix of souls, Benedict became aware they were all connected; humanity formed one being; each of us is an aspect of this wholeness. He was drawn into matrix, which he describes as ineffably beautiful. It radiated a healing, generative love that overwhelmed him. The light conveyed to him that the soul matrix formed a subtle energy level that girded the earth and bound people together. Now he was confronted, he says, with the pure beauty of every human soul and was dumbfounded. He was particularly astonished that no soul contained evil, and the light informed him that soul couldn't be inherently evil. Underlying all human action is the search for love, and when people are driven to evil actions, the root cause is lack of love. Benedict was experiencing profound ecstasy as he was absorbed deeper into the light - reaching another realm that was subtler but also much vaster. He beheld an "enormous stream of light, vast and full, deep in the heart of life." When he asked what it was, the light told him it was the river of life and that he should drink from it to his heart's content.

Fueled by limitless curiosity, he now asked the light to reveal the entire universe to him "beyond all human illusion." He was told to ride the stream of life, and as he did, he passed through a tunnel hearing "soft sonic booms" on the way. His speed accelerated beyond the speed of light as he left the solar system, passed through the heart of galaxy, and became aware of many worlds and many life forms, all in a dizzying rush. At this point Benedict made a critical discovery that what appeared to be travel through space was in fact the expansion of his own consciousness. The appearance of galaxies and star clusters racing past was his own consciousness streaming past one boundary of space-time after another. Benedict describes entire galaxies disappearing into a point, of all life forms making their presence known, of a second light that contains every vibration in the universe. Benedict was actually witnessing the operation of consciousness itself.

Passing into the second light, he experienced a profound shift into silence and utter stillness. It came to him that he could see to infinity. He was in the void, or pre-creation as he calls it and his consciousness was limitless. He was in contact with the absolute, which was not a religious experience but one of the unbounded awareness. He perceived all of creation generating itself without beginning or end. Instead of the Big Bangs constantly generating new universes. Since he was beyond time, this was happening simultaneously in all dimensions. After reaching this epiphany, Benedict's journey reversed itself, step by step, and he woke up in his bed at home with the unshakable realization, now so familiar in the NDE literature that death was as illusion.

Mythology of Death and Afterlife

Every life is framed by two mysteries. Only one of them, birth, is considered a miracle. If you are a religious person, birth brings a new soul into the world from its home with God. If you are not, the miracle is that a single fertilized cell in a mother's womb can divide and subdivide again a mere fifty times to produce a complete new person. A ball of protein and water somehow knows how to shape itself into eyes, hands, skin, and a brain. This nine-month transformation keeps accelerating, so that by the end a million new brain cells are appearing every minute. At the moment the new born emerges, like a space shuttle unlocking from the mother ship, every system that needs to function independently – heart, lungs, brain, and digestive tract, suddenly realizes that the moment is now and not a moment later. Organs detach from total dependence on the mother, and with astonishing precision they begin to act as if they had always been on their own. In a split second life chooses to live. The other mystery that occurs, usually decades later, death, is very difficult. It brings to an end all the things birth struggled so hard to achieve. A thready heartbeat crosses an invisible line and becomes still. The bellows of the lungs, which have pumped some 700 million times, refuse to pump even once more. A hundred billion neurons cease to fire; a trillion billion cells throughout the body receive the news that their mission is over. Yet this abrupt finale is as much a mystery as birth, for at the moment life ends, 99% of our cells are typically still functional, and all three billion cordons, the individual letters in the book of human DNA, remain intact.

Religion does not consider death a miracle. In Christianity death is linked to sin and Satan, the Western equivalent of the Lord of Death. Death is the enemy, and God saves us from its clutches. But with God's help dying is the doorway to a far more important event, the beginning of the afterlife. To the religious mind death brings the presence of God near, and witnesses throughout history have claimed to actually see the soul depart. There is a persistent legend that 21 grams of mass disappear when we die, which must be the weight of the soul. Deepak Chopra (2006:1-169) believes that death accomplishes the following miraculous things:

It replaces time with timelessness. It stretches the boundaries of space to infinity. It reveals the source of life. It brings a new way of knowing that lies beyond the reach of the five senses. It reveals the underlying intelligence that organizes and sustains creation. In other words, death is a fulfillment of our purpose here on earth. Every culture offers a deep faith that this is true, but ours demands a higher standard of proof. The proof exists, but it cannot be physical, since by definition death brings physical life to an end. To see this proof, we must expand the boundaries of consciousness so that we know ourselves better. The very word "after" implies that time hasn't changed at the moment of death, that it still moves in a straight line, carrying a person from earthly time to heavenly time. This is wrong on two counts. First, eternity is not a function of time. In Christianity, sinners consigned eternally to hell wouldn't be punished for a long time. They would be punished outside time. Good people who find salvation also live in that same region where clocks never tick. So our ordinary sense of time has no relevance to what comes "after". Secondly, our everyday sense of time is itself based on eternity. The universe exploded into existence 14 billion years ago, and started the cosmic clock going. Our bodies experience time because of atomic vibrations at the level of hydrogen, oxygen, nitrogen, and carbon, the building blocks of organic chemicals. We measure outside events using the inner clock of the brain, which is nothing but these organic chemicals. Before the Big Bang time wasn't ticking away; a second was equal to eternity. We surmise this because quantum physics has pierced the illusion of time, detaching from the atomic clock to go deeper into the fabric of Nature. Yet the appearance of death is illusory, where all activity ends marks the beginning of a new region, known as virtual reality, where matter and energy exist as pure potential. Creation leaps from the void to complete fullness, just as eternity leaps from timelessness into fullness of time. In the beginning, the spiritual landscape of Sikkim was replete with gods and goddess. There were innumerable nonphysical worlds (*Lokas/Dens*/worlds etc) in their belief system. In the face of such bewildering diversity, the spiritual leaders didn't offer one God. They offered one reality that encompassed every possible experience, both in this life and beyond. They posited that every level of existence was actually a state of awareness. In other words, all worlds, in fact, were formed in consciousness. Therefore, as creators of these worlds, we could experience them and influence them at will. That is the essence of the indigenous belief systems of Sikkim. It was an invitation to participate in an endless experiment. The purpose of the experiment was to test the truth of reality by exploring it within oneself.

Stages of Awakening

The soul is always with us face to face with the fascinating phenomenon of near-death experiences (NDE), which have become a fixed part of popular belief. Near-death is a momentary brush with another reality, or so it seems to those who report the experience. A person is lying in the emergency room or intensive care unit. His heart stops, and for all intents and purposes death ensues. Yet some of these patients, typically those who suffer cardiac arrest, can be resuscitated. When they are, nearly 20% report at least one of the familiar symptoms of NDE, leaving their bodies, looking down and seeing themselves on the operating table, watching medical procedures being performed as doctors tried to restart their hearts, finding themselves in a tunnel, going toward a bright light, feeling the presence of a higher power, hearing or seeing loved ones beckoning them on. How, can a person experience any event after the brain's clock has stopped? Other cultures, however, have ventured even further into the timeless, and they assure us that time may end, but consciousness continues. NDE of *Dawa Dolma* and *Lingza Chokyi* in the *Bardo,* the subtle world of Tibetan Buddhist afterlife in Tibet, and many such NDE are wonderful experiences available with us today. People who come back to life after *Bardo* (intermediate stage) are called *delogs* or *deloks.* One amazing thing about *delogs* is their consistency; the experience of *Dawa Dolma* in the twentieth century mirrors that of *Linza Chokyi* four hundred years previously. They see the same six levels of wisdom (six worlds), and receive messages to bring back to the living. These messages tend to center on being a good Tibetan Buddhist. There are significant parallels, then between the experience of NDE and the *delogs* of Tibet. Since *delogs* provide more detailed and extended accounts, it seems fair to assume that an NDE is just the beginning of the awakening taking place that moves the dying person through all the stages needed for the soul to reveal itself. If we shed the specific geography of Christian heaven, the Buddhist *Bardo,* the many *Lokas,* or divine realms of Hinduism, and *Yumaism's* eighteen Dens, the first stage of the afterlife emerges with certain consistent events (Chopra, Deepak 2006; Subba, J.R. 1999; 2005b).

Crossing Over -How the Afterlife Dawns

(i) The physical body stops functioning. The dying person may not be aware of this but eventually knows that it has occurred.

(ii) The physical world vanishes. This can happen by degrees; there can be a sense of floating upward or of looking down on familiar places as they recede.

(iii) The dying person feels lighter, suddenly freed of limitation.

(iv) The mind and sometimes the senses continue to operate. Gradually, however, what is perceived becomes non-physical.

(v) A presence grows that is felt to be divine. This presence can be clothed in a light or in the body of angels or gods. It can communicate to the dying person.

(vi) Personality and memory begin to fade, but the sense of "I" remains.

(vii) This "I" has overwhelming sense of moving on to another phase of existence.

This sevenfold awakening isn't the same as going to happen. Researchers often call this the "inter-life" phase, a transition between the mental states of being alive and the mental state of realizing that one has passed on. There are many specifics that change from person to person and the persons belonging to culture to culture. Not all NDE's "go into the light". Some patients report traveling to various planets or *Lokas* or *Dens*, in space or to other worlds according to their religious belief systems. Some experience a judgment scene that can be quite harsh, or even hellish; it can also be full of satisfaction however. The nature of the person plays a large part. A child can come back from heaven and report that it was full of baby animals at play; some may be told by god to return to earth. Crossing over is only a transition, however. The full reality of the soul has not yet revealed itself. For *delogs*, still ahead lies the experience of "the mind's pure nature," as Buddhist would call it. Westerners argue over whether the afterlife could be as real as the physical world. Easterners declare that both are mental projections. Westerners limit the human life cycle to a short span between birth and death. Easterners see an eternal cycle of birth, death, and rebirth. Thus, there is huge room for variation even in the same journey. Science is not about knowing the mind of God; it is about understanding nature and the reason for things. The thrill is that our ignorance exceeds our knowledge. Afterlife is created in consciousness. As soon as we talk of consciousness we shut out of science.

Three Wishes

1. Easterners believe that the east is where the sun rises; and is also the way back to the living beings.
2. The role of love is to create.
3. The *Yama*'s role is to destroy. And hence, the *Yama* or *Thakede?ba* or *Sandey* need no love.

There are two paths in life, the path of wisdom and the path of ignorance. The path of wisdom is to pursue the Self (*Atman/*

Soul-complex, Sam-complex). The path of ignorance is to pursue pleasure. Pleasure, being born of the senses, is temporary, and whatever is temporary falls under the sway of death. The physical existence of body is temporary, and thus death is inevitable. But the Self (*Atman*) is the light of immortality. It shines forever. Few are wise enough to see this light, even though it is inside them and nowhere else. The Self (*Atman/ Soul-complex, Sam-complex*) is but the light of your soul. Most people are ignorant, and the Self is muddied by the mind's constant activity and confusion. They can't see the light or reach to the ancestor's village (Chopra, D. 2006; Subba, J.R. 2005b).

Question of Belief

Everyone's basic choices, which have shaped their lives, begin at the level of consciousness. At this level choices aren't simple. They depend on memory and conditioning, on culture and expectation. These entire ingredients factor into what happens in the afterlife is the only some of the belief systems that make a difference center on religion. Looming much larger are the infinite other choices we make every day, for they create our personal reality. The notion of heaven (*Sangrampedang Den* or *Swargha/ Baikuntha* or joining one's Ancestor place *etc.*) keeps things human, and that is one reason it has survived so long. The image of returning home after we die, resting from our labors, and receiving our just reward offers powerful reassurance. Of all possible destinations, heaven is the easiest. It offers reassurance that we will remain physically the same, with our personality intact. Easterners believe that our destination is meeting with the unknown. After the familiar images of "crossing over" disappear, the unexpected unfolds. Consciousness can take a creative leap. In Christ's conception of heaven is present as in other religions. It is an inward experience that can be felt by the righteous. Heaven is also a future. It is returning home to be with God that the righteous weights on Judgment Day. Heaven is personal. It is to be found "within you." At the same time, heaven is universal. It is an eternal abode beyond birth and death, a place outside creation. This teaching was revolutionary because Jesus built a bridge to the soul, exhorting every person to find his or her way across. He is giving us a clue about the kingdom of heaven within. Heaven is an inward experience – an experience in consciousness. Ecstasy represents the limit of happiness that can be felt personally. The Latin root of the word "ecstasy" means, "to stand outside". In common usage people will say, "I was so happy it felt unreal, like it was happening to someone else." Bliss is the quality of soul (Chopra, D. 2006:1-169; Subba, J.R. 1999; 2005b).

Path of Hell

Hell or *Naraka* or *Khema Youngong Den* is payback for sin, but it's also an extension of earthly suffering. When escape is the ultimate reward, staying behind is the ultimate punishment. Christian theology basically says, "Be good or God, will give you more of this life, only worse." The Oriental mythology looked at suffering not as a matter of sin but as a matter of lost freedom. Whatever limits our freedom now will continue to operate after we die. In both cases, you are subject to the power of *Karma*. Originally the Sanskrit word *Karma* meant "action", but it quickly expanded and now imply the eternal struggle between good and evil. At the most superficial level you build good *karma* (personal effect) by being good and bad *karma* (personal effect) by being bad. This matches the Christian concept of choosing between good and evil actions, and being rewarded or punished accordingly. Millions of people, East and West, live by that belief. But *Karma* (Cosmic effect) never ends; it is part of the soul's continuous journey, not just a single lifetime that leads once and for all to heaven or hell. The catch is that no amount of good *karma* (personal effect) can win a person's freedom. The oriental mythology's version of hell is never finding a way out of bondage, which makes it strangely congruent to Christian hell. Perfect goodness is not achievable, and bit by bit the effect of *karma* (personal effect) will turn the saint's life into the sinner's, and vice versa. That is why "glue" might be a better translation of *Karma* (Cosmic effect) than "action". The oriental mythology believes that one can compare *Karma* to a cosmic clock with every gear perfectly meshed. One can compare it to a super-computer keeping track of every action in creation. One can compare it to an eternal judge (for example, *Paoti Mang* in *Yuma* religion) weighing the good and bad results (*Suyo Kheyo* in *Yuma* religion), of every thought and deed. In truth the whole system – universe, brain, lower self, higher self, Atman, God, Goddess, is bound together by *Karma*'s (Cosmic effect's) invisible force. The law of *Karma*, which underlies every oriental mythological belief system, holds that none of us can escape paying our debts, and since we accumulate debts every day, we have no choice but to keep paying them off lifetime after lifetime (Chopra, D. 2006:1-169; Subba, J.R. 2005b).

Being Saved from Sin

According to oriental mythology, punishment in the afterlife is the result of unpaid *Karma* debts. If I commit a crime and don't pay for it here on earth, I will pay by suffering later. The universe will insist on redressing the balance of wrong with right. Hell (*Khema Yongson Den/Naraka*) is the condition of *karmic* suffering. NDE investigators have even found a category of people whom they call "earthbound souls", haunted by evil actions and frustrated desires. A man named George Ritchie, who was given the firsthand look at them, offered prime witness to this.

Whether suffering is created here on earth through physical pain or in the afterlife through psychological torment, the causes remain the same, since they can be traced back to the workings of *karma*. Every culture irrespective of occidental mythology or oriental mythology believes that bad deeds are inescapable in the afterlife. The spiritually mature person pursues a meaningful life through the following self-worth, love, truth, appreciation and gratitude, reverence and nonviolence as specified by the code of religion or belief system they adhere to. To live outside these values or code of their belief system or religion is painful, and if intense enough, perhaps the pain puts a person in hell. So the value of a meaningful life demonstrates the hidden side of *karmic* debts. When you are free of them, your life becomes fulfilled and deeply worth living. Hell or *Naraka* or *Khema Yongsong Den* is farthest from God because it represents the low ebb of consciousness. Satan is a creation of consciousness, and as such he waxes and wanes, he evolves, and he changes in significance. *Karma* or action spins the web. *Karma* is not prison; it is a field of choice. *Karma* keeps our choices honest. "We sow what we reap", but this is far from saying that the forces of cosmic good and evil trap us. Hell or *Naraka* or *Khema Yongsong Den*, like every other location in consciousness, ultimately reflects the state of our own awareness, and freedom from hell is own, like every other achievements, by coming closer to the reality of the soul (Chopra, D. 2006:1-169; Subba, J.R. 2005a; 2005b).

Mind is the Stream of Desires

The *Akashic* field has been interpreted by every culture to make it meaningful to that culture. We have been following the soul's journey into the highest stage it can attain, which is the *Akasha* itself, the source of creativity. Different spiritual traditions envision this end point in different ways. *Yumaism* believes in Eight Dens (worlds/Akashic fields/*Lokas*) above the earth and Nine Dens (*Akashic* fields/worlds/*Lokas/Dens*) below the mother earth surface. Here are seven versions that continue to shape how people experience their spiritual journey: Paradise, ii) The Godhead, iii) The Spirit World, iv) Transcendence, v) Transmigration, vi) Awakening and vii) Dissolution. These are seven settings for the soul, and each possibility is self-created (Chopra, D. 2006:197-214; Subba, J.R. 2005a; 2005b).

Seven Destinations of Souls

(i) Paradise (Heaven, *Sangrampedang Den, Swargha*): Your soul finds itself in a perfect world created by God/Goddess. You go to paradise as a reward and never leave or leave only when your *Karma* account gets exhausted. If you are bad, you go to Satan's home (hell, *Narak, Khema Yongsong Den* etc.) and never leave or leave only after your bad *karma* gets burnt through punishment.

(ii) The Godhead: Your soul returns to God, but not to any particular place. You discover the location of God/Goddess as a timeless state infused with His or Her presence.

(iii) The Spirit World: Your soul rests in a realm of departed spirits (Forefather's village). It rejoins your ancestors and those who passed on before you, who are gathered with the Great Spirit (*Hang Sam, Purkha, Pitri*).

(iv) Transcendence: Your soul performs a vanishing act in which this expression person dissolves, either quickly or gradually. The pure soul rejoins the sea of consciousness from which it was born.

(v) Transmigration: Your soul is caught in the cycle of rebirth. Depending on your *karma*, your soul moves from lower to higher life forms, and even may be born in objects. The cycle continues eternally until your soul escapes through higher realization.

(vi) **Awakening:** Your soul arrives in the light. It sees with complete clarity for the first time, realizing the truth of existence that was masked by being in a physical body.

(vii) **Dissolution:** Eternity is nothingness. As the chemical components of your body return to basic atoms and molecules, the consciousness by the brain disappears completely. You are no more.

There is a good deal of cultural overlap here as one tradition feeds into another. The Muslim vision of eternity as a paradise garden owes its existence in part to the Garden of Eden. Spirit worlds are common all over the globe. The ancient Greeks expected to meet the shades of the departed across the River Styx in Hades, but filtered through time and Christianity. Hades became a punishing hell presided over by Satan while the Greek place of blessed spirits, the Elysian Fields, became heaven. There are invisible spirit worlds found in the ancestor worshippers of Sikkim like in Japan and China. In a prehistoric age aboriginal peoples drifted from South Asia to Australia and the islands of the South Pacific, bringing their spirit worlds with them. With them also came a kind of "dream time" that infused ordinary time, in which material events could be seen as depending upon spiritual events. But spirit world didn't hold in most of the developed religions in the main lands of India, where the dominant belief gathered around three other afterlife:

(a) **Transcendence** (rejoining the sea of consciousness),

(b) **Awakening** (discovering that one's true nature is *Atman,* soul, Sam-complex, Soul-complex, *Sam* etc.), and

(c) **Transmigration** (the eternal cycle of rebirth).

Sikkim and in other remote corners of India the spirit world still holds in many less developed belief systems of tribal communities. Being born in a certain culture, however, doesn't always determine where your soul finds itself after "crossing over". Eternal life, it turns out, is also very personal. Human mind is addicted to repetition. We pursue the same desires today that we had yesterday. Even our thoughts today are generally above 90% the same as the thoughts we had yesterday, according to some studies. On the positive side psychologists point out that the pursuit of pleasure and the avoidance of pain motivate us every day and generally to good effects. We are assured by what we know. Dying forces us outside the wall. We believe that we don't enter the *Akashic* field empty-handed. Whatever our dream is right now, the dream continues. Consciousness is tied by thousands of thread to old memories, habits, preferences, and relationships. You have to know where you are right now, in order to know where you will be tomorrow, and the afterlife is just a special kind of tomorrow. You need to know seven points about you. They are:

(i) What is Your Story? Your story is more than just a list of the events in your life. It is about your self-image, how you are yourself, what shaped your mind, which memories imprinted them on you. Taken together, your story tells you where you are in the cycle.

(ii) What are Your Expectations? Expectations are seeds. Once planted, they manifest into those things we gain from life, or lose. When you become aware of your own expectations, you discover the unspoken limits you have set on yourself. There is a huge difference between those who expect great things and those who don't.

(iii) What is Your Purpose? This is the meaning you are trying to find. If you know your purpose (not the worldly superficial things) to which your life is dedicated.

(iv) What is Your Destination? This is about fulfillment. Human goals are endless; they unfold not like a road that has an end but like a river that flows to join the sea, merging with ever-larger possibilities. If you know your destination, you can envision your highest fulfillment.

(v) What is Your Path? Having identified your purpose and your destination, there must be a way to get there. "Path" has been adopted as a spiritual term, but in fact anyone, spiritual or not, follows certain ways to get where they want to go.

(vi) Who are Your Adversaries? Forward motion is never without obstacles. On your path you will find yourself blocked. At times the adversary is external, but if you examine yourself deeply, you will find it is always internal as well.

(vii) Who are Your Allies? We all bring others with us on our journey. Just as your adversaries did, you may identify these allies as external, but only reflect your own inner strength, just as an opponent reflects your inner vulnerability.

Everything serious and difficult gets postponed, often to their dying day. But self-exploration is the most important thing one can do to prepare for the afterlife. Buddhism sometimes describes its practices as conscious dying. One dies to old memories, conditioning, habits, and self-denial; all the things that the mind uses not to see itself. To experience the *Akashic* field (*Lokas/Dens/* spiritual worlds) requires an expanded state of awareness. Contracted awareness keeps us anchored in daily affairs. The critical thing is to have a life of the soul, and that comes about only through expansion. *Akasha (Dens/talatal/*spiritual worlds) is the home of the soul and therefore cannot be limited in any way. The mystery, strangely enough, is how we manage to restrict the undoubted potential of our own minds. We have variety of choices depending on the qualities of your own mind, which expands and contracts depending on many factors. The key words for such choices are based of Expansion or Contraction of Expression – Repression; self knowledge – Denial; comfortable with uncertainty – crave security; personal insight – received opinion; spiritually oriented – materialistic; self-accepting – guilty, self-denying; individualism – conformity; altruistic, selfless – ego-driven etc. In catholic theology, condemned reincarnation as a heresy by 553 A. D. In occidental traditional, the arithmetic of good and bad deeds is infinitely flexible. For every act that earns bad *karma*, sending the soul downward in its next rebirth, there is a chance to balance the scale through good *karma*. Reincarnation also allows a soul to experience one heaven or hell after another without limit until *Moksha*, or liberation, is achieved. *Moksha* ends the entire cycle of heaven and hell forever, at which time the soul returns to its original state as pure consciousness, a drop of bliss in the ocean of bliss. Here, the quarrels of religion end. Like all earthly attachments, they fall away. Consciousness is consciousness no matter who is interpreting it. *Akasha* (*Lokas/Dens/talatal*) exists beyond choice, beyond mind. This state of unity attracts the dying person towards it. Through the magnetism of the soul, one is drawn to the next stage of a personal dream that is universal at the source (Chopra, D. 2006; Subba, J.R. 2005a, 2005b).

Traveling in Three Worlds

A staunch materialist may consider it impossible to travel to non-physical worlds, but we travel to other states of consciousness all the time, in fact. According to oriental mythology, we move between three levels of awareness that account for all experience: (i) Consciousness filled with physical objects; (ii) Consciousness filled with subtle objects; and (iii) Consciousness filled with nothing but itself – pure consciousness. In each state the soul looks different. In the physical world the soul is centered on emotions and idealism. It connotes warmth of heart, love, and devotion to God. We look to our souls to remind ourselves that we have a divine spark inside, and yet we don't base our lives on it. The soul flickers in and out of our physical body. In the subtle world the soul is spirit, denoting holiness, closeness to God, and freedom from the burdens of physical existence. The soul no longer offers mere comfort; it is the bliss that pain was disguising. The soul is constant now; its guidance can be clearly followed without confusion. The primary feeling is magnetic; one is being drawn inexorably towards the divine. In the domain of pure consciousness, achieving destination is complete. One sees that self and soul are one and is nearest to the Almighty God or Goddess. It has reached to the village or place where forefathers reside (*Sangrampedang Den/Samkhalung/Rumlyang*). After death a person experiences the subtle dimension automatically, yet every dimension is enfolded into the others. Each state of consciousness has its own particular qualities and is perceived as its own separate reality. Accordingly, there are three worlds of Eternity:

(i) Consciousness of physical objects: This is the world of concrete things that we verify through the five senses. It obeys linear time. We appear to ourselves as physical bodies separated in time and space. A life span occupies a limited number of years between two absolute events, birth and death. The laws obeyed in this dimension are strict. Gravity, the speed of light, and the conservation of matter and energy (which can be neither created nor destroyed) form the foundation of every other natural law. If this is your primary world, you have certain powers that allow you to explore it. These include physical strength, willpower, reason, emotional expression, sexuality, and personal authority. To the extent that you use these powers fully, you will be more and more successful. At the same time, you are more likely to become attached to this dimension of consciousness as the only reality. In this world the sky feels like physical space filled with infinity of material things. The soul feels personal but is seen only in short glimpses.

(ii) Consciousness of subtle objects: This is the world of dreams, imagination, and inspiration in all its many forms. We verify this world through intuition, detecting qualities like love and beauty, feeling a subtle presence within and without that is not available to the five senses. A life span in this dimension lasts as long as it can be imagined. The laws of the subtle world are fluid. Events can happen forward or backward. Invisible structures may persist for a long time (for example, as myths and archetypes), but even then, time does not bind them as strictly as in the physical world. Gravity and the speed of light are no longer absolutes. This is your primary world; you will have certain powers that allow you to explore it. These include imagination, memory, artistic ability, spiritual sensitivity, healing abilities, and intuition. The more you exercise these powers, the more successful you will be. However, you may also find yourself detached from the physical world and unable to navigate it as well as someone without intuition and spiritual sensitivity. This will worry you discover that the subtle world is capable of supporting you. The sky feels dreamlike, filled with memories and images, archetypes and gods, spirits and etheric beings. The soul feels like a guiding force leading back to the source. It is sensed constantly.

(iii) Pure Consciousness: This is the world of awareness being aware of itself. There are no objects, gross or subtle. We verify this world through "I am". Existence becomes its own end, its own reward. As an experience, pure consciousness begins with a silent mind; this grows in richness and meaning the longer a person has the experience. The laws of this world apply to creation itself. The seeds of every object and event gestate here. Here is the possibility of time, space and physical things. There is the possibility of mind, as yet without thought or images. Although totally free of anything visible, pure consciousness is eager to give birth; mystics tell us it is pregnant with All That Is. If this is your primary world, you need no powers to navigate it. The flow of time and the expansion of space are neutral events to you; they come and go within your being. You witness them without attachment, although you wish, you can call upon any quality, love, compassion, strength, truth, and experience it in fullness. In this world the sky feels uncreated. Concepts like birth and death, life and death, have no relevance. There is only existence. To be is an all-enveloping experience. Afterlife is not as "afterlife" as we assume. All three dimensions of consciousness are ever-present space.

The sky enclosing itself is pure existence. The soul is impersonal. It is being, with no added qualities (Chopra, D. 2006:197-214; Subba, J.R. 2005a; 2005b).

Living Beyond Boundaries

The afterlife is not just a mystery to be solved. It is an opportunity to expand life beyond boundaries. Awareness begins in an unbounded state with pure consciousness and then cascades, plane to plane, until it reaches the physical world. Each level is in you. At any given moment you could place yourself anywhere; the choice of boundaries or unboundedness is your alone. Therefore journeys to heaven and hell are daily occurrences, not far-off possibilities. The inner and outer worlds are changing constantly. We are touching on subtle experiences every day. Some of the levels we apply to our voyages in the subtle world are: Dream, imagination, myths, archetypes, epiphanies, the shadow, collective consciousness, numinous creation (angels, demons, saints, *Bodhisattvas, Phedangmas,* Deities, Divinities, etc), sacred visions, desires and wishes, and inspiration. These are the consciousness filled with subtle objects (Chopra, D. 2006).

Guides and Messengers

Everything that is real at one level of consciousness is unreal at another. If you make an angel, you must project it, but to do that, you must be in a state of consciousness that accepts angels as real. In India there is a specific region called *Devaloka* or *Sonaingtong Den*, where angels abide, but it is not the same as heaven. *Devaloka* is often portrayed like heaven, a place in the clouds where ethereal beings float, but it is understood that all *Lokas*, or other worlds, are layers of consciousness. Therefore, angels are part of the whole self-system. Similarly, in *Yuma* religion there is Eight Dens (*Lokas* or worlds) above the Mother Earth and Nine Dens (*Lokas*/worlds) below the Mother Earth making a total eighteen *Dens*, and are simply projected layers of consciousness. Each of these eighteen layers of consciousness (*Lokas/Dens*/Worlds) have specific functions to discharge and the *Dens* are governed by different *Mangs* (Deities), *Sammangs* (Divinities), *Sammang Chyangs* (Retinue of Divinities), and enlightened Spirituals. As a believer of *Yuma* religion, you must project it, but to do that, you must be in a state of consciousness that accepts *Mangs, Sammangs, Sammang Chyangs* and Enlighten Spirits of the Eighteen Dens as real. The Almighty Goddess *Tagera Ningwaphuma* often referred them (these gods and goddesses) as *Sijo Ingmi Sa* (messenger Goddess) in *Mundhum* (myths). This is understood that all these Deities (*Mangs*), divinities (*Sammangs*) and retinue of divinities (*Sammang Chyangs*), are projected spiritual conscious gods and goddesses perceived by the learned forefathers during the evolution of *Yuma* religion. Therefore, the *Mangs, Sammangs, Sammang Chyangs* and Enlightened Spirits of the *Yuma* religion are part of the whole self-system. Any one projection of *Dens/Lokas*, and gods or goddesses as messengers affects every level of consciousness and therefore every level of creation. Meaning is never isolated. The Eighteen *Dens* and *Mangs, Sammangs, Sammang Chyangs* and Enlighten Spirits exist because they have been projected in consciousness. Just as a movie requires an image, a projector, and a viewer, so do these messengers. In *Yuma* religion, these are projected in mental consciousness, not in personified images like the gods and goddess of Hinduism. In *Yuma* religion the three elements involved are: the seer or observers are *Phedangmas*, the process of projecting are *Mangs, Sammangs, Sammang Chyangs* and Enlighten Spirits, and the thing projected are *Mundhums* (myths).

In *Yuma* religion, at the soul level all the three roles, the observers (*Phedangmas*), beholds an object (*Mundhum* recited at

Altar) and through the process of observation (*Mangs, Sammangs,* and *Sammang Chyangs*) are enfolded into unity. Almighty Goddess *Tagera Ningwaphuma* is the Creator (through Her Messenger God *Sigera Yabhundin Mang Porokmi Wambhami Mang*) and Her creation. Once She projects Her creation outward, unity turns diversity. This is equivalent of the Big Bang. When the creator begins to look at Herself, instantly there is a three-in-one state: the observer (*Phedangmas*) beholds an object (*Mundhum*) and the process of observation (*Mangs, Sammangs, Sammang Chyangs*). As soon as the three emerge, the entire universe emerges with them. The matter dispersed by the Big Bang is only one facet of an invisible mechanism in which the creator suddenly sees what is possible, and in that seeing the possible comes true in infinite variety. It is surprising that the entire universe contains only 4% visible matter and energy, the remaining 96% being so called dark matter whose function seems to be that it holds the visible universe together in some mysterious way. The creator is invisible and creates the invisible field from which everything visible is organized and upheld.

The mystery of creation lies in the gap between the observer and the observed. Angels (*Mangs, Sammangs, Sammang Chyangs*) exist in this gap; they are the processors of consciousness. They are the servants of God in Biblical term and *Devata* in Sanskrit. They are the agents of creation. The creator does nothing but observe, the messenger gods and goddesses, or *devas* fulfill the imagination of creation of the creator. The *devata* effect or *Mang, Sammangs, Sammang Chyangs* effect regulates every level of reality, and Angels/*Mangs, /Devtas* therefore appear in all the Soul-complex/Self-system. In the physical dimension angels/*Mangs Sammangs, Sammang Chyangs /Devtas* appear as visitors and guides. They deliver messages from God or offer help in times of crisis. In the vital dimension angels/*Mangs Sammangs, Sammang Chyangs /Devtas* sustain Nature by breathing life into creation. They serve as builders of forms; they give each living thing an essential connection to Nature. In the mental dimension angels/*Mangs Sammangs, Sammang Chyangs /Devtas* appear in visions and dreams. They embody the mind of God and connect it to our thoughts. In the ego dimension angels/*Mangs, Sammangs, Sammang Chyangs /Devtas* serve as personal guides and guardians.

In the dimension of bliss Angels/*Mangs, Sammangs, Sammang Chyangs /Devtas* surround God and praise Him constantly. They embody joy in its most exalted state.

All five levels share the need for communication. The creative impulse must cascade from one level to the next. Angels/*Mangs, Sammangs, Sammang Chyangs /Devtas* are really symbols for how information gets passed along and organized. The reality beneath the symbol is the Angel/*Mang, Sammang, Sammang Chyang /Devta* effect. Our own consciousness regulates what is real and unreal; we have stepped into our own projection. Through us, gods/goddesses, angels, and souls come in and out of being. Gods and Goddesses, angels, and etheric beings exist because they have been drawn out of the raw material of consciousness. The workshop where this creation takes place is Void or the Sky/*Akasha/Dens*, the field of consciousness (Chopra, Deepak. 2006; Subba, J.R. 1999; 2005a; 2005b).

The Sky/*Akashic* Field or *Lokas* or *Dens*

Physicists now believe that space is full of activity in the form of invisible fluctuations in the quantum field. These so-called virtual fluctuations account for matter and energy and also for distortions in time and space. Thus, in a curious way the disproved notion of the ether has been revived indirectly. Physics had proven that light, unlike waves rippling across a pond, does not need a medium to travel in. When a photon starts at point A and moves to point B, the journey can be accomplished by the vanishing act: the first photon winks out of existence, changes its location somewhere in virtual reality (the Zero Point Field), and reappears intact in the second location. Since matter and energy are constantly emerging and then vanishing back into the void, the Zero point serves as the switching station between existence and nothingness. Newton had established that matter and energy cannot be destroyed, but they can oscillate in this shadowy way at the subatomic level, as long as the sum total of matter and energy is not altered. This vanishing act occurs only when the cosmos dies billions of years from now by cooling down to Absolute Zero. Matter would exist only as randomly floating particles in interstellar space. In the Earth's ecosystem, life forms constantly relate to each other in exquisite balance. The oxygen given off by plants during photosynthesis, for example, would eventually poison the entire atmosphere, killing off all vegetation that needs carbon dioxide, were it not for the evolution of animals, which consume the oxygen and return carbon dioxide back to plants. This extremely complex balance can be traced back to the void, where every single fluctuation of virtual energy is passed along and absorbed by a virtual particle in need of energy (Chopra, D. 2006).

Creative Leaps

The appearance of life on Earth depended on the sudden ability of a molecule, DNA, to replicate itself. No molecule before it had ever done that. We can explain the evolution of the universe entirely in terms of such creative leaps, or "emergent properties." Before oxygen and hydrogen could discover how to become water, the cosmos had to create atoms, which were not present at the Big Bang, and atoms had to turn into gases, solids, metals, organic molecules, and so on. None of these events were simple combinations like pouring sugar into water. An emergent property, on the other hand, is a creative leap that produces something out of nothing. In spiritual terms the cycle of birth and rebirth is a workshop for making creative leaps of the soul or *Atma* or *Sam*. The natural and the supernatural are not doing different things but are involved in transformation on separate levels. At the moment of death the ingredients of your old body and old identity disappear. Your DNA and everything it created devolve back to their simple component parts. Your memories dissolve back into raw information. None of this raw material is simply recombined to produce a slightly altered person. To produce a new body capable of making new memories, the person who emerges must be new. You do not acquire a new soul, because the soul does not have content. It is not 'you' but the center around which 'you' coalesces, time after time. It is your *Zero Point*. The human spirit is degraded when we confine ourselves to the span of a lifetime and the enclosure of a physical body. We are mind and spirit first, and that places our home beyond the stars. Knowing that I will return to the field one day to find my source provides me with immeasurable confidence in the purpose of life. There can be no present life, for the old cells in my body have to die to make new tissue possible. This is the miracle of creation, which in every second is one thing: life and death joined in an eternal dance. We live in an endlessly re-created universe (Chopra, D. 2006:1-169; Frazer, James 1996; Fergus Fleming et. al. 1996; Ferguson, J. C. and Anesaki, Masaharu 1964; Fung Yu-Lan 1948; Johnson, Paul 1972; Moody, Raymmond. 1976; Subba, J.R. 1999; 2005a:4; 2005b; Sogyal Rimpoche 2002).

PART-II

2

WELL-DEVELOPED MYTHOLOGIES OF THE PEOPLE OF SIKKIM—OVERVIEW

Under the well-developed mythologies of Sikkim, an overview of oriental mythology of Hinduism, Buddhism, Jainism and Sikhism, and occidental mythology of Islam and Christianity has been discussed in brief. Literature is available on these mythologies in abundance and I have not dealt in detail on these mythologies. Since, these mythologies have also been thoroughly discussed in the first chapter, only an overview of these mythologies has been discussed in this work.

Mythology of Hinduism

The *Khasas* and majority of *Newars*, a section of *Khambu-Rais, Gurungs, Mangars, Sunuwars* and *Thamis* amongst the hill tribes or races, and majority of plains-men are Hindus in Sikkim. The *Khasas* could be divided into higher *Khasas* (*Bahun* and *Chhetri*) and the lower *Khasas* (*Kami, Damai,* and *Sarki*) sub-castes. A few *Khasas* namely *Chhetris* and lower *Khasas* (*Kami, Damai* and *Sarki*) are animist also. They worship *Masta* (*Kul Devta*) – ancestor divinity, nature gods and goddesses such as *Bhimsen, Devi, Nag-Nageni, Simey-Bhumey* etc. through their oracular shaman priests known as *Dhami* or *Jhankri*. During 1981 Census, Hindus were 167,780 persons (53.04%), the highest in Sikkim but it includes many faiths of hill tribes/races also.

According to Dr. Pattanaik, D. (2006) the salient features of myth and mythology of Hinduism revolve around the trinity of

Hinduism. He has described the mythology of Hinduism in brief in his book as under:

(i) The circle of *Brahma* and *Saraswati,* in which the nature of the universe is explored;

(ii) The squire of *Vishnu* and *Lakshmi* in which the cultural codes are distinguished from natural laws; and,

(iii) The point of *Shiva* and *Shakti,* in which the soul is realized and matter validated.

The circle of *Brahma* and *Saraswati,* in which the nature of the universe is explored

The circle is the most spontaneous of natural shapes, taken by the horizon, by the stars, the planets and bubbles. It represents the universe, as being timeless, fetterless, boundless, cyclical and infinite world. This universe is the medium through which the divine presents itself; and thus it serves as a window to the divine. The psychological point of view of Jung's circle has also been dealt with in the overview.

For Hindus, *Brahma* is God who creates the world. The world he creates is known as *Brahmanda.* This world is not just the outer objective world governed by mathematical principles. It is also the inner subjective world of thoughts and feelings. According to *Vedic* scriptures, God does not create this world. He simply made all creatures aware of it. Awareness leads to discovery. Discovery is creation. The world discovered by *Brahma* is embodied in the Goddess. She has always existed, even when no one observed her. For *Brahma,* the Goddess is *Shatarupa,* she who takes infinite forms. *Shatarupa* is *Saraswati,* goddess of knowledge, for in her infinite forms she reflects the answer to Brahma's question: who am I? This question is the impulse of creation. It made God open his eyes and look at the Goddess.

For Hindus, all of creation is divine. Everything in nature is therefore worthy of worship. There is no discomfort visualizing God in plants, animals, rivers, mountains, rocks, and in manmade objects such as pots, pans, pestles and mortars. God creates the world as *Brahma*, sustains it as *Vishnu* and destroys it as *Shiva*. A Hindu deity may be just in a cave, a tree growing in an orchard, a river flowing down the plains, a cow wandering in the street, or perhaps an elaborately decorated idol of stone, clay or metal enshrined in a temple. Anything can be God so long as it can respond to the human condition. In many shrines, deities are given human form merely by placing a pair of eyes and a pair of hands on a rock. Eyes represent sense organs and hands represent action organs. This indicates the deity is conscious, sensitive and responsive. A deity may be worshipped in a temporary open-air shrine made of bamboo, cane and cloth that are dismantled after the ceremony. Or it may be placed in a permanent shrine: inside the house, restricted to the family, or in a public space, open to the community. A Hindu temple is not a prayer hall or the space where the faithful gather; it is the residence of God. Each day the presiding deity is bathed, fed, bedecked and adored. Each day the deity grants audience to devotees, accepting their offerings and answering their prayers. In the earliest phase of Hinduism, known as the *Vedic* age, there were no temples. The need for permanent shrines came much later when the nomadic lifestyle gave way to a more settled agricultural life. Temple or no temple, the aim of invoking the divine in all phases of Hinduism has been the same: to cope with the stress of existence. The ritual known as *yagna* was the cornerstone of religious activity in *Vedic* times. Priests, on behalf of a patron, sat around a fire altar, chanted hymns and made offerings of milk and butter into the flames, invoking celestial beings known as *Devas* and compelling them by the power of ritual to satisfy the material aspirations of the patron. Pleased with the chants and offerings, the *Devas* gave victory in battle, brought rains on time and gave children to the childless.

Three Phases of Hinduism

The development of Hindu religion could be described in three phases as follows:

Phase of Hinduism	*Characteristic Feature*	*Approximate Dating*
Age of Ritual (*Karma Kanda*)	Focus on execution of rituals that realizes desire or changes destiny (highly mechanical)	1500 B.C. to 500 B.C. (*Vedic* era)
Age of Speculation (*Gyan Kanda*)	Focus on a deeper understanding of desire and destiny (highly intellectual)	500 B.C. to 500 A. D. (*Upanishadic* era)
Age of Worship (*Upasana Kanda*)	Focus on appeasement and adoration of deities whose grace can realize desire or change destiny (highly emotional)	500 A.D. to present time (*Bhakti* era).

Vedic gods resided above the earth. There was *Agni,* fire, who stood on the ground. There was *Vayu,* wind, who extended between earth and sky. There was *Indra,* who ruled the sky and brought rain by attacking monsoon clouds with his thunderbolt. Then came *Surya,* the sun, *Chandra,* the moon, and seven other celestial bodies or *Grahas* whose movements across the twelve solar houses (*Rashis*) and twenty-seven lunar houses (*Nakshatras*) aroused great curiosity. Not only did they indicate the change of seasons, they also mapped out the destiny of man. It was in *Vedic* times that *Jyotisha-shastra* or astrology came into being. It enabled man to distinguish favourable times from unfavourable times. It foretold future calamities and provided the means to realize dreams or modify destiny using the power of gemstones and rituals that realigned the power of the *Grahas*. The list of astrological deities includes not only *Devas* but also *Rishis* (*Brihaspati* and *Shukra*) and *Asuras* (*Rahu* and *Ketu*). *Rishis* were keeper of *Vedic* lore and, *Vedic* times, those who possessed a deep understanding of this highly revered scripture were considered as powerful as the gods. *Asuras* were enemies of the *Devas,* and resided under the earth. Though *Asuras, Rahu* and *Ketu* were special, they lived in the skies as eclipses and comets influencing the design of the celestial regions and hence influencing the destiny of those on earth. *Rahu* and *Ketu* therefore became worthy of worship, to be appeased rather than adored.

The Gods of Time

The gods of time in Hinduism are as under:

Name of Deity	*Celestial body*	*Associated Mental state*	*Associated Animal*	*Associated Mineral*
Surya	Sun	Leadership	Horse	Ruby
Chandra	Moon	Mood swings	Antelope	Pearl
Mangal	Mars	Aggressiveness	Lion	Coral
Budh	Mercury	Intelligence	Lion with an elephant's tusk	Emerald
Brihaspati	Jupiter	Rationality	Elephant	Yellow sapphire
Shukra	Venus	Creativity	Horse	Diamond
Shani	Saturn	Impatience	Vulture	Blue sapphire
Rahu	Eclipse	Confusion	Serpent's head	Hessonite
Ketu	Comet	Restlessness	Serpent's tail	Cat's eye

The *Vedic* age also saw the writing of *Vastu-shastra,* a treatise that compiled methods of manipulating the forces of space. Attention was given to the *Diggapalas,* guardians of the four cardinal and four ordinal directions. By placing doors, windows, walls and water tanks in various directions, it was possible to enrich a dwelling and make fortune flow in a particular direction. An analysis of the locations of the *Diggapalas* shows a great need for balance. *Indra,* god of freshwater rains, sits on the east, balanced by *Varuna,* god of seawater, sitting in the west. The moon sits in the northeast, balancing the sun, which sits in the southwest. The fire-god sits in the southeast, balancing the wind-god, who sits in the northwest. In the south sits *Yama,* god of death and decay, balanced by *Kubera,* god of treasures and growth, guardian of the north.

Vastu-Shastra

Vastu-shastra assigns the directions with gods as under:

Northwest	North	Northeast
Vayu	*Kubera*	*Chandra*
wind god	god of growth	moon-god
West		East
Varuna		*Indra*
god of seawater		god of rainwater
Southwest	South	Southeast
Surya	*Yama*	*Agni*
Sun-god	god of death	fire-god

The inclusion of earth-bound gods such as *Asura, Nagas* and *Yakshas* in the pantheon of *Vedic* gods is a clear indicator that, with the passage of time, the sky-gazing nomads were becoming increasingly drawn to the mysteries of the earth. As lifestyle became more settled and less nomadic, the ritual of *yagna* was abandoned or abbreviated in favour of the *puja*. With the *puja* came a slightly different approach to the divine. The gods were no longer compelled to do man's bidding; they were appeased or adored and their grace sought with offerings of food, flowers, clothes, jewels, incense and lamps. Though the methods changed, the intention was the same: to realize desires or change destiny or to make a request to obtain the strength to cope with life.

Ritual or *Puja* makes gods more personal. There are *Ishta-devatas* or personal gods, *Kula-devatas* or family gods, *Griha-devatas* or household gods, and *Grama-devatas* or village gods. These gods either protected their worshippers or provided for them. Protector or guardian gods are usually male while progeny or fertility gods are usually female. Once a year, the wild, untamed form of the goddess is unleashed. On this the goddess reclaims her fertility by demanding blood sacrifices. By quenching her thirst with blood she is able to replenish her spent energy and nurture the community for the rest of the year.

The Hierarchy of the Divine

Dr. Pattanaik, D. (2006) has listed out the hierarchy of the divines as under:

<table>
<tr><td colspan="10">Nirguna Brahman = Divine without form</td></tr>
<tr><td colspan="3">Saguna Brahman = Divine with Form</td><td colspan="7"></td></tr>
<tr><td colspan="3">Purusha = Bhagawan = Divine within = Spiritual reality = God</td><td colspan="7">Prakriti = Bhagawati = Divine without = Maternal reality = Goddess</td></tr>
<tr><td rowspan="2">Brahma = creator</td><td rowspan="2">Vishnu = preserver, affirmer Incarnations of Vishnu</td><td rowspan="2">Shiva = destroyer, renouncer sons of Shiva</td><td rowspan="2">Saraswati = knowledge</td><td rowspan="2">Lakshmi = wealth</td><td colspan="5">Shakti = power</td></tr>
<tr><td colspan="2">Kali= wild</td><td colspan="3">Gauri= domesticate</td></tr>
<tr><td>Diggapalas = of space</td><td>Grahas = gods of time</td><td>Devas = sky gods</td><td colspan="7">Asuras/ Nagas/ Yakshas = earth gods</td></tr>
<tr><td rowspan="2">Ishta-devatas = personal gods</td><td rowspan="2">Kula devatas = family gods</td><td rowspan="2">Griha devatas = household gods</td><td colspan="7">Grama devatas = village gods</td></tr>
<tr><td colspan="3">Vira = Guardian god</td><td colspan="4">Mata = fertility goddess</td></tr>
</table>

A male form is essentially incomplete and presupposes the existence of a female form. God cannot be incomplete; hence *Brahma, Vishnu* and *Shiva* have female counterparts. There is *Saraswati* for *Brahma, Lakshmi* for *Vishnu* and *Shakti* for *Shiva*. Together these three couples embody the Hindu understanding of the ultimate divine.

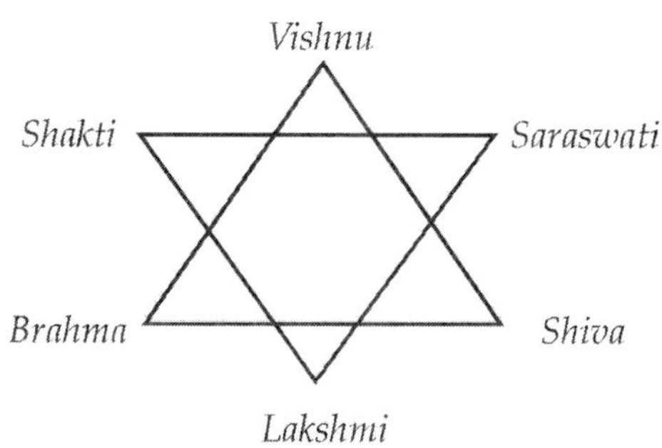

Brahma creates, *Vishnu* sustains, *Shiva* destroys, while *Saraswati, Lakshmi* and *Shakti* embody knowledge, wealth and power respectively. The male forms of the divine are associated with verbs, creating, sustaining and destroying, while the female forms of the divine are associated with nouns: knowledge, wealth, power. Gods are active; Goddesses passive. Goddesses may be knowledge, wealth and power but it is Gods who are knowledgeable, wealthy and powerful. Thus the male form of divinity represents the subject, he who is sensitive to life and he who responds to life. The female form of divinity represents the object, she who is life.

The *Veda* is believed to be of non-human origin, a container of timeless wisdom. *Brahma* sang these hymns out when he first saw *Saraswati*. These were transmitted to humans through seers known *rishis*. The seers who sat around *Brahma* heard four collections or *Samhitas* came to be known as *Rig, Sama, Yajur* and *Atharva*. Of these *Rig Samhita* is believed to be the purest transmission. In the earliest phase of Hinduism, *Vedic* hymns were chanted mechanically during rituals as *yagna* to invoke divine power and change the working of the world. Kings were the patrons of these grand ceremonies. Then a revolution took place. Sages such as *Yagnavalkya* and kings such as *Janaka* challenged the mechanical chanting of *mantras*. They focused on the ideas being communicated through the hymns. As a result, a thousand years after the *Veda* was compiled, the *Upanishad* came into being. This body of scripture is known as *Vedanta*, the pinnacle of *Vedic* wisdom. It states that creation involved the splitting of the primal being that is identified as *Purusha*. The split portion of the *Purusha* is identified as *Prakriti*. The two complement each other. In common parlance, *Purusha* is translated to mean "man" while *Prakriti* means "nature". Thus *Purusha* can also mean "culture" while *Prakriti* can also mean "woman". These translations suggest that in the Hindu world man is equal to culture and woman to nature.

A thousand years after the *Upanishad*, another revolution took place. People became increasingly theistic. Like the mechanical rites of earlier times, the speculations of the *Upanishad* did not satisfy the emotional needs of society. There was need for a divinity that was not merely an abstract force invoked during *yagna* or an abstract idea to be analysed by metaphysicians. There was need for a concrete divinity that could be embodied and personified so that it responded to the human conditions in human terms. To answer these needs, epics such as the *Ramayana* and *Mahabharata* and chronicles known as the *Puranas* came into being. These told the stories of gods and demons, Gods and Goddesses. In them, *Purusha* was personified as *Brahma, Vishnu* and *Shiva* while *Prakriti* was personified as *Saraswati, Lakshmi* and *Shakti*. Stories of Gods and Goddesses were in effect narrative expressions of the interactions between spiritual demands and material needs, between conscious being and evolving environment, between the divine within and the divine without, between *Purusha* and *Prakriti*.

Birth of *Brahma*

In the beginning, on the ocean of milk, within the coils of the serpent of time, *Narayan* stirred out of his dreamless slumber. From his navel rose a lotus in which sat *Brahma*. *Brahma* opened his eyes and realized he was alone. *Brahma* trembled. He wondered who he was. From that desire to know himself, *Brahma* decided to understand what he was not. First he created four boys, the *Sanat Kumars,* out of his thoughts and asked to produce children. They did not know how. They did not understand why. They disappeared. Then came ten grown men, again out of Brahma's thoughts. These men were the *Prajapatis*. They knew how to produce children; they asked their father to give them a wife. *Brahma* split himself into two. From his left half came a creature unlike *Brahma* or his sons. It was a woman. She was extraordinarily beautiful. Her beauty stirred *Brahma* and the *Prajapatis*. The woman walked around *Brahma* to pay her respects, for *Brahma* was her father. *Brahma,* overwhelmed by desire, sprouted three extra heads, two on sides and one behind, so that he could look upon her at all times. Discomfited by her father's stare, the daughter rose to the sky. *Brahma* popped a fifth head atop the other four. This one looked away from *Narayan* towards the daughter. The daughter ran. *Brahma* ran after her. As she ran, the daughter took a number of forms, all female: goose, mare, cow, doe. Afraid of losing her, determined to posses her, *Brahma* kept taking the complementary male forms: gander, horse, bull, and buck. Thus, different types of *jivas* came into being.

Narayan's slumber represents a state when the consciousness is totally unresponsive to the world around. So deep is the slumber that *Narayan* is not even aware of himself. This is the *pralaya,* dissolution, the period before the split between *Purusha* and *Prakriti*. There is neither observer nor observation. Things have no form or name. Space collapses and life entropies into a formless, nameless mass, and the ocean of milk. Time is no longer sequential and the past, present and future telescope into each other. The serpent of time, coils rather than slithers. *Narayan* is the purest conceivable form of *Purusha*. He is consciousness that is uncrumpled, uncreated, unknotted, unpolluted. The waking up of *Narayan*, the blooming of the lotus, the birth of *Brahma* and his sons are various stages in the crumpling of this consciousness. Curiosity about the self is the impulse of this crumpling process. The crumpling gives rise to *Brahma*, the intellect, that is able to distinguish the self from all that the self is not - mind and matter. *Brahma*'s desire for children is the desire of consciousness to have a fruitful interaction with the world, the ultimate goal being knowledge of the self.

The first four sons of *Brahma* are called the ancient ones, *Sanat Kumars*, because they come into being before the creation of the sense organs. Without the sense organs, the mind does not know the material world. The mind unruffled by sensory stimuli is pure; hence the mind-born sons of *Brahma* are described as innocent, pre-pubescent boys. Such a mind has no desire to act. It is incapable of producing children or answering *Brahma*'s questions.

Brahma realizes that for a fruitful interaction with the world, he needs channels that receive stimuli and transmit actions. This results in the birth of the ten sons, the *Prajapatis*, five representing the five sense organs (eyes, ears, nose, tongue, skin) and other five representing the five action organs (hands, feet, mouth, anus, genitals). Following the birth of the *Prajapatis*, *Brahma* becomes aware of the world around him that is the Goddess. This awareness takes the form of a sexual stirring. Unlike the first four sons of *Brahma*, the *Prajapatis* are mature, capable of responding to erotic stimuli.

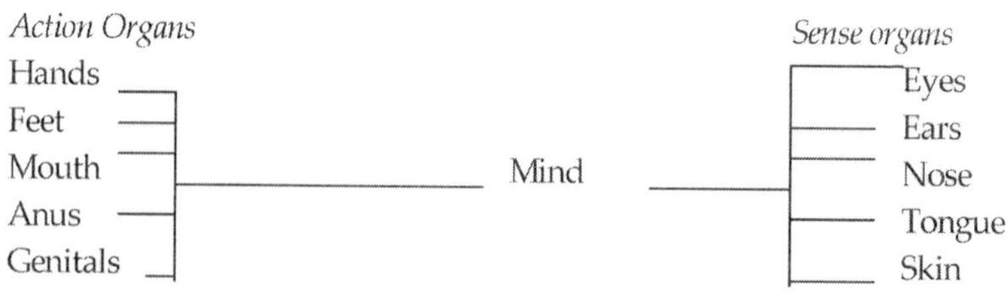

The ten sons of *Brahma* by Pattanaik, D. (2006)

The Goddess exists even during *pralaya*. But no one observes her, as all senses are dormant. This unobserved Goddess is known as *Yoga-nidra,* she who exists during God's dreamless slumber. When *Narayana* wakes up, the lotus blooms and *Brahma* opens his eyes. The senses come alive. *Yoga-nidra* becomes *Yoga-maya,* stimulating the senses. *Yoga-maya* is called *Brahma*'s daughter because she owes her origin to him. If *Brahma* had no questions, if *Brahma* felt complete, if *Brahma* had been self-contained, he would never have 'Looked' for answers: the world has had no observation, and the world would have never been 'created'. Another name for *Yoga-maya* is *Usha,* meaning 'dawn' because her arrival is like the dawn, the hour of awakening. She is also called *Shatarupa,* meaning she of infinite forms. Like the world she represents, the Goddess in mercurial, constantly transforming. She goes around and envelops *Brahma* as soon as she appears. Sensations and actions fill the mind with memories, desires and ideas. These are the three extra heads of *Brahma.* A point comes when the consciousness is so crumpled by external inputs that a fifth head appears, atop the previous four, looking away from *Narayana.* This is the ego; that part of mind that constantly seeks validation and approval from the world around. The narrative emphasizes that the ego has no independent existence; it is a reaction to worldly stimuli. The ego takes *Brahma* away from knowing his true self: *Narayana.* Spurred by the ego, *Brahma* seeks to possess the Goddess, control her. She takes many forms, as is her nature, and slips away like water from a clenched palm. To keep up with her, *Brahma* changes his forms. When she becomes a goose, he becomes a gander. When she becomes a cow, he becomes a bull. In effect, *Brahma* loses his own identity and acquires an identity that depends on the outside world. As the chase proceeds, *Brahma* forgets the reason he created the world in the first place. The objective of self-realization gives way to the quest for self-preservation, self-propagation and self-actualization. The world *chitta* is used for the moulding consciousness; it connects the mind to the soul, *manas* to *atma, Prakriti* to *Purusha. Narayana* is *Param-atma,* the uncrumpled consciousness of God. Interactions with the world, the Goddess, crumple chitta and introduce memories, desires, ideas and ultimately the ego. The sprouting of *Brahma*'s heads represents this crumpling process. The five-headed *Brahma* is *Jiva-atma,* the crumpled consciousness of the unenlightened, ignorant, ego-dominated *jiva*. The four headed Brahma who sings the *Veda* is the crumpled consciousness of the enlightened, wise, soul-dominated *jiva*.

Elements of Creation

The elements of creation could be arranged systematically as under (Pattanaik, D. 2006):

Metaphysical Concepts]	*Mythological Characters*	*Gender*
The soul	*Narayana* (the sleeping *Vishnu*)	Male
Mind's capacity to discern and distinguish things (the intellect)	*Brahma*	Male
Mind's constituents before the appearance of the sources of stimuli: absence of memories, absence of desires, absence knowledge and absence of ego	4 *Sat-Kumars*	Male
Mind's constituents after the appearance of the source of stimuli: presence of memories, presence of desires, presence of knowledge and presence of ego	4 extra heads of *Brahma*	Male
Mind's inward and outward channels: 5 sense organs and 5 response organs	10 *Prajapatis*	Male
Ego	Fifth head of *Brahma*	Male
Material world, the source of stimuli and destination of responses, the external matrix	*Uhsa*	Female

A *jiva* can be defined as any living creature that fears death, hence is constantly involved in acts of self-preservation and self-propagation. A *jiva* contains *jiva-atma*, is sensitive to the environment and constantly engages with it in its quest to survive and find meaning in life. While the original uncrumpled state, *param-atma*, is the same for all *jivas*, the differences in crumpling are responsible for the different personalities of different *jivas*. Crumpling (crookedness) can increase or decrease, depending on how the *jiva* responds to stimuli. In principle, every *jiva* can potentially uncrumple its *chitta* so that the *jiva atma* becomes *param-*

atma. This ability creates a craving for the original uncrumpled state. It makes the *jiva* restless for that perfection, that primal peace, the dreamless slumber.

Param-atma and *Jiva-atma*

The difference between *Param-atma* and *Jiv-atma* are as under:

Param-atma	*Jiv-atma*
Unknotted *chitta*	Knotted *chitta*
Uncrumpled consciousness	Crumpled consciousness
Soul of God	Soul of *jiva*
Unaffected by memories, desires, ideas or ego	Conditioned by memories, desires, ideas of a *jiva*
Witness to a world that is limitless	Witness to a world that is limited
The destination of *yoga* or sensory discipline	The result of *bhoga* or sensory indulgence

Brahma is the grandfather of all *jivas.* His sons marry the many forms of *Shatarupa.* Together they give birth to different types of *jivas.* Through the seed of *Brahma*'s sons flowers *jiva-atma* into the *jiva.* From the wombs of their wives come the different types of flesh. In the following narrative, serpents and eagles have a common father, *Kashyapa.* Hence all possess a crumpled *chitta.* Because they have different mothers, serpents slither on the ground while eagles fly in the air. The difference is superficial, that of the flesh. This difference allows each one to interact differently with nature.

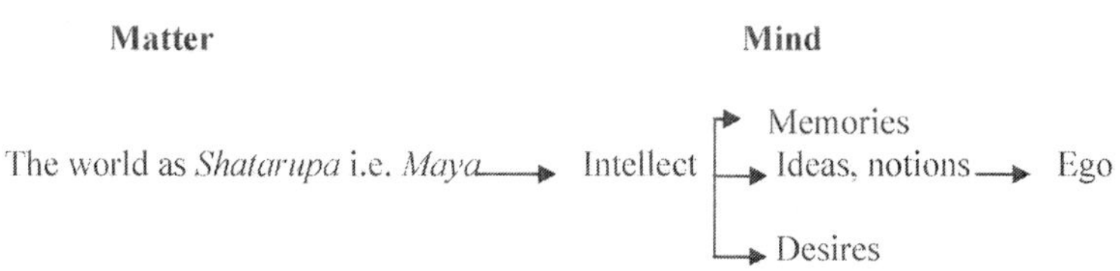

Five Heads of the Deluded *Brahma*

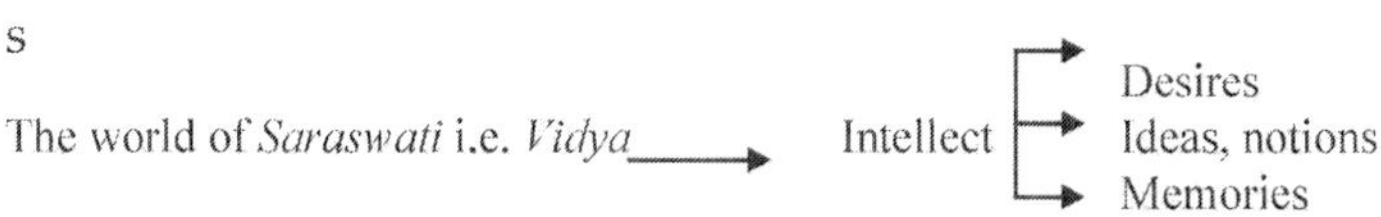

The Four Heads of the Enlighten *Brahma*

Grandchildren of *Brahma*

From *Brahma*'s thoughts came seven seers, the *Sapta Rishis*. One of the seven seers had a son called *Kashyapa*. He had many wives. On *Aditi*, *Kashyapa* fathered the *Devas*, on *Diti* he fathered the *Asuras*, on *Vinata* he fathered *Garuda*, the eagle, and on *Kadru* he fathered the *Nagas*, serpents. *Kashyapa* was also the father of *Manu*, from whom came humans, the *Manavas*. Like *Kashyapa*, *Vaishrava* was another of *Brahma*'s grandsons. He fathered the race of *Rakshasas* and *Yakshas*, malevolent and benevolent spirits. All *jivas* are distributed across three worlds: the Earth, the celestial regions and the subterranean realms, all located below the abode of *Brahma*, *Satya-loka*, the realm of truth.

Devas live in *Amravati*, a city located above the sky in the celestial realm known as *Swarga*, where they are entertained by dancing damsels known as *Apsaras* and musicians known as *Gandharvas*.

Asuras and *Nagas*, commonly described as demons and serpents, live in *Hiranyapura* and *Bhogavati*, cities located under the earth in the realm known as *Pa-tala*.

Manavas live on earth, *Bhu-loka*, along with plants, animals and wild forest spirits such as *Yakshas* and *Rakshasas*. When *Manavas* die they go to the land of the forefathers, *Pitr-loka*, and stay there until it is time to be reborn.

Three Worlds

The three worlds are indicative of the three worlds every living creature resides in simultaneously. There are objective worlds of all individuals: the private world, the social world and the natural world. Then, there are the three subjective worlds: the apparent world perceived by the senses, the imaginary world of dreams, and the conscious world of desires, memories and conditioning. Subjective or objective, every world provokes the *jiva* to act.

Mythological:	*Swarga-loka, Bhu-loka, Pa-tala*
Subjective:	Perceived, Imagined, Sub-conscious
Objective:	Private, Social, and Natural

Significantly, *Brahma* needs to create the three worlds. He merely populates it with *jivas*. God may observe and organize the world, but at no point does he ever create the world physically. Creation is awareness of the difference. Likewise, a *jiva* never creates its world: it is simply made aware of it. The purpose of life then is not to change what one did not create. Rather it is to explore this world, experience it, understand it and by doing so discover the truth about oneself. Of all *jivas*, the *chitta* is most crumpled in the *Asuras* and least in the *Devas*. To indicate this *Devas* are said to reside is a realm that is closest to *Brahma*'s abode while the *Asuras* reside farthest. In terms of degree of crumpling of the *chitta*, *Rakshasa* and *Manavas* are not bad as the *Asuras* and not as good as the *Devas*. The abode of *Rakshasas* and *Manavas* is therefore neither below the earth nor above the sky. It stands in between - On earth. The concept of different types of *jivas* inhabiting different types of worlds is an attempt to represent the plural nature of existence. No two creatures are the same. No two plants, no two animals, no two men or two women are the same. Every creature experiences the world differently. Every *jiva* is unique. But in essence everyone is the same: a *Brahma* sitting on the lotus that rises from the navel of *Vishnu*, looking for answers in three worlds.

According to *Upanishad*, the body has two parts: soul and flesh, *atma* and *sharira*. The *atma* is immortal. Only the *sharira* can die. The soul is surrounded by three *sharira*:

(i) *Sthula – sharira* or the flesh,

(ii) *Sukshma-sharia* or the mind, and

(iii) *Karana-sharia* or the causal body, memory of deeds

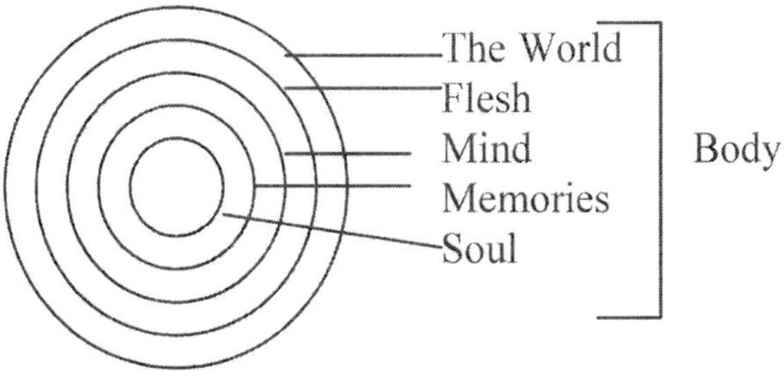

Death happens when *Yama*'s messengers, known as *Yama-dutas*, drag the mind out of the flesh. When this happens, the flesh becomes insensitive and unresponsive to all worldly stimuli. It starts to decay. The flesh needs to be cremated and the skull cracked open so that the soul and the casual body can escape. During funeral ceremonies that follow, the survivors encourage the soul wrapped in the causal body to travel across *Vaitarni* to the land of the dead, where *Yama* rules and the *Pitr* reside. *Pitr* are the ancestors, the dead awaiting rebirth, and subjects of *Yama*. They have no flesh, hence no gender. They have no mind hence no ego. But they have a soul and a causal body. In this form they stand before *Yama*. He determines their fate. Before pronouncing his judgment, *Yama* always consults *Chitragupta*, his accountant, who meticulously maintains a record of a *jiva*'s actions in its lifetime. Being an accountant, *Chitragupta* classifies these deeds as debt or equity. Selfish actions that made demands of the world and indulge the ego are debt-incurring actions. Selfless actions where the ego sacrifices its pleasure for the sake of the world are equity-earning actions. If there are debts that a *Pitr* has to repay, *Yama* ties him with a noose and fetters him to the world, forcing him to be reborn. If there are no debts to repay, *Yama* lets the *Pitr* go, liberated from the obligations of rebirth. Thus rebirth and release are the two possible destinations for the dead. Hindu funeral rites involve the use of both fire and water. The body is cremated and the bones and ashes cast into water. Fire represents the fire of *moksha* or release. The river represents *samsara*, the realm of rebirths. The two possible destinations of the soul are thus symbolically acknowledged. *Yama*, who determines the journey the soul will take, is therefore not merely god of death but also god of destiny. According to the law of *karma*, every *jiva* is obliged to experience the reactions of all actions. *Yama* is the keeper of this law.

Vaikuntha and *Kailasa*

These two represent the Hindu heaven, the destination of released souls. These are located above the three worlds and must be distinguished from *Swargha*, the Hindu paradise, above the *Devas*. *Swargha*, of the Hindu is very much part of *Samsara*, governed by rules of *karma*, fettered by time and space. In *Vishnu*'s heaven – *Vaikuntha* and *Shiva*'s heaven – *Kailasha*, these rules and fetters do not apply. It also distinguishes repaying dept from earning equity through the concepts of *dakshina* and *daan*. *Dakshina* is a fee paid for services. It clears debt. *Daan* is an act of charity. It earns equity. *Swargha* is the abode of the *Devas*, the destination of *jivas* who have only equity and no debts in their karmic accounts books. *Swargha* is a place of opulence and abundance. Every material wish is fulfilled there without effort. Since all needs are satisfied, its residents are forever in a state of delight. Actions that take a *jiva* towards *Swarga* are known as *punya*, merit-generating actions. Actions that take a *jiva* away from *Swargha* are known as *paap*, demerit-generating actions. *Paap* incurs debt. *Punya* earns equity. *Harish Chandra* reaches heaven because of *punya*. *Nahusha* enters *Swargha* because of *punya* but is thrown out because of *paap*. Thus, stay in *Swargha* is not permanent. Just as *jivas* enters *Swargha* by accumulating equity, a *jiva* sinks to *Naraka* under the burden of depts. *Naraka* is everything *Swargha* is not. It is a place of great suffering, struggle and stress.

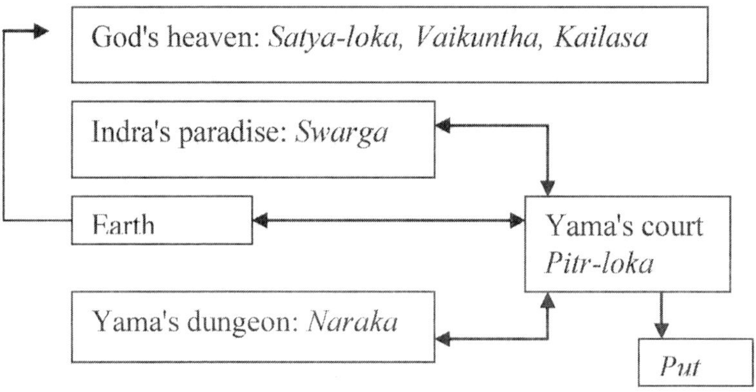

Different Hindu Worlds by Pattanaik, D. (2006)

Constituents of *Swargha*

Constituents	*Description*
Kalpataru	A tree that never withers and bears any fruit one wishes for
Kamadhenu	A cow that provides all one wants
Chintamani	A jewel that fulfils every wish

Constituents	*Description*
Akshaya-patra	A pot that is always full of grain and gold
Amrita	Nectar that keeps the *Devas* healthy and ever youthful
Varuni	Wine that brings dreams of joy without the fear of hangover
Apsara	Damsels well versed in the 64 ways of pleasuring the 5 senses.

The unrighteous *Kauravas* reach *Swargha* while the righteous *Pandavas* reach *Naraka* indicates that the law of *karma* is not easy to fathom. Merits and demerits are earned in complex ways, not all known to man. *Gandhari,* mother of the *Kauravas,* curses *Krishna,* who is God. In being responsible for the death of the unrighteous *Kauravas, Krishna* may be hero for many, but for the mother of those he killed he is villain. *Paap* and *punya* are thus many a time matters of opinion. The story of the *Kauravas* in *Swargha* informs us that there is always hope in the Hindu world, even for the worst of villains. *Paap* can be overcome by *punya;* debt can be offset with equity; desire can override destiny; a resident in *Naraka* can eventually end up in *Swargha.* But there is one place where there is no hope. That place is called *Put.* It is reserved for *Pitr* who are trapped in the land of the dead with no hope of being born. Rebirth can only happen when an offspring or descendant left behind in the land of the living produces a child. Those who die childless have no one in the land of the living that can ensure their rebirth. They are doomed to stay in *Put.* That is why a son and a daughter are known as *put-ra* and *put-ri* in Sanskrit, meaning deliverers from *Put.* By producing a child, a living person not only repays his dept to his ancestors, but he also helps a *Pitr* escape from the land of the dead into the land of the living, provide opportunity of interacting with *samsara,* discovering his or her true identity and being released from the cycle of rebirths. *Pitr* are commonly described as forefathers. But they are simply souls of the ancestors, male or female. As per Hindu mythological vocabulary male forms are used to represent the spirit and soul while female forms are used to represent matter and flesh. The old men represent *atma.* If all their descendents on earth refuse to produce children, they cannot ever get out of *samsara*. They are trapped forever until *Pralaya,* the death of the world.

When a Hindu man or woman dies, his or her children perform the funeral rites known as *shraadh*. During the ceremony, three generations of ancestors are invited to a meal and by offering of rice cakes there is a symbolic reiteration of the promise to produce children and repay the debt to ancestors. If *shraadh* is not performed, the causal body lingers in the land of the living in the form of a ghost or *Preta* unable to cross the river *Vaitarni*. When people are murdered by highway robbers, when a person dies in an accident, and no one knows that they are dead, no one performs their *shraadh,* the causal body of such persons transform into *Preta.* A ghost haunts the land of the living. In the Hindu world, ghosts are not God-less creatures. They are not exorcized. They are in essence *Pitr,* somebody's forefathers. They are angry and restless because nobody has helped them reach the land of the dead and they are not welcome in the land of the living. These *Pretas* require *atma-shanti,* a kind of simple *shraadh* to help their rebirth of the *Preta.*

Rebirth and Release

Rebirth is important. In the womb, the dead are wrapped in flesh and mind so that they once again enter the land of the living and interact with the material world. And without interacting with the material world, the soul can never realize it's true nature hence never get release.

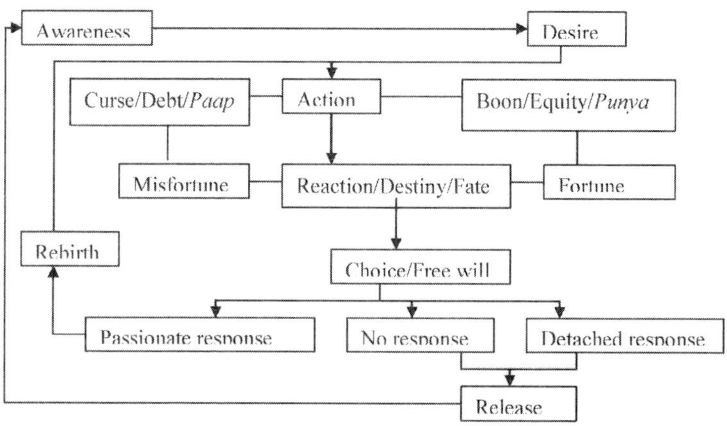

Rebirth and Release by Dr. Pattanaik, D. (2006)

The Square of *Vishnu* and *Lakshmi*

The square, with its sharp edges, is the most artificial of shapes. When drawn within the circle of the universe, it best represents culture. Different cultures have different values; hence the square of culture can be oriented in various ways, but always anchored to the rim of the circle at its corners. All cultures, however different, depend on nature for their survival.

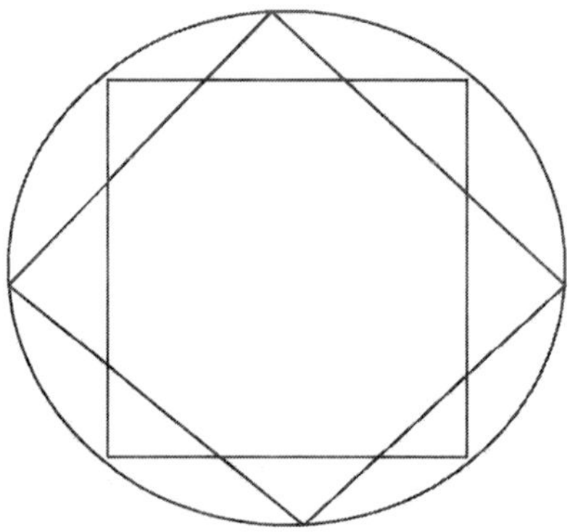

Vishnu is God who organizes the world. *Vishnu* introduces rhythm into nature so that all the changes of *Brahmanda* become predictable, hence manageable. With rhythm come waves and thoughts. For *Vishnu* therefore the Goddess has two forms: *Lakshmi*, the desirable one, and *Alakshmi*, the undesirable one. *Lakshmi* is the fertile and auspicious wave of nature – the day, the waxing moon, the high tide, the spring, the rains and the harvests. *Alakshmi* is the barren, inauspicious trough of nature – the night, the waning moon, the low tide, the hot, dry summers and the bitter-cold winters. *Vishnu* also domesticates nature to establish culture. Within culture, man can look beyond survival and explore his potential. He can generate wealth and create art. Society comes with rules and regulations, roles and responsibilities; milestones that give life direction and standards that create hierarchy. At the top of the hierarchy is *Lakshmi*, all that society admires. Below is *Alakshmi*, all that society shuns.

The value judgment that comes with culture so that the beneficial aspects of nature – those within the square, are appreciated while the rest outside the square are rejected and condemned. A recurring theme in Hindu mythology is the battle between the *Devas* and *Asuras*. The *Asuras* are the incorrigible troublemakers of the Hindu world who need to be constantly defeated by the *Devas*. Both the *Asuras* and the *Devas* invoke God in their quest to be triumphant. Typically, the story begins with an *Asura* invoking God and seeking immortality. God refuses to give such a boon, for all *jivas* are mortal. So the *Asura* asks for a boon that makes him almost invincible, hence almost immortal. Using this boon, the *Asuras* launch an attack against the *Devas* and drive them out of *Amravati*. The *Devas* then invoke God, who defeats the *Asuras* either through force or through trickery. God is thus responsible for the alternating victories and defeats of the *Devas* and the *Asuras*. The form taken by God to defeat the *Asuras* varies from story to story. For *Vaisnavas* it is usually an incarnation of *Vishnu*, such as *Varaha*. For *Shivas*, it is either *Shiva* himself or one of his sons, *Kartikeya* or *Ayyappa* or *Ganesha*. For *Shaktis*, the *Devas* turn to the Goddess when both *Vishnu* and *Shiva* express their inability to defeat the *Asuras*. The peace that follows the defeat of any *Asura* is only temporary reprieve. Soon a new *Asura* appears and repeats the cycle of war and victory. War seems almost a reaction to peace and *vice versa*. God never destroys an *Asura*. The *Asura* is simply put in a place. In the Hindu world, the *Asuras* live under the ground in the golden city called *Hiranyapura*. The *Devas* live in the celestial city above the sky called *Amravati*. The space in between is the battleground. The *Asuras* are the keepers of wealth. All wealth, whether plant or animal or mineral, ultimately has its origin under the ground. Even *Lakshmi*, the goddess of wealth, is said to reside in *Pa-tala*, the realm below the ground.

The *Devas* release the *Asuras'* subterranean wealth. *Surya*, the sun-god, coaxes plants to move towards the sky with his warmth and light. *Chandra*, the moon-god, causes the tide to rise and fall, helping in the harvest of fish and salt. *Indra*, the sky-god, hurls his thunderbolt, forcing monsoon clouds to release rain. *Vayu*, the wind-god, wears down mountains, forcing out rivers. *Agni*, the fire-god, melts rocks and releases metals. Together they draw *Lakshmi* out. The *Devas* can release and redistribute wealth, but they cannot regenerate wealth. That power resides with the *Asuras*, whose priest, *Sukra*, possesses *Sanjivani Vidya*, the secret of resurrecting the dead. He can resurrect the *Asuras* killed by the

Devas; restore the earth's fertility stripped by the *Devas* in harvest time. This makes the *Asuras* not mere enemies, but complements of the *Devas* in the cycle of life. *Asuras* are said to be strong when the sun is making its southern journey from the house of Cancer to the house of Capricorn, when days become shorter and nights colder. *Asuras* are strong when moon is waning. *Asuras* are stronger at night. Together with the *Devas*, the *Asuras* complete the year, the month and the day. *Lakshmi* is sometimes described as *Pulomi*, the sister of the *Shukra*. *Indra* abducts her and installs her as his queen, *Sachi*. But he invariably loses her when he indulges in the pleasures of women and wine, and has to struggle to win her back. For this he needs the help of the *Asuras*.

Comparison between the *Devas* and the *Asuras*

Devas could be compared with *Asuras* as follows:

Devas	*Asuras*
Kashyapa's children by *Aditi*	*Kashyapa*'s children by *Diti*
Brihaspati, lord of Jupiter, is their guru	*Shukra*, lord of Venus, is their guru
Brihaspati, who has two eyes, hence balanced, represents rational thought	*Shukra*, who has one eye, hence imbalanced, represents creative intuition
Live in the skies	Live below the ground
Powerful from winter solstice to summer solstice, as days grow longer and warmer	Powerful from summer solstice to winter solstice, as days grow shorter and colder
Pull wealth above the ground	Drag wealth under the ground
Wealth distributors	Wealth regenerators
Possess *Amrita*, the elixir of immortality	Possess *Sanjivani Vidya*, the science of bringing the dead back to life
Enjoy music and dance and tend to be insecure *Sachi*, a form of *Lakshmi*, is *Indra*'s wife	Tend to be generous and arrogant *Pulomi*, a form of *Lakshmi*, is their sister

The *Devas* and the *Asuras* serve as the force and counterforce of the churn, whose spindle is made up of the axis of space and whose rope is made up of time itself. *Vishnu* realizes the churn. The ocean milk represents the limitless possibilities of the world. All matter is in a state of entropy until the *Devas* and the *Asuras* agitate it. What emerge as a result are treasures representing power, pleasure and prosperity, all things that make worldly life worth living.

Treasures Churned out of the Ocean of Milk

The following treasures were obtained from churning out of the ocean of milk:

Representation of	*Treasures from the Ocean of Milk*	*Name*
Power	Flying horse	*Ucchaishrava*
	Conch-shell trumpet	*Panchajanya*
	Bow	*Saranga*
	White elephant	*Airavata*
Pleasure		Nymph *Rambha*
	Garland of flowers	*Vaijayanti*
	Wine	*Varuni*
	God of love	*Kama*
	God of health	*Dhanavantari*
	Nectar of immortality	*Amrita*
Prosperity	Wish-fulfilling cow	*Kamadhenu*
	Desire-manifesting tree	*Kalpavriksha-Parijata*
	Dream realizing gem	*Chinamani-Kaustubha*
Pot of plenty		*Akshaya-patra*
	Goddess of prosperity	*Lakshmi*
Pollution	Cosmic poison	*Halahala*

Along with symbols of power, pleasure and prosperity comes pollution in the form of a viscid mass called *Halahala*. In some narratives, this is the venomous vomit of the serpent that is used to churn the ocean. Pollution is an inevitable component of any manufacturing process. *Halahala* is a by-product of all the good things that are churned from the ocean. *Shiva* is indifferent to worldly things; he does not distinguish things that are desirable and things that are undesirable. In his eyes, *Halahala* is no different from *Amrita,* the nectar of immortality. He consumes the poison. In *Vaishnava* literature, *Halahala* is embodied as *Alakshmi,* the goddess of misfortune, and the twin sister of *Lakshmi. Alakshmi* always accompanies *Lakshmi. Alakshmi* is the goddess of strife. Unless she is acknowledged fortune always brings with it calamity. Construction of society is always through the domestication of nature and the disciplining of the mind. When the *Devas* pull wealth out of the earth and the *Asuras* pull it back in, another battle rages on earth – the battle between *Manavas* and *Rakshesas*. The battle between the *Devas* and *Asuras* is vertical one, a struggle between the realm above and below the earth. The battle between *Manavas* and *Rakshesas,* on the other hand, is a horizontal one, between culture and nature. *Rakshesas,* like *Asuras,* are often identified as demons. But a more appropriate word for them would be barbarians, *jivas* who follow the law of the jungle, known in Hindu scriptures as *matsya nyaya* or the code of fishes. According to this code might is right, big fish eat small fish. This code offers no reprieve for the weak, the helpless, downtrodden. Only the fit may survive. While the code of *matsy nyaya* is suitable for animals, it is not suitable for humans as humans have the faculty of reason, they can discipline natural urges of sex and violence and tame the instinct to dominate the weak. *Manavas,* the descendants of *Manu,* are expected to follow the code of *dharma.* This code is based on roles and responsibilities. Every creature is bound by duty. This duty bridles desire. It helps in creating a space where even the weakest can thrive.In the realm of *Manavas,* sex is acceptable within marriage for the sake of procreation; violence is acceptable only in defense or the pursuit of food. *Rakshesas* do not respect the laws of marriage. Violence, for them, is a tool to dominate the world.

Rama, embodiment of cultural perfection, kills the ten-headed *Rakshesa* king *Ravana,* who personifies the law of the jungle. *Rama*'s bow is the symbol of poise and balance. Culture can exist only when nature is domesticated. Culture needs to thrive but not at the cost of nature. *Dharma* must not only domesticate nature, it also needs to ensure there is harmony between nature and culture.

In *Rig Samhita,* culture is described, as is *Purusha,* with a head, arms, trunk and legs. Thus culture is a creation of the conscious being, the *jiva.* Society is an artificial construct, not natural phenomena. It involves the domestication of nature by man, for man. It also involves the domestication of man. Nature that is tamed by *dharma* exists outside us as well as inside us. For culture to thrive, the mind needs to be tamed as much as the forest. Taming of the mind involves bridling desire, lust, greed, ambition, and all the forces that threaten civilization. Domestication of the mind involves balancing desire with duty, instinct with intellect, urges with responsibilities. Sex is a natural phenomenon but marriage is a social institution. In nature, any man and woman can have sexual partners. In culture, rules define how man and woman should behave sexually. In the story of Ramayana, Sita's magical powers come from her chastity. *Rama* suffers greatly because he has to choose between the dharma of a king and the dharma of a husband. As king, he must respect his people's wishes. As husband, he can never be unfaithful to his wife. The conflict between cultural demands and natural urges is identified as the root of social change and the cause of cultural decay. Every time *dharma* is threatened *Vishnu* mounts his eagle, the mighty *Gauda,* and comes to earth ready to do battle. The descents of *Vishnu* from *Vaikuntha* to earth are his *avatars* or incarnations. The form in each descent is different because the demands of the world each time are different. The different avatars thus reinforce the idea that rules and regulations that maintain order are not static by nature. They are forged when the demands of desire clash with the quest for order.

Vishnu's Cycle of Incarnations

Vishnu's cycle of 10 (ten) incarnations are:

Form	*Purpose*
Matsya	Fish that rescues *Veda,* plants and animals
Kurma	Turtle that supports the churn to obtain treasures dissolved in the ocean of milk.
Varaha	Boar that raises the earth from the bottom of the sea

Form	*Purpose*
Narasimha	Man-lion who defies classification and overpowers mortals who seek to outwit death
Vamana	Dwarf who claims the sky for the *Devas* and shoves the *Asuras* below the surface of the earth.
Pashurama	Priest who turns to violence to kill women unrighteous kings and unchaste
Rama	King who upholds old rules at the cost of personal life
Krishna	Cowherd/chariotee/stateman who shrewdly changes rules
Buddha	Teacher who propagates compassion.
Kalki	Revolutionary who dismantles the world

Vishnu is the protector, the sustainer, and the preserver of all things. All possibilities of life will stay there until it is time for *Vishnu* to wake up and the world to be reborn.

The Point of *Shiva* and *Shakti*:

The point in which the soul is realized and matter validated. The dimensionless point is the most elemental of geometrical forms. Without the point no circle can be drawn and no square constructed. The dot best represents the soul, the formless divine within us. Just as the existence of the word, presupposes the existence of a witness to the world - the soul.

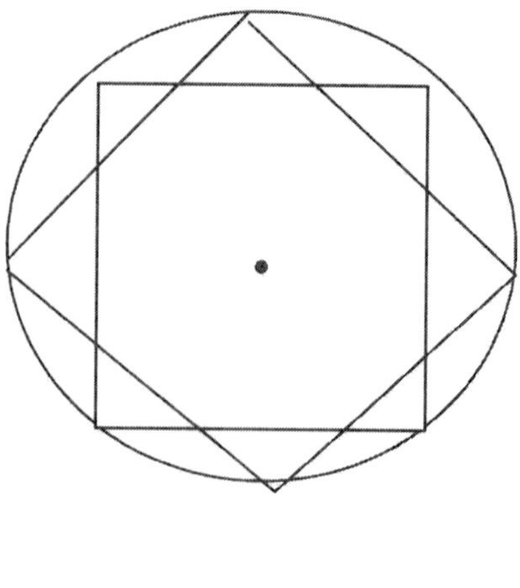

Seasons come and go. Culture rises and fall. Values change. Standards change. Worldly truths seem conditional, relative to space, time and the opinion of people. *Shiva* is god, who is not interested in these worldly truths. He seeks *sat*, truth that is permanent, absolute, and unconditional. So he shuts his eyes to the world, refusing to let memories, desires, ideas and ego crumple his consciousness. Purification of the *chitta* leads to enlightenment. With enlightenment comes *ananda*, tranquil bliss. In bliss, *Shiva* transcends all desires. There is no urge to sense or respond. There is no need for the body or the world. There is no action, no reaction or response. No *karma*, hence no *samsara*. The world ceases to be. All that exists is the *atma*, the uncrumpled pure soul, in self-contained isolation. *Shiva* is therefore god who destroys the world. One is a sterile number. When there is only one there can be no love, no yearning, and no union. Two are required to forge a relationship. Without the other, the self has no meaning. For *sat* to make sense there is need for *maya*, conditional worldly truths. For the stillness of the soul to make sense there is need for the restlessness of energy. The goddess is *maya*, embodiment of all delusions. She is *Shakti*, personification of energy. She is *Adi*, primal, as ancient and boundless as the soul. Depending on time, space and judgments of people she can be as wild and fearsome as *Kali* or as gentle and affectionate as *Gauri*. She is the world *Shiva* shuts himself from. She will stir love in the heart, make him open his eyes and be part of worldly life. Love will connect the divine inside with the divine outside. The yearning and union that follow will validate all of existence. The embodiment of *Adi-Maya-Shakti*, *Durga* is the invincible. She is at once bride and warrior. The one establishes home, provides pleasure, produces children and offers food. The other rides into battle and kills – defending those who submit to her, destroying those who challenge her. She will tame and ride the lion, the lord of the jungle. Her hair will never be bound.

The tension between the stillness of the soul and the restlessness of matter is always acknowledged. If the inner reality of *Purusha* is best represented by male forms; and if female forms best represent the outer reality of *Prakriti*, it follows that sex is the most appropriate metaphor to establish a relationship between them. The recurring theme of 'spilling semen' indicates the spirit's acknowledgement of and interaction with the material world. Refusal to do so indicates the reverse, disconnection between *Purusha* and *Prakriti*. The former is creative and fertile. The later is dangerous, destructive. The *Devas* are ever willing to shed their semen and create new life. They are indifferent to the social consequences of their actions. For *Devas*, no matter the girl asking them to impregnate her is not married. What matters to them is that by making her pregnant they help in rebirth and the rotation of the wheel of *samsara*. Society is a creation of man, not the gods. In nature, sex is not judged; ideas such as marriage and incest are cultural, born of man-made laws that seek to regulate and control sex, making it acceptable only under certain conditions. The *Devas* concern themselves with the production of new life, not its legitimacy.

According to *Tantrik* physiology, the dead are reborn when the white seed of man successfully merges with the red seed of woman. Spilt semen holds the possibility of a new life. Spilt menstrual fluid indicates failure to create that life. Seed, white or red, is thus the most potent substance in nature. The white, the colour of male reproductive fluid, represents *Purusha*; red, the colour of female reproductive fluid, represents *Prakriti*. The earth is red before the rains. After the rains, the earth is green. Red thus represents the virginal *Prakriti* who holds the promise of creating new life. Green represents the material *Prakriti* who has realized that promise and created new life. Men and women, such as monks and widows, who seek *Purusha* and withdrew from worldly life, prefer wearing white clothes. Men and women who seek to celebrate the union of *Purusha* and *Prakriti* and enjoy worldly life prefer coloured clothes; red for brides, green for mothers. Semen, menstrual fluid and water, all are forms of *rasa*. *Rasa* is the fuel of life, the juice of existence. *Rasa* is required to respond to worldly stimuli. The ritual known as *yagna* is aimed to promoting the flow of *rasa* in a particular direction – that of the patron of the *yagna* – so that it enriches and empowers the patron's life. *Shiva* sits with his eyes firmly shut, unresponsive to any worldly stimuli. His sense and action organs are in a state of total suspension. He does not use even a drop of *rasa*. Thus retained in his body, semen, hence *rasa*, transforms into *tapa*. *Tapa* is fire. It is ignited the moment god shuts his eyes to the goddess. *Tapa* and *rasa* is in essence the same thing: *tapa,* the product of separation; *rasa,* the product of union. By sitting on *Shiva*'s head, *Chandra* draws on *Shiva*'s *tapa* to regenerate himself. The practice of igniting *tapa* is known as *patasya.* It involves not responding to any worldly stimuli. He who performs *tapasya* and churns the fire of *tapa* is known as a *Tapasvin.* A *tapasvin*'s eyes are always shut. He does not see the world.

Shiva is the supreme *Tapasvin,* still and unmoving as the mountain he sits on. There is so much *tapa* in *Shiva*'s body that water does not flow around him; it freezes to become snow. *Shiva*'s abode, the snow-capped *Kailasha,* is unfit for habitation. *Daksha,* son of *Brahma,* chief patron of *yagna,* preferred offering his twenty-seven daughters to the *Devas.* The *Devas* are able to rotate the wheel of *samsara,* overpower the *Asuras,* draw and distribute *rasa,* and bring rain, children and harvest, to the delight of *Daksha.* The power to subvert natural law through *tapa* is known as *siddhi.* When a *Tapasvin* acquires *siddhi,* he becomes known as a *Siddha.* Any *jiva* can become a *siddha* if he can overpower the urge to respond to sensory stimuli. Once a *siddha,* a human become more powerful than a *Deva,* capable of doing whatever he wills. A *Siddha* must be differentiated from a *Rishi.* A *Rishi* obtains his power from the *Devas* by chanting the appropriate hymns and making the appropriate offerings during *yagna. Siddha* bypass the *Devas* and go directly to god to get their powers. Plants, animals and women shed their seed during pollination, heat and menstruation whether they want to or not. Hence they cannot retain *rasa.* Unfettered by the cycles of nature, a man can restrain his sexual urges, retain *rasa,* ignite *tapa* and acquire *siddhi. Shiva* may be the lord of *Siddhas,* the supreme *Tapasvin,* but he has no desire to subvert the working of nature. His attention is inward. He seeks not *siddhi,* power over things worldly, but *samadhi,* freedom from all things worldly. *Shiva* uses the flames of *Tapa* to burn all memories, desires, ideas, values and standards that crumple his *chitta.* In the light of the fire *Shiva* sees the true nature of the world around, hence the true nature of the self within. With true knowledge of *Purusha* and *Prakriti, Shiva* feels no urge to act or react. He experiences bliss, *ananda. Shiva* is not just a *Tapasvin.* He is also a *Yogi.* The aim of *yogi* is to unknot the mind, uncrumple the consciousness, and attain the triple state of ***sat-chitta-ananda***: unconditional truth, purified consciousness, and tranquil bliss. *Shiva* is therefore associated with *bilva* leaves, whose three leaves represents *sat-chitta-ananda* and whose stalk holding the three leaves together represents *yoga*. The three blades of *Shiva*'s trident also represent *sat-chitta-ananda* and its staff represents *yoga*. *Shiva* communicates the truth of life through dance. *Dance* is the symbol of life. It is impermanent, lasting as long as the dancer dances. It flows through time and space, unfettered by any dimension or moment. No life can be sustained without consumption of another life. *Daksha* and *Shiva*, the *Rishi* and the *Yogi*, embody two opposing approaches to life. For the *Rishi*, the world is *Shakti*, energy with the power to make existence delightful. For the *Yogi*, the world is *Maya*, delusion. Truth lies beyond the enchanting forms created by space, time and matter. From *Rishis* came *Vastu-shastra*, *Jyotisha*, *shastra* and *Ayur-veda*, sciences that aim to manipulate space, time and body to harness happiness, fortune and health. *Shiva* being the ascetic has no interest in happiness, fortune or health. Space, time and body do not interest him. He prefers the inner fire to the outer fire. His doctrine is *Yoga*, the science of managing the mind, un-crumpling the consciousness and attaining *sat-chitta-ananda* (Pattanaik, D. 2006).

Shiva's Image

There is some image of *Shiva*, the god *Shiva*, surrounded by circles of flame, rings of fire. That is the radiance of the god's dance. *Shiva*'s dance is the universe. In his hair are a skull and a new moon, death and rebirth at the same moment, the moment of becoming. In one hand he has a little drum that goes tick-tick-tick. That is the drum of time, the tick of time that shuts out the knowledge of eternity. We are enclosed in time. But in *Shiva*'s opposite hand there is a flame that burns away the veil of time and opens our minds to eternity. *Shiva* is a very ancient deity, perhaps the most ancient worshiped in the world today. There are images from 2000 to 2500 B.C., little stamp seals showing figures that clearly suggest *Shiva*. He is the archetypal *yogi*, canceling the illusion of life, but he is also the creator of life, its generator, as well as illuminator.

Goddess

When you move to a philosophical point of view, as in the Goddess religions of Hindu, where the Goddess symbology is dominant to this day, and the female represents *maya*. The female represents what in Kantian terminology we call the forms of sensibility. She is time and space itself, and the mystery beyond her is beyond all pairs of opposites. So it is not male and it is not female. It neither is nor is not. But everything is within her, so that the gods are her children. *Upanishads* say, "Thou art the dark blue bird, and the green parrot with red eyes. Thou hast the lighting as thy child. Thou art the season and the seas. Having no beginning, thou dost abide with immanence, whereof all things are born." The Hinduism believes that the informing life and energy of all things is the earth. The earth and we are the same. The male god or the female goddess has made psychological difference in the character of our culture. For example, the basic birth of Western civilization occurred in the great river valleys of the Nile, the Tigris-Euphrates, while the eastern civilization in the Indus and later the Ganges (*Ganga*). That was the name of the goddess. The name of the river ganges is the name of a goddess, for example. And then there came the invasions. These started seriously in the fourth millennium B.C. and became more and more devastating. They came in from the north and from the south and wiped out cities overnight. Just read the story in the book of Genesis of the part played by Jacob's tribe in the fall of the city of *Shechem*. Overnight these herding people, who have suddenly appeared, wiped out the city. The Semite invaders were herders of goats and sheep, the Indo-Europeans of cattle. Both were formerly hunters, and so the cultures were essentially animal-oriented. When you have hunters, you have killers. And when you have herders, you have killers, because they are always in movement, nomadic, coming into conflict with other people and conquering the areas into which they move. And these invasions bring in warrior gods, thunderbolt hurlers, like Zeus, or Yahweh. The sword and death instead of the phallus and fertility, they are equated. In historical terms, it is a very interesting thing to see that Mother Goddess was the queen right across to the Indus Valley in India. From the Aegean to the Indus, she is the dominant figure. Then you have the Indo-Europeans coming down from the north, into Persia, India, Greece, Italy, and a male-oriented mythology coming in, all along the line. In India it is the *Vedas*, in Greece it is the *Homeric* tradition, and then about five hundred years later the Goddess begins coming back in the mainland India. In the Near East, the god who descended into the field of time was originally a goddess. Jesus took over what is really the Goddess's role in coming down in compassion. But when the virgin acquiescence in being the vessel of the incarnation, she has herself already affected the redemption. It has become more and more apparent that the Virgin is equivalent in her suffering to the suffering of her son. In the Catholic Church now she is called the 'Co-savior".

Upanishad from about the seventh century B.C. – which is just about the time she is coming back to force in the Aegean as well, where the *Vedic* gods are together, and they see a strange sort of amorphous thing down the way, a kind of smoky fog, and they ask, what is that? None of them knows what it could be. So one of them suggests, "I'll go find out what that is." And he goes over to this smoky thing and says, "I am *Agni*, the Lord of fire; I can burn anything. "Who are you?" And out of this fog there comes flying a piece of straw, which falls on the ground, and a voice says, "Let's see you burn that." *Agni* finds that he can't ignite it. So he goes back to the other gods and says, "This surely is strange." Well, then, says the Lord of the wind, "Let me try," so over he goes, and the same sort of things takes place. "I am *Vayu* of the wind, I can blow anything around." Again a straw is thrown. Let's see you blow that." And he can't. So he too returns. Then *Indra*, the greatest of the *Vedic* gods approaches, but as he draws near, the apparition vanishes, and where it had been, a woman appears, a beautiful, mysterious woman, who instructs the gods, revealing to them the mystery of the ground of their own being. "That is the ultimate mystery of all being", she tells them, "from which you boys yourselves have received your powers. And it can turn your powers off or on, as It wills." The Indian name of that Being of all beings is Brahman, which is a neuter noun, neither male nor female. And the Indian name for the woman is *Maya-Shakti-Devi*, "Goddess Giver of life and mother of forms." And there in that Upanishad She appears as the teacher of the Vedic gods themselves concerning the ultimate ground and source of their own powers and Being. Hence, it is the female as the giver of forms. She is the one who gave life to the forms and she knows where they came from. It is from that which is beyond male and female. It is from that which is beyond being and non-being. It both is and is not. It neither is nor is not. It is beyond all categories of thought and the mind. When you substitute the male for the female you get a different psychology, a different cultural bias. And it is permissible in your culture to do what your gods do. There are three situations. First, the early one of the Goddess, when the male is hardly a significant divinity, then the reverse, when the male takes over her role. And finally, then the classical stage where the two are in interaction, as they are also, for example, in Hinduism, in India. In ancient times, people learned to live spiritually from the teachers. He was to give you the clues to a spiritual life. That is what the priest was for. Also, that was what ritual was for. A ritual can be defined as an enactment of a myth. By participating in a ritual, you are actually experiencing a mythological life. And it is out of that participation that one can learn to live spiritually. The stories of mythology actually point the way to the spiritual life. You have got to have a clue, a road map of some kind, and these are all around us. But they are not all the same. Some speak only of the interests of this in-group or of that, this tribal god or that. Others, and especially those that are given as revelations of the great Goddess, mother of the universe and of us all, teach compassion for all living beings (Campbell. Joseph 1959; Campbell, Joseph 1962; Campbell, Joseph 1964; Campbell, Joseph 1968; Campbell, J. 1988: 3-36).

Lingam and *Yoni*

In Hinduism, the most common ultimate symbol of the phallus, or *lingam,* as they call it, of the generating god penetrating the vagina, or the *yoni,* as they call it, of the Goddess. In contemplating this symbol, you are contemplating the generating moment it self of all life. The entire mystery of the generation of life is symbolically contemplated in that sign. The sexual mystery in Hinduism, and in most of the world, is a holy mystery. It is the mystery of the generation of life. The act of generating a child is a cosmic act and is to be understood as holy. And so the symbol that most immediately represents this mystery of the pouring of the energy of life into the field of time is the *lingam* and the *yoni,* the male and female powers in creative conjunction.

Mythology of Journey Inward

Heaven and hell are within us, and all gods are within us. This is the great realization of the *Upanishads* of India in the ninth century B.C. All the gods, all the heavens, all the worlds, are within us. They are magnified dreams, and dreams are manifestations in image form of the energies of the body in conflict with each other. That is what myth is. Myth is a manifestation in symbolic images, in metaphorical images, of the energies of the organs of the body in conflict with each other. This organ wants this, that organ wants that. The brain is one of the organs. "I see that I am the creation", says the god in *Upanishad*. When you see that God is the creation, and that you are a creature, you realize that God is within you, and in the man or woman with whom you are talking, as well. So there is the realization of two aspects of the one divinity. There is a basic mythological motif that originally all was one, and then there was separation, heaven and earth, male and female, and so forth. How did we lose touch with the unity? "*AUM*" is a word that represents to our ears that sound of the energy of the universe of which all things are manifestations. You start in the back of the mouth "*ahh*," and then "*oo*," you fill the mouth, and "*mm*" closes the mouth. When you pronounce this properly, all vowel sounds are included in the pronunciation. Consonants are here regarded simply as interruptions of the essential vowel sound. All words are thus fragments of *AUM*, just as all images are fragments of the Form of forms. *AUM* is a symbolic sound that puts you in touch with that resounding being that is the universe (Campbell, J. 1988).

Mythology of Death and Afterlife

Hinduism believed that knowledge wasn't external to the knower but woven inside consciousness. Thus, they had no need for an external God to solve the riddle of life and death. Each person is conscious. Each person has a self. Each person is certain of existence, that is, of being alive. With these raw ingredients, *Vedanta* declares, anyone can come up with firsthand knowledge of anything, no matter how deep the mystery appears. We don't contact the deepest part of ourselves, which the Hindus called *Atman*. The closest equivalent word in English is "soul". Soul or *Atman* is a spark of the divine, the invisible component that brings

God's presence into flesh and blood. The biggest difference between them is that in Hinduism the soul isn't separate from God. Unlike the Christian soul, *Atman* cannot come from God or return to him. There is unity between the human and the divine; awareness of this unity is the necessary step that makes reality dawn. The soul does not belong to me the way my house does, as a possession, or as my children do, as an extension of my flesh and blood. It does not belong to me like my personality, or my memories, because senility and mental disorder can disable the brain and take away both. Human beings have a deep intuition that our destiny is infinite, but we fear death because it tests our wishes and dreams. We fear to be tested because if we turn to be wrong, then all our aspirations feel empty. Dying is not more real than any other moment, but it is more definitive. No matter how rich and gifted you are, death is the great equalizer. Our fault is not that we fear death but that we don't respect it as a miracle. The most profound subjects like love, truth, compassion, birth and death, are equal. They belong to our destiny but also to our present life. For the afterlife to have meaning, it has to be fully as satisfying as this life. Bringing money, power, sex, family, achievement, and physical pleasure to the end is not a trivial thing. Much that we love and depend on will be extinguished when this life comes to an end. And yet we can bring something to that moment (Campbell, J. 1988).

At Home in Consciousness

According to Deepak Chopra (2006), in Hinduism, the five *Koshas*, namely (i) Physical body, (ii) *Prana* (subtle breath or life force), (iii) Mind, (iv) Ego and intellect and (v) Body of bliss, operating in union, give rise to the self, or the self system. Any individual is multi-layered because he is inseparable from the five *Koshas*. Pure consciousness remains wrapped around itself like layers of an onion. Each *Kosha* sheath has its own rules provides us with a structure for the subtle world. Our travels remain within the self-system. The *Koshas* are also shared. The universe has its own layers. Experiencing departed spirit, for example, is made possible by the countless generations that helped create the sub-world. Shared reality is not mystical. You claim your physical body as uniquely your own, but even that is shared. The air you breathe today contains millions of atoms of oxygen that were breathed out in China, for example, just a few days ago. You absorb ideas floating around in the mass media. So the analogy of the onion built in layers breaks down at a certain point. A *Kosha* is not an individual possession. It is a dynamic realm with its own laws and experiences, a realm we can enter alone or with others.

(i) Annamaya Kosha (Physical body)

The physical body is the most separate aspect of the self-system. At birth most babies are very much alike physiologically, but the time has made each of us unique. This material fact underlies a great deal of the separation in the world, as people struggle to grab their share of food, money, possessions, and status. They want to promote the well being of their physical body, to enhance its charm and beauty, and to protect it from the threat of injury and death. At this level first consciousness is biology. It operates silently, without a voice, as it organizes the myriad functions of the body. Yet even here, if we look at what is happening at the cellular level, it turns out that consciousness transcends boundaries. Cells cooperate, communicate, exchange functions, perform acts of self-sacrifice, remain in balance, keep aware of their environment, adapt to change, and know that they survive by being part of a greater whole. Every *Kosa* reveals wholeness and separation at the same time. If we look upon the physical body as the physical world, it is obvious that our bodies are isolated from one another, which keeps us in separation by giving rise to the illusion that we must struggle and compete with every other isolated body. Yet this *Kosa* brings us closer to wholeness through cooperation, physical security in social groups, and shared desires for food, shelter, sex, and physical comfort. The physical dimensions contain action. You live here whenever you see yourself as a body separate in time and space. Yoga uses physical postures called *Asana* that combine balance, strength, and body awareness to bring us to physical consciousness. Nourish and respect your body. Appreciate its incredible inner intelligence. Do not fear it or taint it with toxins. Take time to really be in your body. Take outside and let it play.

(ii) Pranamaya Kosha (Subtle breadth or life force)

Prana means vitality. In the individual, *Prana* is the breadth that sustains life by rhythmically joining us to Nature. We inhale all that is necessary to remain alive, and then exhale it back to wherever it is needed next. There is no equivalent in the West for *Prana*, except a tradition called vitalism that centers on the life force. A subtle flowing life force or intelligence sustains the physical body. At this level consciousness is the binding force that keeps Nature intact. Humans recognize that we are united with all living things. Consciousness does not recognize higher or lower levels of life; it orchestrates diversity into wholeness. When you feel connected to the life forms enveloped in the ecosystem, to environment, pets, an old shade tree, the full moon, a thunderstorm, sunshine, rain, you are feeling the flow of vitality that binds Nature together. When you become aware of the incredible intelligence that knits every cell in the body, it is no longer possible to say, "I own this." You cannot own life, yet you cannot help but be at its center also. Yet in this level separation still seems to dominate over wholeness, which is why human beings continue to depredate the ecosystem without realizing that they are destroying part of their own self-system. This *Kosha* keeps us in separation through imbalance, a disrupted ecosystem, pollution, and urban overcrowding.

This *Kosha* brings us closer to wholeness through vitality, kinship with other living beings, and balance in the ecosystem, and empathy. The *Pranic* dimension connects you to other living things. You live here when you see yourself as part of the web of life, a creature of nature. Yoga uses exercises in soft, self-aware breathing called *Pranayama* to bring us to consciousness of the flow of *Prana*. This is a vital body. Go out into Nature and sink into the feeling that this is your home. Respect and nourish the ecosystem. Do not harm other living things. See Nature without fear or hostility. Reverence for life is the key here.

(iii) Manomaya Kosha (Mind)

The root of the mind is individual ideas and thoughts. This is the level where you process the raw data of the world to make it meaningful. Mind includes emotions, sentiments, memories, and other uses of the brain. Mind is organized into its own invisible body, a body of personal memories and beliefs that we guard from harm as fiercely as we guard our physical body. At this level consciousness finds itself at play in the cosmos without boundaries, for the mind can fly anywhere, imagine anything. Your mind is free to interpret the world any way it wants, and unfortunately some of those ways include ignorance of the self. It is impossible to restrict the mind, yet many people fear its gift of freedom. At this level we come up against the self-created boundaries of belief, fear, and prejudice. Mind is more collective than individual. My mind means my unique thoughts and memories, but 90% of our thoughts are picked up from society and its many outlets. A great many memories are shared, and the very stuff of thought, language, is a collective creation. Mind is the first *Kosha* where wholeness dominates over separation. This *Kosha* brings us closer to wholeness through shared beliefs, social conditioning, religion, received opinions, and common values. This *Kosha* keeps us in separation through divisive beliefs in politics and religion, prejudice, "us versus them" thinking, nationalism, and arbitrary mental boundaries made of fear and hatred. The mental dimension organizes reality through thought. You live here when you see yourself as the sum of your thoughts, desires, wishes, dreams, and fears. Yoga uses the whole field of discrimination called *Viveka* to being us to consciousness of how the mind works. This is therefore the level of evolution in consciousness, both for you and me and for human beings as a whole. We carve out individual niches in collective consciousness, and as a wave of evolution passes through humanity, each of us can decide to catch the wave or ignore it, to embrace it or defend against it. This is the mental body; develop positive uses of the mind. Read and appreciate what is finest in human expression. Become aware that you are wholeness, and allow ideas to come in that support wholeness over separation. Resist us versus them thinking. Examine your autonomic reactions and secondhand beliefs. Find every opportunity to welcome signals from your highest self.

(*iv*) *Vigyanmaya Kosha* (ego and intelligence)

This is the level of identity dominated by "I, Me, and Mine." Society places positive value on someone with high ego drive and will to succeed, but in spiritual circles the ego's reputation is low. Spiritual seekers often feel it is their duty to "kill the ego" and control its impulses. However, if we look at "I-ness" without prejudice against the ego, this level of the self brings identity into being, not all the external things that ego drive makes us pursue. Identity is not a blank slate for long. It becomes filled with attachments and associations depending on what we choose to identify with. This *Kosha* is that level where myth and archetypes operate; giving us stories and models to identify with. The gods play out our primal desires, quests, wars, and loves. Ego also gives us knowledge about identity itself, what it means to be human: I cannot know who I am without family and society. At this level consciousness is self-centered, brought to a focus upon "I". Nothing is more universal, yet ego drives separate us when one person's desires clash with another's. To be fair, this clash develops in the mind, not in the ego itself. When we say ego, we usually mean the ego-personality, which is full of individual desires, dreams, beliefs, likes, and dislikes. This *Kosha* is closer to unity than that. At this level wholeness dominates over separation, as can be seen from the world's shared archetypes and myths. This *Kosha* brings us closer to wholeness through a sense of one humanity, heroic quests and mythic explores, and the need for self-respect, dignity, and inner worth. This *Kosha* keeps us in separation through personal alienation, separation anxiety, loneliness, and repressed emotions that gives rise to shame and guilt. The ego dimension defines your unique identity. You live here when you see yourself in terms of "I, Me, and Mine." Yoga uses mindfulness in all its various forms, such as contemplation and meditation called *Dhyana* to bring a person to consciousness of the "I am" that underlines all experience. This is an ego body. Find a vision; go on a quest. Fit yourself into the larger pattern of growth. Seek ways to evolve personally. Celebrate the vast traditions of spirit and wisdom that unite cultures. Be as humane as you can in every way, following the dictum "The world is my family."

(vii) Anandamaya Kosha (body of bliss)

In Hinduism, bliss is more than a feeling of ecstasy. It was the basic vibration, or hum, of the universe, the ground state from which all diversity springs. It is possible to imagine an afterlife where one no longer has a body, where there is no need for breadth, where the mind does not process data anymore. But there must be a faint sense of both ego and bliss. Ego, says, "This is happening to me." Bliss says, "I feel the spark of creation."

Ananda is the possibility for creation to manifest, and as long as you inhabit the body of bliss, bliss is an intense, dynamic experience and not just a potential. At this level consciousness is the joy of being. Instead of focusing on anything in the external world, our attention comes to rest on the numinous presence that has been described as a golden light suffusing every particle of Nature. In bliss you perceive that separation is only a thin veil. Behind the veil shines the light of pure consciousness. Devotional practices that increase a person's sense of joy can reach as deep as the level of ecstasy. But bliss itself is far from the feeling of happiness or even joy, though in diluted form it can be experienced as both. It is the vibratory connection that allows pure consciousness to enter into creation. This *Kosha* reveals wholeness so entirely – through love, joy, and ecstasy, that separation no longer holds any attraction. One could say that this *Kosha* is pure. Being mixed with just a touch of individuality, just enough to allow someone to live in physical form, and whatever forms the afterlife takes. Without this gossamer sheath you would dissolve into Being and become bliss itself, without an experiencer. The dimension of bliss holds our ultimate fulfillment through love and joy. You live here when you see yourself blending into everything through the power of love, or when you have no other sensation ecstasy. *Yoga* uses sustained periods in a deep state of silence called *Samadhi* to bring the subtle vibration of bliss to the surface of the mind, making a person conscious that the "hum" of the universe is present in every experience. This is the body of bliss. Develop your own practice for transcending and finding bliss. You already know the phrase "Follow your bliss". Now, put it into practice through some kind of "alpha wave" exercise like meditation and deep relaxation. Devote yourself to discovering what *Samadhi*, the silence of deep awareness, is really like. Experience your own being as a reason to be here. The whole question of life revolves around being versus becoming. Becoming is always fractional. And being is total. In the first few years you are a child, and that is only a fraction of the human being. In a few more years you are in adolescence, and that is certainly a fraction of the human being. In maturity you are still fractional, you are not a child, but you are not old yet. Thus, you are a fraction of human being now, and going to become fully human. There is an image in the Upanishads of the original, concentrated energy that was the big bang of creation that set forth the world, consigning all things to the fragmentation of time. But to see through the fragments of time to the full power of original being, that is a function of art. Beauty is an expression of that rapture (a state of great delight or ecstasy) of being alive and every moment should be such an experience. It is not the destination of life that counts, but it is the journey. As Karlfriend Graf Durckeim says, "When you are on a journey, and the end keeps getting further and further away, then you realize that the real end is the journey" (Campbell. Joseph 1959; Campbell, Joseph 1962; Campbell, Joseph 1968; Pattanaik, D. 2006; Zimmer, Heinrich 1969).

3

MYTHOLOGY OF BUDDHISM

Mahayana Buddhism was introduced in Sikkim in the Eighth century A.D. The land was then, blessed by *Padmasambhava* popularly known as *Guru Rimpoche*. He personally consecrated many of Sikkim's sacred landmarks, and blessed *Drakar Tashiding* as the land's spiritual centre. After the mythic blood brotherhood treaty of the legendary leaders, *Khe-Bumsa* - the *Lhopo* (*Bhutia*) leader and *Thekong-Tek* - the *Lepcha* leader during 13th century A.D., the migration of *Tibetans* to Sikkim increased. Later, in the 14th century, the great *terton* (*gter ston* = revealer of hidden treasures) *Rigzin Godemchen* (1337-1408) came to Sikkim and established monasteries and meditation centres at *Sinon* (*Zilnon*), near *Tashiding* and nearby *Pawo Hungri*. The 17th century was a turning point in the history of Sikkim. The Himalayan Kingdom, "the Greater Sikkim" came in existence when the first *Chogyal Phuntso Namgyal* was enthroned at *Yoksom*, West Sikkim in 1642 A.D.. Under the patronage of the *Chogyals* of Sikkim (12 Nos), the monasteries, hermitages and stupas were built and Buddhism was proclaimed the state religion. Since then, Buddhism was the only state religion of Sikkim till the tiny Himalayan Kingdom finally integrated into the Indian Union as the 22nd state of secular democracy in 1975 A.D. (Subba, J.R. 2008a:143-157).

Most of the Buddhists of Sikkim are the believers of *Nyingmapa* sect, *Kargyupa* sect, and *Sakyapa* sect (Red Hat Sects) of *Mahayana* Buddhism. However, the later migrants of Tibet are believers of *Gelukpa* sect (Yellow Hat Sect) of *Mahayana* Buddhism. Out of the fourteen hill tribes races of Sikkim, *Lhopos* (*Bhutias*), a sizeable population of *Lepchas, Tamangs, Sherpas*, a section of *Newars* (*Sakyas*) and a section of *Gurungs* are believers of *Mahayana*

Buddhism. During 1981 Census Buddhist population of Sikkim was 90,848 persons constituting 28.72% of the total population, the second highest religion in the state. Buddhists constitute 5.99%, 4th highest population in the world. *Bonism*, the native religion of Tibet, originated from ancient shamanic rituals and beliefs of the time has been suitably blended in the *Mahayana* Buddhism. Hence, there is no basic difference between the two faiths now (Subba, J. R. 1999; 2008a:143-157).

Buddhism is a well-developed religion, and plenty of Buddhist literature is available in Sikkim. More emphasis will be given on the mythological aspects of Buddhism in brief in this work.

Philosophy of Buddhism

Buddhism was founded by *Siddhartha Gautama* (566-586 B.C.), who taught us the *"Four Noble Truths"*: Viz;

(a) Existence was embedded in sorrow;

(b) This resulted from human desires;

(c) Humans could never fulfill all their desires; and

(d) Hence, the way to end sorrow was to end desire.

Buddhist teachings emphasized on "Self-Awakening", for every individual could seek to attain salvation. According to the philosophy of Buddhism, man is merely a coming together of certain properties or qualities categorized by Buddhists under five heads termed *Skandhas*; Viz:

(i) *Rupa*: organized body;

(ii) *Vedana*: sensation;

(iii) *Samjna*: perception;

(iv) *Samskara*: discrimination; and

(v) *Vignana*: consciousness.

When physical dissolution takes place these components disperse leaving no residue. And since there is no residue there can be no soul. However, when a man dies there will be left over from his life's activities, so to speak, a certain balance of un-required action. It may be good action or it may be bad action; but in accordance with doctrine of *karma* reward or retribution must follow automatically. And it is that fundamental necessity which causes a fresh assemblage of *Skandhas* for the working out of the unexhausted *karma*. Rebirth then is a mere manifestation of the effects of certain causes. The link between death and rebirth is impersonal and imponderable. By treading the Noble Eighth-fold Path a man so lives that his *karma* works itself out, leaving over no balance of un-required action at the moment of death; then he leaves behind him nothing capable of causing a re-assemblage of the five *Skandhas*.

The Noble Eighth-fold Paths are:

(i) Right View;

(ii) Right Aspiration;

(iii) Right Speech;

(iv) Right Conduct;

(v) Right means of Livelihood;

(vi) Right Endeavor;

(vii) Right Mindfulness; and

(viii) Right Contemplation.

By treading these Noble Eighth-fold Paths, suppression of suffering can be achieved. The Noble Eighth-fold Path laid down by *Gautama Buddha* has been transformed into a single narrow track of the mystic incantation ***"om mani padme hum**!"*, by the patron deity of Tibet – *Cheresi*. The repetition of the above syllables bars the doors of the various worlds of existence, Viz:

(i) *Om*, of the heavenly world;

(ii) *ma*, of the world of spirits;

(iii) *ni*, of the human world;

(iv) *pad*, of the animal world;

(v) *me*, of the world of tantalized ghosts, and

(vi) *hum*, of the spaces of hell.

(Risley, H. H. 1894:241-384; Subba, J.R.1999; 2005a; 2008: 143-257; Ranaldshey, L. 1923: 59-78).

Concept of God

Hinayana Buddhism is a moral philosophy designed to overcome suffering, and thus do not believe on the existence of

God. However, *Mahayana* Buddhism does accept existence of Deity, an absolute Supreme Being or Power. Thus, Buddhism originally had nothing to do with God. Yet serving God and having a proper relationship with Him is the whole point of a true religion. The whole basis and origin of Buddhism was religion without God. But religion without God is like an ocean without water or a meal without food, and thus, it violates the whole meaning and purpose of religion. In general, Buddhism rejects the idea of an individual (*Atman*), immortal soul and fosters instead the Buddhist belief in the unity and interdependence of living things and possibility of a harmony achievable by means of compassion. It supersedes the suffering that permeates much of human existence (Subba, J.R. 2005a: 36-37).

Buddhist Concept of Creation of the Universe

This worldview presents a non-theistic approach to existence of the universe (atheistic monism). The world exists because of casual actions. All things are produced by casual actions (*karma*) and all beings are governed and bound by causal actions. They are fixed like the rolling wheel of a cart, fixed by the pin of its axle shaft (*Sutta Nipata* 654). The universe was not created neither is it permanent. Three things identify the true nature of this world:

(a) Impermanence (*anitya*, also spelled *anicca*);

(b) Suffering (*dukkha*); and

(c) Insubstantiality or not-self (*anatma* or *anatta* – no enduring essence in anything).

Ignoring or distorting the three basic facts ultimately leads only to frustration, disappointment and despair... "the clear comprehension of impermanence, suffering and not-self will bring us a saner outlook on life. It will form us from unrealistic expectations; bestow a courageous acceptance against the lure of deluded assumptions and beliefs. By seeing thus, detachment will grow, bringing greater freedom from egoistic clinging."

A fourth doctrine that further identified the nature of things is "*Sunyata*", meaning "emptiness". This term communicates that all things are empty of lasting value or that they are "empty" of lasting value or that they are "empty" of anything substantive. All things are mere appearances, temporary illusions, possessing no lasting reality or substances. So in essence, they are "empty". Realizing this as the basic character of the material world imparts an attitude of detachment that ultimately serves to free a person from suffering. In conclusion, therefore, even though interpretations of these terms may differ slightly from one Buddhist school to another, the following logic is generally accepted: all things are empty (*Sunyata*), impermanent (*Anicca*), devoid of essence (*Anatman*) and marked by suffering (*Dukkha*). Buddhist contend that such a view is neither optimization nor pessimistic, simply realistic (*Nayanaponika Thera* 1997).

Buddhist Concept of Life and Destiny

The concept of life in *Mahayana* Buddhism is same as that of Hinduism. Buddhists believe that, when a man dies, he will return to live as another living being on earth. The cycle of birth and rebirth continues indefinitely until one is released. The *Hinayana* Buddhism believes that a man has no spirit or inner self that lives after death. Only the consequences of past deeds (*karma*) live from life to life. They believe that the ultimate goal or destiny of man is to be released or obtain *Nirvana* from the cycle of earthly destinies. Whether or not this state is conscious is not defined. They deny annihilation, but they also deny existence as individuals distinct from others.

The *Mahayana* Buddhism believes that man has a consciousness that continues from life to life. They believe in a concept of conscious happiness. Everything good or bad that happens to a man is the result of his conduct in previous lives. What happens in future life is determinate by his actions (*karma*) now. Nothing is really a result of a person's environment, the acts of others, or the work of God. All is payment for what the person himself did in the past.

Death

From its inception, Buddhism has stressed the importance of death, since awareness of death is what prompted the Buddha to perceive the ultimate futility of worldly concerns and pleasures. Realizing that death is inevitable for a person who is caught up in worldly pleasures and attitudes, he resolved to renounce the world and devote himself to finding a solution to this most basic of existential dilemmas. Buddhists look at death as a breaking apart of the material of which we are composed. However, Buddhism does not look at death as a continuation of the soul but as an awakening. Dying and being reborn has been compared by some Buddhist as a candle flame. When the flame of one lit candle is touched to the wick of an unlighted candle, the light passes from one candle to another. The actual flame of the first candle does not pass over but is responsible for lighting the second candle. When preparing the death Buddhists generally agree a person's state of mind while dying is of great importance. While dying person can be surrounded by friends, family and marks that recite Buddhists scriptures and *mantras* to help the person achieve a peaceful state of mind. Buddhists assert that all being live beyond the various fluctuations of this life. Death is merely a passage to rebirth in ultimate nature of the mind.

Suffering

The Buddhist teaching regarding suffering is based on the "Four Truths".

(i) Suffering is an essential part of life. Troubles are basic and inherent to life.

(ii) The cause of suffering is human desire. Man suffers because of his desire for personal enjoyment and possessions, but especially because of the desire to continue to exist as an individual, separate and distinct from others. The highest destiny of man is to cease existence as a separate and distinct individual, and enter the state of "*Nirvana*". The earthly life is an illusion, but due to ignorance of man continues to desire to exist. This desire causes rebirth to other lives and since life involves suffering, we continue to suffer.

(iii) The solution to suffering is to eliminate earthly desires, especially the desire to exist as an individual. When desires are renounced and destroyed, rebirth will cease; and

(iv) The steps to defeat these desires are the "Eightfold Path" described above. This is a way of life consisting of eight steps in which one disciplines himself till all earthly desires are eliminated. The idea is to avoid two extremes; avoid indulging in luxury and pleasures, but also avoid self-torture or depriving oneself of necessities. Buddhists believe that many lifetimes are required to reach the perfection.

Salvation and Eternal Destiny

Escaping from suffering is possible only for the one who accepts the above four truths. The eight practices of self-training can be classified in three categories: morality (*Sila*), meditation (*Samadhi*) and wisdom (*Panna*).

(i) Morality means right speech, action and livelihood. It has to generate a perfect state of self-control and contentment.

(ii) Meditation requires perfection in effort (right attitude of the mind), mindfulness (awareness of mental and physical possession), and concentration (introversion and cessation of empirical consciousness).

(iii) Wisdom requires perfection in view (thorough understanding the impermanent nature of the world) and intention (cultivating desirelessness, friendliness and compassion).

Further, there are two complementary types of Buddhist meditation: Calm meditation (*samadhi*) and insight meditation (*vipassana*). The first is aimed at producing deep concentration (*samadhi*) by developing a capacity of the mind to rest undisturbed on a single object of perception. The second aims at understanding the true nature of things, which is characterized by impermanence, suffering and no-self. In other words, calm meditation is about letting them go completely as a result of understanding the nature of the world.

Once one has attained "*Nirvana*", he becomes an *Arahat* (living enlightened one). His *Karma* is buried out and at the time of his death he will cease to exist. *Nirvana* is neither a re-absorption in the eternal ultimate reality, nor an annihilation of a self, because there is no self to annihilate. It is rather an annihilation of the illusion of an existing self. The proper image to describe it is the flame of the candle that is blown out. This represents the end of suffering but at the same time the end of any aspect that may define existence. In general, Buddhism rejects the idea of an individual (*atman*), immortal soul and fosters instead the Buddhist belief in the unity and interdependence of living things and possibility of a harmony, achievable by means of compassion that is able to supersede the suffering that permeates much of human existence. The difference between *Mahayana* and *Theravada* Buddhism is in the concept of salvation and eternal destiny. The first significant difference is a new goal to be pursued in life in the former. Instead of seeking "*Nirvana*" just for oneself in order to become an "*Arahat*" in *Theravada*, the disciple of *Mahayana* Buddhism aims to become a "*Bodhisattva*", a celestial being that postpones his own entrance into '*Parinirvana*" (final extinction) in order to help other humans attain it. He swears not to enter "*Nirvana*" until he fulfills his noble mission. He is a part of a "*Bodhisattva*'s" vow. "I shall accept all suffering for the sake of all sentient beings in all worlds, in all accept all suffering for the sake of all sentient beings in all works, in all states of misery, forever and ever, and still always cultivate foundations of goodness for the sake of all beings. Why?

I would rather take all their suffering on myself than to allow sentient beings to fall into hell. I shall be a hostage to these perilous places – hells, animal realms, neither world, as a ransom to rescue all sentient beings in states of woe and enable them to gain liberation. I vow to protect all sentient beings and never abandon them. What I say is sincerely true, without falsehood. Why? Because I have set my mind on enlightenment in order to liberate all sentient beings; I do not seek the unexcelled way for my own sake (*Garland Sutra*:23). Due to its selfish way of seeking "*Nirvana*", *Mahayanists* considered the *Theravada* school as inferior spiritual path, valid only for those who cannot accept the idea of becoming a "*Bodhisattva*". *Hinayana* is thus known as narrow/inferior path that reduces its goal in becoming an "*Arahat*" (Subba, J.R. 2005a: 95-100).

Buddhist Concept of Soul

Buddhism believes that all things are impermanent, in a constant state of flux, all is transient, and no abiding state exists. This applied to humanity as much as to anything else in the cosmos; thus, there is no unchanging and abiding self. Our sense of "I" or "Me" is simply a sense belonging to the ever-changing entity that is body, our mind, and us. This expresses in essence the Buddhist principle of *anotta* (*anatman*). Buddhists hold that the delusion of a permanent, abiding self is one of the main root causes for human conflict on the emotional, social and political levels. At death, the body and mind disintegrate; if the disintegrating mind contains any remaining traces of *karma*, it will cause the continuity of the consciousness to bounce back an arising mind to an awaiting being, that is, a fetus developing the ability to harbour consciousness. Thus, a being that is born is neither entirely different nor exactly the same as it was prior to rebirth.

However, scholars such as *Shiro Matsumoto* have argued that a curious development occurred in *Mahayana* Buddhism stemming from the *Cittamatra* and *Vijnanavada* schools in India. Although this school of thought denies the permanent personal selfhood, it affirms concepts such as Buddha-nature, *Tathagatagarbha, Rigpa* or "original nature". *Matsumoto* argues that these concepts constitute a non-or trans-personal self, and almost equate in meaning to the Hindu concept of "*Atman*", although they differ in that Buddha-nature does not incarnate. One should note the polarity in *Tibetan* Buddhism between *Shes-pa* (the principle of consciousness) and *Rig-pa* (pure consciousness equal to Buddha-nature).

The concept of a person as a "*Tulku*" provides even more controversy. A *tulku* has due to heroic austerities and esoteric training, achieved the goal of transferring personal identity from one rebirth to the next. Although Buddha-nature does not incarnate, the individual self comprises "*Skandhas*" or components that undergo rebirth. For an ordinary person, "*Skandhas*" cohere in a way that dissolves upon the person's death. So elements of the transformed personality re-incarnate, but they lose the unity that constitutes personal selfhood for a specific person. In the case of *tulkus*, however, they supposedly achieve a "crystallization" of *Skandhas* in such a manner that the *Skandhas* do not "disentangle" upon the *tulku*'s death; rather, a voluntary reincarnation occurs. In this new birth, the *tulku* possesses a continuity of personal identity rooted in the fact that the consciousness or *Shes-pa* (which equates to a type of *Skandha* called *Vinana*) has not dissolved after death, but orthodoxy remains in dispute.

Many *Bonism* adherents believe that the concept of Buddhist reincarnation has been adopted from the shamanic priest tradition of *Bonism* without much understanding of this phenomenon. Many modern Buddhists, particularly in western countries, reject the concept of rebirth or reincarnation as incompatible with the concept of *anatta*. They take the view that if there are no abiding self and no soul then nothing remains to be reborn. If a self does not exist, who thinks/lives now? Buddhists hold the view that thought itself thinks; if you remove the thought, there's no thinker (self) to be found (Subba, J.R. 2005a:123-124).

Buddhist Concept of Afterlife

Hinayana Buddhists assert that a person's *karma* is continuously reborn until they attain *Nirvana*, and that rebirth is undesirable. *Mahayana* Buddhism is more in the line with Hinduism with regard to certain belief on reincarnation. However, Buddhism's state of *Nirvana* is not analogous to the Hindu concept of *Moksha* as *Nirvana* is a state of non-being or voidness and does not focus on the concept of a personal, Supreme Being that is allowed in *Advaita* and is mandated in the strict theistic schools such as that of *Ramanuja* and *Madhva*. At death, each life continues in some other form – human, divine or animal, depending upon the results of behavior in the last life. The goal of Buddhism is to extinguish the flame of wanting or attachment to the sense of self so that rebirth does not occur and *Nirvana* is attained. The greatest Buddhist contribution to afterlife is *Nirvana*. Buddhists believe that *Nirvana* is the end of suffering while you are alive and the end of rebirth after you die. The Buddha said that all forms of life are unsatisfactory and that you will eventually end suffering.

According to Buddhist cosmology, philosophy and origins, Buddhism recognizes as many as 33 heavens and 33 hells listed as possible destinations, but mainly talk the six realms of existence. Buddhist believe to be in the best heaven where everything is just the way you want it to be. This concept of the best heaven is the same as that of the Hinduism-God's heaven: *Satya-loka, Vaikuntha*, or *Kailasa*. As in the case of *Shiva*'s heaven – *Kailasha*, you are put there by repaying dept from earning equity through the concepts of *dakshina* and *daan*. In this heaven, there is no reason to change anything. You are ultimately happy. The problem is that it is not permanent, as is everything in Buddhism. One day in the heaven realm is equal to 400 human years, and your stay is four thousand heaven years, so you will be there a really long time. But, one day the karma that put you in this heaven will be used up. You are only in heaven as long as your *karma* account has merit in it. You can only draw from your *karma* account while in heaven, because they are in no way to make a deposit. You cannot practice generosity or compassion, and you are not striving to gain wisdom. When the *karma* that put you in heaven is used up...you are reborn..... And that would probably make you really unhappy. Who wants to leave a perfect place?.

The second heaven realm, which is a lower one, is where things are almost perfect. It could be just a little better. The concept is the Hinduism-*Indra*'s paradise-*Swarga*. *Swarga* is the abode of the *Devas*, the destination of humans who have only equity and no debts in their karmic accounts books. *Swarga* is a place of opulence and abundance. Every material wish is fulfilled there without effort. Since all needs are satisfied, its residents are in a state of delight. Actions that take the adherents towards *Swarga* are known as *punya*, merit-generating actions. Actions that take the adherents away from *Swarga* are known as *paap*, demerit-generating actions. *Paap* incurs debt. *Punya* earns equity. There is still some desire associated with this heaven realm.

The next realm is the human realm, where we all ended up for whatever reason. This is the best place for us to come because this is the only place where we can become enlightened. We cannot become enlightened in both the above-mentioned heavens, because things are too nice and we have no reason to strive. We also cannot become enlightened in the hell realm because things are too bad and all we can do is suffer. We cannot relax too long in any one mental state, because they will not last.

The next realm is the animal realm. Wanting to have sex, wanting to have food, wanting to have sleep and being confused, marks the animal realm. Those are the four characteristics that we find in the animal realm. So you can see that we are not likely to become enlightened in the animal realm.

The next realm is called the hungry ghost realm, and is often pictured as a giant creature with a large stomach and a pinhole for a mouth. They can never fulfill their hunger. So they are always filled with craving and desire. They can never be satisfied.

In the hell realm, that is where there is the most suffering. We have these little hell bodies. The leaves of the trees are like razor blades. They fall off the tree and cut us into a million pieces. Then our bodies resurrect and we are again cut into little pieces. And there is molten lead and we burn to death. The only way we can get out of the hell realm is to burn off our bad *karma* that got us there through suffering. Suffering is the act of purification that enables us to be reborn in a higher realm.

In the Buddhist model we have specific practices that are necessary to achieve rebirth in heaven. We have specific practices necessary to achieve *Nirvana*. It is a labour intensive practice that requires personal responsibility. A Buddhist looks at life as a continuum, as a process of birth and death. And we are in a constant state of becoming. It is just like the analogy of going to an airport with a suitcase. We put it on the conveyor belt so it can be loaded onto the airplane. But we are not getting onto the plane. That suitcase contains our *karma*. When it gets to its destination, the next person picks up the suitcase. That is what they have to work with. Now they can get more clothing, better clothing if they practice acts of generosity and compassion. Or they can turn the clothing into rags if they have greed, anger, hatred and delusion. I am not going to the next lifetime. My *karma* is. It is not the event that is going; it is the process that is going (Subba, J.R. 2005a: 152-154)

Buddhist Concept of Purpose and Meaning of Life

The goal of human being in Buddhism is to control the process of birth and death and achieve *Nirvana* (release). You can master all the *Samadhi* that allow you free entry into all of these realms, and yet you can still remain unenlightened if you cling to the subtle notions of a self, which means clinging to subject-object dualities. If you can attain enlightenment, then you can become free of the *karmic* pull of the realms so as to control your birth and death, and be able to come and go wherever and whenever you wish. You can also learn how to manipulate things in the realm of interdependent origination in order to accomplish great deeds for the benefit of sentient beings. There is no ultimate rest. What is left is the challenge of perfecting your functioning expression in the universe through countless acts of compassion, whether great or small. Until you become a Buddha, there is also always *karma* to be paid for, so you are always working off bad *karma* and burning up your good *karma* in this process, as well as making new good and bad *karma* instead. Hence, there is a great importance on learning how to act skillfully in the universe so as to create good *karma* for the future, burn away any bad *karma* from the past, or even change it into something positive. The purpose of life is whatever you choose to be, whatever you choose to be accomplishing, what ever you select to build. Life purpose is a subjective thing.... something you choose and define yourself (Subba, J.R. 2005a:177-179).

Buddhist Mythology

Buddhism is a psychological religion. Plenty of literature is available on Buddhist mythology. Hence, there is not much scope to add more on it. A lot more about Buddhist mythology has also been discussed under overview chapter. However, a few important mythological interpretations have been mentioned in this work also.

Buddha goes into the forest and he conferences there with the leading gurus of his day. Then he goes past them and, affirms a season of trials and search comes to the bo-tree, the tree of illumination, where he, likewise, undergoes three temptations:

(i) The first is of lust: In the first temptation, the Lord of lust displays his three beautiful daughters before the Buddha. Their names were Desire, Fulfillment, and Regrets: Future, Present, and Past. But the Buddha, who had already disengaged himself from attachment to his sensual character, was not moved.

(ii) The second of fear: Then the Lord of Lust turned himself into the Lord of Death and flung at the Buddha all the weapons of an army of monsters. But the Buddha had found in himself that still point within, which is of eternity, untouched by time. So again, he was not moved, and the weapons flung at him turned into flowers of worship; and

(iii) The third of submission to public opinion, doing as told: Finally, the Lord of Lust and Death transformed himself into the Lord of social duty, and argued, "Young man, haven't you read the morning papers? Don't you know what there is to be done today?" The Buddha responded by simply touching the earth with the tips of the fingers of his right hand. Then the voice of the goddess mother of the universe was heard, like thunder rolling on the horizon, saying, "This, my beloved son, has already so given of himself to the world that there is no one here to be ordered about. Give up this nonsense."

Whereupon the elephant on which the Lord of social duty was riding bowed in worship of the Buddha, and the entire company of the antagonist dissolved like a dream. That night the Buddha achieved illumination, and for the next fifty years remained in the world as teacher of the way to the extinction of the bondages of egoism. Now, those first two temptations, of desire and of fear, are the experience. The tree is, of course, the mythological world axis, at the point where time and eternity, movement and rest, are at one, and around which all things revolve. It is here represented only in its temporal aspect, as the tree of knowledge of good and evil, profit and loss, desire and fear: these are the two emotions by which all life in the world is governed. Desire is the bait; death is the hook. Adam and Eve were moved; the Buddha was not. Eve and Adam brought forth life and were cursed of God; the Buddha taught release from life's fear. Buddha found salvation beyond death and returned from the wilderness to choose and instruct disciples who then brought their message to the world. The message of the great teachings of Buddha, Christ, Mohammed, differ greatly. But their visionary journeys are much the same.

Religion begins with the sense of wonder and awe and the attempt to tell stories that will connect us to God. Then it becomes a set of theological works in which everything is reduced to a code, to a creed. That is the reduction of mythology to theology. Mythology is very fluid. Most of the myths are self-contradictory. You may even find four or five myths in a given culture, all giving different versions of the same mystery. Then theology comes along and says it has got to be just this way. The Buddha does not show you the truth itself; he shows you the way to truth. But it has got to be your way, not his. The Buddha can't tell you exactly how to get rid of your particular fears, for example. Different teachers may suggest exercises, but they may not be the ones to work for you. All a teacher can do is suggest. Following the middle path of the Buddha, the passage to fulfillment lies between the perils of desire and fear. The Buddhists talk of *Nirvana,* and Jesus talks of peace, of the mansion with many rooms. The place to find is within yourself. The Buddhist *Nirvana* is a center of peace of this kind. Buddhism is a psychological religion. It starts with the psychological problem of suffering; all life is sorrowful; there is, however, an escape from sorrow; the escape is *Nirvana,* which is a state of mind or consciousness, not a place somewhere, like heaven. It is right here, in the midst of the turmoil of life. It is the state you find when you are no longer driven to live by compelling desires, fears, and social commitments, when you have found your center of freedom and can act by choice out of that. Voluntary action out of this center is the action of the *Bodhisattvas,* joyful participation in the sorrows of the world. You are not grabbed, because you have released yourself from the grabbers of fear, lust, and duties. These are the rulers of the world. There is an instructive Tibetan Buddhist painting Wheel of Becoming is represented. What is shown is the mind's image of the world when still caught in the grip of the fear of the Lord Death. Six realms of being are represented as spokes of the ever-revolving wheel; one is the animal life, another of human life, another of the gods in heaven, and a fourth of the souls being punished in hell. The fifth realm is of the belligerent demons, anti-gods, or Titans. And the sixth, finally, is of the hungry ghosts, the souls of those in whose love for others there was attachment, cling, and expectation. The hungry ghosts have enormous, ravenous bellies and pinpoint mouths. However, in the midst of each of these realms there is a Buddha, signifying the possibility of lease and illumination. In the hub of the wheel are three symbolic beasts, a pig, a cock, and a serpent. These are the powers that keep the wheel revolving, ignorance, desire, and malice. And then, finally, the rim of the wheel represents the bounding horizon of anyone's consciousness that is moved by the triad of powers of the hub and held in the grip of the fear of death. In the center, surrounding the hub and what are known as the "three poisons", are souls descending in darkness and others ascending to illumination. The illumination is the recognition of the radiance of one eternity through all things, whether in the vision of time these things are judged as good or as evil. To come to this, you must release yourself completely from desiring the goods of this world and fearing their loss. Every man, woman, or child can cultivate this art, which is the only way to achieve this illumination. Art and religion are the two recommended ways. This is not achievable through sheer academic philosophy, which gets all tangled up in concepts. But just living with one's heart open to others in compassion is a way wide open to all.

The experience of illumination is potentially in every one of us, deep in the unlocked memory box. It is to be unlocked by getting somebody to help you unlock it. It may come from actual human being, teachers, illuminating books. Mythology is the penultimate truth, penultimate because the ultimate can't be put into words. It is beyond words, beyond images, beyond that bounding rim of the Buddhist wheel of Becoming. Mythology pitches the mind beyond that rim, to what can be known but not told. So this is the penultimate truth. It is important to live life worth the experience, and therefore the knowledge of its mystery and of your own mystery. This gives life a new radiance, a new harmony, a new splendor. Thinking in mythological terms helps to put you in accord with the inevitable of this vale of tears. You learn to recognize the positive values in what appear to be the negative moments and aspects of your life (Campbell, J. 1988: 3-232).

The *bodhisattva* represents the principle of compassion, which is the healing principle that makes life possible. Life is pain, but compassion is what gives it the possibility of continuing. He is the one who has achieved the realization of immortality yet voluntarily participates in the sorrows of the world. Similarly, the *Phedangmas in Yuma* religion participate in the sorrows of the people, healing the sick, curing them as desired by the Almighty Goddess *Tageraningwaphuma*. Voluntary participation in the suffering of the world or participation as per the desire of the Goddess *Yuma* is very different from just getting born into it. Buddhism is pre-eminently a pantheistic religion, and teaches that every being, sentient or non-sentient, is in spiritual communion with ourselves and destined, together with us, to attain Buddha-hood. Buddhism denied a permanent resting-place to the soul and taught a perpetual process of change in a man's mortal character. There is a river; on the bank of which the soul could decide whither it would go. The stream was "the River of the Three

Routes", because the way departed thence in three directions, one toward the hells, the second toward the beast life, and the third toward the realm of the "hungry ghosts". On these three roads there were various posts at which the soul was examined by the judges, the *Plutos* of Buddhism; and finally there was the dreadful king-judge, *Yama,* in the hells, who gave sentence of punishment according to the sinfulness of the souls that came before him.

Doctrinal views concerning the paradises of Buddhism, the beliefs in those realms of bliss had a great influence on the popular imagination, and descriptions of those happy conditions are frequent in the Buddhist myths and tales. The descriptions are, however, pretty much alike and say little more than that the paradises are the realms of perpetual splendor and infinite bliss. Yet we can distinguish three main paradises, qualified in different manners and located in different quarters. They were the *"Heaven of Contentment"*, of the future Buddha, *Maitreya* situated somewhere high in the sky; *Sukhavati,* accomplished by the Buddha *Amita,* the Buddha of Infinite Light and Life, situated in the west; and lastly *Grudhra-kuta,* idealized from the Vulture Peak where Buddha *Sakya-muni* is believed to have preached the *"Lotus of Truth."* The first, the Heaven of Contentment, is a paradise still in formation, because the Lord *Maitreya* is to become a full Buddha in the future, and his paradise has been prepared for those who are to be led to the final perfection on his appearance; therefore it is a kind of ante-room for a real paradise. Belief in this heaven is common among the people, and many stories are told of the occasional visits made by human beings to it. The idealized Vulture Peak is placed in the third world and is to be realized by every true Buddhist in this life through his enlightenment in the truths taught in the Lotus.

According to Buddhist cosmology, the innumerable paradises are inhabited by beings of ideal perfection, and the universe, which contains countless worlds, is thronged with spirits, some benevolent and some malicious. There is a Hindu saying "None but a god can worship a god." You have to identify yourself in some measure with whatever spiritual principle your god represents to you in order to worship him properly and live according to his word. This is the reason worship rituals are performed only by learned *Brahamans* (god-heads) in Hindu religion. The same principle applied to Buddhism also. Only learned *Lamas* being certified by the Monasteries perform Buddhist worship rituals. The whole aim of the awakening that comes within is to go past oneself, past one's concept of oneself, to that of which one is but an imperfect manifestation. When you come out of a meditation, for example, you are supposed to end by yielding all the benefits, whatever they may be, to the world, to all living beings, not holding them to yourself. Compassion is the fundamental religious experience and, unless that is there, you have nothing. The idea of Buddha consciousness (inward sensibility of something) is of an immanent (remaining within), luminous consciousness that informs all things and all lives. We unthinkingly live by fragments of that consciousness, fragments of that energy. But the religious way of life is to live not in terms of the self-interested intentions of this particular body at this particular time but in terms of the insight of that larger consciousness. In Buddhist systems, more especially those of Tibet, the meditation Buddha appear in two aspects, one peaceful and the other wrathful. If you are clinging fiercely to your ego and its little temporal world of sorrows and joys, hanging on for dear life, it will be the wrathful aspect of the deity that appears. It will seem terrifying. But the moment your ego yields and gives up, that same meditation Buddha is experienced as a bestower of bliss.

In the Buddhists' view, life consists of a series of successive states of consciousness. The first state is the Birth-Consciousness; the last is the consciousness existing at the moment of death, or the Death-Consciousness. The interval between the two states of Consciousness, during which the transformation from the old to a new being is effected, is called the *Bardo* or intermediate state (*Anterabhava*), divided into three stages, called the *Chikhai Bardo, Chonyid Bardo* and *Sidpa Bardo* respectively. The first, and briefest, is the *Bardo* of the moment of death (*Chikhai Bardo*) when, at the end of a process of sensory dissolution that presages physical death, a profound state of consciousness, called the *"Clear Light"*, dawns. If one is able to recognize the clear light as reality, one immediately achieves liberation from *Samsara,* the cycle of rebirth. If the clear light is not recognized at that time, the consciousness of the deceased person moves into the second *Bardo,* called the *Bardo* of reality – *Chonyid Bardo*. The disintegration of the personality brought on by death again reveals reality, but in this case, not as the clear light, but in the multicolored forms of a *Mondala* of *forty-two peaceful deities* and a *Mondala* of *fifty-eight wrathful deities*. These deities appear in sequence to the consciousness of the deceased in the days immediately following death. If reality is not realized in this second *Bardo*, then the third *Bardo*, the *Bardo* of mundane existence – *Sidpa Bardo*, dawns, during which one must again take rebirth in one of the six realms of gods, demi-gods, humans, animals, hungry ghosts, or in hell. Consciousness is blown to the appropriate place of birth by winds of past *karma* (effect of actions in life). The realms of animals, ghosts, and hell beings are regarded as places of great suffering, while the godly realms are abodes of both pleasure and pain. Buddha preferred the realm of human beings as "*Bodhisattva*" for serving the humanity through compassion and his teaching of middle path is achievable only in this realm.

There is a story of the Buddha, who encountered a woman who had just lost her son, and she was in great grief. The Buddha said, "I suggest that you just ask around to meet somebody who has not lost a treasured child or husband or relative or friend." Understanding the relationship of mortality to something in you that is transcendent of mortality is a difficult task (Campbell. Joseph 1959; 1962; 1988:3-232; Chopra, Deepak 2006:21-250; Ferguson, J. C. and Anesaki, Masaharu 1964; Fung Yu-lan 1948; Sogyal Rimpoche 2002; Subba, J.R. 2005a: 4;).

4

RELIGION AND MYTHOLOGY OF CHRISTIANITY

Sikkim came under British protectorate through the Treaty of Titaliya in 1817 A.D. They also annexed Darjeeling areas of Sikkim in 1835 and dominated Sikkim Administration through the Sikkim *Tumlong* Treaty of 1861. The British East India Company established Political Office in Sikkim in 1887-88 and started interference in the Sikkim administration and other aspects. Church of Scotland missionaries from Kalimpong made several visits to Sikkim in 1880s and the Reverend MacFarlane used the *Lepchas* of Kalimpong, West Bengal, to spread the Gospel among their fellow Lepcha tribesmen in Sikkim. By 1890, a church was established at *Chidam*, South Sikkim for the first time. Thus the Christianity was introduced during the later quarter of the nineteenth century in Sikkim. During 1981 Census of India, there were 7,015 persons, 2.23% Christians of the total population, 4th highest religion in Sikkim. Amongst the Hill tribes of Sikkim who adopted Christianity are mostly from *Lepchas* and *Khambu-Rais*. Christianity ranks the first amongst the religions of the world with 33.56% in 1991. A detail history of spread and development of Sikkim has been described by Mckay (2004) and Subba J. R. (2008a), and hence there is no need of discussing it again in this work. Plenty of literature on Christianity is available through out the world. Further, a number of mythological aspects of Christianity have also been discussed under overview chapter. This work deals only some concepts of Christianity in brief (McKay, 2004: 40:2:25-48; Nunes, Antonio B 1996; Subba, J.R. 2008a:154-157).

Christian Concept of God

God possesses the characteristics of a personal spirit being. The Bible says that God is spirit (John 4:24) and is not flesh and blood (Matt 16:17). However, His characteristics are those of a living, person, individual Being. He lives (John 5:26), loves (John 3:16, Rom 5:6-11), speaks (Matt 3:17), works (John 5:17, 20), knows (Matt 6:8, 32), wills (Matt 7:21), and sees (Matt 6:4,6,18). God is not just an impersonal force, nor does. He needs a physical body in order to possess personal characteristics. God is spirit, not material or physical, and yet He possesses characteristics of a personal individual.

Man is not Divine. Spiritually man is in the image or likeness of God (Gen. 126f, 5:1, 96; James 39:1, Cor.11:7). But our inner being is not Divine, not of the essence of God, and not to be worshipped. To believe we are divine is blasphemous. Peter used to accept worship from Cornelius because Peter himself was a man (CfRev.22:8,9,10.19). Our inner essence is not God. Therefore, it is not right to worship any man, neither ancestors nor religious teachers. God is not a man (Samuel 15:29). There is only one true God. Three separate Beings possess Deity, the Father, Son, and Holy Spirit. But unlike Hindu Deities, these three are completely united in will, goals, purposes, etc. All have complete authority over all aspects of creation (in contrast to one over fire, one over wealth, etc.). Hence they are completely united to form a God (John 17:20,21). The Lord is God and there is none else besides Him (Deuteronomy 4:35-39). Before Me there was no God formed, nor shall there be after Me. I, even I, am the Lord, and besides Me there is no savior (Isaiah 43:10,11). You shall have no other gods before Me (Exodus 20:3). Use of images in worship is forbidden. You shall not make any graven image nor bow to such (Exodus 20:4,5). Since we are God's off-springs, we shall not think the Godhead is like gold or silver or stone graven by art or device of men (Acts 17:29). Unlike Hinduism, the Christians attitude towards ideology is separate (Subba, J.R. 2005a:35-36).

Christian Concept of Creation of the Universe

God created all things out of nothing (*ex nihilo*). He did this by a series of verbal commands (e.g. Let there be light, Let there be a firmament in the midst of the waters, Let the dry land appear etc.) (Genesis 1:3,9). All things in creation continue to be upheld by "the word of His power" (Hebrews 1:3). Enhancing the Genesis account of creation, later scripture explains, "By the word of the Lord the heavens were made, and all the host of them by the breath of His mouth" (Psalm 33:6). "Just as words manifest out of our mouths accompanied by breathe, so in the creation, the spoken commands of God manifested out of Him, accompanied by divine breath". The Hebrew word is translated both breath and spirit, so this is most likely a reference to the 'spirit of God', sent forth during the act of creation to execute His words. The word "host" is probably referring to the multitude of heavenly bodies (stars, planets, asteroids, etc), but could also be a reference to the angelic "host" of heaven. The natural creation is separate from God, not an emanation of his own being. The material world is not an illusion, it is real, a gift from God to be enjoyed in the proper perspective (Subba, J.R. 2005a:70-71).

Christian Concept of Life and Destiny

The Bible guides the lives of the Christians, the reality of death is acknowledged as part of the current human condition affected by sin. Man has only one earthly life and death. It is appointed unto man once to die (Hebrews 9:27). Man lives and dies physically only once. There is a time to be born, and a time to die (Ecclesiastes 3:2). After death, the body returns to dust and the spirit returns to God who gave it (not to another body) (Ecclesiastes 12:7). Although eternal life is a gift that is granted to all who accept salvation through Jesus Christ, faithful Christians await the second coming of Jesus for complete realization of their immortality (John 3:36). While waiting for Jesus to come again, Christians may be called upon to care for the dying and to face personally their own death. When one has died, his destiny is fixed. He cannot pass from one destiny of suffering to one of bliss, nor vice-versa (Luke 16:26). The Bible teaches just one earthly existence. At death the soul of a born again is immediately received into heaven. The promise is given that to be absent from the body is to be present with the Lord. When Jesus returns at the end of this age, the souls of all departed saints will return with him. The resurrection of the dead will take place as well as the translation of living believers. All redeemed, saved persons will then be given eternal forms, glorified bodies that will shine with the radiance of the heavenly world. Those who are unsaved will spend eternity separated from God (Matthew 13:43; 25:34,41)

According to the Holy Bible, the meaning of Adam's sin is that man who was created in the image and likeness of God and infused with breath by His Spirit, when He had appeared on the face of earth, chose death instead of life, evil instead of righteousness. And so death passed upon all men, for that in him (Adam) all have sinned (Romans 5:12), say the Apostle Paul. And having sinned, men brought death also to his children, who shared his nature and life. Physical death began with Adam and Eve, but it did not end with them. Physical death is a universal experience among human being. Spiritual death has also come as a consequence of men's sin. This is the reason why each person who reaches the age of responsibility must be saved if he expects to go to heaven. Each one is spiritually dead until he is made alive in Jesus Christ. This is why salvation is often called a resurrection in Biblical terminology (Eph 2:1). A person is saved when he is raised up from spiritual death, given spiritual life (put in right relationship with God), and made a child in God's divine household. Although eternal life is a gift that is granted to all who accept salvation through Jesus Christ, faithful Christians await the second coming of Jesus for complete realization of their immortality. While waiting for Jesus to come again, Christians may be called upon to care for the dying and to face personally their own death.

Suffering

"Suffering is a part of life" which basically agrees with the first "truth" of Buddhism. However, the Christians believe that suffering exists as the consequences of man's sin or as a temptation to sin. Physical desires of themselves are neither good nor bad. It depends on how we seek to fulfill the desire. The Bible says that every natural desire has a good and proper way to be fulfilled. However, the Bible warns that human desires can be perverted and lead to sin. The way to overcome suffering is not to strive to defeat it yourself, but to trust in God and serve Him. By serving God properly, we can endure suffering in his life. If we remain faithful to God, he will receive an eternal reward in a place where there is no suffering of any kind.

Destiny

The proper destiny of man is not to eliminate all desires from his life but to know God's will and control the desires accordingly. In particular, the desire to exist as an individual is not bad. It is an act of God's creation. In fact, man will always exist in a state of conscious existence as a separate individual. In the resurrection we will have spirit bodies. In eternity, we will be conscious and distinct individuals (Luke 16:19-31)

Resurrection

After Jesus died, His spirit was reunited with His body. Likewise after death, the spirit of each man will be returned with his body when Jesus comes again. It will then be changed to a spirit body to receive as eternal reward. All in the tombs will come forth to the resurrection off life or damnation (John 5:28, 29). Thus, after death comes resurrection, the reunion of our spirit with our own body. The body without the spirit is dead. Death is separation of the spirit from the body. All die as a result of Adam's sin, as a result of Jesus, all live again. Resurrection is the opposite of death; hence the spirit is reunited with the body. Christians believe that man do not become another person, but are resurrected as themselves. This happens at Jesus second coming. It is not something that happens repeatedly before His return nor that happens for different people at different times. Man lives one life and then dies. At Jesus return, the spirit is reunited with the body and man is judged for that one life. There is no other life on earth and no other chance to please God after his life. We most obey in this life to have hope. The wicked go to eternal punishment, but the righteous to eternal life.

Judgment

In contradiction to the doctrine of "Karma", the Bible teaches that on earth, men often do not receive fair or just rewards for their lives (Luke 16:19,25; Matt 5:11-12). Instead, when Jesus returns, He will judge all men and declare our eternal rewards on the basis of our lives, good or bad. After judgment, each one will receive a reward according to the life he lived in the body, good or bad (Corinthians 5:10).

Final Destination

After judgment, men receive their eternal destinies. The righteous receive eternal life, a state of bliss, in the presence of God. The wicked receive eternal punishment, suffering and sorrow, separated from God (Methew 25:46). Hence, both the rewards and the punishments taught in the Bible are to be received after we leave the earth, not while on the earth.

Salvation

Our sins spiritually separate us from God. All people are guilty of sin, disobedience to God's will (Romans 3:23). Because of our sins, we are out of harmony and fellowship with God. He is then not dwelling within us. God cannot be found within the heart of the sinner, for He is not there. Our soul is not part of God, nor are we in fellowship with Him. Because of this spiritual alienation from God, we will be separated from God eternally if our sins are not forgiven (Eph 2:11-19; Rom 6:23). Because of God's love and grace, Deity came to earth in the form of man (Jesus) and died as a sacrifice to pay the penalty of man's sins. Without the faith in Jesus, man cannot be saved (Subba, J.R. 2005a:102-106).

Christian Concept of Soul

Most Christians regard the soul as the immortal essence of a human and that after death; God either rewards or punishes the soul. Different Christian groups dispute heatedly whether this reward or punishment depends upon doing good deeds, or merely upon believing in God and in Jesus. The Bible teaches just one earthly existence. It is appointed for men to die once (Hebrew 9:27). At death, the soul of a born again believer is immediately received into heaven. The promise is given that to be absent from the body is to be present with the Lord (Carinthians 5:8). When Jesus returns at the end of this age, the souls of all departed saints will return with Him. The resurrection of the dead will take place (with souls and new bodies rejoined), as well as the transformation of living believers. All redeemed, saved persons will then be given eternal forms, glorified bodies that will shine with the radiance of the heavenly world. Those who is unsaved will spend eternity separated from God (Mathew 13:43; 25:34,41) (Subba, J.R. 2005a:130).

Christian Concept of Afterlife

Bible teaches us that after death, comes resurrection, the reunion of our spirit with our body. We do not become another person, but are resurrected as ourselves. This happens at Jesus second coming. There is one life only. Beliefs about death vary. The soul may ascend to heaven and be judged by God; or the soul and the body may be raised on the Day of Judgment, at the end of time, and will then be judged.

(i) Catholicism asserts that individuals are saved by declaring faith in God, but are still subject to punishment for unrepented sin at death, which is purified in purgatory.

(ii) Traditional Protestantism asserts that purely declaring their belief in the saving power of Jesus's death and resurrection saves individuals.

(iii) Some others believe that individuals choose their own heaven or hell; if a person chooses to live in a self-created hell on earth, they continue to choose that after death, and God ultimately gives them what they wish: distance from God and joy. On the other hand, people that seek heaven on earth continue to seek heaven after death, and God gives them what they desire: nearness of God, and joy.

The concept of heaven and the road to salvation are diverse based on interpretations of different faiths of Christianity (Subba, J.R. 2005a:155-157).

Christian Concept of Purpose and Meaning of Life

"Be fruitful, and multiply, and replenish the earth, and subdue it" (Gen 1:28), indicated that there are three purposes of man: (i) the propagation of human race; (ii) the care and restoration of the earth, and (iii) the control of our environment. These are the three goals God has set for men (Subba, J.R. 2005a:179-181).

Mythology

Mythology of Christianity has been discussed at length in the overview chapter. Hence, only some aspects of Christian mythology are being discussed in this chapter. In Christianity, the biblical tradition is a socially oriented mythology. Nature is condemned, and hence there is no nature mythology. In the nineteenth century, the Christian scholars thought of mythology or ritual as an attempted to control nature. But that was thought of magic, not mythology or religion. In fact, nature religions are not attempts to control nature but to help you put yourself in accord with it. But when nature is thought of as evil, you don't put yourself in accord with it, you control it, or try to, and hence the tension, the anxiety, the cutting down of forests, the annihilation of native people. And the accent here in Christianity separates us from nature. The process of nature cannot be evil. Every natural impulse is not to be corrected but to be sublimated, to be beautified. The glorious interest in the beauty of nature doesn't know where nature begins and art ends.

Goddess

In the story of the incarnation of Jesus, the father of Jesus was the father in heaven, at least in terms of the symbology. When Jesus goes to the cross, he is on the way to the father, leaving the mother behind. And the cross, which is symbolic of the earth, is the mother symbol. So on the cross, Jesus leaves his body on the mother, from whom he has accrued his body, and he goes to the father, who is the ultimate transcendent mystery source.

We have found hundreds of early European Neolithic figures of the Goddess but hardly anything there of the male figure at all. The bull and certain other animals, such as the boar and the goat, may appear as symbolic of the male power, but the Goddess was the only visualized divinity at that time. Mother Goddess was very potent figure in Hellenistic times in the Mediterranean, and she came back with the Virgin in the Roman Catholic tradition. You don't have a tradition with the Goddess celebrated any more beautifully and marvelously than in the twelfth and thirteenth century French cathedrals, every one of which is called Notre Dame. There were the great female saints. Hildegarde of Bingen, was a match for Innocent, and Eleanor of Aquitaine, who has the statue to match hers. But none of those saints would ever become pope. That is where the paternalistic idea grew. There is one scene of the Goddess swallowing the sun. The idea is that she swallows the sun in the west and gives birth to the sun in the east, and it passes through her body at night. So it would be natural for people trying to explain the wonders of the universe to look to the female as the explanation of what they see in their own lives. In the New Testament "In Jesus there is no male or female, there is neither." And in that yin/yang figure from China, in the dark fish, or whatever you want to call it, there is the light spot. And in the light one, there is a dark spot. That is how they can relate (Campbell. Joseph 1959; 1962; 1964; 1968; 1988: 3-36).

Mythology of Heroes and Heroes

A legendary hero is usually the founder of something, the founder of a new age, the founder of a new religion, the founder of a new city, the founder of a new way of life. In order to found something new, one has to leave the old and go in quest of the seed idea, a germinal idea that will have the potentiality of bringing forth that new thing. The founders of all religions have gone on quests like that. The Buddha went into solitude and then sat beneath the bo-tree, the tree of immortal knowledge, where he received an illumination that has enlightened all of Asia for twenty-six hundred years now. After baptism by John the Baptist, Jesus went to the desert for forty days, and it was out of that desert that he came with his message. Moses went to the top of a mountain and came down with the tables of the laws. These heroic stories are important to the human race. The rituals of primitive initiation ceremonies are all mythologically grounded and have to do with killing the infantile ego and bringing forth an adult, whether it is the girl or the boy. It is harder for the boy than the girl, because life overtakes the girl. She becomes a woman whether she intends it or not, but the little boy has to intend to be a men. At the first menstruation, the girl is a woman. The next thing she knows, she is pregnant, and she is a mother. The boy first has to disengage himself from his mother, get his energy into himself, and then start forth. That is what the myth of "Young man, go find your father" is all about. In the Odyssey Telemachus lives with his mother. When he is twenty years old, Athena comes and says, "Go find your father". That is the theme all through the stories. The story of crucification, which is a fundamental image in the Christian tradition, speaks of the coming of eternity into the field of time and space, where there is dismemberment. But it also speaks of the passage from the field of time and space into the field of eternal life so that we crucify our temporal and earthly bodies (physical consciousness), let them be torn, and through that dismemberment enter into the spiritual sphere (spiritual consciousness), which transcends all the plains of earth.

The story of Jesus, for example: there is a universally valid hero deed represented in the story of Jesus. First, he goes to the edge of the consciousness of his time when he goes to John the Baptist to be baptized. Then he goes past the threshold into the desert for forty days. In the Jewish tradition the number forty is mythologically significant. In the desert, Jesus underwent three temptations:

(i) First, there was the economic temptation, where the devil comes to him and says, "You look hungry, young man! Why not change these stones to bread?" And Jesus replies, "Man lives not by bread alone, but by every word out of the mouth of God."

(ii) And then next we have the political temptation: Jesus is taken to the top of a mountain and shown the nations of the world, and the Devil says to him, "You can control all these if you will bow down to me," which is a lesson, not well enough made known today, of what it takes to be a successful politician. Jesus refuses.

(iii) Finally the Devil says, "And so now, you are so spiritual, let us go up to the top of Herod's Temple and let me see you cast yourself down. God will bear you up, and you won't even be bruised." This is what is known as spiritual inflation. I am so spiritual; I am above concerns of the flesh and this earth. But Jesus is incarnate, is he not? So he says, "You shall not tempt the Lord, your God."

Those are the three temptations of Christ, and they are as relevant today as they were in the year A.D. 30. Now, those first two temptations, of desire and of fear, are the same that Adam and Eve are shown to have experienced in the extraordinary painting by Titian (now in Prado), conceived when he was ninety-four years old. Adam and Eve were moved. Eve and Adam brought forth life and were cursed of God. Christ found salvation beyond death and returned from the wilderness to choose and instruct disciples who then brought their message to the world. The message of the great teachings, Moses, the Buddha, Christ,

Mohammed, differ greatly. But their visionary journeys are much the same.

Journey Inward

The snake is the symbol of life throwing off the past and continuing to live. The power of life causes the snake to shed its skin, just as the moon sheds its shadow. The serpent sheds its skin to be born again, as the moon sheds its shadow to be born again. They are equivalent symbols. Sometimes the serpent is represented as a circle eating its own tail. That is an image of life. Life sheds one generation after another, to be born again. The serpent represents immortal energy and consciousness engaged in the field of time, constantly throwing off death and being born again. There is sometimes tremendously terrifying about life when you look at it that way. And so the serpent carries in itself the sense of both the fascination and the terror of life. Further, the serpent represents the primary function of life, mainly eating. Life consists in eating other creatures. You don't think about that very much when you make a nice-looking meal. But what you are doing is eating something that was recently alive. And when you look at the beauty of nature, and you see the birds picking around, they are eating things. You see the cows grazing, they are eating things. The serpent is a traveling alimentary canal that is about all it is. And it gives you that primary sense of shock, of life in its most primal quality. There is no arguing with that animal at all. Life lives by killing and eating itself, casting off death and being reborn, like the moon or the serpent. This is one of the mysteries that their symbolic, paradoxical forms try to represent. Now the snake in most culture is given a positive interpretation. In India, even the most poisonous snake, the cobra, is a sacred animal, and the mythological Serpent King is the next thing to the Buddha. The serpent represents the power of life engaged in the field of time, and of death, yet eternally alive. The world is but its shadow, the falling skin. The serpent flows like water and so is watery, but its tongue continually flashes fire, so you have the pair of opposites together in the serpent. In the biblical tradition we have inherited, life is corrupt, and every natural impulse is sinful unless it has been circumcised or baptized. In Christianity, the serpent was the one who brought sin into the world. And the woman was the one who handed the apple to man. This identification of women with sin, of the serpent was sin, and thus the life with sin, is the twist that has been given to the whole story in the biblical myth and doctrine of the fall. In the biblical tradition women represent life and are also held responsible for the downfall. Man doesn't enter life except by woman, and so it is woman who brings us into this world of pairs of opposites and suffering.

In the good standard Christian doctrine – at the end of the world there will be a general judgment and those who have acted virtuously will be sent to heaven, and those who have acted in an evil way, to hell. This is a theme that goes back to Egypt. Osiris is the god who died and was resurrected and in his eternal aspect will sit as judge of the dead. Mummification was to prepare the person to face the god. But an interesting thing in Egypt is that the person going to the god is to recognize his identity with the god. In the Christian tradition, that 's not allowed. So if you are saying that the alternative is hell or heaven, well, give me heaven forever. But when you realize that heaven is a beholding of the beatific image of God that would be a timeless moment. Time explodes, so again, eternity is not something everlasting. You can have it right here, now, in your experience of your earthly relationships (Campbell. Joseph 1959; 1964; 1968; 1988; Johnson, Paul 1972; Frazer, James 1996; Fergus Fleming et. al. 1996).

5

RELIGION AND MYTHOLOGY OF JAINISM

Most of the early plainsman migrants to sikkim were asked for supply of quality materials required by the *Chogyals*, Kleptocrats, and British people, who were deputed to the Political Office, Gangtok Sikkim during the *Chogyal* Dynasty of the Himalayan Kingdom. They were the *Marwaris* from Rajesthan state of India migrated during the last decade of nineteenth and the first decade of twentieth century in Sikkim. They were the believers of Jainism and settled mainly at Gangtok, and slowly on other urban areas of Sikkim. Thus, Jainism was introduced in Sikkim along with these plainsmen. During 1981 Census, there were 108 persons (0.03%) Jain believers in Sikkim (0.07% in the world) (Nunes, Antonio B 1996; Subba, J.R. 2005a; 2008a: 154-157).

Jainism Concept of God

Jainism believes that universe and all its substances or entities are eternal. It has no beginning or end with respect to time. There is no need of some one to create or manage the affairs of the universe. Universe runs by its own cosmic laws. Hence, Jainism does not believe in God as a creator, sustainer and destroyer of the universe. However, when a living being destroys all his *karmas*, he possesses perfect knowledge, vision, power, and bliss. He becomes omniscient and omnipotent, and this living being attends Godhood in Jain religion. Thus, every living being has a potential to become a Deity in Jainism. They are known as *Tirthankaras* or *Arihants* or *Jinas* (Jainism, Mirian, 1999).

Jainism Concept of Creation of the Universe

Jainism considers the world eternal and uncreated. The universe is made up of six basic elements or components that are infinitely indestructible. However, these are in a constant state of flux. These fundamental elements are soul, matter, time, space, the principles of motion, and the arrest of motion. Only living matter contains a soul (*jiva* or consciousness). Non-living matter is *ajiva*. To a Jain, matter is reality, not an illusion perpetrated by a creator-god who temporarily takes upon himself the appearance of matter (Jainism, Mirian, 1999).

Jainism Concept of Life and Destiny

The concept of life is same as that of Hinduism. Jainism is a dualistic philosophy, declaring the reality of the individual soul and the matter. There are eight kinds of *karma* that keep the soul trapped in the cycle of birth and fourteen steps to liberate from this inexorable law. Acquired *karma* can be cancelled through *nirjara*. This process includes self-denial, service, mortification of the body, various atonements of sin, and meditation. There are four states of existence (*gatis*) into which souls can be reincarnated. This is determined by accumulated *karmic* merits or demerits. They are Heavenly beings, Human beings, *Tiryancha* beings (animals, plants, lower life forms), and Infernal beings (those tormented in hells). After numerous existences in various forms the *jiva* eventually evolves to the level of a human being. It then incarnates many times as a human being until liberation takes place. Liberated souls rise to the top of the universe. The number of souls is infinite. Jain religion believes that human souls can revert spiritually and be reincarnated in non-human life forms. Once absolute consciousness is attained, this state is eternal and irreversible.

Destiny

The ultimate objective in Jainism is the total freedom from the cycle of birth, life, pain, misery, and death; and achieve the permanent blissful state of one's self. This is known as liberation, *Nirvana*, absolute freedom or *Moksha*. True philosophy in Jainism should result in removing all bondages (*Karma*) in the process of purifying of the soul. The central theme of Jainism considers religion as a science of ethical practice. It conceives the human body as a chariot on which the soul rides towards liberation. Every soul can attain purity and perfection that is Supreme Spiritual individuality by realizing its intrinsic purity and perfection. An individual, in his conduct can be gained by the examples of five benevolent personalities. They are Supreme human beings, pure or perfect souls, master teachers, scholarly monks and ascetics.

Karma

Karma in Jainism is not a mere effect of a particular activity, but a real substance, that flows into the body and envelops it in the dark gloom. From eternity, every living being is in bondage of *karmic* atoms that are accumulated by its own good or bad deeds under the influence of *karma*. The soul is habituated to seek pleasures in materialistic belongings and possessions, which are deep-rooted causes of self-centered violent thoughts, deeds, anger, hatred, greed, and such other vices. These result in accumulating more *karma*.

Liberation or *Moksha*

Jainism believes that right faith, right knowledge, and right conduct together will help attain the liberation of one's Self. Non-violence, truthfulness, non-stealing, chastity, and non-possession/ non-attachment, complete detachment of people, places and material things are the right five great vows for the Jains. Matter is the aggregate of atoms, the source of bondage and the cause of all *karmas*. *Moksha* is the freedom from all *karmic* matter, owing to the non-existence of the cause of bondage and the shedding of all the *karmas*. Thus, complete freedom of the soul from *karmic* matter is called *Moksha*. *Moksha* is attained when the soul and matter are separated from each other. The separation is effected when all the *karmas* have left the soul, and no more *karma* matter can be attached towards it (Jainism, Mirian, 1999).

Jainism Concept of Soul

Jainism believes in soul (*jiva*), an immortal essence of a living being. It is capable of changing its dimensions, expanding and contracting depending upon the circumstances and the nature of *karma* it has indulged in. The soul exists everywhere, not only in living beings, but in inanimate objects as well. They are everywhere in every aspect of the world around us.

Jainism Concept of Afterlife

Jainism believes that the ultimate end and purpose of all life and activity is to realize the free and blissful state of our true being. Adherents of Jainism should result in removing all bondages in the process of purifying of the soul. The human body is considered as a chariot on which the soul rides towards liberation. The conduct of the present life should be aimed to attain total freedom from which there is no return to the birth and death cycle. *Moksha* is the freedom from all *karmic* matters, owing to the non-existence of the cause of bondage and the shedding of all the *karmas*. One who attains *Moksha* is to attain Godhood. Everybody can attain Godhood by realizing its purity and perfection (Jainism, Mirian, 1999).

Mythology

The Jainism mythology is more or less the same as that of Hinduism.

6

RELIGION AND MYTHOLOGY OF SIKHISM

After India's independence of 1947, the Himalayan Kingdom-Sikkim came under the protectorate of India. Indian army were deputed on the boarders of Sikkim mostly on the Northern and Eastern Boarders. The army personals were mostly *Punjabis*, believers of Sikhism. Army cantonment was established at *Living*, near Gangtok, where some of the families were also residing. Along with these personals Sikhism was also introduced in Sikkim. Now, *Gurudwaras* and other worship places of *Sikhism* exist in many working places and settlements in Sikkim. During 1981 Census, there were 322 Sikhs (0.10%) in Sikkim (0.37% in the world) (Nunes, Antonio B 1996; Subba, J.R. 2008a:154-157).

Sikhism Concept of God

Sikhism is a monotheistic religion, founded in the 15th century by *Guru Nanak*. It believes on a single, all-powerful God, who created the universe and everything in it. There is only one God; he is the creator, sustainer and destroyer. The worship place is known as *Gurudwara*. Sikh's scripture is known as *Adhi Granth* or *Guru Granth Sahib*. Sikhs believe that the words of these scriptures are the present day embodiment of the *Sikh Guru* and they treat the book with respect and devotion that they would have given to a human Guru.

Sikhism Concept of Creation of the Universe

Sikhism maintains that this world was created by a divine decree (*Hukam*). With a single command, creation was unfurled (*Japji*-16). The whole creation and individual destinies are maintained and preserved by the complementary principles of justice (*Nian*) and grace (*Nadar*). Sikh doctrine is strongly against the pantheistic notion that all substances, force and laws in this universe are essentially God in manifestation. The universe is not God, but his container. The world is God's own form (*Adi Granth* 922:6). So most *Sikhs* would conclude. This creation is divine since God is present in the creation in His immanent form. Contrary to the Hindu belief that the world is an illusion (*Maya*), and the Buddhist doctrine that all phenomenon in this world are ultimately empty (*Sunyata*) and unreal, Sikhism is world affirming. *Guru Nanak* taught, "Real are Thy realms and real Thy universe. Real are Thy world's and real Thy created forms" (*Adi Granth* p 463).

Sikhism Concept of Life and Destiny

The concept of life is same as that of Hinduism. The goal of human life is to break the cycle of births and deaths, and merge with God. This can be accomplished by following the teachings of the Guru Nanak, meditation on the Holy Name and performance of acts of service and chastity. The five cardinal vices are *Kam* (lust), *Krodh* (anger), *Lobh* (greed), *Moh* (worldly attachment), and *Ahankar* (pride). If one can overcome these, they will achieve salvation. Most *Sikhs* believe in the twin doctrines of *karma* (*karam*) and rebirth. Once souls are released from the cycle of rebirths, they become one with God. In Sikhism the world is real, so the world means something different. *Maya* is the self-deceived state of mind that results from placing too much emphasis on the material world and too little focus on spiritual values. There are five ascending levels on the spiritual paths. They are: (i) *Dharam Khand* – living by God's law; (ii) *Saram Khand* – living a self-disciplined life; (iii) *Karam Khand* – living in God's grace; (iv) *Gian Khand* – living in the revelation and knowledge of God; (v) *Sach Khand* – attaining ultimate truth. Those who achieve this absolute state arrive at the final objective of every *Sikh Sahaj*, the rapturous peace of blending with the divine, which many would say results in final liberation from the painful sequence of death and rebirth.

Sikhism Concept of Afterlife

Each individual has many reincarnations, but being a human means the soul in nearing the end of rebirth. God judges each soul at death and may either reincarnate the soul or if pure enough, allow it to rest with him.

Mythology

The Sikhism mythology is more or less the same as that of Hinduism.

7

RELIGION AND MYTHOLOGY OF ISLAM

After integration of Sikkim into Indian Union in 1975, the people of India inmigrated to Sikkim in large numbers. Of the immigrants, *Muslim* constitute one of the major chunks in Sikkim. During 1981 Census there were 3,241 *Muslims* (1.03%) in Sikkim. They have established many *Musjits* in many important business centers like Singtam, Mangan, Jorethang, Gangtok, etc. (Subba, J.R. 2005a; 2008a:154-157).

Islamic Concept of God

Islam is a monotheistic faith; believe in the Almighty God *Allah*. He is often referred as the creator, the sustainer, the merciful, the compassionate, the judge, the governor, the eternal etc. *Allah* is without beginning, without end, and He alone sees and knows all things. *Allah* is transcendent, yet close to mankind. The *Qur'an* is the Holy book of Islam, and contains all information including history, basic concepts, excerpts, search energies, audio recitations etc. Islam believes that one can only find peace in one's life by submitting to Almighty God – *Allah* in heart, soul and deed. The prime message of Islam is the unity of God that the creator of the world is one and He alone is worthy of worship and that Muhammad is His messenger and servant. Islam's main message is to worship God and to treat all God's creations with kindness and compassion (Subba, J. R. 2005a: 38-39).

Islamic Concept of Creation of the Universe

According to the *Qur'an,* the Almighty God – *Allah* solely created the life-containing universe and He is the Supreme Ruler of the universe. Islam believes that God brought creation into being by the power of a spoken command, "Be" (*Kun*). The material world is separate from God as in the case of Christianity. Mystical *Islam* (*Sufism*) believes that the universe is an expression of God's Infinite compassion and came into existence through the utterance of the Divine command, "*Kun*" (Be). Light God brings all things into existence and sustains them. Everything was created by the sound of the wings of the guardian angel – Gabriel in *Islam*.

This universe – earth and heaven has definite life period and has some definite objectives like other creations of *Allah*. *Qur'an* rejects any notion of eternal universe which other theories like steady state theory holds. The creation of universe from out of nothing or creation *ex-nihilo* is in direct references in the *Qur'an*. "He is the originator of the heavens and the earth" (*Qur'an* 6:101). The information given in *Qur'an* is in full agreement with the findings of contemporary science (Subba, J.R. 2005a:71).

Islamic Concept of Life and Destiny

Islam believes that one can only find peace in one's life by submitting to Almighty *Allah* in heart, soul and deed. The literal meaning of Islam is peace; surrender of one's wills, i.e. loosing oneself for the sake of God and surrendering one's own pleasure for the pleasure of *Allah*. The message of *Allah* was revealed to the Holy Prophet Muhammad 1400 years ago. It was revealed through angel Gabriel and was thus preserved in the Holy *Qur'an*. The Holy *Qur'an* carries a Divine guarantee of safeguard from interpolation and it claims that it combines the best features of the earlier scriptures. The prime message of Islam in the unity of God, that the creator of the world is one and He alone is worthy of worship and that Muhammad is His messenger and servant.

Death

When death approaches, the close family and friends try to support and comfort the dying person through supplication as well as remembrance of *Allah* and His will. The attendance is to help the dying person to iterate his commitment to unity of God. Like Jews and Christians, Muslims believe that the present life is only a trial preparation for the next realm of existence. Basic articles of faith include the Day of Judgment, resurrection, Heaven and Hell. Visiting the graves is recommended for the living to remember death and the Day of Judgment. When a Muslim dies, he or she is washed, usually by family members, wrapped in a clean cloth, and buried with a simple prayer preferably the same day. Muslims consider this one of the final services they can do for their relatives, and an opportunity to remember their one belief existence here on earth.

Death is the will of God so that God uses *Azbrail,* upon him be peace, to take souls of those who are to die. Death releases us from the hardships of worldly life, which is a turbulent, suffocating, narrow dungeon of space that gradually becomes harder through old age and affliction, and admits us to the infinitely wide circle of the eternal, beloved one's mercy. There, we may enjoy the everlasting company of our beloved ones and the consolation of a happy, eternal life.

All human beings have an intrinsic feeling of eternity and so feel imprisoned in the narrow confines of the material world and yearn for eternity. The natural inclination towards eternal happiness comes from an objective reality; the existence of eternal life and our desire for it. The spirit uses the body as an instrument and thus governs and controls all parts of it in a comprehensive manner.

Destiny

Following death, the spirit is taken to the presence of God by the angels for introduction. If it led a good, virtuous life and refined itself, the spirit is brought back to the grave where its body is buried, so that it can answer the questions of *Munkar* and *Nakin,* the interrogating angels. This is the reason, why the Muslims bury the dead body and do not cremate.

Duties

The followers of Islam are known as Muslims and have five main duties to perform, namely:

(i) Bearing witness to the unity of God and Muhammad (peace and blessing on Him);

(ii) Observing the prescribed prayer;

(iii) Payment of *Zakat;*

(iv) Keeping the fasts of *Ramadhan*; and

(v) Performing the pilgrimage to Mecca.

Islam believes that each person is born pure. The Holy *Qur'an* tells us that God has given human being a choice between good and evil and to seek God's pleasure through faith, prayer and charity. Islam believes that God created mankind in His image and by imbuing the attitudes of God on a human level mankind can attain His nearness. Islam's main message is to worship God and to treat all God's creation with kindness and compassion. Rights of parents in old age, orphans and the needy are clearly started. Women's rights were safeguarded. Islam's teachings encompass every imaginable situation and its rules and principles are truly universal and have stood the test of time.

Islamic Concept of Soul

According to the *Qur'an* of Islam (15:29), the creation of man involves *Allah* 'breathing" a soul into him. This entangle part of an individual's existence is "pure" at birth and has the potential of growing and achieving nearness to God if a person leads a righteous life. At death the person's soul transitions to an eternal afterlife of bliss, peace and unending spiritual growth (*Qur'an* 66:8, 39, 20). This transition can be pleasant (Heaven) or unpleasant (Hell) depending on the degree to which a person has developed or destroyed his or her soul during life (*Qur'an* 91:7-10).

Islamic Concept of Afterlife

There is one life only as in the case of Christianity. Most adherents believe the individual awaits the Day of Judgment also as in the case of Christians, when all will be brought back to life and judged. Paradise awaits those who have lived according to the will of *Allah* and those who have failed to do so cannot enter Paradise. Under most traditional Islamic belief, God judges us on the basis of our adherence to the five pillars of Islam, including acknowledgement of God, and living according to God's laws of justice, faith, and mercy, and rewards us according to our acts on earth.

In Islam, life continues after the phenomenal death. The idea of afterlife is very important, without which person would not be able to approach the meaning of spiritual life on earth. He would consider himself as a finite being. *Qur'an* stresses the afterlife specially those who approached life from a spiritual perspective.

Islam's Views of Purpose and Meaning of Life

Islam's view point is that God created man for one purpose and that is to worship God. To Islams, life is like a test. How well you perform on this "test" will determine whether you get into *Jenna* (Heaven) or *Jehenim* (Hell). There is no purgatory or in between in Islam (Blank, Jonah 2001).

Mythology

Mythology of Islam is more or less the same as that of Christianity.

PART-III

8

LASSER KNOWN RELIGIONS AND MYTHOLOGIES OF THE PEOPLE OF SIKKIM

Sikkim is a multi-racial, multilingual, multicultural, secular and democratic state of India. The early adoptees of Hinduism - the *Khasas* have strongly influenced the other races/tribes of Sikkim especially those who migrated to Sikkim after 1774 A.D. Similarly, after the establishment of the Himalayan Kingdom – Greater Sikkim and declaring Buddhism as a kingdom's religion in 1642; Buddhism has tremendously influenced the belief systems of the people of Sikkim – especially the *Lepchas*. Further, after the treaty of Titaliya in 1817 A.D., Sikkim came under British protectorate. Church of Scotland missionaries from Kalimpong started sending the *Lepcha* Christian adoptees, trained for conversion of their fellow *Lepchas* of Sikkim after 1880s. Then onwards some of the indigenous people especially the *Lepchas* were converted to Christianity. Thus, the Lepchas were sandwiched between Buddhism and Christianity, which affected their belief system tremendously.

When we examine the history of Nepal, a section of the *Rajputs* of Rajesthan migrated to Nepal along with the *Royal Shah Vangshi* families, and by 15th century *Yaso Brahma Shah* became the king of *Lamjung*. He had three sons *Narhari, Dravya* and *Narpati*; out of which *Dravya Shah* killed *Kharnka Khasa* king of *Gorkha* province of Nepal, and became the king of *Gorkha* in 1559 (B.S. *Bhadra* 25th 1616). He introduced Hinduism amongsts the *Khasa* subjects. Then, after 13th generation of *Shah Vanshi* kings, king *Nar Bhupal* bore a son – *Prithivi Narayan Shah* in 1722. He succeeded his father in 1742. By this generation, the entire *Khasa* race/tribe of *Gorkhas* (Higher *Khasas – Bahun* and *Chhetri,* Lower *Khasas - Kami, Damai* and *Sarki*) had adopted the introduced Hinduism; forgetting everything of their own belief system accept their *Masta* god (ancestor deity). *Prithivi Narayan Shah* started his first conquest of Nepal in 1744-54 and ended in the East in 1774, extending the *Gorkha* Kingdom right upto Teesta River. The Gorkha unification process distinguished by Stiller, Ludwig F. (1968: 65-82) as Military, Political, Legal and Judicial, Administrative, Cultural and Hindu religious affected the entire hill tribes and races of the Nepal tremendously.

Amongst the most affected tribes or races that have almost forgot everything of their own and are identifiable races/tribes here in Sikkim today are the *Khasas, Newars, Sunuwars, Bhujels, Thami, Majhis, Mangars,* and some *Gurungs*. The tribes who adopted Buddhism leaving aside their *Bonism* long back are the *Bhutias, Tamangs, Sherpas,* and some *Gurungs*. The partly affected tribes by Buddhism are the *Lepchas, Gurungs* and *Newars;* while partly affected by Christianity are the *Lepchas, Khambu-Rais* and *Yakhas.* The *Limboos* are the least affected tribes by other religions and belief systems in Sikkim (Subba, J.R. 2008a; 143-157).

Hence, there are many lesser-known religions, belief systems popularly known as animist mainly by the westerners and the elite people in Sikkim. These are the ancient belief systems of different 14 (fourteen) hill tribes or races of Sikkim, namely: *Lhopo (Bhutia), Lepcha (Rong), Limboo (Tsong), Khambu-Rai, Yakha, Magar, Gurung, Sunuwar, Tamang, Sherpa, Thami, Majhi, Newar* and *Khasa (Bahun, Chettri, Kami, Damai, Sarki)* inhabiting in Sikkim today. The main aim of this work is to collect the valuable information of these lesser known "Belief Systems" or "Religions" and "Mythologies" of the hill communities of Sikkim for the first time for further research and development for the benefit of the people in general.

9

YUMAISM AND MYTHOLOGY OF THE LIMBOO TRIBES

Yumaism belief system was developed in time immemorial and retained generation after generation amongst the aboriginal *Limboo* tribes and some *Yakhas* in this part of the Himalayan region as an oral tradition. In the later half of the ninth century *Ubahang* (849-65 A.D.) - the tribal king of *Limbuwan* propagated *Yumaism* amongsts his subjects in *Limbuwan*, which was followed by his successors; kings *Mabohang* (865-882 A.D.), *Sirijunga Hang* (882-925 A.D.) and *Yongjanga Hang* (925-?). *Yumaism* had become a way of life amongst the *Limboo* tribes in the Eastern Himalayas and thus survived through self-generating tradition of *Phedangma* priestly system in the community. The learned scholars - *Sirijunga Teyongshi Singthebe* (1704-1741), *Lalshore Sendang* (1840-1925) and *Imansing Chemjong* (1904-1976) propagated the faith further in Sikkim and West Bengal. *Yuma* religion has now been developed and spread throughout the Eastern Himalayas amongst the *Limboos* and some *Yakhas* in Nepal, Sikkim, West Bengal, Assam and other North Eastern States of India, Bhutan, Maymar, Singapore, U.K., Canada, and USA. About 4, 00,000 *Limboos* and *Yakhas* are the followers of this religion as their inherent faith in their day to day life. In Sikkim there are 45,000 (14.22%) adherents of *Yum* religion (Subba, C. 1995; Subba, J.R. 1999; 2005a; 2005b; 2008a: 157).

Basic Concepts

Plenty of literature is available on *Yuma* religion. However, some important features of this lesser-known religion could be briefly described as under:

Stages of Development of *Yumaism*

Basically, like any other religion *Yuma* religion has four stages of development as follows:

(a) In its infancy *Yumaism* was Mythological and is in practice even today

Yumaism has an elaborate tradition of reciting oral myths (*Mundhums*) while performing the rituals by the incarnate shamans of the community, collectively known as *Phedangmas*. These oral myths are not composed by a man but are supposed to be the sacred spiritual instructions of the Almighty Goddess *Tagera Ningwaphuma* and her messenger gods and goddesses. These are the sources of understanding of this belief system. These oral traditions are the most important means of cultural continuity in a non-literate society, and are inherited and past down from generation to generation through their shamanic priesthood system – *Phedangmas*. Myths (*Mundhums*) are the power of the great strength and believed to be true holy and powerful scripture. The *Kirant tribes* (*Limboo, Khambu-Rai* and *Yakha*) live on more independently and steadfastly in these oral traditions, than in any other domain. The total corpus of the performed texts of *Mundhums* is myths - sacred, legend, mythological or spiritual instructions, ritual songs and ceremonial dialogues. It generally refers to inherited knowledge concerning the universe creation, creation of living beings, human beings, ancestor etc. It comprises:

(i) Creation of the universe, gods and goddesses.

(ii) Creation of living beings and non-living.

(iii) Creation of human beings and origin of the ancestors.

(iv) The emergence of natural and cultural orders.

(v) The means of communicating through *Phedangmas* with gods, goddesses and ancestors and ritually maintaining the order they have established.

(vi) Continuing to the settlement of the ancestral territory.

(vii) It evokes a way of life predefined by the ancestors, a self-enclosed world, rooted in the past.

(viii) It is the very essence of their culture, the foundation of their identity.

There was no written religious book of the *Kirantas* (*Limboo, Khambu-Rai, Yakha* races) prior to 1961 when I.S. Chemjong started documenting the *Mundhum*. They solely depended on the spoken verses of religious rites by *Phedangmas*. These *Mundhums* have now been recorded, written in black and white and are available in book forms as religious books of *Yumaism*. These are:

(i) *Kirant Mundhum*; I. S. Chemjong 1961.

(ii) *Limboo Jatima Kakhpuja*: Kainla Bairagi. 1991: Nepal Academy.

(iii) *Nahen Mundhum*. Kainla Bairagi: 1994; Kathmandu, Nepal.

(iv) *Samsogha Mundhum*: Kainla Bairagi:1994; Kathmandu Nepal.

(v) *Sasik Mundhum*: Kainla Bairagi.1995. Kathmandu Nepal.

(vi) *Tongsing Tokma Mundhum*. Kainla Bairagi 1995. Nepal Academy.

(vii) *Yakthung re Tendham Mekkhim Mundhum*. J.R. Subba, 1998, Gangtok, Sikkim.

(viii) *Yakthung re Phungsoktimma Mundhum*. J.R. Subba 1998, Gangtok, Sikkim.

(ix) *Sumsemba Tongsingtok Mundhum*. J. R. Subba, 2001, Gangtok, Sikkim.

(x) *Mujoklung Khejoklung Mundhum*. J. R. Subba, 2003, Gangtok, Sikkim.

(xi) *Simering Mundhum*. J. R. Subba, 2004, Gangtok, Sikkim.

(Allen, N.J.1976a:258; Martin Gaenszle, 1991: 223-224; Chemjong, I.S. 1961:21; Subba, J.R. 1998:1-57; 1999:323-397; 2005a:1-21; 2005b:1-136)

Mythology is poetry, and the poetic language is very flexible. Thus, the *Mundhums* in *Yuma* religion are all in classical oral poetry, metaphorical language, flexible, and is often very difficult to understand. Religion turns poetry into prose; and that is the difference between the old primitive *Mundhums* of Limboo classical oral poetic language and *Yuma* religion of the present. The

Almighty Goddess *Tageraningwaphuma* (*Yuma*) is literally up there, and this is literally what she thinks, and this is the way you have got to behave to get into proper relationship with that Goddess up there. All religions have been true for their time. If you can recognize the enduring aspect of their truth and separate it from the temporal applications, you have got it. The sacrifice of the physical desires and fears of the body to that which spiritually supports the body; is the body learning to know, and express its own deepest life in the field of time. One way or the other, we all have to find what fosters the flowering of our humanity in this contemporary life, and dedicate ourselves to that. It is in our-self, let us find out.

Myths inspire the realization of the possibility of your perfection, the fullness of your strength, and the bringing of solar light into the world. Slaying monsters is slaying the dark things. Myths grab you somewhere down inside. Later on, myths tell you more, and more, and still more. We learn them as a child on one level, but then many different levels are revealed. Myths are infinite in their revelation. "Follow your bliss." Find where it is, and don't be afraid to follow it. If the work that you are doing is the work that you chose to do because you are enjoying it, that is it. But if you think, you couldn't possibly do what so and so is doing, then that is the dragon locking you in. Psychologically, the dragon is one's own binding of oneself to one's ego. We are captured in our own dragon cage. The problem of the psychiatrist is to disintegrate that dragon, break him up, so that you may expand to a larger field of relationships. The ultimate dragon is within you; it is your ego clamping you down.

(b) In its Youth *Yumaism* took to Nature's Worship

Nature worship is in every religion of the East, and is the prime essence of this religion. Nature mythology is absent in Western religions. It is because of this, the religion is often known as animist by the westerners. Animism is common in all the religions at the youth state. The nature divinities are worshipped from time to time for health and prosperity. There are many nature divinities such as *Tambhungma, Tenchaba, Yobedangma, Thimennama* etc. in *Yuma* religion. We moderns are stripping the world of its natural revelations, of nature itself. The pygmy legend of the little boy who finds the bird with the beautiful song in the forest. He brings it home. He asks his father to bring food for his bird, and the father does not want to feed a mere bird, so he kills it. And the legend says the man killed the bird, and with the bird he killed the song, and with the song, himself. He dropped dead, completely dead, and was dead forever. The story is what happened when human beings destroy their environment, they destroy their world, destroy nature and the revelations of nature (Campbell, J. 1988). The same legend is applicable to the native people of Sikkim. We ignored our own mythology; compared or adopted the advanced religions and mythologies of our neighbors. Now, many of us have lost our own religion, belief system and mythology for ever.

(c) In its middle age *Yumaism* consisted of worshipping Gods and Goddesses and its form is Theological

Yumaism believes on "Biogenesis" law of creation and the adherents do not worship idols but pray the Almighty Goddess and *Mangs* (gods and goddess); worship of various gods and goddesses of nature (*Tap Sammings*), household divinities (*Him Sammangs*), Clan divinities (*Thokley Sammangs*), departed souls and spirits (*Sam Sires*), and retinue of divinities (*Sammang Chyangs*). For worship, the adherents make temporary altars, made of stone, *Artemisia vulgaris* twigs, banana leaves, *pahengs* etc. as a symbol of deity or divinity evolved from the *Nahangma* myth, invite the divinities for worship/prayer and after the ritual is over they disperse the divinities and then destroy the altars. Now only, they started construction of community worship places like *Mangkhim* (Subba, J.R. 2005a:23-33).

(d) In its matured age religion searches for the essential elements and tends to be Philosophical

This deals with soul-complex, afterlife, *karmic* effects, and relation with the Goddess *Tagera Ningwaphuma*, righteousness, humanity, morality, ethics, and destination after death. *Yumaism* believes on three realm of existence of life – *Iksakhambek Den*, *Sangrampedang Den* and *Khema Yongsong Den*. The *Iksakhambek Den* (Earth) is the only place where the life is in the physical existence; and thus can earn positive or negative *karma*. The existence of life in the other two realms – *Sangrampedang Den* (Goddesses place –

forefather's village/heaven) and *Khemayongsong Den* (place of retribution/hell) is only spiritual (soul form) and hence there is no chance of earning positive or negative *karma* through practice of generosity and compassion. *Sangrampedang Den* is the origin place of every soul but the souls can stay in the center of its origin as long as he has the positive *karma* in his account. Once his *karma* account gets exhausted the souls have to come to the earth realm in the physical form for earning *karma* through practice of generosity and compassion. This is known as *karmic* cycle of birth and death. With the negative *karma* the soul has to undergo to *Khemayongsong Den* (*Naraka*/hell) for retribution and torture. After burning away his negative *karma* in the hell the soul once again get a chance to come to the earth realm for earning positive or negative *karma*. The existence of life and soul in these realms depends not only on positive or negative *karma* but also on the individual's attachment of the origin Goddess *Tagera Ningwaphuma*. Further, the Almighty Goddess upgrades good souls to a higher status in *Sangram Pedang Den* to "*Hang-sams*" (Clan forefathers capable of receiving the souls of the dead) and also "*Sam Sire*" depending on their patrilineal or matrilineal affiliation. These "*Sam Sires*" are sent to the earth as reincarnation on the body of young boys and girls and they serve their community as *Phedangmas* at the will of the Almighty Goddess (Subba, J.R. 1999; 2005a: 7-8; 2005b: 1-137).

According to psychologist Jung, religion evolved through a series of stages – archaic stage represented by shamans, medicine men, and sages; ancient civilizations represented by prophets, physicians, and priests and the religion heritage represented by mystics, theologians and philosophers. All these religious figures, at every stage of history, share one thing in common – the inner experience of divinity. Jung calls this experience, *numinous* (from the Latin, *numen* or *numina*, "the presiding god"). When the shaman hears the voice of the Great Spirit or the Christian mystic experiences – the Christ within; both are referring to an archetype of wholeness, the archetype of self, represented as an image of God. All religions confirm the existence of "something whole", independent of the individual ego and whose nature transcends consciousness. A *numinous* experience of "something whole" is not only the privilege of shamans and priests. It is the aim of anyone seeking wholeness of self. What the *numinous* experience of "inner divinity" really points to is the process of individuation. The archetype of wholeness manifests itself in dreams, myths and fantasies. It occupies a central position in the unconscious and tends to relate all other archetypes to this centre, which is approximate to the God-image (Jung 1933: 111-112).

Life Stages

Yuma religion recognizes eighteen life-stages – right from the day of conception. Various prayer or worship rituals are performed depending on these life stages which has been elaborately described in various literatures available today. At these different life stages worship rituals need to be performed for better health and prosperity of the individual in his lifetime. These stages are:

(i) *Toanayonara* (earthworm form): the life stage from the day of conception to two month stage in the mother's womb;

(ii) *Sumnarathok* (round form): the life stage of the third month after conception in the mother's womb;

(iii) *Linarathok* (bow form): the life stage of the fourth month after conception in the mother's womb;

(iv) *Nyanarathok* (fish form): the life stage of the fifth month after conception in the mother's womb;

(v) *Monasamtingsa* (human form): the life stage of the sixth month after conception in the mother's womb;

(vi) *Toareba* (for male): the life stage from birth to fourth day of the child;

Toarema (for female) the life stage from birth to third day of the child;

(vii) *Tangdhangsa*: the life stage from third day (for female) and fourth day (for male) to the first tooth emergence stage (upto sixth to eighth month);

(viii) *Hachasa*: the life stage up to the emergence of front teeth (up to eighth to ten month);

(ix) *Tanglinghangsa*: the life stage up to joining of forehead bones (fissure on the top of the cranium called *Numbrokpa*) (fifteenth to twenty four month);

(x) *Hinja Pi-cha*: the life stage up to eighth years of age;

(xi) *Choprookpa* (for boys): the life stage up to youth stage (9 to 18 years of age);

Choprookma (for females): the life stage up to youth stage (9 to 18 years of age);

(xii) *Nalinggen thangben sa*: Youth stage (for male);

Sisaagen menchin sa: Youth stage (for female):;

(xiii) *Nalingsang* (for male): the life-stage from marriage engagement to marriage;

Sisaamay (for female): the life-stage from marriage engagement to marriage;

(xiv) *Yembitcha* (for male): married man;

Menchhuma (for female): married woman;

(xv) *Kappoba* (for male): man of 60 years of age and above;

Kappmoma (for female): woman of 60 years age and above;

(xvi) *Tumbhaksa* (for male): man or woman of 60 years age and above with good manners, good character, polite and religious minded;

Tumbhakma (for female): -do-

(xvii) *Tumyanghang* (for male); man or woman of 40 years age or above who knows about the Limboo social, religious, cultural, traditional rites and customs;

Tumyanghangma (for female): -do-

Yehang (for male) man or woman of 40 years age or above who knows about the Limboo religious, social, cultural and traditional rites, customs and capable of advising and guiding the Phedangma priests;

Yehangma (for female): -do-

(xviii) *Tuktuken Tumyanghang* (male): Very old man or woman who officiate the Limboo social, religious, cultural and traditional functions.

Tuktuken Tumyanghangma

(for female): -do-

These life-stages serve for detection of the developing child in the womb, time of womb worship, performing various worship rites in one's life, conducting type of death rituals which differ on the stage of death of the individual, and a host of functions in the society (Subba, J.R. 1999:391-508; 2005a: 8-17; 57-137; 2008a: 310-317)

The Religious Shaman Priests – *Phedangmas*

They discharge both religious shamanic and priestly functions in the society. *Phedangma* is a common term used for the *Limboo* religious practitioners. There are nine types of *Phedangmas*. They are: (i) *Muhikkum Ongshi,* (ii) *Phejiri Phedangma,* (iii) *Somboko Samba,* (iv) *Yeboko Yeba,* (v) *Yeboko Yema,* (vi) *Yuma Sam,* (vii) *Sammundhum,* (viii) *Yepmundhum,* and (ix) *Sidapangdang*. Out of the above, (i) to (v) are incarnate *Phedangmas* while the rest (vi) to (viii) are not incarnate and do not perform shamanic functions but perform some priestly functions in the society. The (ix) above is herbalist. All these *Phedangmas* have their own gear and costumes; and have their functional differences in the society (Subba, J.R. 1998: 19-57; 1999:339-379; 2005a:15-18)

Jung's view about the shaman is that the shaman's spirit "leaves his body" and goes on a visionary pilgrimage, during which he experiences sickness, fortune, death and rebirth. His experiences are similar to Christ's passion, but also parallel the soul's after-life voyage towards rebirth in *Tibetan* Buddhism, the Egyptian Book of the Dead and many other religions (Jung 1933: 114).

The shamanic *Phedangmas* in *Yuma* religion are the ones who communicate myth for the *Yuma* adherents today in our society. They are our spiritual advisors who understand mythology and humanity and are not simply sociologists with a programme for us. There is a major difference between a shaman and a priest. A simple priest is a functionary of a social sort. The society worships certain deities in a certain way, and the priest becomes ordained as a functionary to carry out that ritual. The deity to whom he is devoted is a deity that was there before he came along. But the shaman's powers are symbolized in his own familiars, deities of his own personal experience. His authority comes out of a psychological experience, not a social ordination. In the case of *Yuma* religion, the shamanic *Phedangma* performs both as shaman as well as priest in the society. In the early development of *Yuma* religion, the shamanic *Phedangmas* might have translated some of his visions into ritual performances and thus brought the inner experience into the outer life of the people themselves. This was the beginning of a religion. That is how religion began. We find a shamanic aspect in practically all the hunting and gathering cultures.

Teachings of Yuma Religion

The broad outline of the teachings of the religion has been classified into 6 (six) categories which are as follows:

(i) Good *Karma* alone is not enough for the soul of the dead to join the ancestors or return to the center of origin at *Sangrampedang Den*. The blessing of the Almighty Goddess is equally important. Hence, continuous daily praying the Almighty Goddess to establish a close relationship for the favour blessing in this life and beyond is very essential.

(ii) To earn Good *Karma*/action/*Nuyambok* in this life depends on the individual's moral conduct. *Yuma* religion teaches the individual to be kind to all living beings, love fellow beings, feel grateful to one's saviors, never envy and jealousy to others, revere *Mangs* (Deities) and *Sammangs* (Divinities) as parents, act with immaculate heart and mind, never practice theft, plundering, abetment, quarreling, fighting, murder, lying, slandering and backbiting, never be arrogant and involve in debauchery, look after orphans and poor, never involve in incest and wicked sinful acts, lead a simple and sincere life, avoid pious acts, and practice generosity and compassion.

(iii) The Almighty Goddess, other gods and goddesses can be experienced in life only through our inner eyes, which could be developed through knowledge (*Sikkum* = *Vidya*), intelligence (*Ningwa* =*Buddhi*) and wisdom (*Thona* = *Vivek*). Hence, Knowledge, intelligence and wisdom are the ways to open our inner eyes. The Almighty Goddess "*Tagera Ningwaphuma*" (*Tagera* = from *thogi* = eldest, *Ningwa* = intelligence, *Phuma* = the Supreme) is simply a personification of these ways of opening our eyes. Hence every individual needs perseverance for attainment of knowledge, intelligence and wisdom.

(iv) The Almighty Goddess *Tagera Ningwaphuma* or *Yuma* is a source of energy, light or power or a source and center of creation. With this energy a living being survives in this world and then returns back to its source – the center of creation. This energy/light/power comes to the individual through understanding, communicating, perceiving, listening, doing justice and performing efficiently.

(v) Clean mind is the essence of life. Unsullied mind always remains free of trepidations. Hence every individual should practice self-control, austerity, purity, uprightness, forbearance, generosity, vigour and heroism; and,

(vi) Vicious acts are sin and sin is more powerful. The only way to get rid of sin is the pious acts.

Concept of God or Goddess

Yumaism is a Henotheist or Kathenotheist religion and believes in a single Almighty Goddess "*Tagera Ningwaphuma*" (*Yuma*) while still recognizing other gods and goddesses. She is the creator, preserver and sustainer Goddess and is the Ultimate Supreme Goddess, Omnipresent (in all places at all time), Omniscient (all knowing), Omnipotent (all powerful), Infinite (without beginning or end), and Eternal (force, Light, power existence) having none of the attributes. It recognizes Deities (*Mangs*), divinities (*Sammangs*) and retinue of divinities (*Sammang Chyangs*) (Subba, J.R. 2005a:23-33).

Motherhood is sacrifice. Mother gives every damn thing to her progeny. That is why the mother becomes the symbol of mother earth. She is the one who gives birth to us and on whom we live and on where body we find food. The Goddess *Yuma* in *Yumaism* is sacrifice for motherhood. In *Yuma* religion, the *Mangs* (deity), *Sammangs* (divinities) and *Sammang-Chyangs* (retinue of divinities) are the "*Collective Unconscious Archetype Images*". They have no material existence and reveal themselves only as images. Hence, the adherents of *Yumaism* never worship these *Mangs*, *Sammangs* and *Sammang-Chyangs* in their physical form (manmade idols/statues) but only as Archetype images or Psyche as Jung meant the whole of our being, conscious and unconscious.

Concept of Creation of the Universe

As in the case of many other religions, *Yuma* religion believes that gods and goddesses created the universe. There is an elaborate myth of creation of the universe, creation of earth and the sky – creation of the *Akashic* field in *Mundhum* of the religion. It believes that there are eight Layers of *Akashic* field (atmospheric layers) around the earth, and nine layers below the living earth layer, making a total of eighteen worlds (*Dens*). These eighteen worlds (called *Dens* in *Yumuism*) have specific functions to discharge and are governed by different Deities (*Mangs*), Divinities (*Sammangs*) and Retinue of Divinities (*Sammang Chyangs*), enlightened spirits, and the living beings

They are:

Around the earth (from outermost) the *Akashic* fields are:

(i) *Sangram Pedang Den,* (ii) *Sang Sang Den,* (iii) *Mangkhoma Den,* (iv) *Sey Seywa Den,* (v) *Sunaingtong Den,* (vi) *Mundhang Khara Den,* (vii) *Torongding Tangsang Den,* and (viii) *Samyukna Den.*

The layer of the Living beings, spirits, souls, demons and ghosts:

(ix) *Iksading Khambek Den* (the Earth).

Inside the Earthen Layer (from outermost) underworlds are:

(x) *Khambongba Lungbongba Den,* (xi) *Muroplung Kheroplung Den,* (xii) *Muguplung Theguplung Den,* (xiii) *Murupli Kherupli Den,* (xiv) *Mujikna Kheyongna Den,* (xv) *Musekha Sekhana Den,* (xvi) *Tungutlung Haralung Den,* (xvii) *Sumbodona Lekwadona Den,* (xviii) *Khemading Yongsong Den,* (Subba, J.R. 1998:3-18; 1999: 326-337; 2005b:10-22).

Concept of Life and Destiny

The creator god "*Sigera Yabhundin Mang Porokmi Wambhami Mang*" created the earth and all forms of life on earth. The creator god tried to create an immortal life but could not be successful. The human idols created by elements like gold, silver, bronze etc.

could not hold the vital air. The Almighty Goddess desired to create the self-generating human beings on the earth. Since the self-generating human being was possible only through the dynamic life forms, the creator god was advised by the Almighty Goddess to create male and female human idols with already existing organic materials (pre-existing life forms); and thus obtained the physical form as her own images on the earth. The creator god then created self-sustaining, self-reproducing human being on Her guidance. Thus, the concept of life in *Yumaism* has become *"Biogenesis"*. It believes in the "Law of Biogenesis" – life could be created only from the life or with pre-existing life products with the blessing of the Almighty Goddess *"Tagera Ningwaphuma"*. It also believes that the existence of human life on earth is dependent on the earth's sustainability of environment and a number of other lower forms of life created by the creator god *"Sigera Yabhundin Mang Porokmi Wambhami Mang"* with Her blessing and guidance. Prior to creation of human beings, the messenger god created:

(i) The suitable environment for life both plant and animal.

The equilibrium of oxygen and carbon dioxide was maintained in the environment with the creation of plants and animals.

(ii) Created various crops and flowers;

(iii) Created various animal forms and birds; then

(iv) Created human beings and then defined their final destination (Subba, J.R. 2005a:74-87).

Concept of Soul

Yuma religion recognizes eight-soul-complex known as *"Yetchham thim"*. They are: Two perceptive souls known as (i) *Ni-sam* (the soul of sight), and (ii) *Khem-sam* (the soul of hearing); Three conceptive souls known as (iii) *Sikkum-sam* (the soul of intuition – knowledge/*Gyan*); (iv) *Ningwa-sam* (the soul of mind – intellectual power/*Buddhi*); and (v) *Thona-sam* (the soul of wisdom/consciousness/*Vivek*); and Three vital souls namely (vi) *Si-sam* (the graveyard soul), (vii) *Pung-sam* (the wandering soul), and (viii) *Hang-sam* (the main soul/forefather's soul). The perceptive souls start developing only after the birth of the child and also disintegrate on one's death. The conceptive souls develop only after the individual starts acting and reacting with the living and non-living material world. In many individuals *Sikkum-sam*, *Ningwa-sam* and *Thona-sam* starts developing in later part of his life. The conceptive souls also disintegrate on one's death. The vital souls are hereditary and come to the individual from the origin, forefathers, and also go back or reached by *Phedangmas* to the origin - forefathers at the individual's death. *Pung-sam*, the wandering soul gives you the dream both Archetypes and instincts as described by C. G. Jung (1875-1961). *Si-sam* becomes active only at the time of individual's death. The main soul – *Hang-sam*, is accompanied in the soul journey by the shamanic priests – *Phedangmas* at the time of *Sams-ama* ritual, to reach the soul to the forefather's village and hand over to one of the forefathers, conducted after the burial of the dead at home. The process of soul journey is again repeated to reach and handover *Si-am* and *Pung-sam* souls to forefather while conducting *Sam-chhamma* ritual separating the living souls of the family members and also repeated at the *Sitongsing* ritual at the time of the final death ritual. Further, the soul-images of male and female are always represented by the individual's opposite gender, and is an archetype which can represent the whole of the unconscious. It is inherited, collective and ageless as experienced by the famous psychologist C.G. Jung. In *Yumaism* it is known as "*Mangenna*" which protects the individuals from accidents, etc. The individuals perform "*Mangenna*" rituals to activate it once in every six month or a year (Subba, J.R. 1999:379-381; 583-592; 2005a:113-121; 2005b:22-148).

Concept of Afterlife

Yuma religion firmly believes in the afterlife. The soul of the dead has to be accompanied - soul-journey, reached to the village of the clan known as *Khemayongson Pangbhe* or *Samyukna Den* and handed over to one of the forefathers of the clan who is there atleast more than three years. The ritual of soul journey accompanied by the *Phedangmas* and handing over the soul immediately after the burial of the dead is known as "*Samsa-ma*". During this ritual, the *Phedangma* can retrieve only the *Hang-sam*, while the *Si-sam* and *Pung-sam* cannot be retrieved during that time and reached to the forefather's village at *Samyukna Den*. The two perceptive souls *Ni-sam* and *Khem-sam*, and the three conceptive souls *Sikkim-sam, Ningwa-sam* and *Thona-sam* disintegrate at the time of death. During the final death ritual conducted at any odd day or month but within a year after 8 or 9 days of death, the *Si-sam* and *Pung-sam* souls could be retrieved, accompanied soul journey and hand over to one of the forefathers at *Sangram Pedang Den* through the ritual of "*Samchomma*" by the *Phedangma*. At this time the souls of the dead are separated from the living souls, and again assure success of soul journey and handing over of the souls of the dead by repeating the process through the ritual of "*Sitongsing Khema*". *Yumaism* believes that the souls come from the village of forefathers – *Sangram Pedang Den* and finally they have to be reached to the place of origin. There the souls live as we live in this world but more happily (Subba, J.R. 1999:453-508; 2005a:131-162; 2005b:1-137).

Purpose and Meaning of Life

Yuma religion believes that the purpose of coming to this world is to gain experience, earn positive *karma* through the practice of generosity and compassion, and develop a close relationship with the Almighty Goddess "*Tagera Ningwaphuma*" and finally return to the place of origin – *Sangram Pedang Den* to join our own forefathers. To achieve these targets *Yumaism* believes to discharge the function in life as under:

(i) *Yumaism* has recognized eighteen life-stages of human beings. It has also recognized Almighty Goddess *Tagera Ningwaphuma*, different gods and goddesses as Deities (*Mangs*), divinities (*Sammangs*) and retinue of divinities (*Sammang Chyangs*). These *Mangs, Sammangs* and *Sammang Chyangs* have to be prayed and worshipped at the different stages of life right from conception of the child in the mother's womb to the death. It also recognizes a number of death types, which vary depending on the age of death, cause of death and mental status of the dying individual. Accordingly, death rituals to be conducted also vary. Conducting these rituals appropriately by the family members has been emphasized for better health, prosperity, establishing better relation to the Goddess and earning better *karma* essential for the soul of the individual to return to its' destination safely.

(ii) Fulfillment of legitimate desires, the attainment of success in this world of the individuals, family, and the society as a whole and pursue the six broad teachings of the religion for earning better *karma* are the main purpose of life on earth.

(iii) *Yumaism* has strong belief on attainment of the spiritual goal of securing a place at "*Sangrampedang Den*" after the death. To fulfill the spiritual aspirations of the individuals, family and the society, every individual has tremendous responsibility to create awareness of the spiritual yearnings, providing worship places, capacity building of the *Phedangmas*, easy access to the *Phedangmas* etc.

(iv) Joining of one's forefathers or return to the origin at *Sangram Pedang Den* and the length of your stay over there depends on your positive *karma* and your relationship with the Almighty Goddess *Tagera Ningwaphuma* while you are in this world is very essential in life. It is therefore, extremely essential to practice the teachings of *Yumaism*.

(v) Pray and worship of Almighty Goddess, gods and goddesses on the one hand and the status of the deceased at the time of death greatly affect the afterlife. Hence, proper conduct of death rituals of the deceased ensures the safe return of the soul-complex of the deceased to the *Sangram Pedang Den*.

(vi) In *Yumaism* the existence of human being has been defined only in three realms as (i) Physical existence on the earth as human beings, and spiritual existence in *Sangram Pedang Den* and *Khemayongsong Den*. The path of success both for physical existence and spiritual existence has been defined. It is the choice of the individual to follow for the purposeful and meaningful life and afterlife of the adherents of *Yumaism*.

Mythology of *Phangmuksam* (Pythagorean Tetrakys)

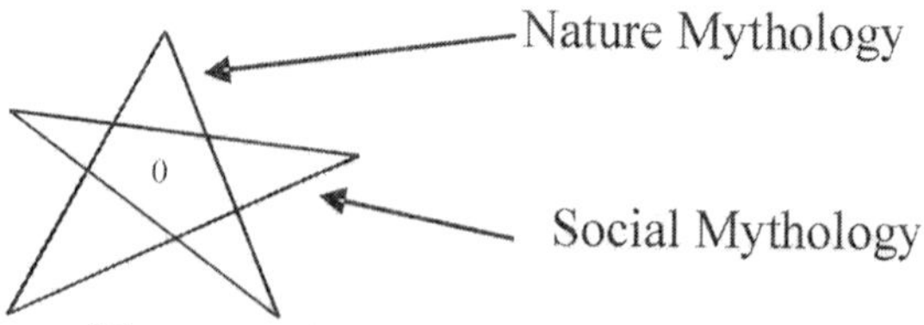

Phangmuksam

Each of this is a triangle composed of ten points, one point in the middle and four points to each side, adding up to nine: one, two, three, four, five, six, seven, eight, nine; representing the nine celestial planets. This is the primary symbol of Pythagorean philosophy, susceptible of a number of interrelated mythological, cosmological, psychological, and sociological interpretations, one of which is the dot at the apex as representing the creative center out of which the universe and all things have come. There are two of these interlocking triangles; one represents the natural world, of which you are a part; while the other represents social world linking you to a particular society. The interlocking triangles represent interlocking of two mythologies; that is Nature mythology and Social mythology linking you to both of these mythologies together. It also represents the belief system of nine *Dens* (world) above and nine *Dens* (world) below the mother earth's fertile layer of soil of *Yuma* religion. It has been placed on the top of the *Yuma Mangkhim* - community worship place and it is known in *Limboo* mythology as *Phangmuksam*. It is often Hinduized as *Panchatatwa* due to five cones of the star formed by its pointed cone and often called *Namuksam, which* is not correct. The five cones of the star are added up to three floor of the *Mangkhim* structure and the fertile layer of the mother earth to represent nine *Dens* (world) of nature mythology of which you are a part. The other triangle representing social mythology is linking you to a particular society for instance, the Limboo society, of which you are also a part. This interlocking triangle constitutes the domain of your *"Physical consciousness,"* and is continuously energized by the center or origin of mind or self or soul or spiritual consciousness or power or energy or the God or the Sun of the planet at the centre. At death you have to be prepared to come out of all your "physical consciousness" and transcendent your "Self" or "Soul" or "the god within you" or "energy" or "power within you" "individual consciousness" to *"Spiritual consciousness"* to join the ultimate source to the Center or Energy or Power or Forefathers at the *Khema Pangbhe* or the God or the Sun of the planet or your Origin. In *Yuma* religion, the learned forefather priests believe that it takes 8 (eight) days for female and 9 (nine) days for male after death for this transformation (intermediate stage), and thus observed 8 or 9 days of mourning of death pollution. In Buddhism, this intermediate period is known as *Bardo* and observe 49 days of death pollution. In Hinduism, the period is observed for 13 days. The observance of death- pollution varies depending on the believe system of the people adhere to.

In *Yuma* religion, there are elaborate mythological rituals for assisting the "Self" or "the Soul Complex" or "Physical Consciousness" of the dead for this transformation. The elaborate rituals are "*Sam Sama*" and "*Sam Chamma* " and "*Sitongsing Khema*" conducted by the learned *Phedangma* - incarnate priests of the religion. This involves collection of the soul complex, retrieving, accompanying the soul, beading goodbye to the household deities, divinities, nature divinities etc., recollecting the memories of physical world right from lower elevation to the higher and higher elevations wild-plants and wild-animals one by one, rocks, stones, hills, mountains, streams, springs, and biding goodbye to the nature divinities; and ultimately reaching to the top of the Everest mountain (*Chombhutlungma* or *Chumjumlungma*). The physical consciousness of the living being can travel only up to the topmost height of the earth. Then, the *Phedangma* priest, requests one of the forefathers to come up to this level and take it to the *Khema Pangbhe* or the God's place or source of origin and take care of the soul of the dead. The forefather also agrees and promises to take care of the soul now onwards. *Yumaism* believes that this elaborate process will help the soul of the dead to reconcile for quick transformation to "*Spiritual Consciousness*" and leave this physical world to join the Ancestors. At the time of final death ritual also, the "Physical Consciousness" or soul-complex left if any in this physical world are also again retrieved, accompanied elaborately this time, separate the soul of the dead from the living souls of the family, accompany both the dead and living souls of the family this time (*Tongsing* could be done only once in three years while *Sitongsing* has to be performed in every death) and reached on the top of the *Chumbhutlungma* (Mount Everest), hand over the dead soul-complex to one of the forefathers for taking it to the Ancestor's Village or God's place or center of origin. They assure the descending of the dead soul through divination at various stages while accompanying the souls. Then, the living souls are brought down by the *Phedangma* priest to the *Moralungma* (K2, the second highest mountain of the world) where there are fortified sacred places of the living people, fortified the living soul-complexes and brought back to the house through the same route. The living souls remain in the physical consciousness while the dead souls are helped for transformation to mental or spiritual consciousness through the rituals of "*Sam Samma*", "*Sam Chamma*" and "*Sitongsing*" this time by reaching them up to the last point of the physical consciousness by the *Phedangma* priests. This is a unique ritual not found in any other religion in this part of the Himalayas (Subba, J.R. 1999; 2005b, 2008a).

The mythological symbol "*Phangmuksam*" is the philosophical way of suggesting the voice of reason. Reason is the way of man. And of course what destroys reason is passion. The principle passion in politics is greed. That is what pulls you down. And that is why we are in the side instead of the top of the pyramid. That is why our founder opposed religious intolerance as early as about 500 B.C. by Buddha, Pythagoras, Confucius and *Lao-tzu*. This is the period of awakening of man's reason. No longer is he informed and governed by the animal powers. No longer is he guided by the analogy of the planted earth, no longer by the course of the planets, but by reason.

Reason and thinking are not the same. Reason is one kind of thinking but thinking things out is not necessarily reason in this sense. Reason has to do with finding the ground of being and the fundamental structuring of order of the universe. The eye of God being reason, the ground of our being as a society, as a culture, as a people, derives from the fundamental character of the universe. That is what the first pyramid or triangle representing natural world is. The other triangle or Pyramid representing social mythology is our society, and they are of the same order. That is God's creation, and this is our society.

Carl Gustav Jung (1875-1961) saw that the *mandala* returned everything to a single central point and interpreted this to mean that the goal of psychic development was the "path to the centre, to individuation". The circular structure of the *mandala* symbolized the self, the totality of the individual, conscious and unconscious, which carries an individual's sense of meaning and purpose as he or she moves towards it (Jung, 1933: 57).

Mythology of Goddess

Myths of the Great Goddess teach compassion for all living beings. There you come to appreciate the real sanctity of the earth itself, because it is the body of the Goddess. Mother or Grandmother is a symbolic image. All of the references of religions and mythological images are the planes of consciousness, or fields of experience that are potential in human spirit. And these images evoke attitudes and experiences that are appropriate to a meditation on the mystery of the source of your own being. In some primitive religion like *Yumaism*, the mother is the prime parent, the source. The mother is really a more immediate parent than the father because one is born from the mother, and the first experience of any infant is the mother. Mythology is a sublimation of the mother image. We talk of mother earth. And in Egypt you have the Mother Heavens, the Goddess Nut, who is represented as the whole heavenly sphere. Similarly, in *Yuma* religion *Tageraningwaphuma* is the Almighty, Omnipresent, Omniscient, Omnipotent, Eternal and Infinite Goddess, who is the ultimate creator, sustainer and preserver Goddess and lives in *Sangram Pedang* Den, the ninth, topmost layer of the atmosphere. The idea of the Goddess is related to the fact that you are born from your mother, and your father may be unknown to you, or the father may have died. Frequently, in the epics, when the hero is born, his father has died, or his father is in some other place, and then the hero has to go in quest of his father.

In *Yuma Mundhum* we find that the Gods and Goddesses separated the father and mother progenitors along with their sons of the Limboo tribes to stay away from each other due to their incest relationship. The father *Sutsuru Suhangpheba* (father), later known as *demi*-god *Sodhung Lepmuhang* had to leave with his nine sons (*Phanghang*) for *Muringla Kharingla Tembhe,* synonymous to forefather's village or heaven or eternal world or spiritual consciousness; and the mother *Tetlara Lahadongna* (mother), later no known as *Thillilung Thamdenlungma* had to stay back with her eight sons (*Sawa Yethangs*) at *Sangarek Nugarek Tembhe* synonymous to the mother earth or physical consciousness. However, at times of difficulty the eight sons as well as the mother had to pray or go to their father time and again for consultation and help to solve their problem. The father sent the learned *Phedangmas* (priests) from there for healing, curing, protection and guidance of his eight sons and their descendents left with her mother.

You are born from your mother, and she is the one who nurses you and instructs you and brings you upto the age when you must find your father. Finding of father has to do with finding your own character and destiny. There is a notion that the character is inherited from the father, and the body and very often the mind from the mother. But it is your character that is the mystery, and your character is your destiny. So it is the discovery of your destiny that is symbolized by the father quest when you find your father, you find yourself. In *Yumaism*, there is an elaborate description how a mother conceives a child in her womb, nursed her son "*Susuwengba Lalawengba*" and finally he became a famous hunter "*Sawa Yukphung Kemba*".

In primitive societies Goddess, the mother earth, was associated primarily with agriculture and the agricultural societies. It has to do with earth. The human woman gives birth just as the earth gives birth to the plants. She gives nourishment, as the plants do. So woman magic and earth magic are the same. They are related. And the personification of the energy that gives birth to forms and nourishes forms is properly female. It is in the agricultural world of ancient Mesopotamia, the Egyptian Nile, and in the earlier planting culture systems that the Goddess is the dominant mythic form. When you have a Goddess as the creator, it is her own body that is the Universe. She is identical with the universe. That is the sense of that Goddess Nut figure that you saw in the Egyptian temple. She is the whole sphere of the life-enclosing heavens. Similarly, *Tageraningwaphuma* is identical with the universe in *Yumaism*. In *Yuma* religion, everything is within the Almighty Goddess *Tagera Ningwaphuma* or *Yuma*, so that the gods are her children or messengers (as it is often known as *Sijo-ingmisa* in *Yuma Mundhum*). Everything you can think of, everything you can see, is a production of the Almighty Goddess *Tageraningwaphuma* (*Yuma*), equivalent to the mother earth. We offer the first harvest of the crops, fruits, root-crops, fish or whatever is produced from the mother earth to the *Yuma Sammang*, the divinity form of the Almighty Goddess – the household divinity to signify the importance of motherhood. In *Yumaism* she is believed to be her own daughter and possess the same attributeless and power as that of *Tagera Ningwaphuma* and worshipped in every household as one of the most important household divinity.

With the scientific discoveries myth is coming back. It means to find what the source of your own life is, and what is the relationship of your body, your physical form, to this energy that animates it. The body without the energy isn't alive. So you distinguish in your own life that which is of the body and that which is of energy and consciousness. There is a story about the overthrow of the mother goddess *Tiamat* and is the key archetypal event, a critical moment in history. The Semitic people were invading the world of the Mother Goddess systems, and so the male oriented mythologies became dominant, and the Mother Goddess becomes, well, sort of Grand-Mother Goddess, way, way back.

According to Campbell, J. (1988) it was in the time of the rise of the city of Babylon. And each of these early cities had it's own protective god or goddess. The characteristic of an imperialistic people is to try to have its own local god dubbed big boy of the whole universe. No other divinity counts. And the way to bring this about is by annihilating the god or goddess who was there before. The one that was here before the Babylonian god *Marduk* was the All-Mother Goddess. So the story begins with a great council of the male gods up in the sky, each god a star, and they have heard that the Grandma is coming, old *Tiamat*, Abyss, the inexhaustible Source. She arrives in the form of a great fish or dragon, and what god will have the courage is, of course, the god of our present great city. He is the big one. So when *Tiamat* opens her mouth, the young god *Marduk* of Baybylon sends winds into her throat and belly that blow her to pieces, and he then dismembers her and fashions the earth and heavens out of the parts of her body. This motif of dismembering a primordial being and turning its body into the universe appears in many mythologies in many forms. In Hinduism, it comes up with the figure of *Purusha*, the reflection of whose body is the universe. *Yumaism* believes that she is a big fish known as *Mujikna Kheyongnama*, who holds up the landmass of the earth. When it moves her head or fin, arises the earthquake. Now, the mother goddess in Old Mother-Goddess mythologies was herself already the universe, so the great creative deed of *Marduk* was a supererogatory act. There was no need for him to cut her up and make the universe out of her, because she was already the universe. But the male-oriented myth takes over, and he becomes apparently the creator. And the interest turned from the Goddess to her son, especially of the male governors of the city of Babylon. So the matriarchal society began to give way to patriarchal society. By the time 1750 B.C. or so, the transformation of the society was complete. There are women today who say that the spirit of the Goddess has been in exile since then.

Some historians believe that most probably the forefathers of the *Limboo Kirantas* might have left the city of Babylon before fourth millennium B.C. or atleast 1750 B.C. retaining their Old Grand Mother Goddess *"Tagera Ningwaphuma"* or *"Yuma"* (Chemjong, I.S. 1948). Thus, they retained the matriarchal society with them, which is still surviving in the remote Himalayas till date. In the history of Western religions, this is an extremely interesting development. In the Old Testament, there is a God who creates a world without a goddess. Then when there come the proverbs, there she is, Sophia, the Goddess of wisdom. She says, "When God created the world, I was there, and I was His greatest joy". But in the Hebrew tradition the idea of a Son of God is repulsive, it is not considered at all. The *Massiah* as the Son of God is not actually God's son. He is one who is his character and dignity is worthy to be likened to the Son of God. There is a similar situation in the case of *Yuma* religion where the *Yuma Sammang* (*Sammang* = divinity) worshipped in every household is considered to be the daughter of the Almighty Goddess *Tagera Ningwaphuma* or *Yuma Mang* (*Mang* = Deity). In fact, She (*Sammang* = goddess) is not actually the daughter of the Goddess *Tagera Ningwaphuma* (*Yuma Mang*), but she is the one who has the character and dignity worthy to be the daughter of the Goddess.

Further, there is no idea of a virgin birth in the Hebrew tradition. The virgin birth comes into Christianity by way of the Greek tradition. Out of the four gospels, for example, the only one in which the virgin birth appears is the Gospel from Luke, and he was a Greek. In the Greek tradition there were images, legends, myths of virgin births; Leda and the Swan, Persephone and the serpent; the virgin birth is represented throughout. The idea of virgin birth is also found in *Yuma* religion. In the *Mundhum, Mujikna Kheyongna* conceived from the Lord of Wind. Similarly, *Irerema Serengdhangma* conceived while drinking a mixture of the rain-water collected on a big stone and also from the urine of the tiger collected on the stone.

Mythology of Heroes and Heroes

Many of the heroes of the society give their lives. For instance, *Sirijunga Teyongshi* gave his life for his commitment on *Yuma* religion, language and literature of his community. But it also says that out of the given life comes a new life. It may not be the hero's life. "I will come again" as *Sirijunga Teyongshi* said while he was being assassinated, but it is a new life, a new way of being or becoming. Such stories of the heroes vary from culture to culture. It is the degree of the illumination or action that makes the different from the East to the West. There is a typical early culture hero who goes around slaying monsters. Now, that is a form of adventure from the period of prehistory when man was shaping his world out of a dangerous, unshaped wilderness. He goes about killing monsters. Thus, the heroes evolve over time like most other concepts and ideas.The world without spirit is a wasteland. People have the notion of saving the world by shifting things around, changing the rules, and who is on top, and so forth. Any work is a valid work if its' alive. The thing to do is to bring life to it, and become alive yourself.

The Journey Inward

The heaven is the desired goal of most people, is within us for those who believe in heaven. But many oriental religions based on "*Karma*" have no concept of heaven and hell. They believe that both the heaven and hell are there on this earth. Many oriental religions believe that they have to join the realm where their forefathers are. For instance, in *Yuma* religion the soul of the dead is retrieved, accompanied the soul by the incarnate *Phedangma* priests and the souls of his living family members in the soul journey up to the top of the physical realm of the mother earth (*Chambhatlungma* = Mount Everest), separate the dead soul from the living souls of the family; conduct divination of correctness of the soul journey when they reach at

Chambhatlungma, and hand over the dead soul to one of the members of their own forefather to take him and take care in the villages of the dead (*Khema Pangbhe*). Now, the living souls of the family members are brought back to *Moralungma* (K2) - the second highest mountain of the world, where there are fortified places of the living souls. There are five numbers in total, *Henjiri Henbonge Chotlung* (fortified place of the Children), *Sangphiri Lingphiri Chotlung* (*Thangben-Menchin Chotlung*) (fortified place of young boys and girls), *Padamlungma Thakedhak Chotlung* (*Yaklasuhangma Chotlung*) (fortified place of women), *Tuttu Tumyang Chutlung* (*Khorung Maklung Chotlung or Sawa Yethang Chotlung*) (fortified place of gentleman), *Senwalung Ngekwalung Chotlung (Phejiri Phedangma Chotlung*) (fortified place of the *Phedangma* priests). The priests pray for their respective *Chutlung*, fortify the souls of the living family members to the respective *Chotlung*. There are elaborate procedures for fortification of the souls of the living. They fortify the souls of the living family members and then brought back to the house in the villages following the same path they started the soul journey.

Unlike in Christianity in the story of *Tetlara Lahadongna* and *Sutsuru Suhangpheba* in *Yumaism*, both male and female are equally responsible for bringing incestuous sin in the society. Male and female discovered themselves as opposites. Male and female is one opposition. Another opposition is the human and God. Same is the case in the story of Man and *Mang* when they went for hunting together and brought *Khamseysey* bird hunted and killed. The prey was thrown to the lap of the *Mang*'s sister that broke the thigh of the Goddess women in *Yuma* religion. Good or evil is a third opposition. The primary oppositions are the sexual and that between human beings and God. Then come the idea of good and evil in the world. To move out into the world, you have to act in terms of pairs of opposites. In *Yuma* religion, on the top of each pyramid is the Mother Goddess, and a dot in the center of the Pythagorean opposite triangle, which is the energy of the transcendent entering the field of time. And then from the triangle there come pairs of triangles in all directions. Out of one come two. All things in the field of time are pairs of opposites. So this is the shift of consciousness from the consciousness of identity to the consciousness of participation in duality. And then you are into the field of time. God is an ambiguous word in our language because it appears to refer to something that is known. But the transcendent is unknowable and unknown. God is transcendent, finally, of anything like the name "God". God is beyond names and forms. The mystery of life is beyond all human conception. Everything we know is within the terminology of the concepts of being and not being, many and single, true and untrue. We always think in terms of opposites. But God, the ultimate, is beyond the pairs of opposites, that is all there is to it. Because we cannot think otherwise, that is the nature of reality in our time, nature of our experience of reality – man-woman, life-death, good-evil etc. For instance, we find the story of separation of gods and humans, soul journey and handing over the soul of the dead to the forefathers/ Demi-gods/Gods etc. This indicates that the soul or god within you is a part of the Almighty God. It belongs to the God, and has to be handed over to the God when the individual dies.

Mythology of Sacrifice and Bliss

The sanctification of the landscape is a fundamental function of mythology. This is evident in many traditions i.e. in *Yuma* tradition. In *Yuma* religion, the indigenous landscape – *"Limbuwan"* (Land of the *Limboos*) has always been identified in *Yuma Mundhum*. To its north lies the land of China-Tibet (*Sinyuk-Muden*), to its south lies the land of Indian Plains (*Teymen Warong*), to its east lies the unending land of the Rising Sun (*Tohi-Nangen*), always the new spirit or positive energy pouring in, and to its west lies the land of the unending land of the Setting Sun (*Tohi-Namdha*). The east direction is always a sign of progress and prosperity while the west being always a direction of degeneration and deterioration. The central place is always a center of origin or sacred main pillar or a fireplace of a house – the place of God or a path for the family, leaving to the spiritual consciousness or *Sangram Pedang Den*. The door always opens to the east. The central place is a cosmic center, with the smoke coming out from the fireplace up through the side holes in the ceiling of the roof so that the prayer of the living as well as the soul of the dead always goes along with the scent of the incense to the nostrils of the God. The landscape, the dwelling place becomes an icon, a holy picture wherever you are, you are related to the cosmic order, sitting always facing north or east and praying gods towards east.

There will always be a surrounding figure with an opening in the east so that the new spirit or positive energy can pour in. At the center of the house, there should always be enough space to circle around the main pillar or the fireplace – the cosmic center. When the *Phedangma* priests sit must face east direction of the rising Sun or the north direction to the place of creation – Kumbhakarna or Jannu Mountain peak (*Phoktanglungma-Pembenlungma*). When the Buddha sat under the Bo tree, he faced east direction of the rising sun. Each clan/*Thar* of the followers of *Yuma* religion have their own fortified place known as *Yiok*. The *Phedangma* priests take the entire offering along with the soul of the person for fortification while conducting *Mangenna* ritual to their fortified place conducted twice in a year; and also while conducting *Nahangma* of the head of the family once in three years. You die to your flesh and are born into your spirit. You identify yourself with the consciousness and life of which your body is but the vehicle. You die to the vehicle and become identified in your consciousness with that of which the vehicle is the carrier. That is the god within you. Death is life and life is death, and that the two are in accord. You have to balance between death and life, they are two aspects of the same thing, which is being, becoming. In the *Mayan* ritual, the idea of sacrifice was to become worthy to be sacrificed as a god. It is a basic theme – that which dies is born. You have to have death in order to have life. This is the origin of the headhunt in Southeast Asia, particularly in Indonesia. The headhunt is a sacred act, a sacred killing. Before a young man can be permitted to marry and become a father, he must go forth and have his kill. Unless there is death, there cannot be birth. The significance of that is that every generation has to die in order that the next generation can come. As soon as you beget or give birth to a child, you are the dead one. The child is the new life, and you are simply the protector of that new life. There is a deep psychological association of begetting and dying. For instance, in *Yuma* religion the protective role of the father starts from the day of conception of the child in the mother's womb. You protect the mother to protect the child being developed in the mother's womb. You prevent her working hard, carrying heavy load, going to dense forest, rivers/streams, mountains, crossing the rope tied to the animal, exposing her in the solar and lunar eclipse, eating fish or meat killed unnaturally etc., etc. You organize pre-natal worship or womb worship for protection from evil spirits at six to seven month of conception. You organize *Mangenna* worship for protection from evil spirits when child is 3 or 4 days old. You perform various types of worship ceremonies such as *Mangenna, Tongsing, Taffeng,* worship of *Him Sammang, Tap Sammang* etc. time to time to protect the child. You are merely a protector of your new life - the Child. Our true reality is in our identity and unity with all life. This is a metaphysical truth, which may become spontaneously realized under circumstances of crisis.

According to the famous psychologist Jung, the unconscious side of the person is the Soul-image. Jung uses the Latin male and female names for the soul, the *animus* and the *anima*. The soul-image is always represented by the individual's opposite. A man's soul-image is female: the *Anima*; while the woman's soul-image is male: the *Animus*. The soul-image is an archetype, which can represent the whole of the unconscious. It is inherited, collective and "ageless". Soul-images appear in dreams, myths and fantasies, but they are also projected. The male's Soul-image has appeared in many forms throughout the ages, but always with the compelling and fascinating secret nature of Eros (love), as an archetype of life itself, represented in images of earth and water. Identifying completely with the *anima* can lead to effeminate homosexuality or transvestism. She can appear as light or dark, virgin or whore and is a source of wisdom. The woman's Soul-image takes the nature of Logos (reason), the search for knowledge, truth and meaningful activity, often represented by images of air and fire. The *animus* is a father figure in a young woman, heroic man as she matures and comforting male figure like doctor, priest as she grows old. Over-identification with the soul-image produces the Sol Niger or Black Sun, the *animus*-dominated woman, obstinate, ruthless and domineering, craving power and irrationally opinionated. Jung believed men were polygamous in their conscious attitude, and so the *anima* compensates as only one woman in the unconscious. She can also appear as a cave, ship, bowl, purse, cat, cow etc. Because women are monogamous to their conscious attitude, the *animus* appears in compensatory form as a group of men. The *animus* can be symbolized by a tower, sword, tree, eagle, lion, and bull etc. (Jung, 1933: 93-96).

Gender Disparity

From the mythological point of view, gender disparity is inevitable. If we look at the modern society, the root of gender disparity lies in our human creation. The females are equated with the vibrant mother earth, while the male with the empty *Akashic* field (the sky). The females have been provided by nature the following advantages:

(i) The nature has provided the females the automatic means of transforming into motherhood, once the menstruation starts. They are the producers of human progeny; providers of nutrition, protectors and caretakers of their young children; and are comparable to the mother earth. They are the first to domesticate wild plants and animals and start settled agriculture on earth.

(ii) The development of the perceptive souls such as *Ni-sam* (soul of sight) and *Khem-sam* (soul of hearing) as well as the conceptive souls – *Sikkum-sam* (soul of knowledge), *Ningwa-Sam* (soul of intelligence) and *Thona-sam* (soul of wisdom) starts developing earlier than the male-child. Thus the child naming ceremony (light showing, and giving instructions to do the works early) is conducted one day earlier than the male-child (in three days after birth) in *Yumaism*.

(iii) When the females die, their physical consciousness transforms to spiritual consciousness earlier than the males to facilitate soul journey to the ancestors or *Sangram Pedang Den*. As a result the judgment of *Suyo-Kheyo* (*virtue* and *vice*) by *Paoti Mang* at *Mundhang Khara Den* also takes place earlier and thus death pollution cleansing (*Yum chama ritual*) takes place on the 8th day of the burial.

Contrary to the above advantages to the females, the males are the killers, hunters, protectors of the family, and simple service providers only. They have no autonomic means of transformation to adulthood in nature. They need assistance of mother, or father or brother in their childhood for transformation to adulthood. The perceptive and conceptive souls mentioned above starts developing in males later than females, and thus birth ceremonies are performed only on 4th day of the birth. On the death of the males their physical conscious transforms to spiritual consciousness latter for soul journey; and hence, the judgment of *Suyo Kheyo* (*virtue* and *vice*) by *Paoti Mang* at *Mundhang Khara Den* takes place later (on the 9th day of burial) than the females. Because of all these advantages in the females, the male-folks are jealous to the female-folks. Out of this jealousy the male-folks resorted to dominate the female-folks by his extra-strength given to the males for hunting and killing in nature. This jealousy slowly led to a male dominated society in the modern world today.

10

MYTHOLOGY OF YUMAISM

Myth Basically Serves Five Functions

(i) The first is the *mystical function*; that is the one, realizing what a wonder the universe is, and what a wonder you are, and what experiencing are before this mystery. Myth opens the world to the dimension of mystery, to the realization of the mystery that underlines all forms. If you lose that, you don't have a mythology. If mystery is manifest through all things, the universe becomes, as it were, a holy picture. You are always addressing the transcendent mystery through the conditions of your actual world.

(ii) The second is a *cosmological dimension*, the dimension with which science is concerned, showing you what the shape of the universe is, but showing it in such a way that the mystery again comes through. Today we tend to think that scientists have all the answers. But the great ones tell us, "No, we have not got all the answers. We are telling you how it works, but what is it? You strike a match, what is fire? You can tell us about oxidation, but that does not tell us a thing.

(iii) The third function is the *sociological* one, supporting and validating a certain social order. And here is where the myths vary enormously from place to place. You can have a whole mythology for polygamy, a whole mythology for monogamy. Either one is this okay. It depends on where you are. It is this sociological function of myth that has taken over in our world, and it is out of date.

(iv) The fourth function of myth, is the *pedagogical*, of how to live a human lifetime under any circumstances. Myths can teach you that. This is the one that everyone must try to relate to. The laws of life, ethical laws, as it should be in the good society. All of what kind of clothes to wear, how to behave to each other, and so forth in the first millennium B.C. So the old story, so long known and transmitted through the generations, is not functioning, and we have not yet learned a new one. The story that we have in the West, so far as it is based in the Bible, is based on the view of the universe that belongs to the first millennium B.C. It does not accord with our concept either of the universe or of the dignity of man. It belong entirely somewhere else in the past. Similarly, it varies from place to place, community to community, and,

(v) The fifth function of myth, is the *mystery of afterlife,* the dimension of the journey inward, the human psychology of source of origin of life, the physical conscious transforming into mental consciousness, concept of soul and journey of soul to heaven and hell, and other such mysteries could be experienced and try to be linked.

We have to learn to get back into accord with the wisdom of nature and realize again our brotherhood with the animals, and with the plants, the water and the sea. To say that the divinity informs the world and all things is condemned as pantheism. The idea is trans-theological. It is of an indefinable, inconceivable mystery, thought as a power that is the source and end and supporting ground of all life and being. Myths and dreams come from realizations of some kind that have them to find expression in symbolic form. And the only myth that is going to be worth thinking about in the immediate future is one that is talking about the planet, not the city, not these people, but the planet, and everybody on it. That could be the future myth is going to be. In this chapter an attempt has been made to understand and analyze the important myths of *Yuma Samyo* (*Yumaism* or *Yuma* religion) through the functional lenses of mythology mentioned above.

Myths (*Mundhum*) of Universe Creation and the role of gods and goddesses

The mainstream religions offer seven explanations for the creation and existence of the universe. They are:

(i) The universe is eternal and uncreated;

(ii) The universe was created by God out of nothing (*ex nihilo*);

(iii) The universe was created by God (or various gods) using a pre-existing substance;

(iv) The universe was created by God, yet is separate from Him;

(v) God created the universe. Though it is not God in manifestation he is the essence of life within it;

(vi) The universe was emanated out of God (*ex Deo*). Therefore, it is a manifestation of God himself;

(vii) The universe is simply the result of casual actions. It was not a creative act of either a personal or impersonal Creator.

Some religions teach the natural creation is an illusion; others teach it is real. Some teach that it has a divine essence; others teach it is separate from God. The various views are defined as follows:

(a) Dualism: the concept that the universe is composed of two distinct parts – mind and matter, or being and non-being, and that there is a distinct difference and separation between the creator and his creation.

(b) Monism: the concept that all things in the universe, natural and spiritual, are of one essential substance. There are three types of monism – the belief that the universe is: purely mental; purely physical; and a mixture of both views.

(c) Monistic Theism: a blend between monism and dualism.

(d) Pantheism: the idea that creation with its substances, laws and forces, is God in manifestation. In the most extreme form of pantheism, God does not exist apart from these – "All is God", and "God is All".

(e) Panetheism: the teaching that even though the transcend creation, yet God is the essence of life within it – "All is in God" and "God is in All".

(f) Pluralism: the idea that reality is comprised of a number of parts. No single belief system can sufficiently explain the nature of the universe and of God.

(g) **Theism**: the view that creation is separate from God that He/She is transcendent, existing apart from the material universe. The life of animate things is distinct from God. It is a gift from God, but it is not a manifestation of God.

Yumaism believes in a combination of (ii) above, but human life was created as per (iii), (iv), (a), (b), and (g) above.

Myth of Creation of the Universe

(a) Creation of Water: In the beginning, there was nothing at all, only the void. There was no universe, no solar system, no sun, no moon, no planets, no earth to live in, and no life. There was only a void, darkness, emptiness or nothingness (*Sunyata*). In *Yumaism*, the "Void" has been described as *"Muatti ratt nesse musunne nesse Musunne ratt nesse khesunne nesse, Muhonglung ratt nesse khahonglung ratt nesse, Lasaphapmaga tunghik ratt ne ro, Namsaphapmaga tunghik ratt ne ro, Muguplung ratt ne khahoplung ratt ne"*. In the void, an attributeless nebulous goddess known as *"Tunghike Mang Pahike Mang"* – the god of dust and mist appeared suddenly and created the nebulous cloud (*Tunghi-Pahik*) in the void. The other gods and goddesses representing the void, loneliness, and some movement, power and existence in the void appeared next were: *Attiya Mang Musunne Mang, Musunne Mang Khesunne Mang, Chokchoke Mang Yangyange Mang, Pamekhosa Mamenkhosa Mang,* and *Allapi Manglo Jallapi Mang*. Now, with the continuous rolling, whirling and bubbling action of the nebulous cloud of the void produced a number of gods and goddesses. This action has been described in the myth as *"Nenjum ireang nengwa ireang, Nenjum phokteang nengwa phokteang, Tunghik lipsingang pahik lipsingang"*. These gods and goddesses were in sequence: *Langmembott mang langdhuti mang, Hukmembott mang hukdhuti mang, Muaunga mang khaunga mang, Uppange mang puppange mang, Acchuni mang Allekha mang, Khambudang mang yeppodang mang, Sawara mang yettunggek mang, Sawathamaga Yetthagek mang, Chankhema mang thobuma mang, Nawara mang chogoplung mang,*and *Mululung mang khalulu mang*. They began to extend a web. *Adhinlung phaphalung mang, Muroklung kheroklung mang, Ijumbu idakha mang* appeared.

Now, the gods and goddesses thought of creating the self-sustaining universe suitable for existence of human beings. But there was no water, no air and wind, no cloud, no earth, no sun, no moon, no plants and animals to sustain the human life. They unanimously thought of creating water first, as water is the first step of creation in the universe. Now all the gods and goddesses danced continuously, sweating profusely and thus dropping their sweat from their face, which ultimately constituted the source of water in the nebulous cloud. Then, *Sawara yettungek mang* milked her own milk from the left breast and rolled it on her hand which manifested into four more gods with one, two, three and four legs namely, "*Nawara thiklangma mang, Nawara nilangma mang, Nawara sumlangma mang* and *Nawara lilangma mang*". These four goddesses bounded and protected the water from all the four sides of it. There again appeared a *Kehike Namhike mang* (god of the brimming ocean), also known as *Mujiri mubokwama* (mistress of the base of the creation, second name of the *Sawara Yetungekma*) and shake her body and a white and black coloured cow known as *Phajiyang Makchiyang Pit* appeared. They also danced and added more sweat on it from their face. The gods and goddesses namely *Khambudang mang yeppodang mang, Ijumbu mang idakha mang, Toktigek mang yangdigek mang, Mullulung mang Khalullung mang*" supported the weight, established the balance and maintained the equilibrium, and stabilized the water, and thus remained suspended in the nebulous cloud. Further, two more gods namely "*Thiksumba mang nisumba mang*" and "*Sumsumba mang lisumba mang*" appeared and added their more sweat from their face by dancing. Then, the goddess *Sawara Yettungek mang* scratched her hair and her hairs fell down in the ocean water of the sweat. These hairs manifested into snake gods and goddesses namely "*Kumakla asek mang, Kuphora asek mang, Kuhetla asek mang,* and *Kuhitla asek mang*". She once again milked her milk from the left breast. The milk manifested into fish gods and goddesses known as "*Padhung letnya, Panganu nyanu manganu nyanu, Chophatangnya thungwangnya* and *Seknyanu nyanu neknyanu nyanu*. Now again *Sawara mang yettungek mang* again milked her right breast. The milk of the goddess continued to flow from the breast, as if the water was flowing from millions of water springs, which now formed the ocean water. These milk streams are known as *Akkam wallimu makkam walli, Tigi wallimu chuwalam wallimu*. Then, some more gods and goddesses were manifested in the ocean water. These were: *Allauta mang challuta mang, Kunuri mang nirajra mang, Aetta mang taetta mang, Huktrakek mang langtrekhek mang, Phakphoke mang mangmange mang, Toktigek mang Yangdigek mang,* and *Nendhoke mang imetang mang.* The gods and goddesses then, took rest for some time and distributed food amongst themselves. While distributing the food, the youngest god *Nendhokke mang imetang mang* was forgotten and was not served any food. With anger the god caused shaking and frightening the ocean, which manifested four frightening, shaking and causing epidemic disease gods *Sapphara mang muyongching mang, Kunuri mang chinuri mang, Kunuri mang tumuang mang, Kunuri mang bimuri mang* and *Chokchoke mang yangyange mang.* Some more gods were also appeared in the ocean. They are *Sapphara mang muyongching mang, Kunuri mang chinuri mang, Kunuri mang tumuang mang, Kunuri mang bimuri mang* and *Chokchoke mang yangyange mang.* Now, the ocean water contains snake gods and goddesses, fish gods and goddesses and full of milk, water and sweat of the gods and goddesses.

(b) Myth of creation of air, cloud, lakes, the solar system: The creator gods and goddesses now thought of creating air, wind, cloud, lakes, the sun, the moon, the stars and other planets. They created froth in the ocean water. Two gods with deformed hands and legs *Huktrakhek mang* and *Langtrakhek mang,* appeared in the ocean and threw some seeds in the ocean. The seed germinated and grew there was known as "*Sattik singma ilam singma- Sathu singma singphek singma*". The tree grew very fast and the full-grown tree covered over the entire ocean water. All of the gods and goddesses gathered there and thought about the creation of the universe. Then, they cut down the tree and prepared seven churners (leg or *Otta* in *limboo*) out of the roots of the tree. (i) The first churner going towards the south of the ocean water inside was known as the leg of the water (*Chophat-thungwa otta*); (ii) the second churner going towards north in the ocean was known as the leg of the mother Earth (*Iksa-khambek otta*); (iii) the third churner going to the east inside the ocean was known as leg of the gods and goddesses (*Mang Sammang otta*); (iv) the fourth going to west direction inside the ocean was known as the leg of the wind (*Sammetang langlo kejongang otta*); (v) the fifth churner going to north-south direction of the ocean are known as the leg of the envy and jealousy (*Tingding linglawet* *otta*); (vi) the sixth going vertically up from the centre of the ocean water was known as the churner of the sky (*Torong Tangsang otta*); and (vii) the seventh going vertically down from the center of the ocean was known as churner of the bottom (*Khema yongsong otta*).

Then, all the churners were connected with the strings and *netii* (*uunga*) made of snake gods and goddesses *Situmbu osek tumbu - Kumakla asek mang, Kuphora asek mang, Kuhetla asek mang, Kuhitla asek mang,* and *Singdung letthap osek letthap mangs".* Then, the gods and goddesses started churning the ocean water suspended in the nebullous. Churning of the ocean water in all the seven directions caused rolling and whirling action in the ocean water. The forces caused by churning of ocean water caused creation of the air- wind (*Kejong Sammet*) and cloud (*Khaamet-thumbon*). The fish gods of the ocean water were also churned and with their fins and heads moved caused vigorous shaking and rolling of the water body. This is the origin of the earthquake. Thus the air, wind (*Kejong-Sammet*) and clouds (*Khaamet-thumbon*) were created by churning, whirling and rolling of the ocean water of the universe in the nebulous cloud by the gods and goddesses.

The gods and goddesses continued to churn the ocean water of the nebulous, causing solidification of viscous material in the ocean water. The force of churning resulted creation of centrifugal and centripetal forces that has created the various planetary bodies of the solar system in this universe from the scattered drops. When the speed of churning increased further the centrifugal force caused the sun, the earth, the moon, the planets, the stars with their satellites appeared and started rotating in their orbits in the nebulous. The gods and goddesses namely *Ijumbu mang idakha mang, Khambudang mang yeppodang mang, Toktigek mang yangdigek mang, Mullululung mang Khalullung mang, Namkejok mang mamandin mang, Lakejok mang kamala mang* and many other gods and goddesses of cosmos balanced the equilibrium of the solar system in the nebulous with centrifugal, centripetal and gravitational forces of the cosmos, and stabilized the rotation, distance, speed of the planets, stars, satellites, the moon to move around the sun in the solar system in their respective orbits. The churning of the ocean by the gods and goddesses also created a number of gods and goddesses in the ocean. They are *Laotima mang phungphahangma mang, Chungjihangba yetchahangba mang, Lakejok kamala mang,* and *Namkejok mamandin mang*. They again churned the ocean and different kinds of gods and goddesses appeared again who were the lords of the earth, sky, air, water and so on. The youngest one was the powerful god *Takdigek yangdigek mang, Nenthakkum imetang mang*. They were tired and felt hungry and thirsty. They began to take foods and drinks. While distributing foods and drinks they forgot the youngest one. He was the god of death and destruction; he even had the power to cause death to gods and goddesses. He got angry and caused floods and erosion (*yongsong thukwa*). A number of water bodies or lakes were also drifted out from the ocean by the force of churning, which created *"Thosu warakma singkhi warakma, Yosu warakma linkhi warakma, Mikchumjum warakma mikyaya warakma, Tappeso warakma lerengba warakma"*, Churning of the ocean also produced sparks and created light namely *"Thosu semi yommba semi, Yosu semi panna semi, Akkam semi parna semi"*. The gods and goddesses now stopped churning the ocean. Thus, the gods and goddesses have created the solar system, the Sun (*Mikthama/Nam*), the Venus (*Sukra/Sringma/Pyanglungma*), the Mercury (*Budha/Thungyaba, Keksuba*), the Earth (*Iksama/Prithivi*), the Mars (*Mangal/ Samyangmuden/ Pungmimi*), the Jupiter (*Brihaspati/Chamthima/ Khawalumba*), the Saturn (*Sani/Pungsam/Thakrama*), the Uranus (*Arun/Phakmasinyuk/Kudapma*), the Neptune (*Barun/Tungdungtheba/ Maksama*), the Pluto (*Rahu-Ketu/Phagna*), the Moon (*Chandrama/ Laba/Singlaba/Okwama*), stars, satellites, air, wind, cloud, water bodies etc. in the nebulous.

However, there was no light, the Sun had no light rays (*Namsang*), the Moon had no Moonlight (*Lasang*), the earth had no soil, no sky, no suitable environment for life to live on the earth. The solar system was composed of only the water, sweat of the gods and goddesses, milk of the goddess *Sawara mang yettungek mang* and other viscous materials.

(c) Myth of Creation of the Earth: The earth was created by the gods and goddesses in the nebulous through churning the ocean. There was no soil, no light, no sky, no environment for existence and sustenance of life. Then, the gods and goddesses joined their heads together for creation of soil on the Earth and suitable environment for the creation of human life and its sustenance. Now, a god namely *"Tiutti mang kautti mang, Kautti mang mautti mang"* appeared and seeded a flowering plant in the earth-ocean, which germinated and started growing very fast. The name of the plant was *"Minuri (or Kunuri) phung samjori phung-Sumbaso singma yangmiso singma"*. The flower-tree grew so fast and big that it covered the entire north, south, east and west of the ocean and flowered profusely. The flower that bloomed in the eastern branch ultimately became the flowers of ladies and gentlemen (*Tuttu tumyang yakla suhangma phung*), the flowers bloomed in the north became the flowers of young men and women, the flowers in the south became the flowers of curse and misfortunes, and the flowers in the west eventually became the flowers of evil spirits and divinities. Then, the cow goddesses *"Phojiyeng pit makchiyeng pit"* felt thirsty and drank the ocean water, and licked and shaking her body that caused to drop some of her body-hairs in the ocean. These hairs settled on the ocean water and laid the foundation of the soil of the earth. It is known as *"Iksa yorong khambek yorong, Hukso nenchinglo tangne nenchinglo"*. When the cow goddess was drinking the earth-ocean water, some saliva of the cow goddess dropped on the cow goddess's dropped hairs. This saliva was manifested into the earthworm gods known as *"Iksa tona khambek tona, Tarong tona tangsang tona"* and became the origin of earthworms. A kind of platform with earthworms on hairs on the surface of the ocean was made. But still there was no earth, and hence were lying on the cow goddess's dropped hairs necked.

Now, the *Minuri* or *Kunuri phung samjori phung* of the earth-ocean bore an elephant size yellow black berry type fruit. The cow goddess now, snitched which manifested into the rainbow and is, also became the origin of rainbow. It also manifested into a number of gods in the form of birds known as *"Phogiya puro magiya pu, Puringla puro kumaey puro,* and *Pulingla puro puroti puro"*. They were created to stay on the tree, and thus the tree was made nice looking and pleasant. They are the eldest birds in the creation on earth. The god-birds were attracted to the fruit and tried to pick it. However, due to flapping of their wings, and fighting each other for the fruit, burst into several parts which formed islands on the ocean. Various kinds of minerals were created in those islands, which manifested into diamond (*hilli*), pearl (*mudhing*), precious stones (*muni*), gold (*Samyang*), silver (*yuppa*), bronze (*sakkong*), lead (*menja*), copper (*kingna*) and iron (*phenje*). Later on, they became the origin of these precious materials on earth.

Then, the goddess *"Wadhinlung mang phapphallung mang-Torang chombhama tangsang chombhama"* hits (*khekhusi*/fires) her own fingers each other, which created the sky. Now, *Wadhinlung phaphalung mang* reacted with the space and became creator god – *Nawara chagaplung mang, Chankhima mang thobuma mang.* Froth began to a mass on the platform, and earthworms were trying to create soils.

Now, another important creator god *'Porokmi mang wambhami mang"* appeared on the earth. He shook out his hands that created the soils known as *"Chukchi khamba yoyong khamba, Sibring khamba thebring khamba, Khambo khamba yupling khamba, Henkham khamba makkham khamba, and Laha khamba rutaak khamba"*. Thus various types of soils were created on earth out of nothing. Now, the earthworm gods started working on these soils. The god *Porokmi mang wambhami mang* again shook out his hands. This created the soil known as *'Sinahik londe Thenahik londe"*. The material in its turn produced the sand known as *"Siyengkha lottu theyangkha lottu"*. The material in its turn produced the stone known as *"Parung thaptu marung thaptu"*. The material in its turn produced another stone known as *"Tambetlung thaptu suyolung thaptu"*. The material in its turn produced *"Wayalungba thaptu chujiklungba thaptu"*. Now, *Porokmi mang wambhami mang* tied the earth with the dub grass-*Cynodon dactylon* (*Samyok*). *Nawara sumbangmu mang* (three divine manifestations), *Nenthakkum imetang mang, Yakchumma mang* (anger showing god), *Yahakma mang* (god difficult to satiate) also helped *Porokmi wambhami mang* to create the earth, rivers, lakes, mountains, trees and forests. Then, the *Wayalungba Chujiklungba* produced the gods and goddesses known as *"Khambongba lungbongba sa"*. These types of personified gods and goddesses are dwarfs and are the owners below the fertile layer of the earth. The adherents of *Yuma* religion had to purchase the land from these gods and goddesses for burying their dead body at this layer. The entire myths of *Yumaism* are based on these gods and goddesses. These gods and goddesses are personified in the myth as dwarfs not able to carry the load of the balls of goat's excreta; users of bamboo leaf as their rain shelter or who could hide in a leaf of bamboo; who had to cut down a fern for wood; who had to hurl sticks at the branches to bring down the peppers; and *siputrukma* (smallest bird) meat eaters.

Then, *Tambitlungma suyolungma* produced "*Tidiklung tadaklung*". *Tidiklung tadaklung* produced the Almighty Goddess *Tagera Ningwaphuma*. *Tidiklung tadaklung* also produced "*Lajiri layangma*", *Chijiklung mamaklung* rocks, and monkeys (*khokchum saba*). It also produced "*Mujilung sinalung – Mujiplungba yodetlungba*". It in turn again produced "*Minuri sinalung*" and that is known as the stone of gods and goddesses. Then, *Tambitlungma suyolungma* produced "*Minulung thaptu mijaklung thaptu*". Now, *Mujiplungba yodetlungba* produced the goddesses *Thosulungma phiyamlungma, Yosulungma mukkumlungma - Sayokhimma yokhimkhimma, Khamjitchhima khamjirima, Lunchichhima lunjirima, Parnanamaro sarenghangma, Phaksereba tigenjongba, Phoktanglungma Pembenlungma* (Mt. Jannu), *Muktikumma senchhegumma* (K2), *Mudoklungma sewachungma* (Kanchanjunga), *Chambhutlungma Chumjumlungma* (Mt. Everest), etc.. They all became rocks and mountains on the earth. *Nasolungma namgenchho mangga, Nasolungma phiyamse mangga, Thosulungma sewalungma,* and *Thosulungma chaphatlungma* were settled on the earth. Now, the earth was created, the sky was created, water was created, air was created. However, the earth was not joined or cemented together properly. The creator god created "*Iksa samyok khambek samyok*" (*Cynodon dectylon/ dubgrass*) on the soils to joined and cemented the soils on earth properly. Thus, the creation of earth is completed.

(d) Myth of creation of the Plants: The god "*Porokmi mang wambhami mang*" thought that creation of plants is essential for survival of the human beings. Thus, he decided to create plants. Then, he went up to the border of Tibet, China and also down to the border of Indian-ocean in search of plant seeds. The goddess "*Tattandi mang pattandi mang*" appeared at "*Tappeso warak lerenba warak*" (mythical ocean) and created the plant seeds. The god "*Porokmi mang wambhami mang*" went there and requested the Goddess for the plants seeds. Finally, he pleased the goddess and succeeded in obtaining the plant seeds from the goddess and brought them in his special bag known as "*Omlari sukwa tettari* *sukwa*". Then, the god seeded the plant seeds on earth, but failed to germinate due to envy and jealousy of a god known as *Chaitari khille mang*. The bodies of the Sun and the Moon were created due to churning of the ocean water of the universe with the Sun and the Moon gods but the celestial bodies were lacking the Moon-light and the Sun-light on them. Now, *Porokmi wambhami* god went to a place known as "*Tappeso warok lerengba warok*" and then to *ladellung*, and then requested the god of the Moon- "*Lakejok mang kamala mang* or *Lakejok mang lamangla mang*" to create the Moon with the Moonlight. The god also went to *namsalling* and requested the god of the Sun – "*Namkejok mang mamandin mang* or *Namkejok mang namsalling mang* or *Namkejok mang namangla mang*" to create the Sun with the Sunlight. They tried to create the Sun and the Moon but had no Sunlight (*namsang*) and the Moonlight (*lasang*) due to envy and jealousy of *Chaitari khille* god. Now, all the gods and goddesses lead by the Sun god and the Moon god requested the god of light "*Thoklingma mang kugapma mang –Tiotti mang paotti mang* ". They pleased the god of the light, who went to the Tibet-China and brought "*Sinyuk ponche pona muden ponche pona*" (garland of ambers, coral beads) and put on the Sun and the Moon. He also went down to the ocean and brought "*Teymen ponchhe pona warong ponchhe pona*" (garland of coral beads, ambers, precious jewels) and put on the Sun and the Moon. Thus, the god provided the Sun and the Moon the warm Sunlight and the cool Moon-light. The Sun started providing Sunlight rising from the east in the morning and provided light and heat on earth during daytime while the Moon started rising at evening from the east and provided Moonlight at night. The gods and goddesses made morning (*tanchoo*) with the appearance of the Sun and evening (*yunchoo*) with the Sun set and appearance of the Moon. Thus, the morning, day, evening and night were created (light and darkness periods) which was necessary for the plant seeds for germination. The Sun-heat provided warmth and light to the seed sown by the god *Porokmi wambhami mang*. Although the Sunlight brought daylight on earth now, it also caused excessive heat and made the earth too dry. Thus, no plant seeds sown by the god *Porokmi wambhami mang* germinated. Now, the god *Porokmi wambhami mang* went to see the seeds sown by him. The seeds failed to germinate. The creator god in despair wept turning his face all around the site where he had sown the seeds. The tears of the god while crying thus provided moisture to the plant seeds sown in the soil. The plant seeds thus germinated from the tears were collectively known as "*Toatisingmasi paramsingmasi* or *mikwa sing*". The plants germinated from the tears of the god while facing to south direction were known as *Sakhi singma* (? *Sendo singma/ Dhobiphul/ Musunda spp.*); the plant germinated from the tears facing the north direction were known as *Phegi singma* (? *Tusare, Debregeasia longifolia*); the plants germinated from the tears of the god while facing to east direction were known as *Sambarak singma lingbarak singma* (? *Gogun/Persek*); and the plants germinated from the tears of the god while facing to the west direction were known as *Chameli thokwaro mikwa thokparo* or *Mempheko sing ga ritti singro* or *Mempheko sing ga hondok sing ro* (? equisitum/*Sallibisalli*).

The gods and goddesses thought that the plants germinated thus were not suitable for the human beings. The creator god asked for guidance to gods *Sinyukhangba, Kandenhangba, Mudenhangba* and *Yonchenhangba*. But they replied that they know nothing. Now, the creator god *Porokmi wambhamai* went to Almighty Goddess *Tagera Ningwaphuma* and told her difficulties faced on the creation of the plants needed for the future human beings; and requested for guidance. The Almighty Goddess said "my dear grandson lacking knowledge, intelligence and wisdom. You are having a big thumb lacking knowledge; having a big toe lacking intelligence; having long fingers lacking knowledge of mathematics; having a big head lacking wisdom; you lie down on my foot to night, you will dream what you have to do".

On the guidance of the Almighty Goddess *Tagera Ningwaphuma*, the creator god went to the north on the high mountains known as *Iwahorana tembhe*, where he met the *Khambongba-Lungbongba* gods *Laphinjongba* and *Namphinjongba*. They were the experts in shot put game (*ponglung leppma*) and were having a heavy *Ponglung* (stone shot) with them. He requested them for the shot but they refused. Anyway he pleased them and obtained the shot and started playing the shot put. *Phaksara tigenjongba* another *Khambongma Lungbongba* god joined him and helped him by marking the distance with a stick (*singbit*). After practicing for some time, now he threw the shot put to the farthest distance on earth known as *"Ladoksurungma Namdoksurungma, Sakhonglung tembhe hongphalung tembhe, Lakhonglung tembhe khongbhana tembhe"* where there was an earthen pot containing full of rainwater known as *"Iksa kunda khambek kunda, Torong kunda tangsang kunda"* – the origin and container of the rainfall. The shot put broke the earthen pot. This caused the creation of "the Wind" (*Sammet-Kejong*), "the Cloud" (*Khamet*) and "the thunder storm" (*MudhokTunghik*). Now, the wind, the cloud, and the thunderstorm produced strong thunderstorm effect in the sky known as *"Mudhak Nandhok Loksu, Torong Tangsang Loksu"* and thus, created the rainfall on the earth surface.

The *ponglung* (heavy shotput) stroking at the *"Ladoksurungma Namdoksurungma"*, broke into four pieces and spread to all the four directions from there. The *ponglung* (shotput) piece going towards the west was known as *"Ighukso ponglung samsogha ponglung"* (the shot put of evil spirits); the one going towards the south was known as *"Chophot thungwa ponglung"* (the shot put of ocean water); the third piece going towards the east was known as *"Thokley sammang ponglung"* (the shot put of the gods and goddesses); and the fourth piece going towards the north was known as *"Menchham yapmi ponglung, Tuttu tumyang ponglung, Nali thangben ponglung, Sisa menchen ponglung"* (the shot put of human beings).

Thus, the rainfall provided soil moisture to the seeds, light and darkness period for photosynthesis provided by the Sun and the Moon, made the plant seeds sown in the soil by the god *Porokmi wambhami mang* germinated and started growing. The various types of plants germinated were known as *Sukpasing mullippasing* (*dhup*, pine tree), *Sammangsing irre-yosing* (*gobresalla*), *Menchensing lumlumbesing* (black juniper), and *Angurising nukappasing* (*chanp*). These are the most precious trees equivalent to the precious stones on earth. Next in the sequence germinated were *"Allapising Challapising* (plants not visible from the necked eyes), *Thokphekwasing kekpeppasing* (rhododendron), *Minurising khayekpasing* (*Rhus insignis*), and *Khebunchesing lumlumbesing* (*dhuppi, Cryptomeria japanica*). The species germinated on the mountains were *Simikla pomikla* (*deonigalo, malingo*), *Khechhingsesing Nambhoyosing* (*kattus, Quercus lanceaefolius*), *Yangsingbasing hayakpasing* (*chilaune, Schima wallichi*), *Yosusingma echesingma* (?),

Yohibungsing hoyekpasing (*phalant, Quercus glauca*), *Tigellesing Menjeppesing* (*gineri*), and *Taoghoksing yechhesing* (?). The plants germinated at the lower hills were *Chuktengosing yangdengosing* (*simal Bombax spp*), *Sabellising yakpellising* (*tooni, Cidrela kingii*), *Minuri sing imsekwasing* (*imli, Echinocarpus aristatus*), *Minurising sasingsing* (*sakhuwa, Shorea robusta*), *Minurising manglokpasing* (*roringga, Erythrina indica*), *Hangpharising makpharising* (bamboo, *Dendrocalamus hamiltonii*), *Minurising Mullabung* (*malbans, Bambusa nutans*), *Phungdura wekdurasing* (?).

A number of food crops were also germinated. They were: *ochha* (paddy), *maki* (maize), *Mangdok* (millet), *Kari* (pulses), *Chembi* (soybean), fruits, vegetables, spices, *hellawakhe* (sweetpotato), *himkhe* (yam), *tambhung khe* (*bontarul*), *tengokhe* (*simal tarul*), *sakchinuthi* (green vegetables) etc. He also created a number of flowers. Thus, the creator god created a number of plants, which he thought will fulfill the requirement of the future human beings.

However, due to envy and jealousy of other gods and goddesses to *Porokmi wamphami* mang, windstorms and thunderstorms occurred continuously on young plants and the plants were broken and uprooted. The creator god also created a number of grasses, shrubs and climbers to bind the soil on the soil surface, and the trees together so as to protect them from soil erosion and windstorms. These grasses and climbers were *Samyok* (*dub*-grass *Cynodon dactylon*), *Thangeiwat mangeiwat* (? a type of climber), *Phensangkitna chupsangkitna* (?), *Minuiwat nekhkiwat* (*pangra, Entada ecandens*), *Sidiiwat madiiwat* (*bet, Calamus spp*), *Minuiwat chuksaiwat* (*Mucuna monosperma*), *Tippura henchhingiwat* (*Entada spp*), etc. Thus, the grasses and climbers protected both the soil and plant trees respectively from windstorm and thunderstorm for the future human beings.

(e) Myth of creation of lower forms of life and birds: The creator god *Porokmi mang wambhami mang* went to *Pu pokheden pudhamlung den* (origin of birds) and created a number of birds and other lower forms of life for the future human beings. They were: *Senjik sengwana pu* (?), *Kerungma pu kuhetla pu* (*rani choro* ?), *Chillikhyak pu mayphedat pu* (*fista, yemapu, Rhipidura hypoyantha*), *Tetatla pu lonapma pu* (?), *Minuri pu korona pu* (?), etc. On the mountains he created *Samdangwa pu lingdangwa pu* (*Danphey,*

Lophophorus impejanus), *Samu muya* (*gidda, Gyps himalayansis*). For the lower areas he created *Sangmorapu lingmorapu* (*mayur, Pavo cristatus*), *Minuripu Supetrukpu* (dove, *Streptopelia chinensis*), *Minuripu Sellokwapu* (*nyawlichro, Megalaima virens*), etc. He also created *Khambu sikchen* (ants), *Lingbu thaba* (white ants), *Simbu osek* (snakes), *Mangjum mangwa* (bees), *Sarum sawa Irum iwa* (wasps), *Minuri lakhochen* (a kind of insect), *Mangnini* (*ghyaunkiri*), *Yahangponghe* (*thulo ghyaunkiri*) etc.

(f) Myth of creation of Mammals: Then the creator god *Porokmi wambhami mang* went to "*Sapokhe den Sadhamlung den*" (origin of mammals) and created a number of mammals for survival of the future human beings. They were: *Toktok pengwa* (deer), *Yasa khire* (*thar, Capricornis sumatraensis*), *Yasa Yongling* (*Jarayo, Cervus duvauceli*), *Yonghong makyu* (bear), *Payet nuge* (tiger), *Kiditongna* (leopard), *Poratongna* (wild dog), *Sumdang tokmi* (elephant), *Utta kenda* (rhinos), *Sera* (*bonel*), *Lasa Phungpit* (yak), *Namsa sangpit* (cow), *Sammenda* (wild goat), *Melluk* (sheep), *Chitalla lakhuna* (leopard). etc.

(g) Myth of creation of Human beings: The three creator and developer gods namely *Chokchokke mang yangyange mang* (creator and developer god), *Singmanglung mang yayiklung mang* (god of earth, plants, water, soil and stones) and *Nawalung mang chosaplung mang* (god of fate and destiny) appeared on the top of the mountain *Phoktanglungma pembenlungma* (Mount Jannu or *Kumbhakarna*, one of the five peaks of Kanchanjunga mountain) for creation of human beings on earth. The top of this mountain is a place of appearing gods and goddesses of *Yumaism* and thus known as *Mangjirima manglondhama* (place of appearing gods and goddesses). This is the final goal of creation, and without it there is no meaning of such creation on the earth. The creator gods turned towards the east and wished the Sun for blessing; turned towards the west and wished the Moon for blessing; turned towards the sky, gazed the stars and wished the stars for blessing.

Then, the gods collectively thought of creating very strong, tough, handsome, beautiful and immortal human beings. Then, the creator and developer god made strong, tough, handsome and beautiful human idols (*choyit*) in his own image at *Mangjirima manglondhama* made of gold (*samyang*) with diamonds (*hilli*), pearls (*mudhing*) and precious stones (*muni*) etc. in it. Then, he put the vital air (*kejong surit sokma*) on the idols but the idols could not hold it. He tried to speak with the idols but in vain. Then, he tried with other materials like silver (*yuppa*), bronze (*sokkong*), copper (*kingna*) etc. but failed. Life could not be put on the idols of such elements (materials). He could not create human beings with non-living materials (elements). In frustration, he threw these idols to all the four directions. The idol thrown towards the south became the divinities known as *khamlung keyja*; the idols thrown towards the east became the divinities known as *thokley sammang* (divinities); the idols thrown towards the west became the divinities known as *khebun linglang*; and the idols thrown towards the north became the divinities known as *taotey lembhe*. Thus the gods failed to create the human being with such materials.

Then, the gods went to the Almighty Goddess *Tagera Ningwaphuma* and reported the story of their failure of creating the human beings. On her advice, the gods went to the cloudy (*Siyakhamit mayakhamit*) high mountains known as "*Sawa tatphaklekhamma*", full of bamboo *Simikla* (*deonigalo, Arundinaria racemosa*) and *Pomikla* (*malingo, Arundinaria maling gamble*) forest. They cut down the bamboo forest, waited a week for drying the bamboos by the Sun, and then put fire on it to produce the fresh ash out of it. They sieved out the fine fresh ash and brought it in sufficient quantity to the creation place of human being. They also collected the fowl's excreta (*wahichellekna/seningwahi*) and rainwater collected on the stones or rock holes or tree trunk holes known as "*wadumbokwa*" in sufficient quantity. The gods followed the advice of the Goddess, which the creator and developer god received in his dream in all his works. Now, they mixed the materials thus collected and made two idols one male (*Laikkumsa pheniangsa*) and one female (*Tungutlisa simbumasa*). They put the various organs with the various organic materials available with them. They put the brain out of "*lonlenwahi*" (thin green layer of soil of marshy land); put eyes out of the seeds of "*Phipha phirik*" (a kind of tree seeds); made the tongue with the leaves of "*samyo cheksingma lingyo cheksingma*" (broom grass); made the ribs and fingers with "*minubungmaha tingnambungmaha*" (?); put the teeth made of "*wabholung sellobhung*' (a type of crystal stones); made ears out of *"singnekhekpen"* (mushroom); made hairs out of *"ikpokla susinggemmen"* (a kind of thatch grass); made eye brow out of *"tagera piju ningwaphu piju"*(?); etc. Now, the gods put vital air (*Sangu sokma*) out of the air (*kejong surit*) on the idols and advised (*sake yektutho*) them to come alive within a fortnight. On the eighth day the female idol came alive and on the ninth day the male idol came alive. Thus, the human idols made as advised by the Almighty Goddess *Tagera Ningwaphuma* came alive. The creator god *Chokchoke mang yangyange mang* was disgusted with the idols they made it now. He wanted to create immortal, strong, tough and beautiful human beings but failed. And now, the gods was successful in creating human beings with such a cheap organic products with the blessing of the Almighty Goddess.

In disgust the creator god cursed the new alive idols by spiting on them. The life idols became lifeless now. Then, repenting on his ignorance asked forgiveness and also blessing once again to the Almighty Goddess. The Goddess advised him in the dream to retrieve the souls of the idols through the ritual of *mangenna* (a boon bestowing prayer) for the revival of the idols. The creator god retrieved the souls of the idols by conducting the ritual of *mangenna* (details of ritual mentioned under the myth of *mangenna*) and the idols were made alive to become the human beings.

Then, the god of fate and destiny *Nawalung mang chosaplung mang* examined the human idols so created. He found that a lot of polishing of the human idols was necessary. They again prayed the Almighty Goddess for advice. Accordingly, they brought the cloth weaved and prepared by the Almighty Goddess herself and put on the human idols. The male human idol was put on with *"taga"* while the female human idol was put on with *"loghe"*. Then, the god of fate and destiny weighed both the male and the female human idols in a weighing balance known as *"ninduli pasanga"*. The weight of the female was less and was not looking good and beautiful. They again went for advice to the Almighty Goddess. Then, they went to *sapchong tembhe* where there were five houses of blacksmiths. They were experts in making the ornaments. The gods asked them to make ornaments of gold, silver and other precious materials and brought to the human creation place. Now, the gods tried to make ear-holes and nose-holes of the female human idol for decking the ornaments made of various materials. First they tried with pointed stones but failing, which they tried with thorns of various plants such as orange (*sarimse*), then with horns of cattle, goat, sheep etc. Finally, they could do it with the thorns of *Sidrakma* or *Sidingba* (*Mimosa rubicaulis*). Now, they decked the female idol with gold, silver and precious ornaments and made beautiful to look at. Thus, the gods finally became successful in creating self-sustaining, self-reproducing human beings.

Thus, the concept of life in *Yuma* religion is "**Biogenesis**" – life producing from life or life products with the blessing of the Almighty Goddess *Tagera Ningwaphuma*, and the human destiny is the death. The concept is just opposite to "**Abogenesis**" – spontaneous generation of life of Hinduism out of the earth, the water, the fire, the air, and the ether (Kainla, Bairagi 1993; Shreng, Ranadhoj 1992; 1993; Subba, C. 1995: 1-284; Subba, J.R. 1998:1-18; 1999: 556-561; 2001:40-88; 2003: 203-275; 2005a:40-73).

Mythological Functions

The myth serves all the five functions of mythology. They are:

(i) **Mystical:** The myth has elucidated the mystery of the wonders of the universe creation in its own archaic way; how the gods and goddesses manifested in the void and contributed the creation of essential components required for existence of life in the universe. It has illustrated the mystery of creation of water, air, wind, cloud, thunderstorms, rain, lakes, earth, snakes, fish, birds, mammals, plants, crops, organic matter, and also the environment suitable for creation and sustenance of human beings on earth in an enigmatical manner.

(ii) **Cosmological**: The myth explains how solar system – the planets, the Earth, the Sun, the Moon, the Stars (*Tanchokpa-Unchokpa*) with centrifugal, centripetal and gravitational forces were created in the void. We are yet to understand many of such cosmological phenomena even with the scientific advancement of today, and we are yet to understand fully the origin and creation of the universe.

(iii) **Sociological**: The myths has become an essential ritual of the community today and is invariably recited/chanted in all the religious rituals involving trance, ecstasy, divination, etc. popularly known as "*Yehang Sema Mundhum*", before performing any other religious rituals in the society. It elucidates both natural and social mythology and unfolds the mystery of human mortality.

(iv) **Pedagogical**: The myths interprets the laws of life and how to live a human lifetime with cooperation, depending on some or all the living and non-living resources created for human survival in its existing environment and in the universe as a whole; and finally,

(v) **Mystery of afterlife**: The myth also describes the mystery of mortality of human life, mystery of afterlife, the dimension of the journey inward, the human psychology of source of origin of life, creation of life through the law of biogenesis, physical consciousness transcending to spiritual consciousness and performing soul journey and other afterlife mysteries.

Myths of *Tongsing* – a link with the Ancestors and the Present Family or Clan

(a) Myth of *Idhuk Samsogha Pakma* (origin of evil spirits of unnatural death): *Saonge Ongehangba* and his friends while looking after the harvest once saw various types of birds and animals destroying the crops. They then tried to chase and kill them, but they found that they had all run away and hid in their secured shelter. They saw the beautiful well-protected nests of the birds and appropriately designed shelters of wild boar and other animals. They also thought about building a house and went to the Supreme Goddesses *Tagera Ningwaphuma* for her instructions. The Goddess suggested them to follow the birds. But when they went to the birds, they told them that they know nothing about constructing a shelter. So, they again went to the Supreme Goddess to tell all about it. She again told them to change their name and ask the birds in disguise to tell the techniques of constructing a house. They changed their name and became *Lokpha Temba Hangpha Temba, Phungden Hangba Laden Hangba*, and *Peybukhangba Lansahangba*, and followed the birds for instructions. They learnt the skill from the birds and animals and began to build a house. They leveled the foundation of the house and tried several trees in the nearby forest for pillars (*sitlang*) but the trees were found unsuitable. They had a sister –*Khappura Mellonghangma*. They asked her to remain at home and cook food (*cha*) and drink (*thi*) for them. The trees they tried were *Khorising* (*kheyer, Acacia catechu*), *Sammangsing* (*Gobresalla, Abies webbiana*), *Yongdengosing* (*Simal, Bombax malabaricum*), *Yohising* (*Lalikath, Glechidion acuminatum*), *Khebhunchhesing* (?), *Sangesing* (?), *Hongesing* (*Lampatey, Duabanga grandiflora*) etc. Finally, they were able to make a pillar from the suitable tree – *Sabensing Yakpellising* (*Tooni, Cedrela tooni*) (note: Subba, C. 1995:162, wrongly mentioned Sal tree – *Shorea robusta*).

They were assisted by all the time by their sister *Khappura Mellonghangma* to make his endeavor successful. She was a charming lady with lustrous black locks and dressed it well by tying into knots plaited in board plaits and decorated it with flowers. She often stuck the comb in her plaited hairs. *Lokpha Temba* and his friends brought the log from the forest and dug a hole into the earth to set the pillar upright to construct this house. They were in full preparation to erect the pillar with the support of his sister. *Khappura Mellonghangma* was holding one end of the pillar on the side of the hole and *Lokpha Temba Hangpha Temba* and his friends were holding another end. When they were about to push the pillar into the hole, *Khappura*'s comb, which was stuck in her plaited hair, fell down into the hole from her head, and bent down to pick up the comb. Her brothers could not hold the pillar in angular position due to its heavy load and it suddenly thrust into the hole and hit her. She died immediately and her spirit became *Sogha* (evil spirit of sudden unnatural death). It was the first case of unnatural death when early human beings were just developing to build their shelter. Any way *Lokpha Temba Hangpha Temba* built the house but because of *Sogha*, the house was soon caught by termite and other woodborer insects (*Mudhak Thaknam*). So, again with the instruction of *Sodhung Lepmuhang*, he brought *Lodenhang* and *Phungdenhang* with their long cylindrical hollow log drums (*Sangsing Ke Hongsing Ke*) to kill the insects, termites, fungus etc. by their *Ke* dance ritual. Drum dancers danced in the new house and made the insects fall on the ground by the power of their ritual dance and summoned the bird – *Temlana Lakhrek* that came immediately and ate the insects. The *Sogha* of *Khappura*

Mellonghangma became known to all as "*Pari Nu Kheknu Nu Khemyangma*" (charming maiden with a comb stuck at her plaited hair) evil spirit since then.

There is also another episode relating to the origin of *Sogha*. One day, *Yakpeso Hilli Hang* (also known as *Tumbariba Wanddung Kemba*) went to the steep rock to collect honey from the comb of rock bee (*Yakhek Mangwa*). He fell down and died unnatural death. He also became a *Sogha*. Since then several types of *Sogha* began to appear in the land of *Sawa Yethang*. Some people died by falling from trees and mountains (*Hilli Yakso*), some died in water (*Chaphat Thungwa*), or while crossing rivers, ponds and lakes or while swimming, some died while collecting woods and fodders, some in landslides (*Kai Sareng),* in hunting (*yukphung*) and some were killed by wild animals and the dead souls of those people turned into evil spirits and thus became *Sogha* of various types. The progeny of *Sawa Yethang* began to suffer from *Sogha*. They sent *Sajuwet Mudangwet Samba* to *Tagera Ningwaphuma* to find the way of overcoming their problems and she told the *Samba* to go to *Sodhung Lepmuhang* and find some *Yeas* (*Yeba, Yema*). He went to *Sodhung Lepmuhang* and he instructed him to approach *Chillima Pesumma Ya, Nenjiri Nemmethuk Ya*. He made a humble request with *Yas* to go down to the land of *Sawa Yethang*. *Yas* in their proper gear flew down swiftly with all their paraphernalia to kill (*Idhuk Setchhene, Sogha Setchhene*), to eat (*Idhuk Chaseni Sagha Chaseni*), and to drive away *Sogha* (*Idhuk Nachchhene, Sogha Nachchhene*). They danced and searched the *Sogha* in the house, around the poles, at the doors and called the female *Sogha* "*Pari Nu Kheknu Nu Khemyangma*" and male *Sogha* "*Tumbariba Wangddung Kemba*", earliest among male *Sogha* to come to the door showing them their tasty foods, coaxing them by producing typical sounds, uttering series of puns for shamanic efficiency and chanting spells. When *Sogha* came there, they started to beat them to kill. *Soghas* began to run away, they followed throughout the way until they reached the end of the earth. Then they blocked the path of *Sogha* at the crossroads of eight paths by making an ocean of eggs, erecting mountains of the broken earthen pots, allowing to grow and cover the mountains, steep rocks and hills by walnut-tree, plants such as *Phoeba lanceolata* (*Sapsing* or *Samsingbung*), *Entada phaseoloides* (*Neghekpa*), *Mucuna monosperma* (*Mangka*), Stinging nettle – *Urtica dioica* (*Sogibung*), a plant

Neyraudia madagascariensis (*Muktubung*) and lighting a fire from white crystallized stone chips (*Phaphalungba Sellonglungba*). When chanting this myth *Yas*, together with their assistants or disciples act out the roles and perform the rituals representing the same *Ya* and possessing the same power.

There is another myth relating to the origin and development of *Sogha* and *Sasik Yangdang* (stillbirths). *Khambongba Lungbongba* divinity *Sigera Yetthukka*'s son was a buzzard (an eagle) without feathers. *Sapjiyongba-Pujichongba* (hunter of animals i.e. aboriginals) made feathers from the stalks of food plants for him, which turned into natural feathers. When he was grown up he came down to the land of *Sawa Yethang* and began to stay at the top of a huge tall *Sabensing Paramsing* (*Cedrela tooni*) covered by creepers at the ravine by the side of *Pipmira* and *Phongwa* river. *Muiyan* (buzzard) began to bring the children of aborigines (*Khambongba Lungbongba*) and *Laik Khambu Mikthakso Hangs* (*Khambu-Rais*) from the surrounding villages and kept at its nest and ate whenever he felt hungry. There were hunters (*Sa Keseppa Sajichong, Pu keseppa Pujichong*) around the ravine and the eagle began to kill them every day. *Mikthakso Palahang*, senior among seven brothers of *Laik Khambu Hangs*, began to consult with his brothers and other *Khambongba Lungbongbas* (aborigines or autochthons) to find out and kill the eagle. They all decided to kill the eagle and went in search of it for several days. The seven brothers of *Khambuhangs* had a beautiful sister, *Sappori Hangma Penparihangma*. She was under the endearing care of her seven brothers and her sister-in-laws were jealous towards her. Taking the advantage of the absence of seven brothers, sister-in-laws took her to the riverside to take bath. They suddenly pushed her into the river. The current of the river took her away and luckily she came out in an islet (*Chukmendo Lekwado*) where the river was flowing on all sides. She could not come out and wail, weep and request the fisherman (*Yonjiyongba*) to take her out of the islet. The fisherman threw his fishing net in full swing towards her but could not entrap her to bring out. He then solaced her crying in his shrill voice that someone would come to rescue her. After a while, another fisherman came there playing with his fishing rod and tried to rescue her, but failed. She was left alone. In the mean time, a *Muiyan* (buzzard), flying in the sky, saw her and flew down slowly making a round above her. She cried and asked him (buzzard) to take her out. She also said that she would look after his children. *Muiyan* (buzzard) took her to his nest. She started to look after his children and soon came to know that everyday the buzzard was eating eight-nine children of *Khambongba Lungbongbas*. She felt that some day he would eat her too. One day she saw his brothers passing through that ravine and she made a shrill cry to draw their attention. The seven brothers recognized their sister's voice and found her in the nest on the top of a tall tree. They asked her how she fell in the captivity of *Muiyan* and she told the whole story. They spread the net at the bottom of the tree and she jumped. She was thus rescued. *Laik Khambu Hangs* devised a plan together with the villagers (*Khambongba Lungbongbas*) and snared the buzzard in a trap at *Likhu Tembhe*. They beat him to death and was thrown away into the river. The river carried him away along its course. At last, the corpse appeared floating around the bank of the river at *Chakra Makra* and the fishermen (*yongkeleppa*) –*Chukjihangba* and *Yandihangba* took it out by their fishing net. They saw its legs shining as gold and its wings as silver. They made a flute (*Mephra*) from its legs and various things from its various parts of the body with the expectation that they would earn power or gain energy (*Hanjum Hangwa*) and wealth (*Kanghi Takma*) by their use. They took it home and found that the bones of the corpse were shining. After sometime, they began to tremble and suffer from illness. They consulted various people everywhere. Eventually, *Pengwana Soingna Ya* identified it as *Muiyan Sire* (eagle/Buzzard master spirit) - as the source of power of *Yeba* and *Yemas, Sambas* and *Phedangmas*. The bones, kept in the floor at the corner of the house, became *Miyong Sire* or master spirit of the wildcat. The feathers and various parts of the *Muiyan* became paraphernalia and decoration of shamans. *Satholakhang Thalaghang* performed propitiation rite (*Theyo Thetnam*) by sacrificing black chicken for the first time.

While the local people became able to set free them from the fear of the *Muiyan*, they cut down the tree – *Paramsing* and destroyed even its roots. The *Muiyan* spirit began to wander on the land of *Sawa Yethang* and caused accidents, natural calamities and immense tribulations to humankind. In the prayer of *Sajuwet Mudangwet Samba* on behalf of *Sawa Yethang, Sodhung Lepmuhang* sent *Telete Tenchhammuk Ya, Telele Tenjiyep Ya* to destroy and control evil spirits such as *Sogha, Sugut* and *Sasik Yangdang. Paramsing* became the source or symbol of *Sogha, Sugut* and *Sasik Yangdang* as *Muiyan* used to stay on the top of it and kill, bring and eat the hunters (aborigines) and children of *Laik Khambu Hangs* from surrounding villages. So, the evil spirits of curse – *Sakhera Panbhanjyangma,* a ghost of killing birds – *Pusese Punengjongba,* an evil hunter spirit – *Sakeseppa Sanenjongba* and a spirit of stillbirths – *Sasik Yangdang* appeared along with *Sogha* on the earth. Because of the envy, jealousy and evil acts of *Sakhera Panbhanjyangma, Pusese Punenjongba* and *Sakeseppa Sanenjongba,* the *Ya* had to drive them away by feeding white crystal stones (*Abha Sellong*). There were still some spirits of *Sogha* and *Sasik Yangdong. Chillima Pesumma Ya,* also known as *Yetchillek Phangchillek Ya* – a *Yema* having a weird power of turning into eight-nine forms or entering into the bodies of various animals, had to persuade them. While chasing, they turned into grasshoppers (*Piyat* or *Piyappa*) and *Yema* became hawk (*Phicho*), and followed. They again turned into deer (*Pengwa*) and she followed them becoming a tiger (*Nuget*) and while they turned into fish (*Padhung Letnya*) into the water, she became a crocodile (*Hikkeba*) and chased them. Finally, she was able to destroy or keep them under control.

Reciting the myth of *Sogha, Sugut* and *Sasik Yangdang, Ya* together with his or her assistants, perform the ritual of cutting down the *Paramsing* (a tree where evil spirits stay) and destroying even every bit of roots of the ominous tree. It is done by making a *Paramsing* of *Muktubung* stick and destroying it into pieces and throwing into the hearth. This ritual is known as *Soghasing Khakma* or *Tangma.* Then, *Yeba* or *Yema* performs the ritual of *Khijo Apma* or shooting at the thread where symbols of *Soghas* and its foods are hung. *Ya* (*Yeba* or *Yema*) coax the *Soghas, Suguts* and *Sasik Yangdangs* by his spells and charms and make them to stay and take the foods offered. In the meantime, *Ya* shoot the evil spirits and drive away from the house towards forests, hills, mountains by crossing the river, sometimes passes through knife's sharp path (*Pheyari Chengchengwa Lam*) of rock-ribbed mountains. Finally, they arrive at crossroads of eight paths (*Yetchiri Yetlamdho*) and after crossing the path they hand over the evil spirits to *Damuhang*. In some myths, *Ya* drive away the evil spirits as far as *Layango Sangyango Den* – a place close to horizon

(*Ladhemic Namdhemic*) – a meeting point of earth and sky (*Iksa Khambek Nuphra*). The *Ya* hands over the mischievous retinue and children (*Sogha, Sasik Yangdang*) of *Muiyan* spirit to *Muiyan* at this place. *Ya* and his or her assistants and disciples block the path and fly back through the same path, destroying the bridge on the way and invoking the nature divinity *Kulang Kemba,* to block the path of evil spirits. On the way back, they also invoke the divinities of hills and mountains to obstruct the path and call on *Tikwagemba* and *Khewagemba* (pheasant and partridge) to confound the track. They also invoke the goddesses of eight rivers (*Yetchiri Yet Ado Mang*) and the confluence of three rivers (*Sumjiri Sum Ado Mang*) in the south to block the path of evil spirits. Thus the ritual of blocking path comes to an end. The belief system about life and death, hardship and sufferings, natural and supernatural phenomena and miracles are reflected in the myth (Kainla, B. 1993; Shereng, Randhoj 1992; 1993; Subba, C. 1995: 156-211; Subba, J.R. 1999: 535-574; 2001: 31-39; 2003:152-202).

Mythological Functions

(i) Mystical: The myth illustrates the followings:

(a) The mystery of how the human beings learned to construct their dwelling houses (shelters).

(b) The mystery of origin of *Sogha* (evil spirit of unnatural death);

(c) The mystery of why *Sobensing* (*tooni, Cedrela tooni*) should not be used for construction of dwelling houses in *Yuma* adherents;

(d) The mystery and tradition of protecting the newly constructed house from wood-borer insects (*Mudhak Thaknam*) through *Hongsing Ke* dance as it was done by *Lodenhang* and *Phungdenhang* who killed the insects, termites, fungus etc. by their *Ke* dance ritual and propitiating *Akwanama* household divinity for initiation ritual in the newly constructed dwelling house;

(e) The mystery and tradition of driving away of *Samsogha* (unnatural death), *Sugut* (evil spirit of parturition), *Sasik* (evil spirit of stillbirths) by *Samba, Yeba* and *Yema.*

(ii) Sociological: The myth has provided us the ritual of *Sam Sogha, Sugut, Sasik Yangdang appma, Pakma, Napma , Paramsing Tangma, lam meppma* etc. for protecting the newly constructed dwelling house from wood-borer insects, protecting the womb of the pregnant woman and also protecting the mother during parturition, protecting the individuals/family/clan from unnatural deaths and, taming, accompanying and reaching the souls of such deaths to their destination of evil spirits. It is believed that unnatural death occurs only at the influence of such evil spirits.

(iii) Pedagogical: The myth has contributed the adherents of *Yumaism* a number of ethical and other customary laws to be observed in the good society such as newly constructed house ritual celebration, unnatural death rituals, womb and parturition worship ritual etc.

(iv) Mystery of afterlife: It has offered the adherents of *Yumaism* belief system of afterlife of unnatural deaths, journey inward, concept of soul of the unnatural deaths (*Sogha*), parturition death (*Sugut*), stillbirths (*Sasik*), soul journey of such evil spirits to *Sam Sogha, Sugut, Sasik Yangdang lam, Khema Yongsong Den* (place of retribution or hell) etc. to be reached by the *Sambas, Yebas* and *Yemas*.

(b) Myth of *Mujina Kheyongnama* (Origin of Curse): *Yumaism* believes in curse (*Manghup mangde*) and a special ritual should be performed to avert the effect of a curse atleast once in three years in a family or a clan. The myth of the ritual is related *to Muji-na Kheyongna-ma,* a divinity of *khambongba-lungbongba* described under the myth of creation of the earth. The *Wayalungba Chujiklungba* produced these divinities known as *"Khambongba lungbongbasa"*. These types of divinities are dwarfs and are the owners below the fertile layer of the earth. They are personified in the myth as dwarfs not able to carry a single piece of goat's excreta; users of bamboo leaf as their rain shelter; harvesters of chilly by using sticks; and *siputrukma* (smallest bird) meat eater etc.

Thus, *Muji-na kheyongna-ma* is one of the earliest women divinities on earth produced by the *Wayalungba Chujiklungba* rock. When she grew up and became conscious of herself, she asked for clothes to the Supreme Goddess *Tagera Ningwaphuma*. She dressed up with "*lokhe*" and then was living at "*Thilli yongsong tembhe*". As she reached maidenhood, her breast, pudenda and buttock developed bigger and she got excited with strong sexual desire. She went in all directions in search of a husband. But she could not find. Once she was resting sadly on a branch of a tree, a gust of wind (*thosuingbennu khanglaingben yosu ingbennu suritingben*) struck at her pudenda. She got pregnant from the wind. The myth also describes beautifully about the pregnancy feelings of women. When she was in the first month of pregnancy (the child in the womb was at *Toanayonara* stage- earthworm form - upto two months old), she felt blue (*Kerung Kohim*). She felt her body itching (*Anduk Saham Lose*) in the second month when the conceived child in the womb was at *Sumnarathok* (round form-third month) stage. She felt irritating even with the blowing wind and rain in the third and fourth months when the conceived child in the womb was at *Linarathok* (bow form – four month) stage. She felt confused of herself in the fifth month when the conceived child in the womb was at *Nyanarathok* (fish form – fifth month) stage. The fetus began to move in the sixth and seventh months and she longed for pungent, hot, sweet and sour tastes during the child in the womb was at *Monasamtingsa* (human form – sixth month) stage. She longed for eating snails at the eighth month as the fetus was developing everyday. After nine months, she felt herself irritated and angry and at the tenth month she felt the natal pain and made up her mind to face the consequences and trained herself for safe delivery. Within the tenth month, she gave birth to a baby.. At the tenth month when *Muji-na kheyongna-ma* got the natal pain, she tied herself with string (*Sidiphekkhanamle madiphekkhanamle*), hanged up at a height in a cave known as "*Chilli yongdong phakkutho*" and gave birth to a child, a son of a wind (*kejong sammet*). She named her child – *Lapotiba lakhemyangba*. She did not know how to rear the child and went to *Tagera Ningwaphuma* for advice as the child was getting lean and thin since its birth every day. The Goddess instructed her to sleep at her feet and have a dream. On the advice of the Goddess *Muji-na kheyongna-ma* went to a place called *Hilli yachho* and brought the leaves of *kekyo-na* (a kind of tree with velvety soft leaves). She went to *chokepho pangbhe* where she requested the residents to make *Sidiyangdang madiyangdang* (a kind of child rearing basket) and brought. Now, she put the plant leaves in the rearing basket and conducted *Yangdang phongma* (child naming ceremony) ritual on the fourth day of his newly born son. She renamed her – *Susuwengba lalawengba*. Now, the child started growing normally.

The myth tells us how nature changes the girl child herself to become a woman as seen in the myth of *Mujina kheyongnama*. Contrary to this the boys need training. The boys have no such transformation in nature and have to be trained to become an adult as seen in this myth described as under: When the child *Susuwengba lalawengba* attended the age of three years, he asked for clothing. His mother gave him *"taga"*. At the age of four – five years, he obtained *"apliba"* (*guleli-matengra*), and started hunting small insects, toads, birds etc. With his *apliba* so made himself, he killed a toad, brought to show his mother and asked whether it was edible meat. She said that the toads are dirty creatures and not edible meat. They are poisonous and if eaten the body get swollen up; and asked him to through away to a marshy place. When the boy attended an age of seven years, he went to a mountain with his *apliba* where a pair of birds known as *Phagiya magiya pu* was sitting on the top of a plant known as *Phongdura yettura*. He killed one of the birds and brought to show his mother and asked whether the bird was edible meat. She said that the bird's meat is edible but he has committed a blunder by killing one of the two birds of the pair. She advised him not to kill the pair birds now onwards. The surviving one of the pair will be in great grief, which should not to be happened. The separation and widowhood is extremely painful which should not be created by his action.

When *Susuwengba lalawengba* attended eight to ten years of age he asked permission to his mother for going to forests and mountain for hunting. His mother advised him that he is the lone child of his mother and should not go for hunting till he is well equipped and learns all the skills of hunting. Then, he began to equip and train himself under the guidance of his mother. He went to a kind of bamboo forest (*mulla poksitna*), where he made the bamboo bows (*lijum li*); and also went to cane forest and obtained cane strings (*lijum nammepma*) required for tension of the bow. Then, he went to *"Sapchong tembhe"* where there were five houses of blacksmith who knew to make arrows. He obtained the arrows from them and trained himself in the art of using bow and arrow. He also went to high mountains and obtained hunting poisons required for the arrows from *Samdang khewa lingdang khewa*. Then, he asked permission from his mother for going and hunting. She advised him that he is yet to become a successful hunter, as he requires hunting animals for assistance. Now, he went to high mountains and obtained puppies of dogs (*tekketongna*), wolf (*poratongna*), jackals (*kiditongna*), bear (*makyotongna*) and tiger (*kebatongna*). He started training them for hunting. Now, he was well equipped with hunting skills and equipments. His mother tried to stop him, but he assured his mother that he would return very soon. Then, he entered into the wild forest. As a hunter, he was renamed as "*Sawa yukphung Kemba*".

One day he met a beautiful lady at the higher hills known as *Thosulungma phiyamlungma,* weaving her loom while chasing a deer with his dogs. The hunted deer was tired and came on the way to her loom. She killed the tired deer with her weaving stick (*tholi*) and hid it. Following the prey the dogs came there but she fed them with some food and drove away. After some time *Sawa yukphung kemba* reached there on the spot. Her maidservant "*Sisari phandari*" told her that a young man is standing on the wall. Meanwhile the dogs earth-out the hidden prey. They met each other, eat the deer meat and took rest. They attracted to each other and came in sexual contact. *Phiyamlungma* also a *khambongba lungbongba sa* gave birth to a son in due time. The child was named – *Sutchhuru suhangpheba* in the fourth day. During her prenatal period *Sawa yukphung kemba* cohabited with her maid attendant "*Sisari phandari sa*" and also gave birth to a son in due time. The child was also named *Samdang khewa* on the fourth day of his birth. Now, the family of *Sawa yukphung kemba* and *Phiyamlunma* lived happily for some time.

One day *Sawa yukphung kemba* again went for hunting at the lower hills following a swamp deer (*baharasingha*) with his hunting animals. While following the swamp deer, he met another charming maiden –*Yosu Mukkum lungma,* again a *khambongba lungbongba sa* who was weaving cloth in her loom. They were also attracted to each other and began to a conjugal life. Later, they gave birth to a girl child. On the third day the child was named *Tetlara lahadongna*. During the prenatal period he again cohabited with her maidservant "*Sadilli dellihangma*" and also gave birth to a male child. The child was named *Lingdang khewa* on the fourth day. They also lived a happy family life for some time.

One day *Sawa yukphung kemba* thought of going for hunting and asked his wives for essential foodstuff for his journey. He asked to both *Yosu Mukkum lungma* and her maid servant as well as *Thosu Phiyamlungma lungma* and her maidservant. One showed the other but no one provided the victuals. In this way, envy and jealousy (*Tingding Nahen*) among his wives surfaced while he was in need of material support. Realizing the fact, he told each of his wives that he was leaving for hunting. In the meantime, each of them asked him about who would take care of them. He told them that *Yosu Mukkum* would be looked after by *Sadilli dellihangma* as usual and *Tetlara lahadongna* would be looked after by *Lingdang khewa*. Similarly, he instructed *Sisari phandari* to look after *Phiyalungma* and *Sambang khewa* to look after *Sutchhuru suhangpheba*. After giving instruction to his wives and children, he started for hunting.

Following a deer, he climbed up to the grassy top of the mountains. He took shelter in a rocky place known as *Yetchirimetho yetladhometho* where a lady called *Kambolli khewasumma* fed him food for a week. Then, he left for *Thokchong tembhe* where stood with his stick for some time and then he died with hunger at *Linkhi yokma*. From the decayed part of his chin bones and teeth became *Chellung khoklung* (symbol of spirits of dead incestuous couple). The hunting animals waited for their master for many days till the corpse started to fall after being rotten. Then, accept the dog, all his other hunting animals - jackal, wolf, bear, and tiger went to the forest at *Hilli-Yaksu*. The dog came back to *Thilli yongsong tembhe* and reported to the mother *Mujina Kheyongnama* in detail about the death of her son. When the mother heard the detail information about his son, and the causes of his death from the dog, she began to lament, recalling her instructions to him not to go far away as he had no father, brothers and sisters. She went to *Thosu phiyamlungma* and her attendant and complained that they had made him stay with them, kept for a long time and did not even give necessary foodstuffs while going for hunting. She cursed them to get ruined from incest (*Tandi, Lungdhung kai choginne*), suffer from stillbirths (*Sasik yongdong pokhenne*), and curse, witchcraft and mental disorders (*Naso thapon pokhenne*). In the same way she also came down to *Yosu Mukkum lungma* and her attendant and cursed them to get ruined from incest, die in young age from thunderbolt, and suffer from evil spirits a various illness. With her cursed to her daughter-in-laws and the evils appeared in this world. She came down and on the way, she died in a cave known as *Thili yongdong phukoma*. Nobody saw her or take care of her and she became *Sugut* or *Sugup* (spirit of causing death at parturition) known as *Khijora luplihangma* (Kainla, B. 1993; Shereng, Randhoj 1992,1993; Subba, C. 1995156-211; Subba, J.R. 1999: 535-574; 2001: 80-118; 2003:203-481).

Mythological Functions

(i) **Mystical:** The myth describes the mystery of the origin of curse and its effect on human life.

(ii) **Sociological:**

(a) It also interprets the mystery of how to live in the society supporting and validating certain social order set forth by our ancestors from time to time.

(b) It elucidates how the girl child transforms into the motherhood by nature automatically, as in the case of transformation of *Mujina Kheyongnama* to become motherhood. The boys have no such transformation in nature.

(c) It also illustrates that the young boys have no such means of natural transformation from boyhood to manhood. The boys need assistance for such transformation. In the myth, the mother provides assistance to the child *Susuwengba Lalawengba* for transformation to attain manhood - *Sawa Yukphung Kemba*. It describes how boys have to be assisted for such transformation by the mother or brother or father or the society, as there is no automatic means of such transformation as in the case of females. It expounds that for the boys, care and assistance of parents is essential for this transformation.

(d) The myth also describes elaborately the psychological feelings of a pregnant woman at different stages of conception as *Yumaism* recognizes 18 (eighteen) stages of human life stages of which five are in the womb of the mother.

(e) The myth has to be recited/chanted by the religious *Phedangmas* during *Tongsing Tokma Mundhum* to be performed once in every three years in the family/clan, which reminds the society of the myth time and again for supporting and revalidating.

(f) The myth also teaches us the art of child care and provides the ritual of *Yangdang Phongma* (child naming ceremony) in 4 (four) days for male and 3 (three) days for female child in the community.

(g) It also interprets the disadvantages of polygamy and the effects of curse to the descendants of human being in the society.

(iii) Pedagogical: The myth elucidate how to live a human life, observing the laws of life, ethical laws, other customary laws as it should be in the good society established by our ancestors. All of what kind of clothes to wear and eat, how to behave to each other etc. and if it is not observed, the individual have to face the consequences not only in this life but also in the afterlife, as in the case of the progenies of *Sutchhuru Suhangpheba* and *Tetlara Lahadongna*.

(iv) Mystery of afterlife: The myth expounds the dimension of the journey inward, the human psychology of source of origin of life and the mystery of afterlife due to the effect of good and bad *karma*. Due to her bad *karma* of curse to her daughter-in-laws and grandchildren, the soul of *Mujina Kheyongnama* became *Sugut* (evil spirit of parturition) after her death.

(c) Myth of origin of Incest (*Lungdhung kai phekma*): The myth is full of lewd innuendoes resulting in disorder, sorrow, tribulations and sin. The myth of *Mujina kheyongnama* represents the accession, the myth of *Ipnana sarengdhangma* represents the culmination, and the myth of *Sutchhuru Sauhangpheba* and *Tetlara lahadongna* is the climax in the origin of incest. In the myth of *Mujina kheyongnama,* following her son's death, she cursed her daughter-in-laws to get ruined from incest, and thus the incest was originated for the first time because of her curse to the decedents of her own son *Sawa yukphung kemba*. The second step in the process of incest culmination is in the myth of *Ipnana Sarengthangma*. She was a lady divinity amongst the *Khambongba Lungbongba sa*, having an extreme libidinous urges, who desperately tries to satisfy her sexual desire and material instinct in the absence of husband. She feeds her breast to the insect (*Yaklapuja* – larva of a pest of colocasia) secretly. She gets lean and thin everyday. Her brother *Phaksera Tigenjongba* tries to find out the reason. One day he finds an ugly, frightening, loathsome insect in his sister's bed and kills it, and throws into the bush. Its blood spread in all directions. The birds and beasts get excited with sexual desire while looking at the amazing body of the insect at the bush. Thus, amorous feeling permeated in all living creatures. There is a wonderful description of such feelings and sharing of feelings in this part of the myth.

In the third part of the myth, there is a climax of incest of *Sutchhuru suhangpheba* and *Tetlara lahadongna*. *Samdang khewa* was serving *Sutchhuru Suhangpheba*. But *Sutchhuru suhangpheba* was envious towards him and was treating badly. Being upset, he was wandering in the hill forest in search of hunting animals for food. On the other hand, *Lingdang khewa* also being perturbed was roaming in the same forest hunting birds and animals. While aiming at their prey cautiously, they identified each other as hunters. They met and were introduced to each other as an offspring of *Sawa yukphung kemba*. Thus they came to know that they were brothers by blood relation and talked about their personal life and maltreatment they were experiencing from their elder brother and sister. They decided to bring their brother *Sutchhuru suhangpheba* and sister *Tetlara lahadongna* into wedlock. They made a bag of colourful orchid blades, a comb of Himalayan bamboo (*Simikla*) and a small bamboo harp (*simikla kom*), which is played in mouth. According to their preconceived plan, *Samdang khewa* talked about a beautiful woman with his brother and told him that she had sent a bag for him. In the same way, *Lingdang khewa* told his sister about a handsome gentleman who had sent a comb and a bamboo harp to her. They arranged their meeting in some lovely place. The two were attracted to each other. *Sutchhuru suhangpheba* laced the bamboo harp that was presented earlier in her blouse just hanging from her breast. She also made him strap up the bag that was presented earlier on his shoulder as if they were embracing. Eventually they came in sexual contact and began to spend conjugal life. Being afraid of the disclosure of their malevolent plan, *Samdang khewa* became a pheasant and ran away to the snow capped mountain peaks, and *Lingdang khewa* turned into partridge and moved towards low-hill forests.

Most of the time *Sutchhuru suhangpheba* and *Tetlara lahadongna* were obsessed with the feeling of sex and spent most of their time in lecherous frolic. They gave birth to seventeen off springs. They also had a bitch. One day, *Lahadongna* got so angry with the bitch that she beat her bitch with a broom fiercely at the door. The bitch ran away a bit far and stayed at the roofed yard in front of the door. *Lahadongna* approached there too and beat the bitch with her skirt. She again ran away in the courtyard. Her mistress rushed there and again beat her by her leg. Being harassed so much; the bitch went to complain to the Moon, the Sun and the Stars. She waited all these heavenly bodies on their way. When the evening star (*Unchhokpa*) came, she complained about her incestuous master and mistress. He told her to approach the Moon. When the Moon came, she complained, but the Moon also told her to approach the stars (*Mudhung khese*). She complained with the stars and they also told her to go to the morning star (*Tanchokpa*). She approached the morning star, but she also told her to approach the Sun. Finally the Sun came and she complained about the misconduct of her master and mistress and expressed her grievances. The Sun held a meeting of all the heavenly bodies and decided to send their messengers a crab (*Sangarung khebok*), reptile (*hondigeksa chunyeklesa*), and a grasshopper (*Seksekyoma*) on earth to find out the fact. Their reliable messengers found them lying in the bed caressing each other (*Tengore kitchhang nessesi, Sakphare yahukpa temsangrot nessesi*) and gave the information to heavenly bodies.

They decided to separate them as incest was not justifiable, and it was only a source of envy and jealousy, tragedy and tribulations, disharmony and degeneration, devils and tried to separate them in many ways by using the sword of a wild cane (*Sidi madi khanglek*), a oak tree (*Minu yohiba khanglek*), a catechu tree (*Minu khori khanglek*), a sal tree (*Minu sosing khanglek*) etc. but in vain. They were finally separated with a *Mimosa rubicaulis* and *harkatto* plants (*Sidingba* and *yukmi khanglek*). They also came to know that *Suhangpheba* and *Lahadongna* were unaware of their consanguineous relation. So they thought the separation would be enough and told to *Suhangpheba* to go to *Muringla Kharingla Tembhe*, upland in the north, together with their nine sons (*Sawa Phanghangs*) and instructed *Lahadongna* to stay in *Sangarak Nugarak Tembhe* with her eight sons (*Sawa Yethangs*).

In the course of the division of seventeen offspring of *Suhangpheba* and *Lahadongna*, a sieve (*Lachillingge-Namchillinge*) made of gold and silver was brought from "*Maywara chosappe chongdho nu*" by the separation committee at *Chumling hara tembhe*. They came in agreement that those offspring who remain on the sieve would follow the father and those who pass down would accompany the mother. Eight of them passed down from the sieve and they became "*Sawa Yethang*" and those who remained on the sieve, they became *Phanghangs*. They became *Phedangmas* or erudite persons (*Phejikkumasi phedangmasi, Sawarabasi yetchhammukpasi, Siphakangsasi yamiangsasi*) forming a group of nine "*Phanghang*". One daughter got in mess; neither could pass nor remain on the sieve. Both sides pulled her and his hands and legs severed from the body and fell down on the earth. It became a *Paramsing* (a tree of evil spirits) and her spirit became "*Samudhungma Yepmudhungma*", one of the master spirits of the *Phedangmas*. She was included in "*Phanghangs*". The name of the *Sawa Yethangs* were: *Tappeso Lummehangba, Phurupso Theyonghangba, Sogimso Songmihangba, Lalaso Pangbonhangba, Sangenhang Pangenhangba, Niyara Thokchonghangba, Khetchuwet Upanghangba* and *Setchhere Seninghangba*.

After separation, *Sutchhuru Suhangpheba* renamed himself and became *Sodhung Lepmuhang*. *Tetlara Lahadongna* also renamed herself and became *Thillilung Thamdenlungma* (also *Yosulungma chungutlungma* or *Mujiri Mubokwama*). They played different roles to save human beings on earth. They made a solemn commitment not to meet again (Kainla, B. 1993; Shereng, Randhoj 1992,1993; Subba, C. 1995: 156-211; Subba, J.R. 1999: 535-574; 2001: 119- 134; 2003: 320-325).

Mythological Functions

(i) Mystical: The myth describes the mystery of the origin of incest in the human society. The myth of *Mujina Kheyongnama* represents the accession, the myth of *Ipnana Sarengdhangma* represents the culmination, and the myth of *Sutchhuru Sauhangpheba* and *Tetlara lahadongna* is the climax in the origin of incest. Mystery of sex is beyond the boundary of human understanding. Sex is essential for reproduction, but the intense desire of sex as in the case of *Mujina Kheyoungnama,* the extreme libidinous urges of sexual desire and maternal instinct as in the case of *Ipnana Sarengdhangma,* and the obsess feeling of sex and spending most of the time in lecherous frolic as in the case of *Sutchhuru Suhangpheba* and *Tetlara Lahadongna* (the human progenitors) is the mystery of sexual desire and maternal instinct inexplicable to human beings.

(ii) Cosmological: The *Phanghangs* left with their father to *Muringla Kharingla Tembhe* – an *akashic* field in the sky while the mother stays back at *Sangarak Nugarak Tembhe* – the Earth.

(iii) Sociological: The myth provides the rituals of incest and elucidates to interpret the laws of life and the ethical laws required to be observed for its survival, supporting and validating for social order. Hence, the myth insinuated that incest was not justifiable, and it was only a source of envy and jealousy, tragedy and tribulations, disharmony and degeneration, devils, and needed a change in the human evolution. Having an intense desire of sex, extreme libidinous urges to satisfy one's sexual desire and maternal instinct, the obsess feeling of sex and spending most of the time in lecherous frolic as described in the myth leads to social disorder, which needs to be corrected.

(iv) Pedagogical: The myth counsels the laws of life and ethical laws, as it should be in the good society is essential. It admonish how to live a human lifetime under any circumstances.

(d) Myth of origin of Fire (*Mukkum Semi sepma mundhum*): After separation of *Sutchuru Suhangpheba* (*Sodhung Lepmuhang*) and *Tetlara Lahadongna* (*Thillilung Thamdenlungma*), *Sawa Yethangs* were left with their mother at *Sagarak Nugarak Tembhe*. They had no father with them. They were unaware of fire and they were eating raw foods mainly yams and other root crops (*Su, khe, lawakhe, phungkhe, tengokhe, yakkhe,* etc.), which caused them to suffer from various illness. They discussed the problem with their mother. The mother told them to go to *Pittolung Kamdoklungma* to find a fire (*Mukkum Semi*). Only the youngest among the sons, *Setchhere Senihangba*, got ready to go there. He went there and watched the fighting between black and white bulls (*Phajiyeng Makchiyeng Pit*) throughout the day and night following his mother's instruction. He saw sparks coming out of their horns while they were fighting. The sparks going to the sky were known as the fire of lightening (*mundhang seri semi*). The sparks going towards the east were known as the fire of the divinities (*thokley sammang semi*); the sparks going towards the west and falling on the white crystallized silica (*Avolung Sellolung*) were known as the fire of evil spirits (*idhuklung samsogha semi*); and some sparks were dropping on white shining stones (*Avolung Mijallung*) and dried cow-dung. He brought those sparks falling on the dried cow-dung at home and they began to cook their food (roots and yams). They started to eat cooked food and began to feel well and happy. One afternoon when most of the *SawaYehang* had gone for day work, suddenly a gust of wind blew away the fire to a thatched roof and the roof was caught on fire. Six houses: *Thosu chongbang him, Yosu petthe him, Nasu ekang him, Nasu tehim him, Nasu lingkhim him* and *Nasu sakkong him* were destroyed and eight people including tobacco smoking through hobble-bubbles (*Yuppare yet khatabaha*), millet beer drinkers in wooden vessels (*hanglithokmaga thi kethungbaha*) and enjoyers of warmth at the hearth with legs keeping wide open (*Lang harda mi kejabaha*) were burnt to death. Because of causing disaster (*Mudhung chekya*), *khambongba lungbongba sa* decided to fine (*Samban kupma*) *Sawa Yethangs*. Eight brothers (*Yethangs*) discussed among themselves and asked their mother to find the ways to get rid of the problem. Their mother suggested them to consult their father. Only the youngest son *Setchhere Senihangba* who brought the disastrous fire to *Sawa Yethangs* got ready to go to see their father as he was thought to be responsible to bring the fire and not taking precaution or not adopting adequate safety measures. He was unaware about the residence of his father. So he asked his mother to accompany him and show the route to his father's land *Muringla Kharingla Tembhe*. They went together to the father's place and before approaching to *Sodhung Lepmuhang, Thillilung Thamdenlungma* hid in nettle thicket. The son told his father about the whole story of how the fire caught the houses and what consequences *Sawa Yethangs* had to face. Being worried about the difficult situation of his sons, he sent ***Mugoplung Khegoplung Samba*** with his youngest son. He also came to know from his youngest son that his mother was hiding somewhere in the way. The son returned from the father's land with the *Samba* who had with his complete costumes (*phengbo, aplak* without *kawri, yaboto, yesim, pangphoyee, yejephe, wasang, yaburko, yeponghe, yethala, laphija* etc.) and with all necessary equipments; and had the knowledge and power to put out the blaze, extinguish it and cure the burns. *Mugoplung Khegoplung Samba* came to the land of *Sawa Yethang* and put out the fire with the water collected in the holes of tree-trunks and rocks (*Singdum lungdum pokwa*), thin green layer of soil from marshy land (*longlenwa hi*), blood of fish (*padhung letnya*) and pig (*kubhak*), leaves and branches of trees and creepers chanting spells (*sapsing/ kaulo, muktu, Siding-yukmey* etc).

When the samba put out the fire, the land of *Sawa Yethang* became without fire. They became helpless. So the youngest son *Setchhere Senihangba* who knew his father's land again went to his father's land and brought ***Suketling Tangetling Samba*** by pleasing him. Now the *Samba* began to search fire in various trees growing at the top of the mountains and down to the low plain areas including *Sukpasing, Sammangsing, Menchhingsing, Lumlumbasing, Thokphekla Kokpheklasing, Yohibasing, Khechingse Nambhoyosing, Yangsinba Hayakpasing, Agori Nugappasing, Sabensing, Hangangsesing, SosingSingma, Sakpha Hangpha, Imsekwa, Tengosing* etc. (for common and botanical names see Subba, J.R. 2002). Eventually, they tried in *Isewasing* (*Rhus semialata*) and found the spark of fire. He gave it to *Sawa Yethangs* and they began to eat cooked food. But they did not know to offer foods to their Tutelary deities. They began to suffer from various illnesses. They again consulted their father and brought ***Phungjiri Phungappo Phedangma*** who performed harvest rituals and they became well. To overcome the day to day problems of life and to help them to worship nature and ancestors, they brought ***Nenjirima Nembothangba, Tetlara Laphungyangba*** and ***Miktikke Samsui Phedangmas*** in the land of *Sawa Yethangs*. But still they could not get rid of the evils of incest, envy and jealousy, curse, diseases and sin. So, they brought ***Sajuwet Mundangwet Samba,*** who freed them from all such evils (Kainla, B. 1993; Shereng, Randhoj

1992,1993; Subba, C. 1995:156-211; Subba, J.R. 1999: 535-574; 2001: 135-146; 2002; 2003:275-301).

Mythological Functions

(i) Mystical: The myth illustrates the mystery of the origin of fire, realizing how important the fire was in the evolution of modern human society.

(ii) Cosmological: It also describes that the fire originally was of cosmological origin, but it was not safe for use, as the early man did not know how to extinguish it and produce the fire again when he needed. Hence they extinguished the cosmological fire once for all. Finally, they discovered the fire on earth for their livelihood with the help of an erudite *Samba*. Then onwards, this fire could be obtained whenever they needed and extinguished when they were not in need. This became a fire for their livelihood to the early human beings.

(iii)Sociological: The myth has provided the ritual of *Mi Sam Sepma*, which describes the advantages of use of fire when in need and the effect of its misuse also. The myth is recited or chanted in every *Tongsing Tookma* ritual once in every three years. It also expounds the role of father as well as of mother in the growth and development of offspring and society as a whole, which is essential for the development of a good society. The myth has provided not only the fire for livelihood but also harvest rituals for offering of foods to their tutelary divinities, worship of natural divinities and ancestor deities, rituals for solving their day to day problems and the rituals to get rid of the evils of incest, envy and jealousy, curse, diseases and sin of the early men.

(iv) Pedagogical: The myth interprets the laws of life; and the need of ethical laws set forth by our ancestors such as use of fire when it is needed, offerings of newly harvested crops, fruits etc.to gods and goddesses etc. These laws have to be observed sincerely in a good society.

(v) Mystery of afterlife: It also describes the inward journey and the mystery of why there was a need of a learned *Phedangmas* and *Sambas* for solving the problems of unknown miseries of day to day life in the society

(e) Myth of Origin of Devils, Evil Spirits and Ghosts (*Sangdok Aplek Pokma*): *Sodhung Lepmuhang* came down a little distance to send his son *Setchhere Senihangba*. Suddenly he saw his separated wife *Thillilung Thamdenlungma* hiding in a nettle thicket. He sent down his son with *Mugoplung Khegoplung Samba* and met her. Though he had a wife *Laoti Phungphahangma* after the separation of his earlier wife and also he had promised to the celestial bodies not to see his separated wife again, he could not resist himself when he saw his former wife. They began to indulge in sexual pleasure (*Netti kuphung wamma*) again violating the incest taboo. They came at sexual contact several times at several places. They gave birth to insects, crabs, snails, frogs, lizards and various creatures according to the places where they performed sexual activities due to curse and incest. When they indulged in sexual activity at a marshy place, they gave birth to crabs (*Sangarung kheboksa kengyasa*); when they came to sexual contact on the top of stone-wall, they gave birth to lizard (*hondigeksa chunyaknyaksa*); when they came in sexual contact on the firewood heap, they gave birth to *Gadela* fish (*seknyanunya sapchakkenya*); when they indulged in sexual contact on the tree top, they gave birth to *Minuhangba Inuhangba* evil spirit having gold and silver cap; when they came to sexual contact on the east, they gave birth to *Tappesoba lungmahangba* evil spirit; when they came in sexual contact on the north and south, they gave birth to various spirits and ghosts causing torments and devastations such as *Thosodingma Chammahangma, Hillelema Hingdenmukma,* and *Abolungdhung kapsalungdhung, Lairoba Namiroba, Lambangaba nambangaba, Lakhemyangba Namkhemyangba,* etc. evil spirits; and when they indulged in sexual contact on the *tappeso worok lerengba worok* (mythical ocean) in the west, they gave birth to cruel divinities (spirits) of executing curse - *Sakherama pandendingma, Sakherama pedeingma* and *Sakherama mukhemlungma* and evil spirit of causing illness and diseases-*Chambekoma chamdangmatimma.* In the same way when they intercourse in the low plains of the south and high land of the north, they gave birth to another spirit of causing serious illness and misfortunes – *Sakhera Mukhemlungma* and *Sakhera Bebeingma* respectively. They also gave birth to several divinities including *Tappeso Lareso Hangba* a horrifying and difficult to see, which represented curse and malediction (*Lavak ekma*), incest, illness, crimes and sin (*Sogen soma*) and various sources of human sufferings. They eventually quarreled on the division of their progeny and died, which further caused death in young age.

The myth relating to the origin of *Lungdhung Kai* ends here. Then, come the myth of its impact, consequences and overcoming it. It is the most obscene and exotic portion of the myth. The incestuous relation of *Suhangpheba* and *Lahadongna* left the impression that there was no any barrier for sexual relationships and sexual pleasure is the ultimate goal or accomplishment of all living beings. Such relationships behaviors and lifestyles caused tremendous problems in the life of *Sawa Yethangs*. It was due to curse laid on their ancestors. So, the shamanic priests have to perform the ritual of averting curse. In this context they present the wonderful description of sex organs and sexual acts of various animals such as dog, goat, sheep, bull, horse, elephant, frog, duck etc. in their myth chanting and dramatization.

According to myth, *Sakherama Panphendingma* is the principal divinity of curse or making the curse to happen. Feeling extremely embarrassed by her, progeny of *Sawa Yethang* went to *Sawa Leyomkemba* who by his male organ or penis, used to throw the branch of a tree to the target, slash down the branches of the tree, clear the clouds in the sky and roam carrying his genital on his shoulder. They brought him to control her and get rid of incest and evils. Chanting this myth in detail, *Samba* or *Yeba* remembers with reverence the contribution of premordial *Yea Tetlara Tenchiyeppa Yea* and perform the ritual of destroying *Chellung Khaklung* (symbolic representation of incest) and killing or propitiation of several evil spirits, divinities, devils, ghosts and witches of incest origin. At the same time, they also perform the ritual of killing *Thakpa Kubu* (weevil and other insects) reciting the myth of its origin – killing of *Sakhera Panbhajyangma* by *Setchhere Senihangba* with his *Khambuling Nahangma Tu* (spear that helps to win war), a weapon given by his father. They also invoke *Laden Hangba Maden Hangba* to kill *Thakpa Kubu* and call *Temlana Aphrek Pu* to eat them (Kainla, B. 1993; Shereng, Randhoj 1992;1993; Subba, C. 1995156-211; Subba, J.R. 1999: 535-574; 2001: 119-136; 2003:320-324).

Mythological Function

(i) Mystical: The myth illustrates the mystery of the origin of a number of devils, evil spirits and ghosts (*Aplek Sangdok Aplek Pokma*) in the society and describes how the early men overcame from them. It also suggests the ways and means of overcoming their malevolent effects performing various rituals for it (*Aplek Sangdok Aplek appma*).

(ii) Cosmological: The myth has cosmological origin.

(iii) Sociological: The myth has provided the ritual of *Chellung Khaklung* (symbolic representation of incest) and killing or propitiation of several evil spirits, divinities, devils, ghosts and witches of incest origin. It also explains the need of supporting and validating the social orders, performing rituals once in every three years to neutralize harmful effects of these evil spirits, devils, witches of incest origin.

(f) Myth of Origin of Divinities (*Lahi-Namhi Kubokma*): In the formative period of solar system in the universe creation, eight Suns began to shine on *Pungling Tembhe, Khapling Tembhe, Laphinjong Pangbhe, Namphinjong Pangbhe, Aya Chimling Tembhe* and *Iwa Hara Tembhe*. The eight Suns were *Chikcho Namba, Thanam Namba, Wasa* or *Asa Namba, Chungji (Thinam) Namba, Sikiring Namba, Yukling (Thebiring) Namba, Khekkek (Aya) Namba, and Kamdong (Kambong) Namba* (Shereng, Randhoj 1992). The descendants of *Khamjiri khambongba Lungjiri lungbongba* (the gods and goddesses of earth below), to whom the load of the balls of goat dung was heavy enough to carry, who could hide in a leaf of a bamboo, who had to cut down a fern for wood, and who had to hurl sticks at the branches to bring down the peppers began to suffer from the unbearable heat. The entire earth, plants etc. were dry. First of all, they talked with the senior birds – *Khowa* (?) and *Siya* (?) and asked whether they could kill or control the Suns. But the birds told them that they were spending most of their time in clouds (*Sikhamitma thekhamitma*) and did not know anything about killing the Suns. They consulted various animals and birds, but all of them expressed their inability to do so. They approached *Lepmeyung Lapodhuk* bird (a naked bird without wings and feathers) and the bird told them if they could provide wings and feathers, he would kill the Sun. In *Iwa Hara*, they met a rat (*Hellere* *hensuba Maklere maksuba*) and the rat agreed to make a tunnel to go to the Sun if he were given remuneration. They committed that the rats will have enough opportunities when human beings will grow crops in the later days. They approached an insect that cuts the young bamboo shoots (*Phadyondyok*) and the insect showed its willingness to open up the hole in the bamboo and to glue the piece of it to move towards the Suns. It was not enough. Finally they arrived at a place where porcupines (*Khamlung ai*) were living almost naked (*mullek lekchak*). The decendants of *Khambongba Lungbongbas* dressed and equipped the porcupine with all the feathers and spines of various birds, animals and plants. Its spines became shining arrows of various shapes and these arrows became very poisonous.

Then the teamwork began. The insects and rats opened the hole in a bamboo for the porcupine to go close to the Sun. The porcupine reached close to the path of the Suns and waited in ambush. The sun *Chukchi Namba* appeared; he shot his spines which stroke at *Chukchi Namba*'s heart. It yelled in pain, and the sound echoed in the sky. The blood fell on the earth which became *Toktele Thungthangwa Sammang*, a smith or artisan divinity. One arrow stroke to the eyes of the second Sun –*Thanam* (*Namba*) and its blood of that sun fell down at *Kejiko Kelanga Pun* (*Siringwa*). It became a *Misek Sammang* a divinity of spark and rain, also known as a divinity with injured eyes. Similarly, he shot the third Sun – *Sikire Namba* and the blood of that Sun fell on *Mundakkum Sewa Chong* (mountain top). It became *Tangsang Lawa Lisang Lawa* or *Toksongba Sammang* a hunter divinity. He shot the fourth Sun –*Kamdong* (*Kambong*) *Namba* and the blood of it fell at *Mujiri Thajiri Thalong* and a new divinity emerged –*Tetlere Tenseghama-Kakjiri-Maklanghangba*. Similarly, *Kappelli Yobadangma*, a divinity of forest appeared from the blood of *Wasa* (*Asa*) *Namba* which fell on rocks of the eastern side (*Toi Nangen Lungma*). *Piporima Yangkhonjoma*, a divinity flying in air (*Sammet langma kejong langma*) appeared from the blood of the Sun *Yukling* (*Thebring*) *Namba* which fell on the rocks of the western side (*Toi namdha lungma*). When the seventh sun *Chungji* (*Thinam*) *Namba* was shot, its blood fell on *Muhik Khamhik* soil and it became a divinity of life-flower, *Netti Phungwa Sammang*. Several drops of blood fell on the earth and several divinities appeared at several places. The blood that dropped on

Lagrin Namgrin Tembhe became *Singla Mangwa Sammang*, a divinity of leprosy (*Chokmelle chokmendet papmelle papmendet*). In the same way, *Apliso Poyamlungma, Keba* and *Sigilungma* divinities appeared from the drops of blood that had fallen in *Changelung Chiyenlung*. A cedrela tree (*Sobensingma*) became a tree to *Sogha* (*Soghasing*), Rhododendran became a tree of *Nahensing* (a tree of envy and jealousy) and trees like *Takhapsing, Echesing* became the trees of tears (*Mikwasing*) as the blood drops fell on them. The blood drops fell on flowers also and became the flowers of various divinities. The dead body or organs of the seven Suns became planets (*Lahi Namhi*), the ethereal divinities affecting the life on earth. They become the sources of joy and sorrow, pleasure and pain, happiness and misery, hopes and fears, success and failures having profound impact on human destiny. The literal meaning of *Lahi Namhi* is the shit of the Moon and the Sun. In the popular sense, it is planet or celestial bodies as well as ominous or imprecatory tears of gods and thus planets are associated with bad days or misfortune and distress.

The Eighth and the last Sun *Khekkek* (*Aya*) *Namba* hid away and the porcupine could not find him. The porcupine returned and the descendants of *Khambongba lungbongba* welcomed him and promised him to allow playing and eating in future the crops grown in the field by their descendants as remuneration for his service. As the only sun was hidden, there was darkness everywhere. The stars were able to light their path only. The shining tree at night – *Minu Sendosingma* and the insects with light – *Odhingama* and *Tumbari* (Glow-worm and fire-fly) were able only to light themselves. All the living creatures had to face a lot of troubles and so, they decided to send a delegate (*sijoingmi*) to please the only Sun now and to appear in the sky. Some birds and insects tried to meet the Sun but they could not find him. A louse entered into his body and tickles him, but in vain. A bat went to the Sun and started dancing, laughing, crying before the Sun. The Sun saw the peculiar creature – neither bird nor animal with wrinkled face, hanging below, made him laugh a bit. Some rays of light appeared and the dawn began. As there was no threat of anything, the last Sun came out and thus the day and night began once again.

Some of the myth narrates the trees decided to send their delegates when birds and insects could not succeed to find the hidden Sun. They send various trees: *Wasoma, Sibukma, Sukpa Sammang sing, Yangsingba* etc.. Ultimately, the pine attempted and became successful due to his loud and long voice. The Sun responded him and agreed to come out.

As the *Lahi Namhi* (planets or celestial bodies associated with disaster, distress, misfortune, sorrow, privation and misery) began to move, *khambongba lungbongbas* began to suffer from heavy floods and landslides. It caused destruction of forests, trees, domestic as well as wild animals, birds, insects, reptiles and aquatic animals. The *Sawa Yethangs* brought ***Tetlere Tenchhiyep Yea*** to the land of *Sawa Yethangs* who cracked down on the evil spirits of incest – *Chellung Khoklung,* and divinities –*Lahi Namhi,* the sources of illnesses, death, sorrows, distress and misfortune and threw away to the western lands – *Chulaphe Pangbhe Lappiyo Pangbhe, Khetaphe Pangbhe Laphiyan Pangbhe, Sikwaden Pangbhe Pakwaden Pangbhe,* chanting this myth in course of performing this ritual (Kainla, B. 1993; Shereng, Randhoj 1992;1993; Subba, C. 1995156-211; Subba, J.R. 1999: 535-574; 2001: 119-136; 2003:346-384).

Mythological Function

(i) Mystical: The myth describes the mystery of the origin of various divinities (*Lahi-Namhi Kubokma*) and their benevolent and malevolent effects in the society. It also educates us how to take the benefit from the benevolent divinities and overcome the malevolent effects of these divinities.

(ii) Cosmological: It elucidates the cosmological dimensions of solar system and the natural calamities of drought that had affected the early human beings; and how they overcame from that hardship. Such natural calamities are the part and parcel of life on earth but the hardships could overcome through mutual cooperation of all the living beings on earth.

(iii) Sociological: The myth has furnished the adherents a means of supporting and validating a social order performing a ritual of *Chellung-Khaklung* during *Tongsing Tookma* once in every three years. The myth also enlightens us how we can overcome the worldly hardship through mutual cooperation of all living beings on earth.

(g) Myth of Growing, Accumulating and Separating Flowers (*Phung Letma, Phungma* and *Changma*): A flammingo (*karangwa*) came flying in a beautiful lake at the mountaintop and sat on a hillock just in the middle of the lake. It looked around and abandoned the night soil. By the grace of god, flower-plants grew there and flowers began to bloom in due time. The seeds of the flowers spread in all directions and the place became scenic when flowers bloomed all around. A goddess – *Kheyuncho Yunchoda* appeared in the garden. Three beautiful maidens also appeared there. Among them, *Phungletima* began to plant flowers, *Phungbitnama* began to remove weed and boulders from the roots of the flower plants, and *Phungamlama* began to sprinkle water on the plants. While weeding the garden, the seeds of the flowers scattered on the mountains. By those seeds, *Sekmuri* (celery, *Apium graveolens*), a flower of human life and several fragrant flowers of ladies and gentlemen, grew there. Similarly the flower *Menjai* (*mennoye*/cuscuta?), which can be offered in worship ceremonies and flower of *Phedangmas –Namyoba* (*Artemisia vulgaris*); flowers of *Samba – Sapsing* (*Phoeba lanceolata*) and *Muktubung* (*Neyraudia medagascariensis*); and the flower of *Yaba – Tiamla Theamla* (*Cymbidium spp* orchids) also grew in the mountains. The flowers of evil spirits (*Chuwat phung*, Hyacinth, *Hyacinthus orientalis*), flowers which are not used in worship – *Lekwasen Kopi Phung* (white water lilly, *Nymphaea alba*), a flower which is not used by men and women – *Yamsampha* (?), *Tabe Phung* (*angeri, Melastoma normale*?), a flower to be offered to the dead body only – *Mikchiri Phung* (?) and the flower of tiger – *Ondong Phung* (*Ocimum basilicum*) also grew there. These are the flowers to be segregated and to be thrown away towards the west. There also grew the fragrant flowers *Khirabe* (*bhuinchampa, Kaempferia rotunda*) and *Mahangma* (*Dahlia pinnata*) which keep the body cool and *Singjango-Wetjango* (*dawri, Luculia gratissima*) – a flower of sisters, *Thopara* (marigold, *Tagetes erecta*) – a flower of brothers, *Hukjiri Huk Kaklem Phung* (panchaunle, *Orchis latifolia*), *Mukum Phung Kewa Phung* (*Tulipa spp*), *Maroti Phung* (*Plumeria accuminata*), *Lungdhakke Lunglengwa Phung* (epiphytic orchids ?), *Thokphetla* (*Rhododendron spp*), *Kokphetla* (*Michelia spp.*), *Sinikka Pejamma* (?) and *Ingnamma Chomena* (Jasmine, *Jasminum officinale*) – flowers of life to be protected from draught and frost.

Separating Flowers (*Phung Semma*)

Now, the flowers have to be separated and the flowers of the evil spirits have to be thrown away. Thus, *Khodina leppena phung* (lotus) is a flower of drinking water (*chophat thungwa*), *Jimiyo lamiyo phung* (?) is a flower of star (*mundhang khese*), *Ladok mandok phung* (sunflower) is the flower of the Sun, *Kunuri lilam phung* (orange colour lily, *Nymphaea indica*) of altar (*ekku sangbhe*), *Miktikke phung* (a king of climbing flower?) of divinities, and *Maroti phung* and *Mahangma phung* (dalia) are also flowers of divinity and human life. Similarly, *Singjango wetjango* is a flower of mountain ridges (*koi phangjong*), *Ondong Phung* of tiger (*Phayet nuget*), *Sangopi-lingopi* (?) of steep slope (*Hilliding yakso*), *Yakkawa phung* of forest trees (*Tabu singlang*), and *Pangboti kunata phung* (*jatamashi*), *Sellere semmukti phung* (?) are the flowers of various divinities. In the same way, *Sangdong phung* (*Samyok*) is the flower of earth for saving from floods (*Yongsang thukwa*) and landslides (*khamjuna khamlek*), *Kaodi sellengwa phung* (?) is the flower of *Chellung Khoklung* (incest) and *Sekmuri phung* (celery) is the flower of human beings, of young men and women. *Samba/Yea* while separating the *Sekmuri phung*, calls on the mythical gardeners *Yepling Kemba Toring Kemba* to remove the weeds and take care of *Sekmuri* flower and also invokes the singers – *Mangden Hang, Kewa Phungba* and *Kambolingma Khewasuma* to watch the flower garden from *Salgekna Pu* (*balchey charo*/the Sun birds) and look after it. He invoking Tenjiri ***Tenchhiyep Yea***, throws away the flowers of illness, misfortune and distress causing spirits and divinities. He also throws away the evil spirit and misfortune causing divinities with flowers and blocks their paths. He prays for the plant of *Sekmuri* to ever grow, its buds always sprouts, and always remain blooming and finally prays for the welfare and prosperity of his clients.

Accumulating Flowers (*Phung Summa*)

In *Yumaism*, the life of a human being is compared with a flower garden. Once, the flowers are separated and the flowers of illness, misfortune and distress causing spirits and divinities are thrown away by the *Samba* or *Yea* invoking Tenjiri *Tenchheyep Yea*, and asked the mythical gardeners (*Yapling Toring Kemba, Maden Hang, Kewa Phungba and Kambolingma Khewasumba*) to take care of the human flowers in the garden, he starts accumulation of human flowers on the garden represented by flower-vase (*phungsari*) altar prepared for conduct of this ritual.

The *Samba* says that "we have thrown away *Chellung-Khoklung, Sokhim Soma, Labhak Yekma, Tingding Nahen, Sasik Yongdong, Lungdhung Kai* etc. and now we accumulate and add more and more human flowers in the garden in the absence of which we human being fall illness, misfortune and distress". He accumulates and adds various flowers on the flower vase. They are: sunflower (*Ladokphung namdokphung*), *Minuri Samjori phung* (?), *Sampoyong phung* (?), *Sangophey Tewama phung* (?), *Maroti Mahangma phung* (*maroti*), *Mukkum phung Sayem phung* (Tulip), *Lilam phung* (?), *Minuri Sangdong phung* (?), *Singjango wetjango phung* (?), *Lekwama phung* (?) etc.

Now he invokes the mythical flower gods *Samboko Samhanglaba* and *Phungboko Phunglangaba* and invites for planting the flowers at different places of the Himalayas. The myth also demarcates their land of habitation. They first find the flower *Kawdi Leppetna phung* (?) and plant on a marshy place of drinking water but failed to grow over there. Now, they tried to grow this plant and planted on marshy place of the origin of *Tusroti Umroti Pumma* (Brahamputra River). The flower could not survive. Then, they tried to grow to *Mugangling Kangwama Pundho* (origin place of *Kangwama* river). There also the flower could not survive. Then, they planted on the origin of *Kettok Meywama Pundho* (*Meywa* River). The plant gave out atleast one leaf but could not survive. Then, they planted the plant (lotus) on the origin of *Sindolungma Ainametho*, the plant gave out two leaves but could not survive. Finally, they became successful in growing the flower plant only in the damp areas at the alpine basin of river *Aruna Baruna* (Arun River). The plants grew in due time and became a big tree whose branches shaded the land of all directions. Beautiful flowers began to bloom in the tree and birds began to come here. A beautiful maiden known as *Nettinhangma Phungdiwama* appeared there who was singing a song, plucking the flower and looked charming with flowers in her head. Another handsome young man from the northern land of *Sinyuk-Muden* (China-Tibet) also appeared there. He wanted to marry her and tried to please her. She hid in the flowers and could not find. He tried to bring lightening thunderstorm to destroy the flower and find out the maiden but failed. Then, a gentleman from low land named *Akwasoba Yangsotemba* married her. They gave birth to a beautiful maiden known as *Phungbokoma Phungyarimma Phungbokoma Phungphayemma*. Now, *Phungbako Phunglangaba* and *Samboko Samhanglaba* distributed the flowers to the people. A gentleman *Laik Khambuhang* made futile attempt to marry the maiden but she hid in the flower. In distress *Laik Khambuhang* directed *Phungbakko Phunglangaba* to cut down the flower-tree. While cutting down by axe, birds like *Sellokwa* (Himalayan barbet), *Supetruk* (dove), insects like *Mangnene* (cicada), *Yahangponghe* (big cicada), *Lalakhokcheng* (long sound producing insect) etc., appeared from every bit of the tree. These are the birds and insects of creating gloominess, sadness, and sentimentality. At another stroke, there appeared *Mangjiri Mangganjyaba* and *Mangjiri Mangganjyama*, two male and female singers, but they could not survive due to jealousy and envy. ***Chillima Pesumma Yea*** was invoked and finally the singer *Kewa Phungba* and *Mangdenhangba* came out from the chopped pieces of the flower tree. Then they became the singers of life flower revered by young men and women. One of the branches of the tree fell into the water and fisherman (*Yongjiyongba*) took it out. Various musical instruments were made from the branches. At the time of the falling of the tree, there also appeared *Yepling Kemba* and *Toring Kemba*, gardeners as well as singers of life. While felling the branches of the tree hit the offsprings of the flower gods and goddesses. They began to suffer from ailments. *Kewaphungba, Yepling Kemba, Toring Kemba* sang a song of flowers (life) and they became well again. Chanting this myth, *Sambas* or *Yeas* begin to sing the song of *Sekmuri* flower, a flower representing the human beings, to make it fresh and lively (Kainla, B. 1993; Shereng, Randhoj 1992; 1993; Subba, C. 1995: 156-211; Subba, J.R. 1999: 535-574; 2001: 149-158).

Mythological Functions

(i) Mystical: The mystery of human life is compared with a beautiful flower garden in *Yumaism*. Hence, the myth explains the mystery of the origin of flower growing – seeding, weeding, irrigating and transplanting in a suitable place and environment. Some flowers are useful while others are harmful to the human beings. And hence, the flowers are accumulated and separated. The harmful flowers are weeded out from the garden while the useful ones are grown, protected in the garden, so that the human garden always remain fresh, vibrant and blooming.

(ii) Sociological: The myth explains how the *Phedangmas* (the learned priest) help us to keep our flower garden (human life) always dynamic, vibrant and proactive in the society, supporting and validating certain social order set forth by our ancestors. He performs *Phungwa Changma* (refreshing the human flowers) rituals for the youths to add more and more human flowers in the garden once in every three years, in the absence of which we human beings fall illness, misfortune and distress. He accumulates and adds various flowers on the flower vase. It explains the natural human desire of youthfulness, desire of beautiful life-parters, and the desire of the songs of happiness. But life-flower cannot sustain blooming throughout. Sooner or latter, life ends with the songs of sadness which remains in our mind for ever as the day start with the Sun raise and end with the Sun set only to rise the next day.

(iii) Mystery of afterlife: The myth explains the dimension of the journey inward, the human psychology of youth, songs of happiness and sadness, the mystery of afterlife. Life is beautiful like flower but it is short.

(h) Myth of *Irere Idhuknama* and Origin of *Se-akkum A-akumnama*: *Sodhung Lepmuhang* and *Laoti Phungphahangma* (second wife of *Sutchhuru Suhangpheba*) gave birth to such mysterious son and daughter who had incestuous relation from the womb. They were *Pajoiba Tendhumyangba* and *Irere Idhuknama*. They also gave birth to two sons named *Lagerekpa* and *Namgerekpa*. Because of their incestuous relation, they were sent to another human world – *Khetchhuwa Upanga Pangbhe*.

When *Pajoiba Tentumyangba* and *Irere Idhuknama* became matured enough, they realized that they should not lead a conjugal life. *Idhuknama* suggested his brother to bring a wife from outside of consanguineous relation. He went to the north and brought a beautiful woman but because of his sister's jealousy and unhappiness, the woman went back. He went to all directions and brought a woman from each direction, but they all went back as they found his sister unhappy and envious to them. Finally, he went to *Yosugen Changenhangba Musagek Sagek Somellahang* (surpent king of the underworld) and brought his daughter *Lupli Adenhangma*. Their marriage became successful. The marriage was sanctified and observed with sacred contact in the presence of gods, tutelary deities, his father *Sodhung Lepmuhang*, ladies and gentlemen with certain condition of *Khemjong* and *Najong* (divorce agreement).

In due course of time, *Lupli Adenhangma* gave birth to a child, whom they named *Lapoti Laphungyangba Nampoti Namphungyangba* on the fourth day of his birth. He was also known as *Ekerang Takerang*. *Pajoi Tentumyangba* and *Lupli Adenhangma* used to go to work in their field (*Lunglengmaden Sathamaden*) and *Irere Idhuknama* had to look after the baby. Once while working in the field, milk began to flow from *Lupli Adenhangma's* breast and she remembered her child. She came back to the house at the daytime. All of a sudden, she heard that her child was crying and *Irere Idhuknama* was reviling the child as "a son of unknown father and promiscuous mother, heavy growing overnight, always crying, a son without a traceable descent, a son of a father who chops meat on the pillar" and so on. She was making the cradle swing by her foot with utter despise. *Lupli Adenhangma* got irritated and sad and told her husband all about it when he was in his bed at late evening.

Pajoi confirmed that his sister was ill-treating and slandering his child. He got so irritated that he wanted to kill her with his sword immediately, but *Lupli Adenhangma* stopped him to follow devious means. Following the suggestion of his wife, he went to the hill ridges and collected various kinds of flowers both good and ill causing. These were: *Pangboti phung* (jattamanshi), *Mukkum phung Kewa phung* (tulip), *Mahangma phung* (dahlia), *Kunori Lilamma phung* (lotus), *Miktikke Sambayo phung* (a climbing flower), *Sellengwa phung, Maroti phung, Ladok Namdok phung*, and *Ondong phung Sahetphung* etc. including *Soma phung* (ill causing flowers) and made eight bunches of flowers. He came home with bunches of beautiful flowers and distributed the good flowers to the young ladies. *Irere Idhuknama* was charmed by the beauty of the flowers and asked her brother to give her the flowers. He threw the ill causing bunch of flowers in her breast. She began to feel sickness with the pain in breast. She consulted all the *Phedangmas*, but none responded properly because of intimidation and graft of *Pajoi*. Her breast began to rot. *Pokthimba* (owl), a self-begotten *Yea* with a power of accuracy in divination (*Mangmangdi Yea Khakelon Yea*), came to her along with his retinue of *Khamputruk pu* (*Khamse-se*, Great scaly breasted Wren-babbler, *Pnoepyga albiventer*), *Chokhikpa* or *Chillikhey Pu* (drongo, *Dicrurus spp*), *Sulkhekma pu* (Minivet), etc. and told her the cause of her illness and, the day of her death. *Pajoi* came to know that *Pokthimba* had disclosed his wicked plan and cut off its head with his sword. But being a powerful shaman, its head was reconnected. He cut the tails and feathers of other birds and drove them away into the forest. Because of lack of cure, *Irere Idhuknama* died of breast rot (*angsuk nubun kire ang, yagu chongsi pero*). After her death she was named *Tetlara Laphiaongma*.

Lagerek and *Namgerek* kept the dead body of their mother on the banana leaves (*tetlawet lajongwet chongtho*) and tied it on bamboo bars which were tied again between two parallel bamboo poles. They took it to some far away place to bury. But *Khambongba-Lungbongba* (the first progeny of the earth i.e. autochthons), the owner of the land, did not allowed them to bury the corpse in the earth. They took the dead body of their mother to the river. But the creatures of the water protested them and warned that living beings of land are not allowed to destroy their corpses into the water. The two brothers went to the forest and thought of hanging their dead mother on a tree but the birds did not allow them to keep the corpse on a tree. Finally, they took the dead body in a mountain and placed it in a crevice. There was no custom of observing death rituals. Following this myth, the *Yuma* adherents perform *Kham-ingma* ritual (purchase of graveyard) at the time of burial of corpse from the owners of the land – *Khambongba Lungbongba*. The two brothers came back and began to work in their fields. But every morning they found that all their unfinished works were done perfectly. They were astonished and tried to find out the reasons. Two birds *Torona* (Koel, *Eudynamys scolopacea*) and *Khukwa* (Cuckoo, *Cuculus micropterus*), nestling in a *Hamyangsing* (a kind of fig tree) close to the field, told them that their mother comes at night and accomplishes the unfinished work. They watched the field at night and found her. The supernatural power of reanimating a corpse – *Zembie* told that she could not find the ways to the ancestral world and was roaming on the earth without a place to stick on or any destination to proceed to. She suggested her sons to ask their grandfather

Sodhung Lepmuhang for the ritual of formal separation of dead souls from the living ones and show her destination.

At about the same time, *Sodhung Lepmuhang* got the information of the death of her daughter from the hornet (*Mangjum Mangwa Kak*), a wasp (*Ijum Iwa Kak*), and a blue fly (*Lepmu Sikcha*) respectively and was confirmed by the last message. He came down to the land of his son *Pajoi* and killed his son and his daughter-in-law *Lupli*. His son became a thunderbolt (*Mundhang Seri*) and daughter-in-law a spirit of marshy land (*Senglama Yolama*) or a rainbow (*Namdhingo*). He even killed his grandson *Laphung Yangba Namphung Yangba* by knocking him down at the hearth (*Sumhatlung*) and pressed him under the earth by his foot at the bottom of the main pillar. The grandson called him and asked what mistake he had committed. Realizing the fact that his grandson was innocent, he granted a boon to him to become a divinity of main pillar- ***Saaklungma Akwanama***, protector of the house as well as household and told him that people will offer enough foods to satiate him. After killing his son, daughter-in-law and grandson, he was cooled down. He felt sad in the death of all his offspring. Tears rolled down through his checks. So, the ritual of cleaning tears by water (*Mikwa Sangma*) began since then.

Following the instruction of *Sodhung Lepmuhang*, his grandson *Lagerek* and *Namgerek* took out the dead body of their mother from the cave and buried in the soil below the fertile layer of the earth-purchasing graveyard from *Khambongba Lungbongba*. Then, they conducted *Samsama* ritual (ritual for reaching the soul to its destiny) inviting *Phedangmas* and observed mourning period for their mother for eight days from that day. Then, they got purified by the *Phedangmas* on the eighth day. They also constructed a cemetery (*cha-thi pimaden*) on the graveyard for the graveyard soul – *Sisam*, and a resting place (*cha-thi pimaden nu nasingma ten*) or platform (*Lagaklung kaklung* or *Koknambhe* and *Namgaklung kaklung Kaklung* or *Iknambhe Tembhe*) for resting of the *Pungsam* soul of the dead, which can be useful for resting for the passer bye later on. *Sodhung Lepmuhang* also instructed his grandsons to perform *Khauma, Sam chamma* and *Sitongsing khema* ritual at the presence of consanguineous as well as affinal relatives, villagers, clan leaders and elders at the end. He also told that only with these rituals, the soul of the dead is separated with the living beings. The myth also relates the material relationships between human beings and divinities. But because of vast differences in behavior, lifestyles, food habits, needs and exchanges of goals, the relationships and affinity between human being and divinities could not last long.

There is another myth on the vast differences in behaviour, lifestyle, food habits, needs and exchanges of goals. In early formative years the gods and goddesses (*Khambongba Lungbongba* – dwarfs) and human beings were together on earth. They used to get married each other and lived together. Once a man (human being) married a *Khambongba Lungbongba sa* (woman) and was living a happy conjugal life. One day the man, brother-in-laws and their friends went together for hunting. One group lead by the brother-in-laws (dwarfs) of the man drove the prey while other group lead by the man was ready to kill the prey if any from the other side. In the process, the man could not see any prey but saw only a small bird known as *Khamse-se* (*Pnoepyga albiventer*) coming towards him. He killed that bird and put it in his bag. He was looking for a bigger prey. After sometime his brother-in-law group reached to him and asked the prey. He said he did not see any prey. But the group tracked down the small bird prey to him and charged him for lying. He explained them that he was looking for a bigger prey but the brother-in-law's group did not believe it. Meanwhile they eviscerated the small bird and distributed amongst them. The man got the left thigh of the bird. He got back to home and angrily threw the meat to his wife. The meat broke the thigh of his wife. This event caused a quarrel between the man's group and the brother-in-law's (*Khambongba Lungbongba*) group and finally they decided to separate each other groups. They put a barrier between the two groups with several layers of banana leaves (*Lajum*) and then with ferns (*Kattakwa*) so that neither of the groups see each other. Thus the human beings and divinities separated each other due to their differences in behaviour, lifestyle, food habits, needs and exchanges of goals (Kainla, B. 1993; Shereng, Randhoj 1992; 1993; Subba, C. 1995156-211; Subba, J.R. 1999: 535-574; 2001: 12-30; 2003:377-414).

Mythological Functions

(i) Mystical: The myth elucidates the mystery of the followings:

(a) The mystery of origin of *Akwanama* – an important divinity of main pillar of the house in *Yumaism;*

(b) The mystery of system of the first marriage sanctified and observed with sacred contact in the presence of gods, tutelary deities, his father *Sodhung Lepmuhang,* ladies and gentlemen with certain condition of *Khemjong* and *Najong* (divorce agreement).

(c) The mystery of burial system of the corpse below the fertile layer of the soil;

(d) The mystery of protecting our environment (air, water, fertile soil and other living media of lives on earth) by a system of burial below the fertile layer of the earth surface for survival of all the living beings;

(e) The mystery of purchase of burial land from the gods and goddesses of soil - *Khambongba Lunbongbas,* the owners of that world below the fertile layer of the earth's surface;

(f) The mystery of the system of observing 8 (eight) days mourning for female and abstaining from eating pungent spices – ginger, garlic, salt, oil, meat, food etc. for the first time during the death pollution period;

(g) The mystery of separating the soul of the dead person from the living souls, accompanying the soul journey and handing over the soul of the dead person to the ancestor deity through the ritual of *Samsama, Khauma, Samchomma* and *Sitongsing Khema;*

(h) The mystery of system of purification of death pollution through *Khauma* for the first time; and

(i) The mystery of *Mikwa-Nangwa Sangma* (wiping away of the tears) from the mourners for the first time.

(ii) Sociological: The myth has offered a system of rituals to the adherents of *Yumaism* for all above (a) to (i) in the society. The myth is recited or chanted in all the cases of death, burial and death pollutions. The *Akwanama* is propitiated every now and then, as it is the boon bestowing and protecting divinity of every household.

(iii) Pedagogical: The myth has contributed the adherents of *Yumaism* a number of laws of life, ethical and other customary laws to be observed in the good society as above.

(iv) Mystery of afterlife: It has furnished the adherents of *Yumaism* belief system of afterlife, journey inward, physical consciousness transforming spiritual consciousness which takes place within 8 (for female) or 9 (for male) day after burial, concept of soul tradition (*Yetchham Thim*), soul journey to the ancestors (*Sam Yukna Den*), mistery of linkage to *Sangram Pedang Den* (heaven) and *Khema Yongsong Den* (hell) etc.

(i) Myth of *Kesami-Namsami* (Origin of *Yum sa Chama* ritual)

The myth of *Kesami-Namsami* is the story of two offspring of *Ipnana Sarengdhangma*, the sister of *Phaksera Tigenzongba – Khambongba Lungbongbas*. *Kesami* is the personification of an animal character (tiger-son in particular) while *Namsami* is the personification of a man (with human character) of the two sons of the woman. *Kesami* is also known as *Laphakke Phakkehang* and *Namsami* as *Mukkumyongba Warechongba*. Because of their contrasting conscience, attitude and opposite character, temperament and habit, it became impossible to live together for them as they grew up. Jealousy between them eventually brought them to a bitter fight of life and death. Deeply shocked by the tragic quarrel of her sons, *Ipnana Sarengdhangma* was watching the two flowers – the *Ondongphung* (*Ocimum basilicum*) representing the tiger or animal and *Sekmuriphung* (Celery, *Apium graveolens*/ Umbelliferae Family) representing the human being. *Namsami* was trained in using bow and arrow. He went to *Sapchong Tembhe* for hunting and finally reached *Subhawa Tembhe*. He climbed up to the eighth branch (*Yetporak*) of a *Tengosing* (*Bombax malabaricum*) and made a safe place to stay and launch an attack by arrows. *Kesami* arrived there tracing him throughout the hunting areas and started to climb the tree to kill his brother. *Namsami*'s seven arrows failed to strike him and reached almost close to *Namsami*. *Namsami* was left with only one arrow, the eighth one. So he thought of a trick and told his brother the tiger to open his mouth so that he would jump into his mouth. The tiger *Kesami* believed on his brother's request and open the mouth. In the meantime, *Namsami* threw his poisonous arrow in full speed into the mouth of *Kesami,* which struck the heart and the tiger fell down. He was not quite sure that his brother *Kesami* was dead. Because of fear, he waited till the flies began to buzz on the corpse. He came down from the tree and took out the skin out of the body. *Ipnana Sarengdhangma* found the *Ondongphung* withered away and confirmed that only her human son could survive. *Namsami* took the skin to *Kesalung Namsalung Kookma* and tried to dry it in the sun. But it did not dry up till it was taken to *Seho Namlang Tembhe, Angsarang* and was spread on the hot rays of the sun. When it was dried, *Namsami* went to different places showing the skin of the tiger and getting something in return. He went to north and brought salt, went to east and brought ginger and garlic, went to the west and brought foods and he went to the south and brought money and meat. Thus he collected salt, ginger, garlic, foods, meat and money by showing and exchanging the tiger skin. But both mother and son began to feel sick and become lean and thin when they ate all those things. His mother inquired about the things that he had brought from different quarters. *Namsami* told the truth and his mother called the gentlemen of the village to assemble and find out the way out for them. All the gentlemen and ladies of that land assembled and told them the instruction of *Sodhung Lepmuhang* about the death pollution to be observed and death rites to be conducted. They also told them that they have to restrain from them all those foods, spices and meat up to nine days as *Namsami* has brought those things by exchanging the skin of the tiger. They also instructed them to observe mourning and perform death rite, as the tiger was a brother of *Namsami.* They again assembled on the ninth day (now deteriorated to four in many places after the epidemic disease broke out causing death of several people during the first decade of nineteenth century) and conducted purification rite and allowed the mourners to take restricted or pungent foods again. *Phedangmas* say the tradition was established from this event. They also relate the myth of *Irere Idhuknana* and to follow the instruction of *Sodhung Lepmuhang* about the death pollution and death rites (Kainla, B. 1993; Shereng, Randhoj 1992; 1993; Subba, C. 1995: 213-234; Subba, J.R. 1999: 453-508; 2003:329-345).

Mythological Functions

(i) Mystical: The myth elucidates the mystery of the followings:

(a) The origin of a tradition of *Yum Sa Chama ritual* of abstaining from eating pungent spices – ginger, garlic, salt, oil, meat, food etc. during mourning period, and the mystery of purification of death pollution through *Khauma* and *Sitongsing Khema* (separating the soul of the deceased person) in *Yumaism;*

(b) The myth has identified a belief system of the human life-flower – *Sekmuri* (celery, *Apium graveolens*) and evil-flower *Ondongphung* (*Ocimum basilicum*) and the mystery of separating it.

(c) The mystery of the ritual tradition of observing 9 (nine) days mourning for male after burial (not after death day);

(d) The mystery and ritual tradition of separating the soul of the dead person from the living souls, accompanying the soul journey, and handing over the soul of the dead person to the ancestor deity through the ritual of *Samsama, Khauma, Samchomma* and *Sitongsing Khema* through *Phedangma*. The myth explains the destiny of life to be directed to the deceased soul otherwise it turns into *Letchham* (undestined soul).

(v) Sociological: The myth has yielded a social tradition to the adherents of *Yumaism* performing all above (a) to (d) rituals in every death in the society. The myths are recited or chanted in all the cases of death, burial and death pollution rituals.

(vi) Pedagogical: The myth has offered the adherents of *Yumaism* a number of ethical and other customary laws to be observed in the good society as above. The myth also elucidates that the effect of envy and jealousy to each other leads nowhere in the human society.

(vii) Mystery of afterlife: It has produced the belief system of afterlife, journey inward, physical consciousness transforming mental consciousness which takes place within 8 (for female) or 9 (for male) day after burial, concept of soul tradition (*Yetchham Thim*), soul journey to the ancestors (*Sam Yukna Den*), and the linkage to *Sangram Pedang Den* (heaven) and *Khema Yongsong Den* (hell).

(j) Myth of *Tongsing* or *Yagrangsing Phongma* (Soul Journey)

In the beginning of the ritual, *Samba* makes the introductory remarks in course of his myth recitation by mentioning that the creator god *Mujoklung Khejoklung Mang* sent *Phunjiri Phungappo Phedangma, Sajuwet Mudangwet Samba, Chillima Pesumma Ya, Nenjiri Nemmethum Ya, Langdimma Sodimma Ya* to the earth to save *Sawa Yethangs* and their progeny, the children, young men and women, the people in general. *Phedangma, Samba* and *Ya* came to the land of *Sawa Yethang* with all their necessary equipment and power of knowledge and skills. Following the great tradition of primordial *Phedangmas, Sambas* and *Yas,* the shamans, who is performing the ritual together with his associates, says that they have to do those jobs because they have been assigned to do them when they were in the wombs of their mother. He invokes his master spirits standing at the pole, beating drum or brass plates and often trembles violently. His associates always accompany him. He calls on the powerful spirits (*Sires*) of *Samudhung Yepmudhungma, Sumdang Tokmi* (elephant), *Phaet Nuget* (tiger), *Makyu Yongong* (bear), *Mangjum Mangwa* (hornet), *Irum Iwa* (a kind of wasp), *Sarum Sawa* (wild bees) to carry the *Tongsings /Yagringsings* and ask *Chillima Pesumma Sam* (collecting and leading soul) to collect the souls of everyone to start the journey in a swarm following the path of *Karangwa* (long distance flying migratory birds - flamingo) moving along the path just like a rainbow (*Namdhingo*).

The journey starts from the *Tongsings*. They move towards *Kesing* (bamboo altar) climbing the several steps there and then descend to the floor or courtyard. They enter the house (*PitchhuhimYandhahim*) and reach the main pillar where *Akwanama* stays and move towards the hearth (*Sumjiri Sumhatlung*). Then they proceed towards the hooks (*Segeng Thegeng Churima*) and small bamboo baskets hung on top of a hearth and to the sooty beams. They climb the upper story of the house and reach to the axle of the roof. From the ridge of the roof, *Samba* watches the village in the light of the moon and stars and tells what he has seen, whether good or bed signs, in the village.

The members of the journey consist of (Souls of *Sambas, Sanglangobas* -helpers, clients and their relatives, the master spirits etc.) descend from the *hangsitlang* (main pillar) to fireplace to the axle of the roof to the courtyard. They move towards ancestral land along the path through the hills covered by *Katekwa* (fern), *Namyoba* (*Artemisia vulgaris*), *Parsekpa* (*Saurauia napaulensis*), *Khesungba* (yeast plant, *Polygala arillata*), and many plants starting from lower elevation to higher elevation of the mountains. Sometime, they have to go through the shining path covered by *Sellobung* (*Thysanolaena spp.*), and sometime through the sunny path shaded by *Khechchingse* (Chestnut tree, *Castanopsis spp.*). Sometimes, they move through the path covered by white flowers of *Tabebung* (*Lyonia ovalifolia*) and through the jungles of *Khephunchhe, Yohibung* (*Quercus glauca*), *Yangsingba* (*Schima wallichi*), *Ajising* (*Bauhinia variegata*) etc. When they find *Sellobung, Muktubung* (*Neyraudia madagascariensis*), *Toppasing* (*Perrea gamblei*) and *Phangphangbung* (?), *Samba* recalls his *Sam Sire* (master spirit) with reverence. They must be careful, as there are spear grasses on the way. They also find *Hangangse* (*Ghorakhari*) trees covered by black fruits, even making the path dark and they must proceed cautiously as evil spirits stay or rest on these trees. They even find a place on the way covered by the flowers *Chuwat Phung* (Hyacinth, *Hyacinthus orientalis*), the flowers of dead persons, and they are supposed to take good care of all the souls not to miss or loose any. While moving ahead on the track, they reach to a place where the white flowers of *Kokphekla* (magnolia tree) and colourful flowers of *Thokphekla* (rhododendron) make the surrounding pleasant. They also find pine trees and places covered by mist and cloud in their ascending journey and they have to protect *Tuttu Tongsings* (men's *Tongsing*) and *Suhangma Tongsing* (women's *Tongsing*) from the wind and rain. Various kinds of birds and beasts can be seen on the way. While moving further towards the highland, there come a place full of springs where there are fountains in row. They are the fountains of Supreme Goddess *Tagera Ningwaphuma*, and fountains of *Tuttu Tumyanghang* (gentlemen), *Yakla Suhangma* (ladies), *Sawa Yechchham* (revered souls), *Siphak Yemi* (shamans) etc. These are the sources of clean water and the deep sanctuary of snake and tortoise divinities (*Se-ak Lungdhung Akwama Lungdhung*). There are also the villages of players of musical instruments, wood cutters and carpenters, bamboo-crafters, herders, potters and fair dames looking after poultry, piggery and weaving clothes. The team members of the journey should be careful with the broken pieces of earthenwares because the evil spirits may hide in these broken pieces. After crossing the beautiful land of fountains, they pass through the marshy land. There is a log just like a seesaw, placed on the track to cross the marshy land. They have to jump through it. In the meantime *Samba* lets the fire (*Mukkum semi*) to advance along the path to destroy the possible attacks of envy and jealousy (*Nahen*), as well as other evil spirits and clear the path. They ascend the steep slope following a narrow track and reach *Henjiri Hemponghe Chotlung*, a delightful place where the souls of the children play happily.

The journey further ascends crossing the shaded nook and corners and reaches the *Sisa Menchhin-Nali Thangben Yepmaden Chotlung*, a prestigious place of young men and women to enjoy, play and sing and thus make their life happy, meaningful and prosperous. Probably in the past, this was the place where young men and women assembled and sang songs to make the flower of life fresh and lively and young men used to play a game of throwing of a heavy stone *Ponglung* (shot-put) and women used to weave handloom. When they reach this place, *Samba* stops his myth recitation and begins to sing a *Hakpare* song (*Samlo*) and perform the ritual of *Phungwa Changma* (growing flowers). In this ritual, various divinities including *Sodhung Lepmuhang* and caretakers of the flower garden *Phungbakko Phung Letima, Phungjiri Phungwanama* and *Tibakkoma Tiannama* are invoked and the weeds and boulders are removed from the roots of the flowers by incantation to make the flowers ever fresh and brilliant. The owners (young maiden) of the *Phungsari* (small water vessel decorated with the bunch of flowers) carry their *Phungsari* on their head and make several rounds at the pole following the instructions of *Samba*. This ritual is performed to save the flowers from envious eyes and make the life illuminating and fascinating (Kainla, B. 1993; Shereng, Randhoj 1992; 1993; Subba, C. 1995:156-211; Subba, J.R. 1999: 535-574; 2001: 152-180; 2003: 415-431).

Mythological Functions

(i) Mystical: The myth explains the mystery of a system of the incarnate *Phedangmas* of *Yumaism* (shamans such as *Muhikkum Ongshi, Phejiri Phedangma, Sambokko Samba, Yebokko Yeba, Yebokko Yema*) for transcendenting the physical consciousness to spiritual consciousness for divination and performing such rituals which require trance, ecstasy, soul journey, handing over the souls to deities, blocking the evil spirits, calling the master spirits and asking them to perform some spiritual works etc. The shamans cannot perform the aforementioned works unless he or she is capable and transcendenting his or her physical consciousness to spiritual consciousness with the help of his or her incarnate soul (*Yeming* or *Sam Sire* or *Samudhung Yempmudhung*). They are collectively known as *Siphakyemi sa* (people having souls of the dead person, reincarnated in the new body).

(ii) Cosmological: The shamans have their own cosmological worlds/*Lokas*/ *Dens* in the universe as "the *Akashic* fields" in the atmosphere or "underground world/*Lokas*/*Dens*" where they perform transcendent journey with living or dead souls, and master spirits in spiritual consciousness.

(iii) Sociological: The myth has contributed a numerous rituals in the society.

(iv) Pedagogical: It has provided the laws of life, ethical laws and other customary laws in the society.

(iv) Mystery of afterlife: It has expounded the dimension and belief systems of the journey inward, the human psychology of soul origin, physical consciousness transcendenting to spiritual consciousness, concept of soul journey to different *Akashic* fields and underground world, reincarnation of the souls of the dead persons etc.

(k) Myth of *Ponglung Lepma* (throwing of shotput)

Ponglung Lepma (throwing of shotput/stone) is a prestigious game representing the adventurous endeavour of young people. Today it is performed as ritual in the reminiscence of divine attempt attached with prestige and welfare of humankind. According to its myth, a great wave of desecration passed over the earth. To cause a rain, *Porokmi Wambhami,* the creator god, threw *Ponglung* towards the end of the earth aiming at the horizon. It stroke at *Sakhonglung Khongwa Lakhonglung Khongwa* and broke the earthen pot, which caused rain, and thus the earth was freed from draught. Before throwing the stone from *Iwa Hara* (*Siphak Tigenjong/ Horana Tembhe*), he came in contact with *Khambongba Lungbongbas – Laphingjong Namphingjong* that he had to cross the limit set by them and the stone should not be broken. If the stone did not cross the limit, that would cause downfall and humiliation and if the stone is broken into pieces, they would turn into evil spirits and ominous planets causing harm to the stone thrower according to the condition agreed by both partners. It was also agreed that if the thrower succeeds in his attempt, that would mean a victory, progress and prosperity. *Sakphera Tigenjongba* (one of the *Khambongba Lungbongba*) set the trail limits and *Porokmi Wambhami* crossed the limits every time, eventually breaking the earthen pot full of water. By this attempt of the creator god of *Ponglung Lepma*, the earth became verdant. Following this myth, young men have to perform this ritual imitating the action of throwing stone to some particular distance according to the instruction of the *Sambas* (Kainla, B. 1993; Shereng, Randhoj 1992; 1993; Subba, C. 1995156-211; Subba, J.R. 1999: 535-574; 2001: 177-181; 2003:448-463).

Mythological Functions

(i) Mystical: The myth describes the mystery of how the creator god *Porokmi Wambhami* or *Yembhami* played a shotput game to bring the wind, thunderstorm and rain in order to germinate the plant seeds on earth, and make the earth vibrant with plants and thereby enabling the survival of other living beings. It also explains how the survival of gods and goddesses and animals including man are closely associated with the survival of the plants. The oxygen given out by the plants in the atmosphere is essential for survival of animals while the carbondioxide given out by the animals in the atmosphere is essential for the survival of the plants. The mutual benefit of the plants and animals is what the myth explains for the existence of both the species in this physical world.

(ii) Cosmological: The myth has a cosmological origin.

(iii) Sociological: The myth has provided the society the ritual of *Ponglung Lepmma* to be performed once in every three years during *Tongsing Tookma* ritual. It has also provided us the sport of shot put game. It has also provided us a variety of plants for multiple uses for human survival.

(iv) Pedagogical: The myth has furnished laws of life for survival, ethical laws of protecting the plants, forests etc., and customary and religious laws for the use of plants in various religious rituals, house construction, use as food-crops, use as good and evil flowers etc.

(v) Mystery of afterlife: The myth interprets the journey inward, the physical conciousness transforming into spiritual consciousness and journey of souls.

(*l*) Myth of *Khema Tongsing Semma* (separating the *Tongsing* of the dead persons)

After presenting the flowers of young people at their place of *Chotlung* (prestige and perfection) – *Sang Odhamlung Pangbhe* (*Sangphiriphiri Lingphiriphiri Pangbhe*), the journey moves ahead crossing a river. The river is known as *Sadhunge Thungwama Ahang* and described as a border between phenomenal and nominal world. The god of that river is known as *Makchiso Kulang Kemba* who allows constructing a bridge over the river to let pass the souls and controls the wayfarers of two worlds. *Samba* has to invoke this god to build a bridge while crossing it and not to let evil spirits to come back to earth while coming back after completing the rituals in the supernatural or nominal world. *Achumbung Aroti Mang, Singsara Taoding Mang* is invoked to build a bridge (*Singsa Tayo*) on the river so that they can go further upward. *Samba* now being afraid of evil spirits, ill motives, traps and attempts of envious others to make them unsuccessful, sends the fire (*Mukkum Semi*) to clear the path. The paths are narrow and look like sharp edge of a sword. Sometimes it looks like a cleft similar to the print of cow's hoof and sometimes as way of waterless canyons. The team of the journey moves even upward and reaches the crossroads of three paths (*Sumlamdo*). These are the paths of (i) *Sasik Yangdang* (spirits of stillbirths), (ii) *Naso Thappan* (devils, witches etc.) and (iii) their own path leading to *Chotlung*. They have to follow their own path by the right hand side.

They ascend further and reach another crossroads of eight paths (*yetlamdo*) with their shining equipments. Again the paths of (i) *Sogha* (spirits of unnatural deaths) and *Sugut* (spirits of women died while giving birth to a child); (ii) *Khema Yongsong Pangbhe* – Ancestor's Village (world of dead souls of normal death); and (iii) *Mangs* (Deities), *Sammang* (Divinities) and *Sam Sire* (master spirits) separate from the crossroad. The *Samba* and his assistants reach the souls of respective deaths while conducting death rituals through the ritual of *Sitongsing*. The path of *Khema Yongsong Pangbhe* is covered over by the trees of *Chongjipbung* (*Gurpis, Leucosceptrum canum*) and *Medibung* (*Lekh Chandan, Mahonia napaulensis*). *Samba* blocks all the paths leading to evil spirits invoking his *Sam Sire* and follow the main path from right hand side. Now the *Samba* invokes the *Phupuruba Tagesemba*, the divinity of separating the paths, and performs the ritual of separating the *Tongsing* of dead persons from the living ones. He cuts the thread, which joins the two sticks representing the *Tongsing* of living and the dead persons. He takes out the *Khema Tongsing* (sticks representing the dead persons) along with the soil where it is planted and cuts into pieces with the sword and throws away in the western side. He washes the *Tongsing* (*Muksing*) of living persons with clean water and performs the ritual of purification of his clients and their relatives. Death ritual of *Mikwa Sangma*, dealt elsewhere, is related with this ritual. Purification is done with the branches of some *Sapsing* (*Jhankri Kaulo*) by sprinkling the water of eight sources of eight directions or *wadumbokwa* on each of the family members of ritual organizers and the branches are also thrown away in the west. The ritual of destroying the bridge over a river on the way to *Khema Yongsong Pangbhe* is also performed and it is believed that the dead souls cannot return back to earth due to lack of bridge.

Thus leaving the path of dead persons, they move forward (upward) from the central path carrying rest of their equipment. Still the path looks difficult and winding. They reach to (iv) *Henjiri Hembonge Chotlung* (symbol of power, prestise and progress), which is a *Chotlung* of children and the souls of children are placed before it. Then they move again upward and reach at the center – (v) *Sangphiri Lingphiri Pangbhe, Chotlung* of young men and women, where the young men throw *Ponglung* and the young women weave the looms at close to the spring called *Sangsanglung Saodham*. On the left hand side, there is a path leading towards the land of origin of *Phedangmas, Sambas*, and *Yas*, a land of their *Chotlung* (power, perfection and prestige), which is known as (vi) *Sengwalung Ngekwalung* (*Siphakjong Sakphera Pangbhe*). Now the *Sambas*, together with his assistants, reach that place and rest for a while there. He performs the invocation ritual of his *Sam Sire* (master spirits) offering an upper portion of the pig carcass (*Hoktang*) on the altar built at the top of the pole. Before the sacrificial ritual, they thrash the new crops from its plants, measure the quantity, husk it, winnow it and offer to all divinities, *Sam Sires* such as *Telele Tenjiyep, Merumna Yeyangna*, etc. and *Ke* (drum). Four young men and five young women participate in the rice pounding drama (*Yia Hakma, Thamma, Yekma, Somma*) following the instructions of *Samba* and they perform their circumambulating the pole several times. This dramatization of rice pounding gave rise to *Yia Lakma* (paddy dance) tradition in the *Limboo* community.

They again come to the crossroads and begin their journey towards the land of ancestors by equipping themselves with all their paraphernalia. Eventually they reach the land of peace and perfection, the land of the sun and the moon, the land of accomplishment and fulfillment (*Lingpitma Den, Podema Den*), a sacred place with enchanting scenery (*Niyara Numa Sesema Den*). It is the destination of the journey and a place of (vii) *Chotlung* of ladies (*Yakla Suhangma*) - *Yosu Padam Lungma*; and (viii) *Chotlung* of gentlemen (*Tuttu Tumyang*) – *Thosu Wadhan Lungma*. The ritual of shaking the *Tongsing* of women decorated with necklaces and *Tongsing* of men decorated with swards conducted for their prosperity and well-being (Kainla, B. 1993; Shereng, Randhoj 1992; 1993; Subba, C. 1995:156-211; Subba, J.R. 1999: 535-574; 2003: 432-447).

Mythological Functions

(i) Mystical: The myth describes the mystery of the soul journey and the detail route of physical consciousness along with the souls of both living and dead person, and master spirits transcending to spiritual consciousness. The team crosses the river separating the phenomenal and nominal world, then lead to the crossroad of three paths, then leads to the crossroad of eight paths. The *Phedangma* then separates the soul of the dead person from the souls of the living members of the team and hand over the soul of the dead person to the ancestor deity.

(ii) Cosmological: In the myth the *Phedangmas* (shamans) have their own cosmological "*Akashic* fields" or worlds/*Lokas*/*Dens* and underworlds or /*Lokas*/*Dens* where they perform soul journey in the spiritual consciousness.

(iii) Sociological: The myth has furnished a number of rituals in the society, such as *Samsama, Tongsing, Samchamma, Nahangma,* etc.

(iv) Pedagogical: It has interpreted laws of life, ethical laws and other customary laws in the society.

(v) Mystery of afterlife: It has provided number of belief systems such as soul journey, origin of soul, joining of soul to the ancestors in the afterlife, mystery of *Sangram Pedang Den* (heaven) and *Khema Yongsong Den* (hell) etc.

(m) Myth of *Warak Tingma* (Filling up of the Lake of life)

Sodhung Warak (lake of life) represents the life of human being. *Samba* chants the myth and performs the ritual of filling up this lake. He makes the barrage strong enough by putting more soils of various places for barricading. The lake must be full of water. So he brings the water of the great oceans situated in four different directions, water of different rivers, fountains and wells and pour into the lake. Now the lake becomes full of water and the earth becomes verdant. The flowers look fresh and nice. But that is not enough. Again he has to put fishes and various aquatic animals into the lake along with small rocks (*Pokla Lunglang*) to make places for fishes to live, rough and smooth sands (*Siyengha Thiyengha Lung*) and black and white stones (*Phagiyalung, Makkhiyalung*) to make places for fishes to play. Now the lake becomes perfect and full of every thing. Envy and jealousy (*Tingding Nahen*) may cause harm to it. So he closes the path of envious spirits all around it. Finally, he invokes the goddess *Muaklungma Akwanama Khesewana Wapharama* to protect and look after the lake. This ritual has lead to rear a white hen in the house. The meat is forbidden to eat but the meat of its progeny can be eaten. A ritual of *Phungwa Lingma* (growing flowers) is also performed for adults at this place of *Chotlung*. The plants of the flowers are weeded, new soils are added, and water is sprinkled on them.

Now the travelers (souls of the men and women clients, *Samba* and his assistants) of the journey reach the destination - *Chotlung*. *Samba* performs various rituals at this place of enjoyment, dancing and vociferations (*Ihuma Den Tenduma Den*). He invokes *Mujoklungma khajoklung* (creator god), *Sodhung Lepmuhang* (tutelary deity), *Kamboling Nehangma* (power divinity), *Harara Pitchhama* (goddess of dance and skill), *Tagera Ningwaphuma* and *Tiwakoma Tianghangma* (vigilant goddess) to guard the place and not to allow the *Khakchum Soba* (monkey) and *Muphik Phikwa* (kite) to enter there. Then, he asks all souls to raise and get assembled and start the descending journey back to the *Kesing* (altar). They have to come down by the same path requesting *Samdang Khewa* (pheasant) and *Lingdang Khewa* (partridge) to confuse the track for evil spirits and *Makchiso Kulangkemba* to drag at their feet. They drive down like hawks without leaving anyone behind. After the description of descending journey *Samba* invokes various divinities to offer blessings on his clients (Kainla, B. 1993; Shereng, Randhoj 1992; 1993; Subba, C. 1995156-211; Subba, J.R. 1999: 535-574).

Mythological Functions

(i) Mystery: The myth describes the mystery of *Sodhung Warok Tingma* (barricading the lake) comparable with human life in the spiritual consciousness. The lake of life should always be kept filled with water. To beautify and make the barrage of the lake strong enough, soils are brought from different places, water is brought from different places and added in full, fishes are added, stones of various types are brought and added in it etc.

(ii) Sociological: It has unfolded the concept and belief system of *Chotlung* (a place of power, prestige and energy) of every individual. The myth is recited/chanted in every *Tongsing* ritual in the society.

(iii) Pedagogical: It has furnished us the customary law. If some one is insulted he has to provide *Mangenna* or *Nahangma* for raising his or her head high.

(n) Myth of *Silam Sakma* (Blocking the path of death)

When the people of *Sawa Yethang* land began to suffer from various illnesses and death in the formative years, they approached the Supreme Goddess *Tagera Ningwaphuma* for help. She sent *Sigonda Thegonda Samba* to the earth to cure illness and avoid deaths. He came to the earth and turned down the deaths at *Chimling Hara Tembhe* where some of the progeny of *Sawa Yethang* were living. They again began to suffer from the pangs of sorrows and untimely deaths. They again went to the Supreme Goddess and the Goddess sent *Thappura Theyonge Samba* to that land. The primordial *Samba* performed the ritual of blocking the paths of death by using a special instrument made of tasseled sticks of *Muktubung* (*Neyraudia madacascarensis*) placed in crossed position and tied by thread and a net weaved around it.

Today this ritual is performed with sacrifice of a pig. One rupee silver coin also is thrown in overturning motion in the open air to let it fall on the ground and the overturning of a coin in the expected side is believed to have blocked the path of death. *Samba* distributes the symbol of *Silam Sakma* to all of his clients chanting the myth. They take it with them in their home and keep at the top of the hearth or door so that death will not enter into their houses (Kainla, B. 1993; Shereng, Randhoj 1992; 1993; Subba, C. 1995156-211; Subba, J.R. 1999: 535-574).

Mythological Function

(i) Mystical: The myth of mystery provides the belief system of curing illness and blocking the path of untimely death in the household/clan.

(ii) Sociological: It is recited or chanted in every *Tongsing* ritual in the society. It has furnished the individuals a symbol of *Silamsakma* batch or a symbol of the society of *Yumaism* adherents.

(iii) Pedagogical: It has provided a customary law of hanging a *Silam Sakma* symbol at the main door of the house.

(o) Myth of *Tingding Nahen* (Envy and Jealousy)

Tingding Nahen is one of the most frightening evil spirits for the *Limboos*. Failures and most of the ailments are attributed to this spirit. This ritual is conducted for easy life free from illness and other fatal epidemics, as well as for good health and long life, better crops and prosperity, abundance of livestock, solidness of food grain, expectation of off springs and annihilation of enemies and envious persons. This ritual is either performed in the beginning or at the end of any ritual.

The myth of *Tingding Nahen* (envy and jealousy) originates right from brothers of *Sawa Yethang* at their land when the youngest brother *Shechhere Senihang* was much favoured by his father *Sodhung Lepmuhang* than other brothers. This was followed by the envy and jealousy of the wives of *Sawa Yukphung Kemba.* The *Nahen* was added up as the descendants of *Sawa Yethang* increased. Thus, the *Sawa Yethang* descendants started suffering from *Nahen.* They went to the Supreme Goddess *Tagera Ningwaphuma* and asked for suggestion. She asked them to go to *Sodhung Lepmuhang. Sodhung Lepmuhang* sends *Sambas – Mikhappu Chama Thekong Samba* and *Namdhingo Suyekten Samba* for protection of *Sawa Yethangs.* However, the descendants of *Sawa Yethang* continued to suffer from *Tingding Nahen.* They again went to *Sodhung Lepmuhang* and brought *Sajara Ya Lungdongba Ya.* He licked and ate away *Tingding Nahen* of various types such as *Tingding Nahen* of diamond, pearl, precious minerals, land, plants, youth, water, soil, divinities, etc. from the descendants of *Sawa Yethang* and thus they were made free from *Tingding Nahen.*

Following this myth the people now, perform *Tingding Nahen Sakma* ritual (blocking envy and jealousy). To bar the path of *Tingding Nahen,* the branches of the plants of *Sidingba* (*Mimosa rubicaulis*), *Manglokpa* or *Henchhing* (*Erythrina indica*) and banana plant are planted in one line on the cross paths or at the main path where the track from the house of *Tongsing* performers meet and the sticks of *Muktu* (*Neyraudia madagascariensis*), branches of *Sapsing* and *Yukmiba* (*Ricinus spp*) are interlaced horizontally as well as vertically. *Samyok* (*Cynodon dactylon*) is planted at the bottom of the plants. A winnowing tray made of bamboo splits is kept there and is covered by banana leaves and a *Phungsari* (flower vase) and an egg are placed on the cushion of the banana leaves. Various household goods believed to be the sources of envy and jealousy are also kept there. *Samba, Yeba* or both, with their assistants perform the ritual by sacrificing a black coloured cock and its blood drops are sprinkled on the banana leaves. They worship *Tibakko Tiannama* who looks after *Tongsing,* help to drive away evil spirits and become *Akwanama* to save the house, and they offer millet beer, liquor, husked rice grains and the head, wings and legs of the cock to her. At the same time, her associates such as *Khanjoma*, the female divinity of low land, *Warakma*, female divinity of water or lake, and *Toksongba*, the hunter divinity of high-land are propitiated by offering chickens. It is believed that these divinities cause natural calamities, various sorts of pernicious epidemics, famine, minor illness or major diseases and many other problems if they are not duly propitiated (Kainla, B. 1993; Shereng, Randhoj 1992; 1993; Subba, C. 1995:156-211; Subba, J.R. 1999: 535-574; 2001: 192-199; 2003:452-469).

Mythological Functions

(i) Mystical: The myth describes the mystery of origin of envy and jealousy in the society and it is believed that the cause of failures and most of the ailments are attributed to this spirit.

(ii) Sociological: The myth has provided to society the ritual of conducting it for easy life free from illness and other fatal epidemics, as well as for good health and long life, better crops and prosperity, abundance of livestock, solidness of food grain, expectation of off springs and annihilation of enemies and envious persons. The *Samba* or *Ya* block the path of the spirit of envy and jealousy by performing the ritual.

(p) Myth of *Tappheng* (proprietary rituals of nature divinities)

Pappheng is a proprietary ritual of nature divinities for the protection of family or clan members specially the children. It is conducted almost every six months during low season (at the time of cherry bloom season) and high season (at the time of peaches bloom season) or at least once a year. It is also known as a ritual of defending oneself from evil spirits causing various illnesses. In this ritual, various divinities are invoked and sacrifice rituals are held. Most important among them are *Mundangwa Siringwa Sammang* or *Misekpa Sammang*, *Makchiso Manglangba Sammang - Tambhungna* including her retinue, *Chheppuwama Samenja Patnayoba Thimendhung Mangshengla – Piporima Yangkhonjoma*, *Warakma* and *Toksongba*. The myths of these nature divinities are as follows:

(i) Myth of *Mundangwa Siringwa* or *Misekpa Sammang*

It is a hunter's divinity. It is popularly known as *Pung Sammang* also. The divinity described as *Tasanglaba* appeared at

Soraba Aplangwa Pumma and propitiated by *Sajara Lungdang Ya*. Other nature divinities are propitiated to ward off them, but it is propitiated to come and accompany the hunter to chase wild animals. Hunters have to offer the drops of blood or some small pieces of meat of the hunted animal to it first. It is the god of fire or lightening as well as thunderbolt causing rain. It is usually propitiated offering egg or chicken for protection from heart attacks, accidents, respiratory problems, epidemics, calamities and other illnesses. *Tanghangba Phedangma* was the first to propitiate this divinity. Since then every hunter have to invoke him while entering into the forest. The nature divinity (god of forest, hills and mountains) is the son of *Lagurung Namgurung* born from *Lahi Namhi* (planets). When *Namba* (Sun) fell down at *Kejiko Kelanga Pun* (*Siringwa*) due to the arrow shot by the porcupine, the blood of the Sun manifested into this god. He has one *chyang* known as *Hilly Yaksosaba* to whom he pushed down from the steep rocks and died.

(ii) Myth of *Tambhungna*

This natural divinity is believed to be an eternal and all pervading female divinity having more malevolent roles than benevolent character. She is considered as mistress of the earth or nature (*Laje Dangma*), and goddess of the forest (*Tambhungna*). She is propitiated as the controller of natural phenomena. Forest, trees, precipices, caves, thickets are her abode. When some rituals are performed outside the house, it is necessary to propitiate her to protect the rituals from evil spirits and their obnoxious acts.

She was originated from the blood-drops of the Sun (*Wasa Namba*) fallen on *Sungsa Kharda Tembhe*. Once she was wandering in the hill areas, *Makchiso Kulang Kemba*, chief of the *Kui-kudap* came there in course of hunting. She turned into a deer and began to run into the forest. *Makchiso* followed her and shot his arrow aiming at her. The dear turned into a beautiful maiden. As he came there to grab his prey, he found a dead body of a pretty girl in spite of deer. He was amazed and felt that he has killed his sister. He tried to resurrect her. He took the dead body to the confluence of seven or eight rivers and asked *Koka Mang* (*Phakmurama*) to give her life back again. When she became alive, *Koka Mang* told them to marry (*Igeding Chumding*) each other. But *Makchiso* wanted to treat her as sister. So, he refused to marry her. *Koka Mang* kept both of them into a closed room (*Wayading Saksang*) for several days. Thus they came in physical contact and gave birth to *Cheppuwama Samenja Patnayo* and *Thimendhung Mangsenghang*.

Tambhungna visited from place to place. Nobody knew her. She began to stay at *Khamlung Tana Phukko* (cave by the hill-side of the river-*Embiri Thangwama* or *Yangthangwa*) and started to trouble to progeny of *Sawa Yethang*. *Samdangwa Karangwa Phedangma* identified her as *Tambhungna –Yobadangma* (mistress of the earth), *Senjekum Semmethumma* (mistress of the day), *Yakwadangma-Hangwadangma* (mistress of agriculture and good luck or power), *Mangwadangma* (protector goddess). She is also regarded as *Yetchillekma, Phangchillekma* – a pretty woman in eight-nine forms. She is prayed with due ritual before starting the agricultural activities in the field and after the crops get ready for storage asking for bumper crops.

She is known to cause various illness dizziness, nausea, vomiting, etc. She is usually propitiated with eggs and fried unhusked rice (*Chebhong*) sprinkling pure water around the place of worship. She is sometimes propitiated with three full grown chicken and three eggs put in small bamboo baskets (*Phurlung*). She is usually addressed as the mistress or sovereign of fish, honeycomb of wild bees, varieties of crops and fruits. It is believed that she captures the soul (*Pung Sam*) of human beings and hands over to *Khonjoma*. When the soul comes under the captivity of *Khonjoma*, it is difficult to recover.

Tambhungna has several off springs or *Chyangs*. They are *Samyang Nondangwa, Yuppa Nondang Yetnondang, Aphanacho, Chomanama, Simijangma, Tajumbowa Takeyokpa, Lichumbowa Likeyokpa, Samenja Pannayoba Thimendhung Payonama* (*Mangsekrama*), *Harandi Yojammasa* etc. It is also believed that *Tambhungna* is a composite term of seven young sisters remains sited on the right flank of *Singbung* (*Devithan*). Out of the seven, the three namely *Latibureni, Chomkibureni* and *Bonbureni* execute the commands of causing illness and harm to the people. However, the opinion varies from place to place and person to person on *Tambhungna*.

(iii) Khonjoma or Senghama

Pipporima Yangkhonjoma or *Khonjoma* or *Senghama* is a divinity of low land of the south, originated from the blood of the Sun -

Yukling Namba which fell on *Toi Namdha Lungma* rocks of the west. She is the divinity who brings the curses to fruition. She is also a source of power and strength. She is also invoked as the mistress of the earth. If she is not propitiated properly she causes illness of eyes, nose, throat and various organs, dizziness and other mental problems. *Phatrahang Phedangma* identified her as divinity coming from the low land to the hill regions to cause illnesses to those who do not propitiate her. Most *Phedangmas* say that it is difficult to bring back some one's soul if captured by her. Her altar was made in *Liwado Lisum Thegukokma* (*Charkhola Chukchuli*) to propitiate her for the first time and the ritual included the sacrifices of a chicken preferably a black one, a pig and egg offering.

(iv) Toksongba

Toksongba is a powerful divinity of high mountains and hunters. He is a *Sammang* or a god of divinities. *Toksongba Sammang* or *Toksang Lawa Lisang Lawa* was originated from the blood of the Sun - *Sikire Namba* when it fell on *Mundakkum Sewa Chong* mountain. All *Limboos* irrespective of their *Sammang* background or clan revere him. All inhabitants of high lands also revere him. *Tanghang Penkhang* met him and began to worship him. His altar is on *Sekthok Nangthok Kookma*, a mountain top where snow falls usually. He has an associate *Thosangla Lisangla* (also a *Chyang*). He is invoked for bestowing power and success for adventurous attempts.

(v) Warakma

It is a female divinity of lake (*warok*) recognized by *Sunamal Ongsi* of *Kedemba* group (clan) of *Limboo*. In her propitiation rite, it is said that she is a Supreme master spirit (*Mangmangwa Sire Kedhumma*) – *Sibhakyami Phokwama*, who came down from *Sodhung Lepmu Tembhe* to a pleasant place at the confluence of *Mangmanwa* River and *Maiwa* River where *Yas* of various localities were assembled and they were performing a wonderful dance. She also began to dance with them. But the *Yabas* and *Yemas* did not recognize and reckon her. She caused them to cease trembling and possession and moved to other places where *Yebas* and *Yemas* were dancing and trembling. The same thing happened, as they did not recognize her. She flew away where she was finally injured by Shamans of other pantheon and thrown away into the river. She came out of the water in the plain areas and collected various spirits of low land to form a retinue. She climbed the hills and made her abode at *Sangphi Lingphi* lake. As nobody cared her, she caused illness of cold, heat, severe pains in different parts of the body, stomach swelling, food poisoning, dizziness, headache etc. to the local people. In course of the divination, *Sunamal Ongsi* identified her as *Pharere Phawessangma, Maklere Makwaisangma, Sangphi Lingphi Warakma* and propitiated her with black chicken to save the local people. The place is still known as *Warak* in *Miwakhola*.

(vi) Tenchhama

Tenchhama is also a divinity of low land originated from the blood of *Kambong Namba* (*Lahi Namhi*) fallen at *Mujiri Mulung Thajiri Thalong*. She is also revered as the mistress of the earth and controller of the nature. She is propitiated by offering uncooked rice, egg, millet beer and a male chicken. She causes pain in stomach, joints, dizziness, and headache if not propitiated (Kainla, B. 1993; Shereng, Randhoj 1992; 1993; Subba, C. 1995: 156-211; 236-290; Subba, J.R. 1999: 509-574; 2001: 1-11; 2003:20-101).

Mythological Functions

(i) Mystical: The myth describes the mystery that the earth (*Iksading Khambek*) is inhabited not only by human beings, plants and animals but also by gods, goddesses, and natural divinities or spirits (both malevolent and benevolent), and they dwell in all places of rivers, streams, rocks, plants, trees, stones, soils, forests, lakes, ocean, caves, mountains etc. The myth unfolded that many of such natural divinities have been identified, which forms an important part of natural mythology. The myth traces each of its origin, the *Phedangmas* (the shaman priests) who identified it and performed rituals for harnessing the benefit out of these divinities or propitiated for cure or healing sickness, or avoiding its harmful effects etc. for the first time.

(ii) Cosmological: The myth illustrates that most of these divinities have cosmological origin.

(iii) Sociological: The myth has furnished a number of proprietary rituals to be performed from time to time in the society.

(iv) Pedagogical: It has interpreted ethical laws of protecting, sustaining and giving due respect to all living and non-living things in nature.

Myths of *Sappok Chomen* (Ceremonies Preceding the Birth)

It is a rite of womb worship for the protection of a child in the uterus. It is also a rite of propitiating gods for the good health of the mother and baby in the womb as well as successful delivery of the baby. There are wonderful descriptions in the myth of *Mujina Kheyongnama* that reflect the psychology of pregnancy. These accounts show the physical as well as psychological condition of an expectant mother. There are several such instances, which draw attention towards pregnant women to take care of her. The myths of *Sappok Chomen* includes (i) myths of *Muiyan Sire, Miyong Sire, Tingding Nahen, Sogha, Sugut, Sasik Yangdang;* (ii) *Kui-Kudap*, a group of nature divinities; (iii) *Him Sammang* (guardian divinities) including *Theba Sammang;* and (iv) *Apchara Pakchanama, Wagongma,* and *Mangenna.*

There is a group of divinities known as *Kui-Kudap*. They are *Mundangwa Siringwa, Tenchhama, Khanjoma, Wajangma* and *Toksongba*. These divinities are known as nature divinities as well as hunter divinities and are believed as having a prominent role to cause infliction of pain and sufferings to human beings. Altar for each of the divinities is constructed on a clean elevated floor and covered with banana leaves. A stone is erected along with two small sticks poles on the altar for *wajangma*. One pair of bamboo sticks filled with water and fermented grain (*peheng*) representing *Tongba* are placed on the altar decorated for each divinity. A pair of chicken, both male and female and two eggs are necessary for each of the divinities, but a well grown-up male chicken is enough for *Toksangba*. The myths of these divinities have been described under myths of *Tappheng*.

(i) Myth of *Yuma Sammang*

There are variations in the myth of *Yuma Sammang* from place to place and from person to person with the special emphasis on their own geographical context and myth of the clans who perform the ritual. The myth of *Yuma Sammang* is a long one, but *Phedangma* makes it short according to his or her convenience.

She first appeared as *Kangohangma* in *Mangjiri Mangowet* (Mongolia?), to protect the human beings. Then, she moved to *Sinyuk Muden* and *Lhasa Tembhe* (plateau of China and Tibet?) along with her retinue. Again she moved to the southern side and reached to a big lake at *Wailasho Phullaso* surrounded by hills – *Tangwara Pengwaphang*. She broke the lake and went further to the south and reached the confluence of three rivers where she took bath. She appeared in several places such as *Yadakkum Sewachang, Hangchum Hangwa Pangbhe, Kesalung Namsalung Kokma,* with her looms, and reached *Yetchiri Yet Ado* (confluence of eight rivers) to take bath, and again appeared in *Laikkum Khambu Pangbhe, Thimendhung Payo Pangbhe, Takhokma Tembhe* (plain region), *Kochia-Mechya Pangbhe, Takhong Tembhe* of *Marong Hang* and finally in *Yashok*. Several names including *Manjiri Manganjyangba,* primordial member of human race and *Uba, Chyangba, Khechiba, Thapmiya, Muregan, Libhukpa Phedangma, Waresu Lingkhim Hang, Samdangwa Karangwa Phedangma, Senchhengo Nuphedap Hangba* etc. and finally *Jaijite Kharbalya Mabohang* are referred who recognized and propitiated her. The final incident is usually dealt with in length. *Kharbalya Mabohang* was possessed by the spirit of *Yuma* related her story through him and preached about the god and religions and prescribed precepts to be followed by humankind. This story is narrated in the course of invocation. The instructions of *Yuma* have become guidelines for their way of life.

Phedangma prays and eulogizes her as *Abu Yarin Chadhang Dangma* (goddess of foodcrops), *Thakchung Thapsang Dangma* (goddess of weaving skills), *Sanghi Thobu Dangma Lingkhi Thobu Dangma* (goddess of long life and empowerment), *Thabu Dangma Yanglep Dangma* (goddess of wealth and prosperity), *Abu Dimma Sai Dangma* (goddess of reproduction), *Mujoklung Khejoklung Dangma Nawa Chait Dangma* (lord of the universe, whole creation); *Kamlungding Chempha Dangma* (goddess of all gods), etc. and ask for her client to give her back the vital air or soul (*sigi sosam*) and not let it stray, keep her away from evil spirits, make her life full of strengths and vitality, keep her womb safe and lead to safe childbirth. *Yuma*'s worship is necessary in all ceremonies and only with the backing of *Yuma Sammang,* other divinities or spirits can be propitiated or exercised.

(ii) Myths of *Him Sammang*

Him Sammang (the divinities of house)- *Khawalung Thakphut Mang, Khabeso Thappu Mang* is a god sent by Supreme Goddess *Tagera Ningwaphuma* to look after the houses of human beings, save and care them and bring prosperity and well being to them. He is addressed as *Labelung-Nambelung* (god having the vital element of the Moon and the Sun), *Lokphamang-Singkhimmang* (god of the human shelter), *Menchham Yapmi Dangba* (lord of the human race), *Phungjiri-Phunggappomang* (savior of the flower of life), and is described as coming from *Sinyuk Muden Laze* (china Tibet) to the land of *Khambus* and *Limboos* via *Chenje Lungma Tembhe*. He came along with his retinue – *Phanaga* (snake divinity), *Pangrima, Chamatima, Yotokla Thotokla* (divinities of low season and high season), *Sayanla Muden Mang, Phakmura Mang, Saba* (monkey divinity) and many others. It is invoked to stay on his altar and offered various things; pig, chicken, beer, cooked rice and many other small items. On behalf of the pregnant woman, *Phedangma* prays for her protection and prosperity in the similar ways as in the evolution of other divinities.

(iii) Theba Sammang

Theba (grandfather or primogenitor) *Sammang* is a divinity of power, energy and vigour. He came down from *Parung Marung Tembhe* through the way of *Labhingjong Nambhingjong* to *Nambhun Yiak* to *Idhung Yiak* visiting the various areas of mighty mountains- *Wathinlung, Champhatlung, Kewalung* and *Phaktanglung* (Mount Jannu) and haunts of wild animals and fowls – *Sepangden, Pupangden*. He came down from north to the hill areas of the south crossing various rivers and forest lands and barriers in course of hunting and finally reaches *Idhung Yiak* where he pretended to get ensnared in a trap spread out by *Chukniba* and *Latiba*, the ancestors of *Pebakkhum Nembang*.

Theba made acquainted of himself with *Chukniba* and *Latiba* by disclosing himself his real form, power, valor and identified as ancestor. They were amazed by the thespian and worshipped him as their guardian deity. *Theba* entered into the body of *Chukniba* and *Latiba* and began to speak, instruct and encourage the human beings. His devotees succeeded in accomplishing extraordinary works. Since then, *Theba Sammang* became the

Sammang of all the *Limboos* through the spread of female progeny of *Nembang*. He is imagined in a form of great warrior, skilful hunter, and tall and mighty figure. He is invoked by sacrificing a pig or a grown up male chicken.

(iv) Myth of *Apchara Pakchana*

Apchara Pakchana or *Labhakcha Nambhakcha Pakchana* is the divinity of crossroads. It is said that in early days, even men used to give birth to a child carrying fetus in their thigh instead of uterus. *Apchara Pakchana* was also a pregnant man carrying a fetus in his thigh. He used to stay at cross paths and people provided him foods. After his death, his soul became divinity of cross paths. If he is placated, he protects the womb, otherwise causes problems to both unborn baby and expectant mother. *Phedangma* propitiates this divinity by chanting his litany and offering a male goat or a pig or four chicken and four eggs with *Sapthok* (fermented beer in banboo). It is believed that if this divinity is appeased, he will not inflict and trouble on his suppliant, rather helps to bring back the wandering soul to her body and thus brings long life, happiness and good fortune.

(v) Myth of *Wagongma*

Wagongma is female protector divinity of pregnant women. It is believed that human soul travels from place to place and if it is hurt and lost somewhere, human body will loose its vital air. Myth relates that pregnant women's soul stays in the lake of life (*Yumikma* or *Segep Surungma*). *Wagongma* is worshipped to protect the wandering soul and help and instruct *Tetlara Lajokhang* to bring the soul back to the body of pregnant woman. It is usually performed close to the river or on a rill. Bamboo poles are erected on their right side of the fork of a river or on rill and a kind of raised level stage are constructed on it to make the altar. A pair of chicken and pigeon is offered to this divinity. It is believed that she causes *Sugut* (death of mother at parturition) if she is not propitiated properly.

The myth says that in the early days, there were two persons – a brother and a sister. Once, the sister told her brother to bring some beautiful flowers for her. The brother went to the mountaintops in search of *Semphung* (Petunia, *Petunia spp*), *Pangbok Phung* (Jatamasi, *Nardostachys jatamasi*) and fell down into the

Tamar (*Embiri Yangthangwa*) river. His sister fell in grief in the sudden bereavement of loving brother and she followed the river current, wailing and lamenting, in search of her brother. Finally she found the corpse of her brother at *Serek Surungma*. She burst into tears, lamented and adorned the dead body with *Semphung* (Petunia) and *Pangphokphung* (*Jatamasi*) – the flowers of high land, and *Khechingse* (*Castanopsis spp*) and *Singjango* (*dawri, Luculia gratissima*) – the flowers of low land and said to the departed soul of her brother to become savior of all women (sisters) expecting childbirth – the protector at the critical moment. She also told the departed soul to become a master spirit of water and play on the golden and silver bridges over the lake and river. Since then, he is known as *Wagongma* divinity. It is believed that the divinity is propitiated for protection of both expectant mother and child in the womb, for the welfare, prosperity, long life and safe delivery of the suppliant (Kainla, B. 1991; Subba, C. 1995: 93-102; 236-290; Subba, J.R. 1999: 391-410; 509-534; 2001: 1-30; 2003: 1-101).

Mythological Functions

(i) Mystical: The myth describes the mystery of womb worship to be performed when the child is developing in a human form (sixth month to birth) for the protection of a child in the uterus. The myth has identified the above-mentioned divinities that could be helpful for the protection of the child in the uterus and the expectant mother. It also describes the mystery of the origin of the divinities. Womb worship has been considered as one of the most important worship of life in *Yumaism*.

(ii) Sociological: The myth has furnished the womb worship rituals in the society. The myths are chanted or recited during worship performances for protection of the developing child in the mother's womb.

(iii) Pedagogical: It has interpreted customary laws. Womb worshipping means accepting the fatherhood of the developing child that certifies the parenthood of the developing child.

Myths of *Yangdang Phongma* (Naming of a Child)

The myths of *Yangdang phongma* is for protection of the baby and happy announcement of a new guest who has descended on earth with prayers of the Supreme Goddess *Tagera Ningwaphuma* for the bestowal of safe, prosperous and happy long life to the new born baby. The house gets impure for three days for the female baby and four days for male baby until a ritual of *Yangdang Phongma* is performed. It is a ritual of purification of the mother, the baby, the house and the close relatives and giving name to the baby and showing the baby the light of the day especially for initiation of perceptive souls known as *Ni-Sam* and *Khem-Sam* souls. Usually *Phedangma* officiate the birth ceremonies.

Mother takes a bath in the warm water early in the morning and the baby is also cleaned properly. *Wadum Pakwa* – water of the seven springs or *Chirakphek Chwa* (water in which gold has been washed) or rain-water collected from stone, rock, tree holes is sprinkled in and outside of the house and to the members of the house through a small bunch of *Samyok* and *Namyoba* for purification. *Phedangma* performs the ritual of purification with the aspersion of holy water. *Tumyanghang* support and accept the purification procedure. After purification, the worship of supreme divinity *Yuma* and other guardian deities are performed and prayed for the protection of a new family member. *Mangenna* of the newborn baby is also conducted for the first time and a name is given to the baby. After this, a ritual of showing light to the baby begins. No specific myths are involved but only conventional ritual is conducted in this ceremony (Subba, C. 1995: 103-106; 236-290; Subba, J.R. 1999: 391-410; 509-534; 2001: 1-30; 2003: 1-101; 2005: 74-130; 2005: 22-32).

Mythological Functions

(i) Mystical: The myth describes the mystery of *Yangdang Phongma* (child naming ceremony) rituals in *Yumaism*. This is a ceremony of accepting the parenthood of the newly born child, naming it and providing security to both the newly born child and the mother in the society. It is one of the most important ceremonies of life of the child in *Yumaism*. Because on this day the two perceptive souls *Khem-sam* (soul of hearing) and *Ni-sam* (soul of sight) are initiated and starts developing in the newly born child. The three conceptive souls *Sikkum-sam* (the soul of intuition), *Ningwa-sam* (the soul of mind) and *Thona-sam* (the soul of wisdom) also start developing in the child from this day onwards.

(ii) Sociological: The myth has furnished worship rituals of *Yangdang Phongma* (child naming ceremony) for the protection of both the newly born child and the mother in the society. The ritual is performed on the third day for female and on the fourth day for male child.

(iii) Pedagogical: The myth has interpreted customary laws of accepting fatherhood of the child. If the father does not accept to this ritual ceremony means the child delivering women has to reveal the father of the newly born child. In such cases *Tumyanghangs* and *Yaklasuhangmas* have to settle the case of fatherhood of the child.

Myth of *Mangenna* – warding off Evil Influences

Mangenna is one of the important rituals usually performed every six months at the beginning of winter and summer. *Mangenna* means an act of worship to raise one's head for a person feeling dejected and suffering in hardship in order to encourage him. According to the famous psychologist Jung, the soul-image of a person is opposite in sex, which means a man's soul image is female while the woman's soul-image is the male. *Yumaism* also believes this type of soul-image and worship the soul-image through *Mangenna*. *Mangenna* means worship of that soul-image known literally as "sister" or "brother", which denotes the celebration to commemorate their invaluable support of their soul-image for success and prosperity. The myth of *Mangenna* is the power or energy of the earth, often incarnated and revered as *Khambuling Picchamma,* an agile lightening goddess emerged from earth. According to the myth, *Sechchhere Senehang,* the youngest among *Sawa Yethang,* went to his father *Sodhjung Lepmuhang* to ask for invincible power. *Sodhung Lepmuhang* gave him swords representing invincible power (*Amukkum Mukkum Sam*) – *Ngerere Nahangma,* a boon-bestowing god (*Hangwa Mang*). He weaved two swords with two hands in air and sparks appeared while the two swords clashed. The spark that flew towards the sky became *Ngerere Nahangma Sam* (divinity) and the spark that fell to the earth became *Khambuling Picchamma* (earth divinity). Thus *Khambuling Picchamma is Mangenna* (sister) of *Nahangma Sam*. In short, she is *Mangenna* and symbol of the power of the earth.

Mangenna is done to protect oneself from accidents, obnoxious acts, disputes, fighting, wars, envy and jealousy and to succeed in the desired attempts. The origin of this ritual is traced back to the myth of cosmology. When the creator god *Porokmi Wambhami* was trying to create pretty, immortal human beings, he made several attempts by designing the human body from precious metals (gold, silver, bronze, copper etc.), then from soil (abiogenesis). Human forms of precious metals could not speak and come alive. He could not make immortal human beings by abiogenesis means of creation. He threw it in different directions and they became divinities. Human beings made from the earthen clay were not well developed, they grew up so small that they had to through sticks with force to bring down red peppers from its plants, or had to cut down a fern with axes, and a single goat-drop would be enough load for them. He threw under the earth and they became "*Khambongba Lungbongba*", sons and daughters of the earth. They are the masters of the earth. Finally, the creator god went to the Almighty Goddess *Tagera Ningwaphuma* for advice. With Her instruction the creator god developed human beings from *Simikla-Pomikla Khappu* (kind of high altitude bamboos ashes), water collected in the tree trunks, rocks and stones and other biotic substances (biogenesis means), who spoke and became lively. Being unhappy and dissatisfied with his final accomplishment, he spat at the newly created human form in extreme compunction. Because of utter humiliation, those human beings died immediately. Thus human beings became mortal. The god *Porokmi Wambhami* became anxious once again, went to the Supreme Goddess *Tagera Ningwaphuma* and confessed his mistakes and asked for instruction to revive the human creation. *Tagera Ningwaphuma* instructed him to perform "*Simerima Mangenna*" rite to give the newly created human beings a life again. Since then *Mangenna* became a ritual of giving life, vigor, strength, prosperity, a ritual of defending oneself from the evils, recollecting the gods with reverence and invocating them for their support in time to crucial events of life and death of forefathers.

There are various forms of *Mangenna* done in various occasions, especially on occasions of *Sappok Chomen* (Womb-worship), *Yangdangphongma* (rite of giving name), *Metkkamma* (marriage) and *Chotlung Phongma* (ritual of progression). Today, a rooster is sacrificed for woman and a hen for man.

The *Phedangma* or *Samba* performing the ritual should know the history or mythical accounts of the particular clan for whom the *Mangenna* is going to be performed. He should recite the myth of migrations of the ten *Limboos*, and the establishment of each of the ten *Limboo* in a certain area. The myth begins with the land of human creation – *Munaphen Tembhe* (North of Persian gulf). Some of the myth narrators mention that god first created human settlement at *Mangjiri Mangowet* (Mongolia), while other mention that god first created human beings at *Phoktanglungma Pembenlungma* (Mount Jannu – one of the five peaks of Mount Kanchanjunga) *Mangjiri Manglondha Den*. Eventually they grew in great numbers and dispersed in different directions in search of a better land to live in. Most of the myths indicate that one of the branches of that community moved towards *Lhasa* from their place of origin and settled down there for generations. Again one of the branches of that community migrated towards south and entered into some valley, then to the plain regions of India, particularly to *Kashi* or to a location close to the confluence of eight rivers (*Yetwado*).

They settled down in *Yetchiri Yetchwado Tembhe* (Kashi or Koshi?) for about twelve generations. There is no clear description about their settlements there. They grew in great numbers and finally eighteen brothers, some count up to twenty-nine brothers, moved to different direction from there (Kashi or Koshi?). Now one has to trace or relate their clan to one of these brothers and should know the events of migrations of their ancestors from place to place till they got fortified in some suitable location (*Yiok*).

Mangenna myth recited in *Miwa Khola* and *Tamar Khola* – the watershed areas of *Miwa* and *Tamar* River by most of the *Phedangmas* and *Sambas*, the eighteen brothers are *Shandhunge, Mundhunge, Chongbanglingba, Hamyungba, Hamsenba, Kajungba, Kaneba, Phatlemiba, Yanchamiba, Khetchryaba, Khechiba, Thapmiya, Muregan, Lapsangmi, Phedenmi, Pomenhang, Sapmenhang* and *Nerbahang*. Among them *Sandhunge, Mungdhunge, Chongbanglingba, Thapmiya, Muregan, Kajungba, Kaneba, Phatlemiba* and *Yanchamiba* moved towards the eastern side and the rest to the western side. Those who migrated to the western side, moved towards the north and entered into the present Nepal Himalayas and spread out up to the west of Arun River. The other branch migrating to the eastern side, eventually moved towards north-western side and scattered in different places of the eastern side of Arun River. In search of ancestral land, these people even reached Digarchia (Tibet). They stayed there for a few decades (some say for few generations) and experienced a bitter struggle between the followers of *Bonism* and *Yumaism*. Followers of traditional faith the *Yumaism* adherents were defeated, fell in complete disorder and had to face great misfortune. They ran away and some of them arrived at the river *Kanwa* (*Kaveli*) and some reached the belt of *Phawari* (river *Phawa*), *Yangthangwa* (river *Tamar*), *Ketakkum Miwa* (river *Miwa*) and *Sindolung Maiwa*. It is difficult to relate this event with that of the struggle between followers of *Yumaism* and *Bonism*/ Buddhism described in detail in the story of *Lhasahang* in *Yuma Sammang* myth of I.S. Chemjong (1961), but inconsistent presentation of the scene of strife between these two communities of followers in the myth recitation by well-versed *Phedangmas* and *Tumyanghangs* in myths reveals some common elements in the myth and these mystical sketches reveal that religious strife had caused further migration.

Now the story has to relate to particular clan. For various clans (*Mingsra*) of *Limboo* of *Miwa Khola*, the myth of migration follows this way: *Sadhunge, Mundhunge* and *Chongbanglingba* first appeared at *Nila Chyambuk*, the source area of the river *Miwa*, and then moved towards *Sodhowarak* (the lake). They slowly came down to the *Abhan* river basin, then to the place called *Singrathak*. As the time went on, they slowly moved down to the *Nyayok, Tangen, Tardung, Tinjong, Ammijakpa, Khengjuwa, Sarekma, Yumikma, Papung*, and finally to *Homulungjangma*. The three brothers *Sandhunge, Mundhunge* and *Chongbanglingba* then separated from *Homulungjangma* and moved to different directions. *Mundhunge* went to *Libang*, built his fort (*Yiok*) at *Sarajangma* and settled down there. *Shreng Chongbang, Samyangkham, Langwa, Mademba, Hangam* (two types), *Norbo* (two types) and *Kedem* (two types) were the descendants of *Sandhunge*. *Shreng Chongbang* crossed the river *Miwa* and reached *Mashreng*, where he built his fort. The other brother, *Chongbang Lingba* went to *Maiwa Khola* following a bird *Samdangwa* (*Lophophorus impejanus*) and built a fort at *Chikwa* and his descendants settled down in *Maiwa Khola* areas. The descendants of *Thapmiya* and *Muregon* came down along the *Basin* of *Tambar River* and some of them made a fort (*Yiok*) at *Khambochang* and some of them at *Lunjiri Lumbang* at *Hangdewa.* Four subgroups of *Phenduwa, Nugo, Muringla, Palungwa, Hellok, Lingkhim, Chemjong, Labung, Anchhangbo, Sabehang, Phambu* etc. are the descendants of *Thapmiya* and *Muregan. Kajunba* and *Kaneba* came to the source of *Kangwa* (*Kaveli*) river and followed the river basin down to the low hills around the river. *Phatlemi* and *Yanchhami* followed the source of river *Phawari* (*Phawa Khola*). Their descendants developed their forts (*Yiok*) at various places. First of all, they got fortified there for their protection and made new habitat to settle down permanently. Their descendants grew in great numbers and developed villages. These forts (*Yioks*) are known as *Mangenna Yiok.* They again moved to different places of their choice to occupy more land and these places are known as *Pangwana Den* (land of wondering and playing). Various *Yioks* are described before coming to the final *Yiok* which is known as *Mangenna Yiok*. Usually the myth ends at *Mangenna Yiok* with brief description of movements towards *Pangwana Den* or just naming the place or village where *Mangenna* performer (client) is living. (It is the story of migration of the *Limboos* from the origin in band or tribal sociological stage as hunter-gatherer to the places of first settlement with settled agriculture. Those places of first settlement of the band or tribal stages of a particular clan of the *Limboos* are known as *Mangenna Yiok* which are considered as the symbol of the power of the earth for that particular clan). *Mangenna Yiok* varies from clan to clan.

Through his litany now he takes the entire altar from the place of residence (*Pangwana Den*) to the place of *Mangenna Yiok.* Then, he sacrifices the chicken at the altar of *Mangenna*. The performer tries to propitiate *Tagera Ningwaphuma, Sodhung Lepmuhang* along with their retinue – *Sumjiri Sumhatlung Mang, Angsu Yukmi Mang* (Fire god) etc. and offers the various things including chicken on behalf of the client. He supplicates the divinities for his client to avoid hardships and unhappy incidents while going away, save from *Sogha, Sugut, Yetchham, Pungsam* (evil spirits) and various types of *Sires.* He asks *Akwanama,* the divinity of the mail pillar of the house and other guardian divinities to remain witness of the ritual and prays the divinities to keep the promise by defending his client in time of distress and bring prosperity on him as in the past (C. 1995: 107-119; Subba, J.R. 1999: 583-592).

Mythological Functions

(i) Mystical: The myth describes the mystery of origin of *Mangenna*, which means an act of worship to raise one's head for a person feeling dejected and suffering in hardship in order to encourage him. The soul-image of a person is opposite in sex, literally as "sister" or "brother", which denotes the celebration to commemorate their invaluable support of their soul-image for success and prosperity. It is the power or energy of the earth, often incarnated and revered as *Khambuling Picchamma* (earth divinity), an agile lightening goddess emerged from earth.

(ii) Cosmological: The origin of this myth is traced back to the myth of cosmology. The creator god *Porokmi Wambhami* or *Yambhami* tried to create an immortal, strong and beautiful human beings but failed to design from precious metals (gold, silver, bronze, copper etc.), and then from soil (abiogenesis means of creation). Finally, the creator god developed human beings from *Simikla-Pomikla Khappu* (kind of high altitude bamboo ashes), water collected in the tree trunks, rocks and stones (*wadumbokwa*) and other biotic substances (biogenesis means of creation), which spoke and became lively. Being unhappy and dissatisfied with his final accomplishment, he spat at the newly created human forms in extreme compunction. Because of utter humiliation, those human beings died immediately. Thus, human beings became mortal. The god *Porokmi Wambhami* became anxious once again, went to the Supreme Goddess *Tagera Ningwaphuma* and confessed his mistakes and asked for instruction to revive the human creation. *Tagera Ningwaphuma* instructed him to perform "*Simerima Mangenna*" rite to give the newly created human beings a life again. Since then *Mangenna* became a ritual of giving life, vigor, strength, prosperity, a ritual of defending oneself from the evils, recollecting the gods with reverence and invocating them for their support in time to crucial events of life and death of forefathers.

(iii) Sociological: The myth has furnished a ritual of *Mangenna* to the society, which is performed in every six moths to the individual, during womb worship and child naming ceremony, along with *Nahangma* ritual also, etc. There are various forms of *Mangenna* done in various occasions, especially on occasions of *Sappok Chomen* (womb-worship), *Yangdangphongma* (rite of giving name), *Metkkamma* (marriage) and *Nahangma* or *Chotlung Phongma* (ritual of progression). The *Phedangma* or *Samba* performing the ritual speaks the history or mythical accounts of the particular clan for whom the *Mangenna* is going to be performed. He recites the myth of migrations of the ten *Limboos* from their origin, and the establishment of each of the ten *Limboos* in a certain area. The myth begins with the land of human creation, to *Munaphen Tembhe* (plains of North of Persian). Usually the myth ends at *Mangenna Yiok* with brief description of movements towards *Pangwana Den* or just naming the place or village where *Mangenna* performer (client) is living. Through his litany now he takes the entire altar from the place of residence (*Pangwana Den*) to the place of *Mangenna Yiok* (e.g. *Changthumbo yiok* for *Pondhak* clans). Then, he sacrifices the chicken at the altar of *Mangenna*.

(iv) Pedagogical: The myth provides genological accounts of different clans of the Limboo society, which is useful for ascertaining marriage proposals. The society usually follows 7 to 8 generations of consanguineous relations apart for marriage.

Myth of Marriage

During marriage of the *Limboos*, more of social formalities are involved than of the myths. In the course of the performing *Metkkam Thim* (ritual of the auspicious moment of marriage ceremony), *Phedangma* places great emphasis on the union of two souls and respect, support and love for each other. After the ritual of solemn commitment from bride and bridegroom for conjugal fidelity, mutual cooperation and maintaining a line of descendants with dignity, *Phedangma* addressing to the distinguished gentlemen and ladies to remain as witness, and asks the father and mother of the groom whether they will behave properly to their daughter-in-law or not. They also express their assurance for proper behavior towards the bride and commitment for sincere, cordial and affectionate relationship. This social ritual is known as *Sakey Yeksimma*.

Once this ritual is over, the *Phedangma* performs the ritual of *Mangenna* of bride and groom sacrificing a pair of chicken. Then, the bride and groom are taken around the *Hangsitlang* (main pillar) with *Chabrunggey* (*Chyabrung* dancers). Now, the *Phedangma* starts *Yehang Sema* ritual. Then, the *Phedangma* performs the rituals of

Li-toong Sikma – Thetlang Kamma., Ondong Sanang ritual and then *Phungwa Changma* ritual respectively. This completes the *Metkkam Thim* (Subba, J.R. 1998a).

After the completion of *Metkkam Thim*, and other social formalities, *Phedangmas* and other *Tumyanghangs* sing *Phungnawa Samlo* (songs of flowers) throughout the night. The various myths sang during the *Phungnawa Samlo* has been described in various myths elswhere. They recall the mastersingers, *Kewa Phungba Mangden Hangba* with reverence who set convention of singing *Phungnawa Samlo* by the command of *Sodhung Lepmuhang*, the patron deity of *Sawa Yethang* at the marriage of *Pajoi Tentumyangba* and *Lupliadenhangma*. The various myths sang by the well-versed *Phedangmas, Sambas* and *Tumyanghangs* are:

(a) Myths of *Suchchhuru Suhangpheba* and *Tetlara Lahadongna* – incestuous relationship between brother and sister;

(b) Myths of *Pajoi Tentumyangba* and *Lupliadenhangma* – a marriage union outside the kinship complying with incest taboo;

(c) Myth of *Samba Sutlung Phungba* (*Wayoading Khokling Sakpa*) and *Sekngayang Phekngayangma* (*Selliyong Phetliyonghangma*) – a marriage union based on mother's consent, mutual preference and love, and social approval.

These stories of various eons relate the development of marriage institution and narratives are full of pathos, eroticism, heroism, humor, serenity, affection, amazement, and abhorrence. These myths are quite long, and the first two myths have been described elsewhere. So the third myth is as under.

In this myth, a lady *Sekngayang Phenkngayangma, Khajiri Khayangphekma*, mother of *Sekngayang Pheknagayangma*, is pleased with *Samba Sutlung Phungba* because of his services to her satisfaction. She commits to give away her daughter to marry him when she reaches maidenhood.

(i) First episode of *Phungwana Samlo* – growing of flowers of bride and groom: To relate the upbringing of *Sekngayang Phekngayangma* there come the wonderful description of rising flowers. *Phungbakko Phunglangaba* and *Sambokko Sanglangaba* try to grow various kinds of flowers at different places. They start from the spring area of *Tusroti Umroti Pumma* (Brahmaputra), then at *Muhenlung Hengwa* river, *Mugangling Kangwa* river (Kabeli), *Muphalung Phawari* river (Phawakhola), *Embiri Yangdhangwa* river (Tamar khola) but fail. When they try at the spring area of *Ketakkum Mewa* river (Mewa khola), only one small leaf appears and when they try at the spring area of *Sindholung Maiwa* river (Maiwa khola), only two leaves appear but cannot grow further. So, finally, when they try to grow flowers at the source area of *Ayana Kujuli-Arun Barun* river (Arun and Barun), the plant begins to grow as expected. After twelve months, it becomes big enough and its branches straggle out in all directions. Birds begin to come and stay at the bushy branches. Beautiful flowers bloom there and there appears a beautiful lustrous maiden singing with flowers (*Phungbakkoma Phungdiwama,* sometimes plucking flowers *Phungbakkoma Phungnilima* and placing flowers on her head to look nice *Phungbakkoma Khemphungmyangma*. A handsome youth, *Abaso Patala Hangba* marries her. They give births to four exceedingly good-looking girls (nymphs) playing on flowers – *Phungbakko Phungphayetma, Phungbakko Phungyarima, Phungbakko Phungsikama* and *Phungbakko Phungtiwama. Sinyuk Mudenhang,* king of north and *Laik Khambuhang,* the local king, became fascinated by the beauty of those girls and intend to marry them. When they try to find them, they disappear in flowers. The gently blowing wind disperse the seeds of the flowers in all directions. Various kinds of flowers grow on the hills, representing various lives and human sentiments.

At last *Phungbakko Phunglangaba* and *Sambakko Sanglangaba* cut down the flower tree at the behest of frustrated *Laik Khambuhang*. From every bit of the tree, there appears a variety of birds and insects known as *Sellokwa* (Great barbet), *Siputruk* (dove) birds and *Mangnenema* (cicada), *Yanghangponghe* (great cicada), *Khakchyangba* insects etc. with pathetic songs. Different kinds of musical instruments also are made from the branches of that tree. There appear two male and female singers – *Mangjiri Manganjyaba* and M*anganjyama*. But because of jealousy they could not survive and famous singer *Kewaphungba Mangdenhangba* appears afterwards. They set the tradition of singing a song of flower laying emphasis on *Sekmuriphung* (celery), a life flower for the happy and prosperous life. The song of the growing and taking care of it usually referred to love affairs, youthfulness, amusement, brevity of life and human sentiments. At the end of this part of the myth, the singers have to identify *Sekmuri Wadayo Phungma* (celery), the flower of young men and women among hundreds of flowers of different kinds and should try to keep it always fresh and lively.

(ii) Second episode of *Phungwana Samlo* – balancing the characters of bride and groom: There is another episode narrated in the course of singing *Phungwa Samlo* to balance the characters of man and woman who are going to marry. Emotional, libidinous and physical factors are not only the deciding factors for the stable marriage union. Both psychological and spiritual components have to be considered. *Sawa Yethang*, eight famous founder leaders of human settlement, approach to Supreme Goddess *Tagera Ningwaphuma* with their prospective wives for the blessing before getting married. The Supreme Goddess wants balance between the prospective husband and wife and weighs them in a weighing scale (*Nenduri Passanga*). *Sawa Yethangs* stand at the right hand side and their life mates on the left. They are weighed and the equalization process begins and balance is maintained through dressing up, ornamentation and through the blessings by Supreme Goddess to cover up the imbalance found while weighing. This episode is related with the myth of *Yupparung*. The new bride and groom have to pass through this process. The leading singer has to forecast their future of conjugal life by examining the various aspects of balancing process. This part of the myth has a symbolical significance.

(iii) Third episode of *Sekngayang Phekngayangma*: When *Sengayang Phekngayangma* becomes well grown-up. *Khajiri Khayangphekma*, mother of *Sekngayang Phekngayangma*, tells her nubile daughter that she had already given her to *Samba Sutlung Phungba* and the settlement was reached through a kind of contract (*Chwaphun*). *Sekngayang Phekngayangma* refuses to accept *Samba Sutlung* as her husband and complains that he is old, uncultured and is leading a different way of life. She goes to the north in search of a well matching husband and approaches to *Sinyuk Mudenhang* and requests to marry her. Expressing his unable ness, *Sinyuk Mudenhang* sends her back with the expenses for the way for taking trouble. She again goes to the southern side, approaches to *Temen Warakhang* with the request to marry her. He also expresses his inability and sends her back with the expenses for her way. In the same way she approaches to the kings of east and west, but she becomes disappointed every time. Finally she enters into the country of *Sawa Yethang* and persuades each of the leaders – except her as his wife. They all show their unwillingness and send her back with expenses for the way for taking trouble to approach them, as they were aware of the situation, matching of the couple and beguilement of maidenhood.

After serious deliberation, *Sekngayang Phekngayangma* realizes that *Samba Sutlung Phungba* would be a best mate for her life though there are some differences in many respects between them and she approaches to him. Being aware of all her endeavors, *Samba Sutlung Phungba* pretends to remain indifferent of her request for a short while, but becomes pleased to find her as her bride. The marriage becomes successful.

With the end of these stories, the leading singer has to recite the benedictory portions of the myth with special references to the examples set by legendary heroes and heroines and other predecessors. The contents of the benediction include best wishes for health and happiness of the couple abounding progeny, better relationships with all relatives and success in the performances in household business. The delineation of bride's painful separation with mother, father and other kith and kin, assimilation with new members of the new family circle, adaptation with new circumstances, assuming new responsibilities and a new situation of finding mother, father and everything in her husband alone gives a sentimental touch to the benediction. *Phungnawa Samlo* ends with the completion of benedictory notes at the dawning of the day. It is also said that *Phunjiri Phungappo Phedangma* initiated the tradition of singing *Phunawa Samlo* by making two flowers, representing bride and groom, fresh and lively (Subba, C. 1995: 119-145; Subba, J.R. 1998; 1999: 411-452).

Mythological Functions

(i) Mystical: The myth illustrates the mystery of marriage in three different episodes Viz: (a) incestuous relationship between brother and sister without any formal marriage; (b) a marriage union outside the kinship complying with incest taboo – the first marriage sanctified by the gods and goddesses, and the society as a whole; and; (c) a marriage union based on parent's consent, mutual preference and love, and social approval. These stories of various eons relate the development of marriage institution and narratives are full of pathos, eroticism, heroism, humour, serenity, affection, amazement, and abhorrence.

(ii) Cosmological: The myth of origin of sexual relation or institution of marriage is cosmological. The progenitors – *Sutchhuru Suhangpheba* and *Tetlara Lahadongna* (brother and sister) had to be separated with their children, as the sexual relation was not acceptable in the society. They were separated with their children. The father, *Sutchhuru Suhangpheba* had to go to *Muringla Kheringla Tembhe* with their nine sons – *Phanghangs* (ancestor land somewhere in the *Akashic* field) while the mother *Tetlara Lahadongna* had to remain at *Sangarak Nugarak Tembhe* (on the mother Earth). The second marriage union outside the kinship of *Pajoi Tendhungyangba* and *Lupli Adenhangma* was witnessed by gods, goddesses and the society but was not successful due to envy and jealousy of *Irere Idhuknama* because of her sexual relation with *Pajoi Tendhungyangba* when they were in their early life. Finally, the third marriage was successful as they finally reconciled their differences and married happily with love and the social approval.

(iii) Sociological: The myth has furnished the society a marriage union with mutual love and certified by the society. These myths are recited or chanted during marriage union, the tradition of singing *Phungnawa Samlo* by making two flowers, representing bride and groom, fresh and lively. *Mangenna* and other worship rituals and social formalities are also performed to solemnize the marriage union. These rituals and social formalities include: *Singok Kakma* if elder sister is still unmarried, *Metkkam Mangenna, Sakey Yekma ritual* with *khorilung nu khekkhekna, Yehang Sema, Li-toong Sikma - Sodhung Thetlang kamma, Ninduli Pasanga Sikma, Ondong Sanakma, Phunwachangma, Hangsitlang coppma* etc. After *Metkkam thim, Limellung* social formalities have also to be performed.

(iv) Pedagogical: The myth has interpreted the laws of life, ethical laws and other customary laws of *Limellung* and *Najong-Khenjong* (divorce laws).

Myth of *Nahangma* or *Phungsook Timma*– Anointing the Family Head

Nahangma is a ritual of restoring martial quality of the head of the house and thus bringing good health and harvest to his family. It is a ritual of raising head of the chief of the family and a ceremony to enable him to make successful attempts for the good fortune of his family. It is often conducted to recuperate from deteriorating health and depressing and overcome difficult situation. It is conducted usually in every three years. The best season to perform *Nahangma* is either the beginning of low season (November – December) or high season (March – April). It is an invocation rite for "*Mukkum Sam*" (soul of energy) of the head of the family to gain new strength, vigor to overcome weakness and obstacles.

The various myths commences with the origin of *Nahangma.* These are:

(i) The myth begins from creation of the universe, the gods, the living creatures and finally the human beings. This is also known as the myth of *Yehangsema* (it has been elaborately discussed in the myths of creation).

(ii) The myth relating to amorous experiences of *Sawa Yukphung Kemba, Sutsuru Suhangpheba* and *Samdang Khewa* at the high land and *Tetlara Lahadongna* and *Lingdang Khewa* at the low land; and the origin of *Sawa Yethangs* and *Sawa Phanghangs* (described elsewhere);

(iii) The myth of *Porokmi Wambhami* and *Ponglung* (Shot-put), and

(iv) The myth of soul journey, impounding of ocean water (*Tungut Warak Tingma*), flower collection, and bring the souls back to the house.

(i) Myth of *Porokmi Wambhami, Ponglung* and Origin of *Nahangma Sam* or *Chotlung*

Once being worried with the drought on earth, the creator god *Porokmi Wambhami* (*Yambhami*) went to the Almighty Goddess *Tagera Ningwaphuma* for advice. On her advice the creator god went to play stone throwing (shot-put sport, stone-ball replaced by iron-ball at present) game with the descendants of *Khambongba*

Lungbongba – Labhinchong, Nambhenchong at *Iwa Hara Tembhe* after consulting *Sinyukhang Kandenhang, Mudenhang Yonchhenhang*. When he was playing, the stone (*Ponglung*) stroke with the distant earthen water pot and the clouds were formed, the rain started and the earth became verdant, plants and food crops began to grow. He again threw the stone to the remotest distance, end of the earth surface, known the land as *Shakholung Tembhe Khongkhama Tembhe, Nangkholung Tembhe Kholungma Tembhe*. The shot put stone (*Ponglung*) broke into four parts. One of the parts fell in the eastern side and it became the *Ponglung* or symbol of power of divinities. The another part fell in the western side; it became the Ponglung of *Idhuk Samsogha* (evil spirit of unnatural death). The other part, which fell in the ocean of southern side, became the *Ponglung* of *Sakmura Khingkha Lingmura Khingkha* or spirit of curse or accursed persons. The other part of the *Ponglung* fell to the northern side in front of *Sodhung Lepmuhang*. He again threw it towards *Sangarak Nugarak Tembhe*, the land of *Sawa Yethang* and fell at *Khambuchong Yiak – Ngerere Nehangma Yiak*, where *Sawa Yethangs* were inhabiting. *Sawa Yethangs* began to experience sickness and misfortune. They approached to the Supreme Goddess *Tagera Ningwaphuma* to find the panacea of their illness and misfortune and she advised them to consult *Yetchhamba Phedangma* (erudite shaman in all rituals or sacred performances) for their problems. *Phedangmas* through their divination told that the *Ponglung* was a symbol of power, strength, progress and source of energy of the Sun and the Moon (*Namsakhe Ponglung, Lasakhe Ponglung*) if properly respected or revered and a omen of illness, envy, jealousy, anger and incest (*Sokhim Ponglung, Somathik Ponglung, Chellung Ponglung, Khoklung Ponglung*) if not cared and respected.

Ultimately *Sawa Yethangs* came to know that the *Ponglung* was a divinity, a source of invincibility, unfailing power and eternal energy (*Kamboling Nahangma Sam, Harara Lingemma Sammang*) and a **Chotlung** (symbol of power, prestige and progress) of human beings. *Tappeso Lungmahang* eldest among *Yethang* presented a sword or revered it with a sword (*Sinyuk Muden Phe*); second one *Phurupso Thayonghang* revered with ginger; fifth one – *Sangehang Pangehang* with pepper; sixth one – *Thilliso Thejonghang* with *Kuringlung Yum* (salt from mine), seventh one – *Miyara*

Thokchonghang with banana leaves, *Saptok* (fermented local beer), *Chirangphekwa* and *Hangappa* (consecrated water pot decorated with plant leaves and flowers), and the last youngest one *Sechchhere Seninghang* revered it with *Paga* (turban). When they revered it in this way, it became a *Tumyanghang Ponglung*, a *Nahangma Sam*, and a *Chotlung* of the *Limboos*.

With the completion of the myth of origin of *Nahangma*, *Phedangma* moves to the altar of *Mangenna* and performs the ritual by sacrificing two chickens for each of the family members.

(ii) Myth of Soul-Journey towards the domain of *Nahangma*

The *Phedangma* now moves to the altar of *Nahangma* to begin his journey towards the domain of *Nahangma*. He invokes powerful master spirits, *Sam Sires* (spirit representing the power of some animals, sometimes doing good to humankind if placated properly and doing harm if not propitiated or dually respected) of various types, to accompany him and defend from evil spirits of *Nahen* (jealousy and envy), *Sogha, Sugut* and *Letchham* (soul of corpses living in the tombstones), *Pungsam* (wandering soul) on his journey. Through his incantation, he makes the *Sires* ready to carry heavy loads of equipments and objects of offerings and other items necessary on the journey and tell them to walk in front of him forming a procession while ascending the wonderful world of *Nahangma*. But he alone carries the souls of his clients safely through out the journey. The shaman (*Phedangma* or *Samba*) starts his journey from the central pillar (*Hang Sitlang*) where the *Akwanama* divinity lives and protects the house. He then proceeds to the hearth (*Sumhatlung*) and a fire is sent forward through the chimney of ridge beams full of soot to clear the path. Sires are sent just behind the fire carrying the loads, clearing the path and driving away the evil spirits.

Then the *Phedangma* or *Samba* and others, who are accompanying him, move to the second floor, arrive at the roof and shaman calls *Muiyan Sire* (Buzzard/Hawk Master Spirit) to help him. The shaman, along with his team, comes from the eaves of the roof down to the place where the water falls and thus land down to the earth to move in the inner yard. Then they start their journey through the path of *Namyoba* (*Artemisia vulgaris*), *Kattakwa* (fern), *Hangangse* (*bahrakhari*), *Parsekpa* (*Saurаunia napaulensis*) and various types of plants and flowers. The names of the plants, flowers, birds and animals indicate that the journey moves towards higher altitude through a winding path. There comes the wonderful description of the scenery, the soil, the villages around and they have to cross a river, *Sangdhunge Thungwama Ahang*, requesting the divinity – *Achumbung Aroti* and *Singsara Taodingmang* to construct a bridge (*Singsa Tayo*) across the river. They see some villages on either side of the path where men and women were busy in their occupation of poultry, piggery, animal farming and bamboo works etc. They ascend further and reach to the crossroads of three paths (*Sumjiri Sumlamdo*). Now, the *Phedangma* or *Samba* separates the procession and let (i) the spirits of *Sasik Yangdang* (stillbirths) follow one of the paths; and (ii) *Naso Thapan* (other evil spirits or devils) the other path. (iii) The main procession moves towards the domain of *Nahangma*. The shaman always remains at the back chanting hymns and evoking master spirits to defend the souls of his clients from time to time.

Then, the procession moves further ascend to the hill top and arrive at the crossroad of eight paths (*Yetchiri Yetlamdo*) where the *Phedangma* or *Samba* makes all the participants of the journey to be separated and follow their own paths – (i) the path of evil spirits - *Sogha* and *Sugut*; (ii) *Khema Yongsong* (world of dead souls); (iii) *Sammang* (divinities) and *Sam Sires* (Master spirits); (iv) *Phedangmas* (all *Shamans*); (v) Children; (vi) Youth; (vii) Women and (viii) Gentlemen. After blocking the paths of dead persons, evil spirits and other divinities, *Phedangma* or *Samba* now again lead the procession forward through the path of right hand side along with his two master spirits namely *Samethungma Yepmethungma* and *Tibhakko Tiannama Nettiso Phungdingnama*. They reach to *Henjiri Hembonge Chotlung* (symbol of power, prestise and progress), which is a *Chotlung* of children and the souls of children are placed before it. Then they move again upward and reach at the center – *Sangphiri Lingphiri Pangbhe, Chotlung* of young men and women, where they throw *Ponglung* at close to the spring called *Sangsanglung Saodham*. Then they move to reach *Padam Lungba Thakkethak Pangbhe,* a *Chotlung* of women, where women are presented in front of it. Now they approach close to the *Chotlung* of *Tuttu Tumyanghang* (gentlemen or respected laymen), the domain of *Nahangma*. On the left hand side, there is *Sengwalung*

Ngekwalung, a *Chotlung* of *Phedangmas* (all types) and on the right hand side; there is a special place for *Sawa Yethang*, now *Tuttu Tumyangs*, known as *Khorung Maklungchong Pangbhe*. *Awari* and *Chappari* rivers flow on two sides of the domain of *Nahangma*. Now *Phedangma* or *Samba* place his client (descendants of *Sawa Yethang* or descendants of ten *Limboos*) at an appropriate place before the altar of *Nahangma*, and performs liturgy procedure of blocking the spirit of jealousy and envy (*Nahen Sakma*). He straightens or maintains the bed or sitting place of *Nahangma Sam* properly with the help of his sword, adds soil of various lands through incantations if the place has been denuded and prays for the better life of his client.

Again here, life is represented by *Tungut Warak* (ocean or great lake), and *Phedangma* brings the soil of various lands by his incantations to make the embankment strong enough and brings the water of various rivers, lakes and oceans to make it always full of water. He also puts fishes and other water creatures to make it nice to look at. He blocks the evil spirits such as *Soba* (monkey), *Muiyan* (buzzard), *Phikwa* (kite), *Nahen* (jealousy and anger) and *Letcham, Phungsam* (not destined souls) with his sword shouting and yelling. Thus he makes the life of his client indestructible, invincible and full of vigor and ever progressing. Sacrificial rituals are completed. Divination is done. At the time of sacrifice *Phedangma* usually mimes a war dance, raises the sword *Pheja* high and yells out as the place of *Nahangma* is known as sacred place of dancing, yelling and jumping (*Lapchangmaden, Ihumaden, Tendumaden*).

Phedangma invokes the gods and goddesses *Mujoklungma Khejoklungma, Tagera Ningwaphuma, Sodhung Lepmuhang, Khambulingma Nahangma, Harara Pichamma* and others and ask to accept what has been offered. He comes to solemn agreement with *Tibhukkko Tiyangnama* to protect the altar atleast for three years. He prepares for his return and raises the souls of all with the help of the *Sire-Samethung Yepmethung*. At this moment he is seized by trance again, violently trembles as in the time of invoking powerful master spirits while beginning the ascending journey and other critical moments of the ritual performances. One of the master spirits speak through his mouth and the oracles usually contain the prophesy relating to illness, accidents and deaths of family members, close relatives or some people in the village. *Phedangma* together with the souls of other persons follows the same path while descending. They also collect the souls of women, young men and women and children on the way while descending. With the help of primordial gurus – powerful *Sambas, Phedangmas,* he along with other souls, make a dive of a hawk down to the crossroad of eight paths, block the path of the souls of dead persons and call upon *Samdang Khewa* and *Lingdang Khewa* (pheasant and partridge) to obstruct them. They come down to the river and ask the divinity *Makchiso Kulang Kemba* to watch the bridge and obstruct the evil spirits if they come down. *Phedangma* now come down along with the souls of his clients together to the inner yard of his client members of his journey. He enters to the central pillar of the house and completes his soul journey. Finally he destroys the altar of *Nahangma* and thus completes the ritual (Subba, C. 1995: 145-155; Subba, J.R. 1999: 575-592; 2001: 147-148; 2003: 479-494).

Mythological Functions

(i) Mystical: The myth elucidates the mystery of origin of *Nahangma* and the purpose of performing this ritual. A number of rituals are involved for conducting this ritual. The *Ponglung* (shotput-stone) thrown away to a distance place by the creator god *Porokmi Wambhami* broke into four parts. One of it fell to the northern side in front of *Sodhung Lepmuhang*. He again threw it towards *Sangarak Nugarak Tembhe* (the mother Earth), the land *of Sawa Yethang* and fell at *Khambuchong Yiok – Ngerere Nehangma Yiok,* where Sawa Yethangs inhabited. Ultimately *Sawa Yethang* came to know that the *Ponglung* (shotput-stone) was a divinity, a source of invincibility, unfailing power and eternal energy (*Kamboling Nahangma Sam, Harara Lingemma Sammang*) and a ***Chotlung*** (symbol of power, prestige and progress) of human beings. *Tappeso Lungmahang* eldest among *Yethang* presented a sword or revered it with a sword (*Sinyuk Muden Phe*); second one *Phurupso Thayonghang* revered with ginger; fifth one – *Sangehang Pangehang* with pepper; sixth one – *Thilliso Thejonghang* with *Kuringlung Yum* (salt from mine), seventh one – *Miyara Thokchonghang* with banana leaves, *Saptok* (fermented local beer), *Chirangphekwa* and *Hangappa* (consecrated waterpot decorated with plant leaves and flowers), and the last youngest one *Setchhere*

Seninghang revered it with *Paga* (turban). When they revered it in this way, it became a *Tumyanghang Ponglung*, a *Nahangma Sam*, and a *Chotlung* of the *Limboos*.

(ii) Cosmological: The myth deals with cosmology of creation of the universe, soul journey to the *Akashic* fields/worlds/*Lokas/Dens* and underworlds/ *Lokas/Dens* etc.

(iii) Sociological: The myth has furnished a number of rituals and practices in the society. The myth has provided a practice of constructing altar of the divinities with a symbol of *Ponglung* (shotput-stone) and pegging *Artemisia vulgaris* twigs at its sides, and use of banana leaves, ginger, *Kuringlung Yum* (crystal stones), *Saptok* (fermented beer), pepper, water pot with flowers and *Artemisia vulgaris* twigs for all types of divinities in *Yumaism*. The myth has also expounded the use of *Muden Phe* (knife), and honoring the guests with *Paga* (turban) in our society, which is in practice since then.

(iv) Pedagogical: The myth has interpreted the laws of life, ethical laws of respecting the honorable guests with *Paga* (turban), customary laws of keeping *Mudenphe* (khife) etc.

(v) Mystery of afterlife: The myth has also described the dimension of the journey inward, belief system of soul journey to the *Chotlung* in life, which is believed to be in the *Akashic* field/ *Mangkhoma Den/TapLoka*. The same route leading to ancestor's village has to be followed in the afterlife also.

Myths of Death Rites

Yumaism recognizes eight types of deaths depending on the age, cause of death and condition of the mind of the deceased at the time of death of the individual. They are:

(i) *Lamdoba:* death of the child just after his or her birth;

(ii) *Susuna:* death of a child before appearance of his or her milk teeth;

(iii) *Tanglinghangsa*'s death: death of a child after appearance but before shedding of milk teeth;

(iv) *Sogha*: death due to suicide;

(v) *Sokup* or *Sugut*: death caused by violence or child birth;

(vi) Nahang: individual killed in a war;

(vii) Yok's death: death of a servant;

(viii) Kuso Lamba: a natural death of an individual.

In the case of (i) and (ii) a simple burial takes place and no pollution is observed, while in the case of (iii) besides burial death pollution is observed till the next morning of the burial. No myths relating to this type of deaths are involved and the soul of the dead is allowed to follow their own fate. In the case of *Sogha* (iv), the deceased body's clothes are not removed; the body is tied in a bamboo pole, and directly carried to the burial place either from the place of suicide or from the police inspection spot. The dead body should not be brought to the house in general. In most of the cases, burial takes place at the site of suicide or nearby riverside. The burial rituals are not observed. The deceased body is buried face-side down. The *Phedangma* puts *Muktus* (flowers made of *Ghungring*) on the deceased's nose, mouth, ears, toes of both the legs, and he gently taps on it with chanting myths. All his or her belongings are put inside the grave. Once the burial is complete, *Phedangma* pegs down five *Muktus* (2.5' to 3' long stem of *Ghungring*) and ties with red, white and yellow threads on the top. The *Yeba* or *Yema* through myth gives warning to the soul of the dead not to come out from his or her grave and trouble the people. The people returning from the burial are purified and cleaned by *Siding-Yukmay* twigs (*Mimosa rubicaulis* and *Ricinus communis*) and water before they reach to the deceased's house. On the evening of the burial, the *Yeba* or *Yema* perform the ritual to drive away the soul of the dead and reach to the path of *Sogha Lam* (evil spirits) located in the *Akashic* field (located at *Yetlamdho*), and block its path of return. It is believed that this type of death occurs only with the influence of pre-existing *Soghas* (evil spirits). No pollution is observed in such deaths.

In the case of *Sokup* or *Sugut* (v) the dead body may be brought to the house. It is believed that this type of death also occurs due to the attack or influence of pre-existing *Sokup* or *Sugut* (evil spirits) and could have been avoided with protective measures taken by *Yabas* and *Yemas*. In the case of death due to childbirth, the child is separated from the mother's womb and placed at one side in the burial. The death body of the woman is buried face upward but the face should be covered with her hairs, and the hands should be folded crossed on the body. The *Phedangma* pegs-down *Muktus* same as that of *Sogha* described above. If death occurs after new child naming ceremony then, the death is considered normal. The *Yeba* or *Yema* separates the soul of the deceased from the evil spirits same night of burial and reach to the path of *Sokup* or *Sugut* at the *Akashic* field as in the case of *Sogha* and blocks its return. No pollution is observed in this case also.

In the case of *Nahang* death, the burial is observed same as that of *Sogha*. In the case of *Yok's* death his or her descendants observe rites as that of normal death.

(viii) Kuso Lamba (natural death):

A number of myths are involved in this case. These include:

(i) Funeral procession (*Chesama*); purchase of burial ground (*Kham ingma*) and taking out the soul of the dead person (*Sam Lopma*) – myth of Irere Idhuknama's burial by her sons *Lagerekpa Namgerekpa* (described elsewhere);

(ii) Giving away the soul (*Sam*) of a dead person to ancestors (*Sam-sama*), observation of death pollution, eating salt, spices, meat, ginger, chilly and other forbidden foods (*Yum-chama*) – Myth of *Kesami –Namsami*;

(iii) Final purification rites – myth of *Samchomma, Khauma, Sitongsing Khema,* wiping away of the tears (*Mikwa Sangma*) etc.

When someone dies a normal or natural death, open floor in front of the main door is cleaned to keep the dead body there usually facing westward. The body is laid out in full length and is washed with *"Lisijetti"* (water containing *Artemisia vulgaris* twigs, gold-wash, *Lwang* (Clove, *Syzygium aromaticum*) and *Jaifall* (fruits of Nutmeg, *Myristica fragrans*). Old clothes are taken off and dead body is shrouded with plain white cloth. A bamboo stretcher (*Chedhap*) is prepared to place the dead body. When the procession reaches the graveyard (*ipungden*), they keep the dead body on the ground placing head westward. Now they have to build a new home for the dead person. Digging starts from backside and done conveniently afterwards. A coffin is constructed of flat stones after digging the ground in exact size of the dead body. Before placing the dead body into it, the ritual of *Kham Ingma* or purchasing of the burial ground from the owners of that layer of the earth (below the fertile layer), the divinities *Khambongba Lungbongba* is performed. After that the body is placed into the coffin with the head to the west. Now, the ritual of *Samlopma* (taking out of the soul) is performed. Then stones cover the box properly (Note: details of (i) above and myths has been described elsewhere).

(ii) Myth of *Sam Sama* (soul journey and handing over the soul of the dead to his or her ancestors)

Cooked rice, meat or egg and two *Tongbas* (bamboo cans filled with fermented millet beer) are prepared for ancestor deity (*Hang-sam*). A small basket loosely woven from bamboo splits (*Khengchuri*) is made (three tiers for female and four tiers for male woven in height). It is also known as "*Samsakek*", hung on the top of the hearth. Seven pairs of rice grains husked by hand at the back/without looking at it are kept in *Khengchuri*. Cooked rice, meat or eggs, *Tongba* and other items of offerings to the soul of the dead are kept ready. *Phedangma* after protecting himself through his incantations starts to search the soul of the dead person. *Yumaism* believes in *Yetchham thim* (eight souls). It is believed that the two perceptive souls – *Ni-Sam* (soul of sight) and *Khem-Sam* (soul of hearing) and three conceptive souls – *Sikkum-Sam* (soul of intuition), *Ningwa-Sam* (soul of mind) and *Thona-Sam* (soul of wisdom/consciousness) disintegrate at the time of death, while the vital soul *Pung-sam* (wandering soul) and *Si-sam* (graveyard soul) run away from the dead body at the time of death. Only the *Kunu-sam* or *Hang-sam* (the great ancestor-soul) could be retrieved by the *Phedangma* during *Samsama* ritual with difficulty. Some one has to support him in the ritual. He calls upon the soul not to wander in the villages, hills and forest but to enter the house and accept the food, which is offered by his close relatives or family members. He asks the soul of the dead to remain seated on "*Sam Yukna*" (seat of soul) on the altar. All the relatives and villagers who are staying around mourners or persons observing funeral rites, have to support *Phedangma* from time to time by calling the dead person to enter the house and have the seat. The door is kept open and a corridor is provided to move toward "*Sam Yukna*". This is an effort to retrieve *Pung-sam* and *Si-sam* of the dead person also, but it is believed that usually the two souls fail to enter the house that day. *Phedangma* makes the soul of the dead person agree to enter the house (*hang-sam* of the dead person) and at this moment he violently trembles and suddenly picks up the soul from the air on his sword while entering and makes the soul to remain on his or her seat. He also makes a circle mark around the seat by his sword so that the soul would not run away. By then, he is possessed by the soul of the dead person and the dead person begins to express his or her unsatisfied desire, longing expectations, aims and even secret dealings with other persons through the mouth of *Phedangma*. The *Phedangma* and the mourners offer the foods and other things to please and satiate the dead soul. The food supposed to have been taken by dead is put into the hearth by collecting through the sword used in this ritual.

The *Phedangma* chants incantation to make the dead soul go upward to the *Akashic* field from the *Khengchuri* and living souls to remain downward. With this myth he cuts down the rope made of bamboos splits that hangs the *Khengchuri* and put the *Khengchuri* into the hearth. He then leads the dead soul to the roof. The dead soul is accompanied by living souls gathered there. From the roof, they land down on the ditch like place where water from the eaves falls. The earthworm is asked to help the dead soul to cross the ditch and the soul is lead through the path of fern (*Dryopteris fillixmas*), Scott (*Kattewa loriba*), worm wood fleabane (*Namyoba, Artemisia vulgaris*), bamboo bush and various trees around the house and village. *Phedangma*, chanting the names of different types of plants and trees grown in various altitude where they reach each step, lead the soul of the dead person together with the souls of living persons to the top of a mountain and invokes to all divinities and spirits not to block the path. *Phedangma* also gives the description of the path in his own typical traditional style of rhetorical language. Various types of rocks, soils, birds and beast can be seen on the way. They also find pine trees and places covered by mist and cloud in their ascending journey and they have to protect the souls of the dead and livings. They ascend further and finally they reach to a place where neither the trees can be seen nor the voices of the bird could be heard. The land on either side of their journey is covered with frost (*Sekyayang Pakwayang*), hailstones (*Phanthumba*) and snow (*Nangthumba*).

They further move towards the clouds (*Khami*) by passing the villages of the people of various occupations. At the top of the village only the coniferous shrubs could be seen. While moving further towards the highland, there comes a place full of springs where there are fountains in row. They are the fountains of Supreme Goddess, *Tagera Ningwaphuma*, fountains of *Tuttu Tumyang* (gentlemen), *Yakla Suhangma* (gentlewomen), and the various *Sibhak Yami sa* (*Phedangmas*). These are the sources of clean water and the deep sanctuary of snake (*Osek Tumbus*) and tortoise (*Okwanatumbus*) divinities. After crossing the beautiful land of fountains, they pass through the marshy land. They have to jump through it. Now, they reach to a place with a fountain called *Singoppi Mengoppi Odhan* (*Wathan*). The *Phedangma* makes the dead soul to bathe at this fountain to purify the soul. Now, they ascend the steep slope following a narrow track and reach *Henjiri Hemponghe Chotlung* (fortified place for children), where the souls of the children play happily. The journey further ascends crossing the shaded hook and corners and reaches the *Sisa Menchin-Nali Thangben Chotlung* (fortified place of the young people). The place is known as *Samodhamlung Pangbhe* or *Sangphiriphiri Lingphiriphiri Pangbhe*. They further move towards the clouds by passing the villages of the people of various occupations such as *Thosu Chongbang Khim, Yosu Pethey Khim, Chokephokepho Thingey Kepho Pangbhe* etc.

Now, they reach to a big river where the *Phedangma* invokes the divinity *Achumbung Aroti Mang Singsara Taoding Mang* to build a bridge on the river so that they can go further upward. The river is known as *Sadhunge Thungwama Ahang* and is known to be a boarder between the phenomenal and nominal world. The god of that river is known as *Makchiso Kulang Kemba* that is invoked to allow *Singsara Taoding Mang* to construct a bridge over the river to let pass the souls and control the wayfarers of the two worlds. The team of the journey moves even upward and reaches the crossroads of three paths (*Sumjiri Sumlamdho*). These are the paths of *Sasik Yangdang* (spirits of stillbirths), *Naso Thappen* (devils, witches etc) and the normal path of their own. The *Phedangma* blocks the paths of *Sasik Yangdang* and *Naso Thappen* invoking *Phupuruba Tagesemba*, the divinity of separating the paths and the team follows their normal path from the right hand side.

They ascend further following the normal path (*Kudopma lam*) and reach crossroads of eight paths (*Yetchiri Yetlamdo*). Now the *Phedangma* invokes the *Phupuruba Tagesemba,* the divinity of separating the paths again. If the deceased is an unnatural death, then the *Phedangma* reach the soul of the dead person to the path of *Sam Sogha lam* and asked him to follow that path, blocks the path and return; if the deceased is *Sam Sokup* or *Sugut,* the *Phedangma* reach the soul of the dead person to *Sam Sokup* or *Sugut lam* and hand over the soul of the deceased to Damuhang divinity and blocks the path and return. If the deceased is normal death, then, the *Phedangma* blocks the paths of *Sam Sogha* and *Sam Sugut* or *Sokup* and lead the team further from the right hand side to the land of normal dead persons known as *Samyukna Den* (*Khema Yongsong Pangbhe*), where dreadful watchmen *Haha Mang* (god of laughter), *Habe Mang* (god of crying), *Hadok Mang* (god of sadness) and *Hasu Mang* (god of greed and love removing), etc. watch and guard the place of ancestors village. The path is covered over by trees of *Chongjipphung* (*Ghurpis, Leucosceptrum canum*) and *Mediphung* (*Mahonia napaulensis*).

Now, the *Phedangma* invokes *Phenjetet Kejang Khing Khinglung Samba* (terrible *Samba* wearing iron net), *Sehotet Kejang Khangkhanglung Samba* (*Samba* wearing leather clothes) and *Siwetet Kejang Chingchinglung Samba* (frightening *Samba* wearing stinging nettle cloth) to help him to make them open the gate of *Samyukna Den*. Money (*Khongkhokma yang*) kept in *Samdakhong* and foods prepared in course of performing the ritual are offered to please them. The dead soul is lead towards the place of *Hang Sam* (soul receiving ancestor) to hand over the soul of the dead. The *Phedangma* invites one of the *Hang Sam* to receive the soul of the deceased. When the ancestor opens the door, he is requested to take food and drinks offered. The ancestor deity is made satisfied by offering food and drinks and he takes away the new member. Finally, he requests the ancestor deity to take care of his new member. Now, the *Phedangma* attends trance by possession of ancestor deity and speaks through him that he should not worry about the deceased. He will take care of him. He speaks only a few words and says that he is returning. Then the *Phedangma* with other living souls descend from the same route down to the house describing the routes briefly, from where they started their ascending journey.

While returning, the *Phedangma* invokes *Singsara Taoding Mang* once again to destroy the bridge constructed on the river and *Makchiso Kulang Kemba* not to let evil spirits to come back to earth while coming back after completing the ritual. The *Phedangma* perform various natural dances of deer, *ghoral*, bear, birds and butterflies etc. to confuse the deceased's souls and evil spirits through change of their footsteps which otherwise may follow them to the earth. They also request *Samdang Khewa* and *Lingdang Khewa* to confuse the track for evil spirits and *Makchiso Kulang Kemba* to drag at their feet. The origin of *Ke-Lang* dance or *Chyabrung* dance is the outcome of the nature dances of various types of animals, birds, insects, frogs etc. performed to confuse the dead souls and evil spirits while returning from the ancestor villages. With arrival of home, the myth of *Samsama* ends.

(iii) Myth of *Kesami-Namsami* – Death Pollution

Mourning is observed for 9 (nine) days for men and 8 (eight) days for women and salt, oil, ginger, chili, meat etc. are not taken by family members and close relatives of the deceased person based on the days of coming alive (in 8 days for female and nine days for male) of the first human being created by the creator god *Porokmi Wambhami* and accordingly on the advice of the demi-god *Sodhung Lepmuhang*. However, the days of mourning has been deteriorated or reduced following the devastating plague of the first decade of 19th century to 3 (three) days for female and 4 (four) days for male and observed accordingly now in many places. The persons observing the mourning period do not take salt, pepper, ginger, oil, meat and egg. They take simple food and fruits and do not use metal plates for this purpose. They should not talk to those whose mother tongues or ethnicity differs. They should not play, entertain, worship or bow down to senior relatives. They should not wear *Paga* or turban and women should not comb their hair and wear ornaments and colourful garments. This ritual is known as *Neth Yukma* or *Nepma*. Mourning period starts immediately after the burial and not after the death of the person. All the kins and family members are purified and provided the restricted foods on the 8th (eighth) or 9th (ninth) day depending on the sex of the individual. This ritual is known as *Yum-ninghe-chama Thim* (tradition of taking salt and oil). In this ritual, ginger, garlic, pepper and meat (preferably pork) are fried and kept in a small leave plates separately. All the plates of prepared spices and meat are placed on a winnowing bamboo tray and two bottles of millet beer and locally brewed liquor are kept there. A folded white cloth almost half meter is placed on the bamboo tray and coin of five rupees is kept on top of the cloth along with the new clothes and *Paga* (turban) of those who are observing the mourning ritual. The mourners have to face the west and *Phedangma* starts his myth facing towards them. Other kins, affinal relatives and gentlemen should be present on that occasion. *Phedangma* chants the myth, addresses the gathering and affinal relatives for their consent and performs the ritual of purification. *Yumchama* ritual is conducted on 8th or 9th days along with *Khauma* and *Mikwasangma* or only *Yumchama* ritual is performed on this day and the final rite *Khauma,* accompanied by *Mikwasangma,* is performed in a convenient time. In course of the performance of *Yumchama ritual,* Phedangma relates the myth of *Kesami* and *Namsami* with this event while chanting the myth.

Kesami the tiger and *Namsami* the man were two offspring of a woman named *Ipnana Sarengdhangma,* the sister of *Phaksera Tigenzongba* (*Khambongba Lungbongba sas*). *Kesami* is also known as *Laphakke Phakkehang* and *Namsami* as *Mukkumyongba Warechongba.* Because of their contrasting conscience, attitude and opposite character, temperament and habit, it became impossible to live together for them as they grew up. Jealousy between them eventually brought them to a bitter fight of life and death. Deeply shocked by the tragic quarrel of her sons, *Ipnana Sarengdhangma* was watching the two flowers – the *Ondangphung* (*Ocimum basilicum*) representing the tiger or animal and *Sekmuriphung* (Celery, *Apium graveolens*) representing the human being. *Namsami* was trained in using bow and arrow. He went to *Sapchong Tembhe* for hunting and finally reached *Subhawa Tembhe.* He climbed up to the eight branches (*Yetporak*) of a *Tengosing* (*Bombax malabaricum*) and made a safe place to stay and launch an attack by arrows. *Kesami* arrived there tracing him throughout the hunting areas and started to climb the tree to kill his brother. *Namsami*'s seven arrows failed to strike him and reached almost close to *Namsami. Namsami* was left with only one arrow, the eighth one. So he thought of a trick and told his brother the tiger to open his mouth so that he would jump into his mouth. The tiger *Kesami* believed on his brother's request and open the mouth. In the meantime *Namsami* threw his poisonous arrow in full speed into the mouth of *Kesami,* which struck the heart and the tiger fell down. He was not quite sure that his brother *Kesami* was dead. Because of fear, he waited till the flies began to buzz on the corpse. He came down from the tree and took out the skin out of the body. *Ipnana Sarengdhangma* found the *Ondangphung* withered away and confirmed that only her human son could survive. *Namsami* took the skin of the tiger brother *Kesami* to *Kesalung Namsalung Kookma* and tried to dry it in the sun. But it did not dry up till it was taken to *Seho Namlang Tembhe Angsarang* and was spread on the hot rays of the sun. When it dried, *Namsani* went to different places showing the skin of the tiger and getting something in return. He went to the north and brought salt, went to the east and brought ginger and garlic, went to the west and brought foods and he went to the south and brought money and meat. Thus he collected salt, ginger, garlic, foods, meat and money by showing and exchanging the tiger skin. But both mother and son began to feel sick and became lean and thin when they ate all those things. His mother enquired about the things that he had brought from different quarters. *Namsami* told the truth and his mother called the gentlemen of the village to assemble and find out the way out for them. All the gentlemen and ladies of that land assembled and told them that they have to restrain from all those foods, spices and meat up to 9 (nine) days as *Namsami* has brought those things by exchanging the skin of the tiger his own brother. They also instructed them to observe mourning and perform death rite, as the tiger was a brother of *Namsami*. They again assembled on the ninth day and conducted purification rite and allowed the mourners to take restricted or pungent foods again. *Phedangma* says the tradition was established from this event.

(iv) Myth of *Lagerekpa Namgerekpa*

Phedangma also relate this ritual with the myth of *Lagerekpa Namgerekpa. Sodhung Lepmuhang* and *Laoti Phungphahangma,* a human progenitor demi-god and demi-goddess, gave birth to a daughter *Irere Idhuknama* and a son *Pajoiba Tentumyangba.* These two, brother and sister, came into incestuous relation from their early age and they also gave birth two sons – *Lagerekpa* and *Namgerekpa*. Because of their incestuous relation, they were sent to another human world – *Khetchhuwa Upanga Pangbhe*. When Idhuknama and *Tentumyangba* became mature enough and realized that their relationship was against the wishes of gods and goddesses, *Idhuknama* suggested his brother to marry a girl outside consanguineous relation, as they have to live in the world of human beings. (Note: The myth has been described in detail elsewhere and need not be repeated here).

With the end of the myths, *Phedangma* deals with the present context. He says that death is inevitable and so the person was departed from us. The family members and relatives observed the mourning till today restraining from salt, ginger, garlic, meat and other pungent foods and clothes. He addresses the gentlemen and distinguished ladies for their consent to permit some or all of the items of foods to eat and to participate in some or every activity. All the men, women and even affinal relatives give consent what has been proposed by the *Phedangma* on behalf of the mourners. With the end of his address, he tells all to taste the foods and spices kept on the bamboo tray and to share by all. This ends the ritual of *Yum Ninghe Chama*.

(v) Myth of *Sam-chomma, Khauma*

This is the final rite of death ceremonies. It should be performed within a year. In the early days a suitable time was usually considered the period of winter after harvest but now-a-days *Khauma* is done in any odd day or odd month after *Yumchama* ritual. Dates are decided and the formal mourning period begins with all restrictions. All the relatives and participants of the funeral processions are invited. There is a custom of constructing a cemetery on the graveyard (*Ibungden*) and also a resting platform known as *Kaknamphe Iknamphe* or *Lagaklung Kaklung Tembhe, Namgaklung Kaklung Tembhe* on the way or at a suitable place. The cemetery if constructed is always with three-step or four-step bench like cemented cemetery. The resting place may be wooden or stones and earth or cemented structure. A tablet of stone (*Iksap*) is placed there with the inscription containing the information about the deceased person and those who constructed it. Construction of cemetery and platform should be completed one day before *Khauma*. Myth of cemetery and platform are in the belief system of *Yumaism*. *Yumaism* believes that out of the eight souls of a human being, the two vital souls known as *Si-sam* (graveyard soul) and *Pung-Sam* (wandering soul) cannot be retrieved to handover to the ancestor deity by the *Phedangma* during *Samsama* ritual. The *Phedangma* can retrieve them only after the judgment has been delivered by the *Paoti Mang* for his or her final destination in 8 (eight for female) or 9 (nine for male) days mourning period. The cemetery constructed is for invoking, inviting and feeding the *Si-sam* (graveyard soul) by the family members and close relatives one day before the *Khauma* ritual time. Similarly, the *Pung-sam* (wandering soul) wanders around the earth and the platform is a place where the *Phedangma* invokes, invites and the family members and close relatives feed the soul one day before the final *Khauma*. These two vital souls are finally retrieved and hand over to the ancestor deity by the *Phedangma* by conducting *Sam Chomma* and *Sitongsing Khema* rituals during the day and night of *Khauma* respectively.

Myth of *Sam-Chomma* is just a repetition of *Sam Samma* myth for retrieving, accompanying and handing over the *Si-sam* and *Pung-Sam* souls of the dead person to the ancestor deity.

Khauma Ritual

Once the *Sam-Chomma* ritual is over the *Phedangma* invite all the invitees, villagers, kith and kins assembled in a field and the mourners are made to stay in the middle facing the west. *Phedangma* addresses the mass giving the description of all the efforts made to save the dead person and the way how the close relatives or descendants observed the mourning period with hardships, difficulties and restraints and ask for their opinion and consent to bring light on their lives. The people around him discuss the myths relating to eventual death of human beings and related rituals for the separation for the dead soul with the living ones. *Phedangma* explains that the assembled gentlemen have a power of decision, which never fails citing the example of related myths. Thus, *Phedangma* and others come to the conclusion that the council of *Sawa Yethangs*, eight wise leaders is represented by their descendants with the same traditional authority of giving decisions relating to death and departed soul.

Finally they end their discussion with approval of allowing the mourners free from all restrictions of food, clothes, decoration, entertainment, marriage and worships and considering them free from the impurity caused by the death of close relative. *Phedangma* completes the *Khauma* ritual with the declaration that the departed soul is separated with the living ones. He breaks the stick, which he was holding, and throws away.

(vi) Myth of *Sitongsing Khema*

Phedangmas, Sambas conduct the ritual of *Sitongsing Khema* at night, which has been described under the myth of *Tongsing*. The myth of ***Sitongsing Khema*** is to accompany the souls of the dead person, separating with the living souls and reached to *Samyukna Den* and hand over the deceased soul to the ancestor deity. The ritual is conducted at night in every death ritual. However, full *Tongsing* is conducted only once in three years. Hence, when death occurs in a clan within three years period, then *Sitongsing Khema* is to be conducted. But if death occurs in a clan beyond three years period a full *Tongsing* has to be conducted. The myths of *Sitongsing* and full *Tongsing* is the same as described elsewhere under *Tongsing* and need not be repeated here.

(vii) Myth of *Mikwa Sangma*

This is the last rite of death ceremonies, which is usually performed by *Samba*. The literal meaning of *Mikwa Sangma* is to wash out the tears or stains of tears from the face and these rituals symbolically indicates the total separation of dead soul and forgetting the deceased person and thus remain happy without the phantasmagoria of death. If it is not performed with *Tongsing*, it is known as "*Tapmikwasang*" and if it is performed with *Tongsing*, it is known as "*Simikwasang*". The later is more common than the former today.

First of all, *Samba* invokes *Akwanama*, the god of the main pillar and *Yuma*, the Supreme Goddess, for their permission to start the ritual. He chants the myth of *Pajoiba Tentumyangba* who threw a bundle of *Mikjiri* flower aiming at *Irere Idhuknama*'s breast, which caused her untimely death. *Lagerekpa Namgerekpa* wept in the departure of their mother. Plants, insects and birds began to weep on the tragedy fallen to them. *Irere Idhuknama* began to come out of her body to see her sons at night and to assist them in their works. *Sodhung Lepmuhang* came to know the tragic death of his daughter and her *Letchham* (un-destined soul) just roaming around those lands to which she belonged. He came down to the *Khechhuwa Upanga Pangbhe,* where *Lagerekpa Namgerekpas* were living. Following the instruction of Supreme Goddess *Tagera Ningwaphuma,* he told his grandsons, *Lagerekpa Namgerekpa,* to perform the funeral rites. He also suggested them to ask *Nawara Suling Samba* to conduct the ritual. *Lagerekpa Namgerekpa* followed the instruction accordingly. The *Samba* performed the funeral rites of their mother and washed the stains of tears of their faces. In course of myth recitation, *Phedangma* says that the descendants of *Sawa Yethang* are following the same procedure since then on.

In the meantime, *Samba* sprinkles the water from various springs and rivers on those persons who have been newly purified. Ritual sprinkling is done with four bundle of twigs *Sapsing* (*Phoeba lanceolata*), *Sidingba* (*Mimosa rubicaulis*) and *Yukmi* (*Ricinus sp.*) in practice. The newly purified members face the west and the *Phedangma* sprinkles the water from head to the feet by the twigs (Kainla, B. 1995; Subba, C. 1995: 213-1235; Subba, J.R. 1999: 453-508; 2005a: 74-162; 2005b: 55-137).

Mythological Functions

(i) Mystical: The myths describe the mystery of death rituals performed in the *Limboo* society. It relates a number of myths illustrating origin of the rituals, reason why we should perform these rituals - the whole gamut of death rituals for afterlife of the deceased person, and also for health and well being of the living family members and the close relatives.

(ii) Cosmological: The myths deal with the cosmological origin, how did the mortal life was creator god created, how the *Phanghangs* (nine ancestor-brothers) had to leave for the *Akashic* field *Muringla Kharingla Tembhe,* and *Yethangs* (eight ancestors) had to stay with the mother at *Sangarak Nugarak Tembhe* (on the Earth). It also expounds how after death the soul of the individual has to be reached to the ancestor world in the *Akashic* field (*Samyukna Den*) and handover to the ancestor deity (*Hang-sam*).

(iii) Sociological: The myth has furnished the death rituals of performing rituals for proper guidance of the soul of the dead person such as (a) *Chey sama,* (b) *Samsama,* (c) *Yum-Ninghe-Sa*

Nepmma, (d) *Yum-Ninghe Chama*, (e) *Ibungden chokma*, (f) *Lakaklung Kaklung Namkaklung Tembhe Chokma*, (g) *Sam chomma*, (h) *Khauma*, (i) *Sitongsing Khema*, (j) *Mikwa-Nangwa Sangma* etc. These rituals unfold the rituals of purification from the death pollution; and finally, for better health and protection of the living members and close relatives.

(iv) Pedagogical: The myth has interpreted laws of life rituals, ethical laws and other customary laws of death pollution and death pollution purification.

(v) Mystery of afterlife: The myth also explains the dimension of afterlife such as the journey inward; the physical conscious transcending into spiritual consciousness which takes eight or nine days in *Yumaism* belief system; and soul of the dead person joining to its origin (ancestors). It also unfolds that if the soul is not guided properly it remains in the physical consciousness as *Letchham*. Separation of the soul of the dead person from the living members and close relatives by the ritual of *Khauma, Samchomma* and *Sitongsing Khema,* and providing proper guidance to the soul of the dead person for transcending it into mental consciousness, accompanying it to the *Akashic* field - the *Samyukna Den* and handing over it to the ancestor deity is essential in *Yumaism*. The living family and close relative (mourners) have to be given moral support by conducting ritual of *Mikwa Nangwa Sangma*.

Myths of Supernatural Powers and Spirituality

(a) Myths of *Mang* (Deity), *Sammang* (Divinity) and *Sammang Chyang* (retinue of divinities)

Yumaism recognizes three categories of supernatural powers. They are:

(i) *Mangs* (gods, goddesses or Deities); (ii) *Sammangs* (incarnations or manifestations of gods and goddesses or spirit/ soul forms of supernatural powers or Divinities); and (iii) *Sammang Chyangs* (retinue of *Sammangs* or retinue of divinities).

(i) *Mangs* (Deities)

The *Mangs* are the Deities or gods and goddesses of creation of the universe and are considered as creators, preservers and sustainers of the universe. They are incorporeal, eternal, unstained, almighty and attributeless. They are indefinable absolutes, formless, beyond human sensory perception and are prayed for specific purpose and they discharge their responsibilities in specific time. They are imagined as supreme power, ultimate sources of existence as well as extinction of celestial, formless and beyond imagination but often imagined in any form suitable to their specific roles in specific time. They are beyond sensory perception and are indefinable absolute. They are only prayed and never worshipped with any type of sacrifices or offerings. Several names of *Mangs* (Deities) are mentioned in the course of the myth recitation of genesis. Each *Mang* appears in each situation and because of his presence certain things or creation happens. For Example:

Attiya Mang Musunne Mang (a god of void), *Mu-unga Mang Khaunga Mang* (a crawling god), *Lang Membot Mang Langthuti Mang* (a moving god without legs), *Sawara Yettungek Mang* (god or goddess with eight legs or names), *Hukmembat Mang Hukthuti Mang* (a skilful god without hands), *Allapi Mang Jallapi Mang* (a formless and attributeless lightening and shining god), *Upangek Mang Prapangek Mang* (striding and supplementing god), *Achuni Mang Allekha Mang* (infinite and eternal god), *Khijora Menjora Mang* (god in thread form), *Ijambo Mang Idakha Mang* (net-like spreading god), *Khambudak Mang Ijambo Mang* (soil arranger god), *Tunghikke Mang Panghikke Mang* (god of dust and mist), *Sawara Yetthegek Mang* (god with eight heads), *Wadhinlung Mang Phaphalung Mang* (god in white egg-form), *Changhima Mang Thobuma Mang* (boon bestowing goddess), *Muroklung Mang Kheroklung Mang* (god of nether and ethereal existence), *Mujoklung Mang Mubokwama Mang* (creator god), *Thiksumbha Nisumbha Sumsumbha Lisumbha Mang* (foe destroyer several gods), *Thanget Mang Langet Mang Namget Mang Namdha Mang* (gods of north, south, east and west), *Huktrakek Langtrakek Mang* (gods working hardly by hands and walking hardly by legs), *Tioti Mang Paoti Mang* (god of judgment at death), *Laoti Phungphahangma Mang* (goddess of flower), *Chungchihangba Yechhahangba Mang* (orphan god), *Nenthakkum Mang Imetang Mang* (frightening and shaking god), etc. *Tagera Ningwaphuma* – the ultimate Supreme Goddess, Omniscient (all knowing), Omnipresent (in all places at all time), Omnipotent (all powerful), Infinite (without beginning or end), and Eternal Force, Light or Power of existence, which has none of the attributes. She guides *Sigera Yaphundin Mang Porokmi Wamphami Mang* (creator god) to materialize the creation of all living and non-living things including the human beings and send other gods and goddesses to help him in his mission of creation. To complement the roles of *Porokmi Wambhami*, various gods such as *Kunuso Chayetso Mang* (creators god of physical forms), *Uttandi Pattandi Mang* (creator gods of crops), *Sambang Kepma Toklama Mang* (meditating god), *Chakchakke Mang Yangyange Mang* (developer god), *Sing Mang Lung Mang* (gods of trees and rocks), *Nawalung Mang Chosaplung Mang* (god of destiny and fate), *Thappura Theyonge Mang* (god of the hearth), *Mataso Imetso Mang* (soul controller god), *Yetchiri Yet Ado Mang Sumjiri Sum Ado Mang* (god/goddess of confluence of eight or three rivers), *Nawara Sumlammo Mang Nawara Yetlammo Mang* (god/goddess of the crossroads of three or eight paths), appear with their respective roles. Similarly, *Sumsuba Mang* created the gods and goddesses of water, *Wasumbu Mang* created the stars, *Bebesong Mang* created several divinities (*Thakligen Sammang*), *Benam Song Mang*, *Belasong Mang*, *Kumpha Mang*, *Metha Mang*, *Beli Mang*, *Lokpha Mang*, *Champha Mang*, *Rupi Mang* and *Paoti Mang* created cosmological planets, ocean, air, rain minerals, and other living and non-livings in the universe. *Haha Mang*, *Habek Mang*, *Hadok Mang* and *Hasu Mang* are described as gods leading towards the land of death and damnation – *Khemading Yongsong Den*. Finally, *Sodung Lepmuhang* becomes the protector, rescuer, nourisher god who recently interacted with the human beings and he is also described as the progenitor of human beings.

In the myth of genesis, several gods and goddesses are referred to have played their specific roles to make the creation perfect. Only a few details are presented about them and the semantic interpretation of their names has become the most appropriate way to understand their attributes. *Tagera Ningwaphuma* is the only Goddess who is revered most and whose name is referred to several times on several occasions. In the myth of genesis, all the above mentioned gods and goddesses also pray for blessing and success in their respective role of creation to the Almighty Goddess *Tagera Ningwaphuma*. This indicates the Supremacy of *Tagera Ningwaphuma* in the creation of the Universe; and also indicates that all the gods and goddesses are Her messengers (*Sijoingmi Sa*). Thus, all other *Mangs* (Deities) are prayed in the context of propitiating *Tagera Ningwaphuma*. Further, Mangs are prayed in the context of propitiating *Sammangs* (divinities) but worship ceremonies or rituals are not conducted for *Mangs*. Litany and eulogy of *Sammangs* indicate that *Sammangs* possess the power and attributes of various *Mangs* for the worldly matters or in the Physical consciousness. *Yumaism* believes in two categories of supernatural, as in any other religion or belief system. *Mangs* (Deities) are supernatural powers of **Spiritual consciousness** like *Bhahma, Vishnu* and *Maheswara* of Hinduism. On the other hand, *Sammangs* (divinities) are the supernatural powers of **Physical consciousness** as in the case of *Saraswati* for knowledge, *Luxmi* for wealth, *Durga, Ram* or *Krishna* for *Sakti* or sustenance of the universe in Hinduism. Nobody bothers about the spiritual consciousness in his physical existence on earth, and hence the *Mangs* (Deities) are just prayed casually. The man exists in the physical consciousness on earth, and bothers mostly on the *Sammangs* (divinities) to fulfill his physical requirements. Hence, he prays, eulogizes, propitiate, worship with offering to the *Sammangs* (divinities) only on earth.

(ii) *Sammangs* (Divinities)

Sammang (Divinity) is different from *Mang* (Deity). The word "*Sammang*" is the conjoint of *Sam* (spirit/soul) and *Mang* (Deities), which means spirit/soul gods or goddesses. The *Mangs* (Deities) have manifested or incarnated in many gods and goddesses in spirit or soul forms, representing many divinities having various levels or realms of authority. *Sammangs* are often called "*Thokley Sammang*" which means a supernatural power (godlike power) in various physical forms. They are divinities imagined or described in various forms with certain roles. There are also *Sam Sires* or spirits or Soul-form gods and goddesses or master spirits with certain but extraordinary powers categorized as *Sammangs*. There are various references in myth on the origin of *Sammangs*. Some of the *Sammangs* are the incarnations of *Mangs*. One of the reference expatiate that the first trial models of human creation from various precious metals could not become human beings and were thrown away by their creator god and it became *Sammangs*. Next the creator god tried with soil. It also failed to become human beings. They were also thrown away and it became the dwarf *Sammangs* known as *Khambongba Lungbongba sa* the owners of the soil below the fertile layer of the earth. Other references depict that some of the *Sammangs* were created from various parts or drops of blood of seven suns that were shot down by the porcupine to save living beings on earth from draught and heat. There is also a reference relating to the origin of *Sammangs* in the myth of *Ponglung Lepma* (shotput throwing). The myth describes the origination of some of the *Sammangs* as a result of breaking away of stone while it was thrown away by *Porokmi Wambhami* in the space. It is said that that *Khambongba Lungbongba* (gods and goddesses of soil or earth) appeared after *Mangs; Sammangs* appeared after *Khambongba Lungbongba*; human beings appeared after *Sammangs*; and *Sires* appeared finally. There are several *Sammangs* (divinities) associated with certain rituals. Among them, some are adored inside the house consisting or making an altar in the appropriate place and some are worshipped or propitiated outside the house with their set rituals. Again, some of them are tutelary divinities of particular group (clan or thar) of *Limboos*. *Yuma Sammang* is the only common divinity of all *Limboos*. She is considered the divinity form (physical consciousness or Divinity) of *Tagera Ningwaphuma* (Spiritual consciousness or Deity) and incarnate or daughter having equivalent power to the Almighty Goddess. So, *Yuma Sammang* is the supreme divinity of unlimited powers, intellect, wisdom, and abounding wealth. She is venerated highly and is prayed in every ceremonial rite for the accomplishment of the particular missions. Quite wonderfully, most of the *Sammangs* are related to particular group of *Limboos* and they follow the matrilineal descents. So, *Limboos* were anxious about *Sammangs* when they thought of marrying a girl from a particular clan in the past. The immediate offsprings of a new couple has to propitiate the *Sammang* of both of his father and mother. Mother's *Sammang* will be a new *Sammang* for that family.

There are several *Sammangs* who are worshipped inside the house and are provided special altar or a sacred place to stay for them. *Yuma Sammang, Theba Sammang, Khawalung Thakphut Mang* (*Him Sammang*), *Akwanama, Kappoba, Mudemba,* etc. are most frequently invoked *Sammangs* among them. It is believed that they always accompany the human being, protect them and bring good luck and prosperity for them. Some of them are revered as guardian deities. They are invoked in different ways, sometimes

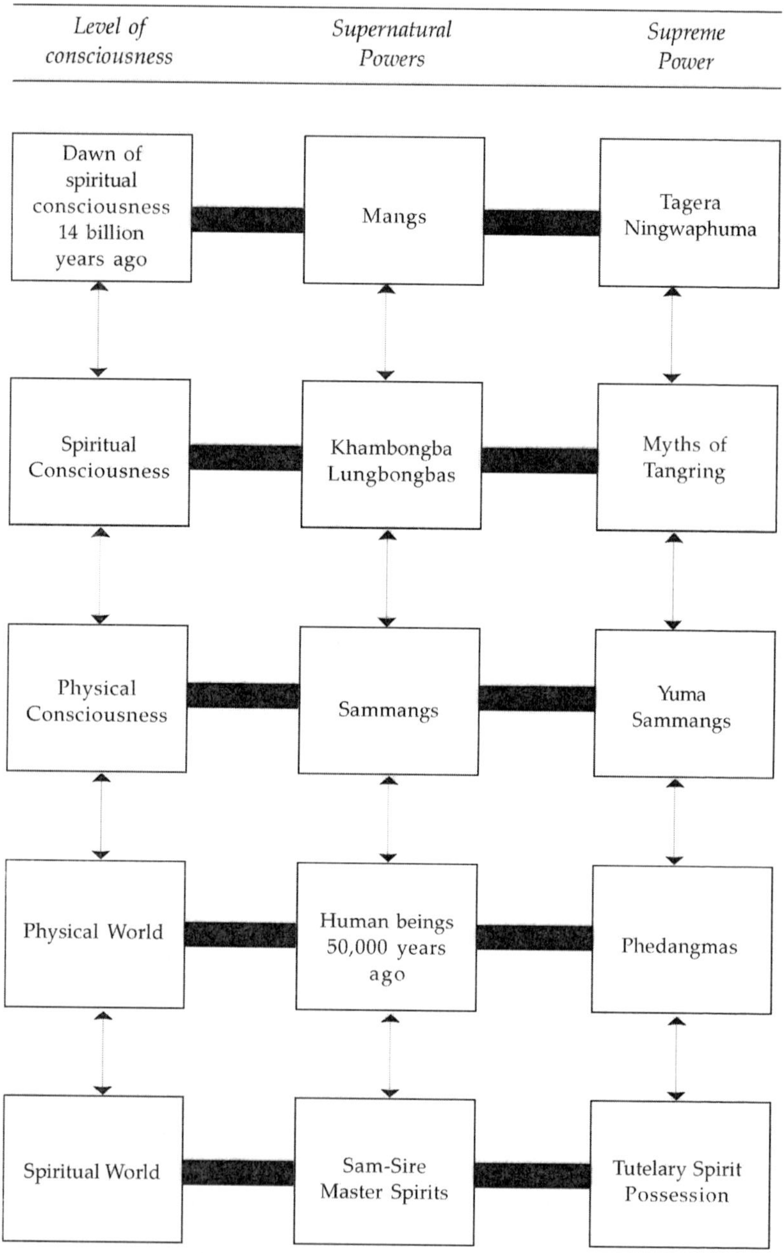

Origination of Supernatural Powers in Yumaism

with sacrifices and sometimes by offering just the fruits, flowers and incense, and sometimes with a long ritual with set rules and fetishes and sometimes, with just praying for few minutes by burning dry leaves of *Sukpa* (twigs of pine trees of high land) or *Namyoba* (*Artemisia vulgaris*) in glowing embers. *Yuma Sammang* is the main tutelary divinity who even controls other divinities or protects her devotees from ill-doings of other divinities and evil spirits.

Sammangs (divinities) are considered to have both constructive as well as destructive powers. Guardian divinities are saviors, obstacle removers, suppressor of evil doers and symbol of heroism and vigor. The other *Sammangs* who are supposed to stay outside the house are numerous. Some of the most frequently propitiated *Sammangs* among them are *Tambhungna, Khanjama, Toksongba, Wajongma, Warokma, Senghama (Phatagekma), Misekpa, Soba Sammang, Chanema, Phakmura, Sakmurama, Singlamba, Dungdunge, Payonglungma, Syanima, Thungdangba, Payohangba (Kusang), Phaksingdangma, Pichchhama, Nangepma, Yangphuma, Lummayeppa, Miksangchakpa, Dokhuma, Hampangma, Thema, Tahangma, Mangduma, Khawama,* etc. They are also known by various names and forms from place to place.

They are worshipped with offerings. *Sammangs* are considered to have both constructive as well as destructive powers. Divinities are saviors, obstacle removers, suppressor of evildoers, and symbol of heroism and vigour. Some of the *Sammangs* are the models of compassion, love, nurturance, inspiration, motivation, intellect, creativeness, growth, advancement and some are of fear, hatred, envy, jealousy, curse, retrogression, degeneration, decadence and annihilation. There are several *Sammangs* with their typical myths and rituals. Some are related with particular groups of *Limboos* and only the *Phedangmas* of the particular clan are competent to deal the particular myth. *Tongsing* myths are the oldest myths on the life of *Khambongba Lungbogba Mangs* while the myths of *Sammangs* are comparatively recent ones based on human ancestors. In the former part, *Tagera Ningwaphuma* (Deity) is the Supreme Goddess and in the later part *Yuma Sammang* (divinity) is the supreme divinity, incarnate or daughter of *Tagera Ningwaphuma.*

Sam Sire

Sires or *Sam Sires* are also another category of *Sammangs*. They are actually the *Sam Sires* and master spirits of *Phedangmas*. They are the souls of the departed persons – incarnation possessed for life and the Master spirits. They are the source of power for them and without their support in due time, they cannot perform the rituals. They are the sources of power for the shaman priests and without their support they cannot perform shamanic rituals. The popular ones are: *Mamgmang Sire* or *Sammethungma Yepmethungma* (tutelary *Sire* of *Phedangmas*), *Muiyan* (eagle/hawk) *Sire*, *Makyu* (bear) *Sire*, *Pora* (wild dog) *Sire*, *Phungpit* (Yak) *Sire*, *Miyong* (cat) *Sire*, *Tokmi* (elephant) *Sire*, *Keba* (tiger) *Sire*, *Ta-angwa* (flamingo) *Sire*, *Mangjum Mangwa* (wild bee/hornet) *Sire*, *Sangwa* (buffalo) *Sire*, *Yurum Yuwa* (poisonous wasp) *Sire*, etc. Although *Sires* may cause troubles of serious nature, but they are useful and benevolent also in many ways. They contribute to the human welfare by performing ritualistic as well as other functions beyond the capacity of ritual performers and ordinary people.

(iii) Sammangchyangs

Sammangs also have their own retinues which are known as "*Sammang Chyangs*". They are the retinues of *Sammangs*. There are hundreds of *Sammangchyangs* forming a coterie of attendants around each of the *Sammangs*. Most of them are known as malicious, obnoxious, detrimental and wicked. They have to be propitiated before initiating the invocation rite of the main divinities so that they may not cause disturbances beforehand. The best-known *Sammangchyangs* are cosmic retinues of *Nahen*, malevolent spirits such as *Sugut*, *Sogha*, *Sasik* etc. They should be driven away before commencing worship of any *Sammang* with rice, ash, white sand etc. (Subba, C. 1995: 236-290; Subba, J.R. 1999: 509- 535; 2005a: 22-39).

Mythological Functions

(i) Mystical: The myth describes the mystery of the origin of *Mangs* (Deities), *Sammangs* (Divinities), *Sammang Chyangs* (retinue of divinities) and *Sam Sires* (Deities and master spirits).

(ii) Cosmological: The myth explains that most of the Deities, Divinities and retinue of divinities have cosmological origin.

(iii) Sociological: The myth has furnished a number of rituals to be performed in household (for *Him-Sammangs*) and also away from household for nature divinities (*Tap-Sammangs*) and clan-divinities (*Thokley-Sammangs*), and are related to both nature (nature divinities) and clan of the society.

(iv) Pedagogical: The myth also interprets customary laws.

(b) *Yuma Sammang* or Yuma (divinity) or Origin of *Yumaism* or *Yuma* Religion

Yuma Sammang (Divinity) is described as the incarnation or daughter or manifestation in the divinity form of *Tagera Ningwaphuma Mang* (Deity); and thus, she is timeless, infinite, eternal, omnipresent, omniscient, omnipotent goddess having the same power as that of the Almighty Goddess *Tagera Ningwaphuma Mang*. She is intuitive light, and she is regulator of both the phenomenal and nounmenal world. Different appellations have been used for her in different context. She is known as *Thillilung Thamdenlungma* (progenitor as well as all pervading goddess), *Sawara Yettungekma* (a goddess appearing in many forms), *Nawara Chagaplungma – Lajiri Layamlungma* (creator of primeval rocks and daughter of mountains), *Iksa Khambek Tarong Tangsang Sumboklama* (mistress of earth and firmament or a goddess of nourishment and heat and cold), *Lokpha Singkhim Dangma-Mujiri Mubokwama* (mistress of the house and a primordial goddess of inner world), *Phajiyang Makjiyang Mangma* (a colourful goddess), *Tetlara Lasoding Mangma* (boon bestowing goddess), and *Tagera Ningwaphuma* (timeless, infinite, eternal, omnipresent, omniscient, omnipotent goddess). Each appellation bears certain attributes and roles in the course of the creation, nurturance and preservation of universe including the earth and living as well as non-living things on earth. The liturgy procedure of *Yuma* religion involves shamanic practices and austerities, complex rituals (with blood sacrifices seen even today) and use of fetishes with magical overtones.

The myth of *Yuma Sammang* recited in the invocation rite presents a picturesque description of her peregrination from the land of early human migration to *Muna Tembhe* (plain areas of Persia), *Mangjiri Mangowet* (?Mongolia) to the land of the progeny of *Sawa Yethangs* through *Sinyuk Muden* (China-Tibet), various places of *Temen Warong* (south) and holy region of Himalayan ranges. An extensive account on *Yuma Sammang* and her homilies are presented in the myth compilation of Chemjong (1961). The myth alludes that *Limboos* were the followers and devotees of *Yuma Sammang* through eternity, and *Limboos* (*Susuwa Lilim Yakthungs*) were always empowered and protected throughout their adventurous migratory journey from *Muna Tembhe* to *Sinyuk-Muden* to their land of last settlement in the sacred Himalayas. According to myth, *Kanden Hang* in *Sinyuk* (China); *Mukkeguba Munaphen Hang*, and *Lasa Hang* in *Muden* (Tibet); and the tribal kings *Uba Hang* (849-865 A.D.), *Mabo Hang* (865-880 A.D.) and *Sirijunga Hang* (880-915 A.D.) who ruled *Limbuwan* propagated the uncanny powers of *Yuma Sammang*, her teachings, code of ethics and instructions. The sermons of *Sirijunga* reveal that he was also a devotee of *Tagera Ningwaphuma* and he revered her much in the form of *Nisammang* or goddess of intellect (Chemjong, I.S. 1965). Through the scrutiny of manuscripts and other written documents, Chemjong (1948) has also reached the conclusion that the king *Sirijunga* of *Limbuwan* has introduced *Limboo* (Kirat) script, emphasized on education and advocated for the religious awakening on the last quarter of 9th century to early decades of 10th century. Thus, *Yuma Sammang* or Grand-mother goddess has always remained as the source of inspiration, motivation for the *Limboo* tribes from remote antiquity to throughout the course of history.

After the elapse of hundreds of years, *Phalgunanda Lingden* once again advocated the teachings, instructions, great maxims and canons of *Yuma Sammang* and reinterpreted the code of conducts, rites and rituals, customs and usages adopted by *Limboos* through centuries as her followers. However, his movements against killings of animals and birds, sacrifices in the ritual, use of intoxicating substances and introduction of oblation in the burning fire or fire cult and Hinduisation of replacing *Phedangmas* by his trained disciples and radical modification in traditional rituals met with much resistance and could not influence the common people.

Though the religious faith founded on the cult of *Yuma Sammang*, seems to have its source in the remote antiquity, only a few preceptors and propagators cum devotees are recalled in the course of myth recitation. This is exhibited in the expression addressed to her such as *Sinyuk Hangma* (Chinese goddess), *Kanden Hangma, Muden Hangma, Yanchhen Hangma, Thak Thakkumma* (weaving maiden), *Mabo Hangma, Lingden Hangma, Thapmiya, Muregon, Kajungwa, Kaneba, Phatlemi, Khechiba, Uba Hangma,* etc. are some of the prominent figures who identified or *Yuma Sammang* spoke through them (*Yuma Sammang Thanchhingma*) (Shreng, Randhoj 1993). Various *Phedangmas* identified her and invoked her on behalf of the local inhabitants. The people suffering from illness became well and desiccation turned into fertility, exhaustion into rejuvenation, destruction into creation, distress into jubilation, evil into good and death turned into life when they invoked and propitiated her.

Though the myth of *Yuma* differs from place to place and person to person (which is natural in oral tradition), the account of her peregrination in the myth indicate that she appeared during the period of social anarchy and moral interregnum as a light in the dark in the hoary past and started her journey from *Muna Tembhe* (Plains of Persia) to *Sinyuk* (China) and with her retinues, devotees, followers and cattle and fowls towards *Muden* (Tibet). She moved towards the south from there and destroyed a lake surrounded by mountains and hills on her way to south. She moved from place to place in the mountainous region in search of better place to spread her loom, to guide people for civilized way of life and left some of members of her journey there. Some of them were *Sammangs* and some of human beings. The big mountains such as *Phaktanglungma* (Mount Jannu, *Kumbhakarna*), *Kewalungma* or *Moralungma* (K2), *Chomjonglungma* or *Chomphutlungma* or *Chomolungma* (Mt. Everest), *Senjelungma* or *Seseylungma* (Kanchanjunga), *Sewalungma,* etc. became the abode of *Yuma Sammang* since then. She then went down to the confluence of eight rivers where she performed the lustration. She moved from place to place in the plain region of *Temen Warong* (south). She created some sisters known as *Kashihangma, Pattagekma, Khanjama, Temphoma* etc. there and assigned their duties to look after nature and other living creatures. She finally came to the confluence of seven rivers (*Koka Braha*) and entered into its basin, reached its springs and flew to mountains visiting various places of *Khambu, Yakkha* and *Yakthungbas*. Probably most recently she was recognized by *Jaijite Kharbalya Phangdangma* and established an altar in *Yasok. Mabohang*, who found her, became a great devotee of her and preached and propagated her instruction, maxims and percepts to all the people of his land.

The myths of *Yum Sammang* are chanted in different tunes. The myth portion is chanted in one musical tune and litany and propitiatory invocation with offerings are chanted in different tunes. The musical elements of the myth recitation make the myth more melodious and pleasing. Various kinds of fruit, root and tuber crops are considered best offerings for *Yuma*. The worship of *Yuma* is performed in a quit place inside the house decorating the altar with one water pot infixed with flowers and lighted one small lamp. *Namyoba* (*Artemisia vulgaris*) will be necessary to be included in the bunch of flowers. A holy water (*Wadumbokwa* = rainwater collected on tree-holes or stones or rocks) is sprinkled by a *Namyuba* twigs to purify the altar and incense is burnt in glowing ember there in course of the invocation ritual. Physical presence near by or clothes of the upper part of the body of those persons, who have organized the ritual, are kept in front of the altar and *Phedangma* invokes *Yuma* on their behalf. *Yuma* is worshipped on most occasions. She is invoked during the time of illness, distress and difficulties. She is invoked in time of harvesting season and sowing season. *Limboos* do not eat any food crop without offering it to *Yuma* when it gets ready for eating. Even fruits, ginger, yams and other root crops are offered when it is ripe and ready to eat. Among domestic animals, pig is necessary to offer to *Yuma* when it is killed. So Phedangma has to be present to kill a pig. *Yuma* is always invoked in the proprietary rites of other *Sammangs* also for the success of the particular attempts. Sacrifices of domestic animals and fowls to *Yuma* have become common practice today, though such practices seem to have started very recently out of greediness of *Phedangmas*.

The myth tells us that various rules and customs were laid down to govern the Limboo society. The rules were based on certain ethics, norms, values and conscience through which a religion developed. Prominent figures in this connection are the Demi-god *Sodhung Lepmuhang* – a patron deity, *Sawa Yethangs* (eight Limboo ancestors and leaders) –the primogenitors of the Limboos, the *Yuma* incarnates – *Kanden Hang, Mukkeguba Munaphen Hang,*

Laso Hang, Sirijonga Hang, Yongjonga Hang, Mabo Hang, Sirihonga Singthebe who were always inspired and guided by *Tagera Ningwaphuma,* a Supreme grand-mother Goddess in *Mang* form (Deity) popularly addressed as *Yuma* in its *Sammang* (divinity) form in the world at present. The pious people of the period had direct contact with *Tagera Ningwaphuma* and they developed various rituals of life cycle and death with her guidance. They interpreted the natural as well as supernatural phenomena with the insight bestowed upon them by her and became able to develop certain values and ethics for human society. At the latter phase, *Yuma* spoke on essential issues and instructed to the common folk through these enlightened people. Following this tradition, *Phedangmas* (all types) come in touch with *Yuma* (referred to both *Yuma Sammang* and *Tagera Ningwaphuma*) through their unrelenting practice of séance, necromancy and austere pursuit of applied myths. It is believed even today that *Yuma* speaks to her devotees through these professional people. The oracle deals with philosophical, religious, ethical, social and various aspects of human relationships and relationships between life and death, natural and supernatural world, and eschatology as well as metempsychosis.

Oracles or instructions of *Yuma* are too much scattered and oral tradition of myth has made even more difficult to systematize and give correct interpretation. However the norms and values, that guide and govern the *Limboo* community, the belief system, the basic theological elements of rituals, the witty sayings retained in the memory of many *Phedangmas* provide the base for the redaction and exegesis of the theological and religious concepts behind *Yuma Samyo* or *Yuma* religion. Some of the enthusiastic writers (Chemjong, I.S. 1961, Shreng, 1992; 1993; Subba, J.R. 1998; 1999; 2005a) have tried their best to deal in this subject.

Six *Yuma* Religion Teachings

The broad outline of *Yuma*'s teachings are divided into six categories as follows::

(i) The Origin and Destination of Human Life (Souls)

The origin as well as the destination of human life (souls) is ***Sangram Pedang Den.*** We came in our physical existence with the blessing of *Yuma* and return to the center of origin, Her place "*Sagram Pedang Den*" after our physical death. Safe return to our destination is possible only through establishing a close relationship with *Yuma* (*Yuma Sewa*) through simple prayer and good *Karma* (*Nu Yambok*).

Sangram Pedang Den is the sacred, bright (*Sese Sangsang*) and cheerful place (*Sododing Siling Tembhe*) without the Sun, The Moon and the stars where *Tagera Ningwaphuma* stays. It is the ultimate land of immortal gods, goddesses and souls. It is the destination of lives on earth for absolute beatitude. It is the ultimate destination of Human Souls. Only the people with righteous deeds (*Nu Yambok*) go straight to this place for eternal communion with the Almighty Goddess, otherwise most of the dead souls have to face a trial in *Mundhang Khara Den*, where judgments (*Suyo Kheyo*) on the actions of virtue and vice take place. Till their day of judgment, they have to stay in *Sam Yukna Den* – a land of ancestors. *Sendige Pekesappa Mang* (god of destiny, secretary of gods) maintains the records of all human activities and submit to *Pasti Mang*. *Paoti Mang* makes the decision. *Tunhikke Mang* supervises the process to make the judgment rightful and accurate. Following the injunctions of judgments on 8th day (for female) or 9th day (for male) of the burial of the deceased individual, some of them have to come down to the earth and enter into the womb of the human beings; and some have to go to the *Khema Yongsong Pangbhe* in retribution of their evil deeds and sinful acts. The souls of perpetrators of heinous acts and crimes do not find way either to ancestors or to the human womb and roam in ethereal form suffering from various spirits and also causing harm to the lives on earth. They are eventually captured by brutal and cruel gods – *Haha Mang, Hasu Mang, Habe Mang* and *Hadok Mang* and taken to the *Khema Yongsong Pangbhe* for further punishment and torture. Finally they are allowed to find rebirth in trivial creatures as the human beings.

(ii) The Moral Conduct of Human Beings

As a human being, one should be kind (*Lungma Tukma*) enough towards all living creatures (*Sangu Sokma Keyakpa*), one should love (*Nanumma*) his or her fellow beings, feel grateful to one's saviors, never envy (*Tingding Nahen*) to others, revere *Mangs* (Deity gods and goddesses) as father and mother, act with immaculate heart and mind, and should never practice theft

(*Khupma*), plundering (*Napma*), abetment (*Lengma*), quarreling (*Khema*), fighting (*Thokma*), murder (*Sepma*), Lying (*Illek Chokma*), slandering (*Taphemba Papma*) and backbiting (*Cheya Eplek*). One should not be arrogant (*Angding Loma*), coveteous (*Kekhimba, Kekhimma*), and involve in debauchery (*Chalammma*). One should always look after orphans and poor (*Yechchha Yangkesaba/ Yangkesama*), be just towards widows (*Keeppa/Mimeduma*), and never involve in incest (*Kai Lungdhung*) and wicked sinful acts (*Layo Lasot*).

(iii) Knowledge (*Sikkum*), Intelligence (*Ningwa*) and Wisdom (*Thona*) are Gods

Works performed by good conscience (*Nosang*) will be fruitful and lasting. Stupidity (*Adong Lam*) leads to misery (*Yangsama*) and ruin (*Inugen Minde*). One should lead a simple and sincere life (*Tondon Lam Langhekma*) to remain happy and prosperous (*Hangwa Phungwa*) throughout his or her life. Distress (*Ingekwa Sarekwa*) and difficulties suddenly fall upon wicked persons, and death and diseases attack them. In due course of time they have to face litigations (*Mapma*) and their wealth and riches (*Yangsa Kundhe*) will be wasted. Knowledge (*Sikkum*), intelligence (*Ninwa*) and wisdom (*Thona*) are the only means to reform human beings (*Menchham Yapmi*), improve natural surroundings (*Laze Singbung*) and enlighten and civilize (*Khaot Tapma, Khasam Chokma*) the people. Lack of perseverance for the attainment of knowledge, intelligence and wisdom leads to paucity of knowledge, intelligence, wisdom and good conscience, and such disposition produces arrogance (*Angdhing*), conceit (*Henchhing*), selfishness (*Khakkhawa*), which leads to the loss of money (*Yang*), power (*Hangwa*), prestige (*Ing*) and health (*Yamjik*). This again causes the loss of knowledge, intelligence, wisdom and conscience eventually leading towards the darkness (*Khamak*) and destruction (*Mapma*).

(*iv*) *Yuma* is a Light (*Khaot*), a source of Power or Energy (*Mukum*) and a source of creation (*Nawa Chait*)

Only the bright soul (*Khaot Sam*) causes light and light and darkness never co-exist. When the light comes, darkness vanishes naturally. *Tambhungna* represents the darkness and to drive it away, one has to search *Yuma* – the eternal light. The light comes in the form of power of understanding (*Ichchingma Sam*), communicating (*Tachengma Sam*), perceiving (*Omepma Sam*), listening (*Pankhemma Sam*), doing justice (*Kharon Chokma Sam*) and performing efficiently (*Nurik Chokma Sam*). When the light come the theft (*Khupma*), spoliation (*Napma*), quarreling (*Khema-thokma*), war (*Thong*) and evil thinking and actions will vanish inevitably as its source, the darkness, disappear. *Yuma* loves her creation (*Chait*), nourish (*Thumma*) them, protect (*Tangsepma*) and preserve (*Nomma*) from evil spirits, enemies and annihilation. These, who have this understanding, never deviate from the path of devotion to *Yuma* and discharge their day-to-day responsibilities sincerely and properly. Righteous deeds bring forth beneficial results. Those who resort to wicked, unjust means the fruit of such acts will be troublesome.

(v) Clean Mind is the essence of Life

One must have a clean mind. Unsullied mind (*Sese Ningwa*) always remains free of trepidations. One should save others to save one-self, raise others to raise one-self. Gods live in the hearts of small children and they speak through their babbling tongues. So, one should love the children to love the god. Life is just like a *Sekmuri* flower (Celery) – beautiful but transient (*Thiknamba*), with sweet smell but fugacious. One should enjoy it overcoming hankering, lust, anger and dejection. One should make it ever fresh through self-control (*Ningwa Khengma*), austerity (*Mudasek*), purity (*Sese*), uprightness, forbearance (*Nasethapma*), generousity (*Ningma*), vigour (*Sam*) and heroism (*Thak Ing*). One should respect the elder and look after them. One should for see the eventuality of life by taking pleasure in serving elders and helpless. One should always respect the guests and should provide whatever he or she has. One should always try to satisfy those who are hungry and thirsty. If some one does not provide even water to thirsty person or animals or birds he is a great sinner. One should always try to give, not to take. This disposition will lead him or her to prosperity, contentment and quietude. One should be able to sacrifice one self for justice, goodness and welfare of others.

(vi) Vicious acts are sin (*Layo Lasot*) and sin is more powerful

The only way to get rid of sin is the pious acts (*Sese Samyo*). Retribution (*Samban*) of such acts are meted out to the evil doers by the king or laws in lifetime and by god after life. Everything are evanescent including prosperity (*Numa Tama*), wealth (*Kapma*

Yakma), prestige (*Ing*) and power (*Hang Tumyang*). One should take these facts into consideration while in actions. One should not quarrel even if someone instigates for it. If people are cooperative, the society will prosper and remain happy. One should never involve in physical violence (*Chepma Hipma*) as nobody knows the impending pleasure and pain (*Inugen Tukkhey/ Lakhe*), progression and retrogression (*Numa Phenma*). One has to face eventual death one day. So, one should act keeping this truth in mind. If one is afraid of god, he never commits vicious acts and crimes. These are some of the basic tenets of faith in Yum religion.

Mythological Functions

(i) Mythical: The myth describes the mystery of origin of *Yuma Sammang*. This also provides the basic understanding of the *Yuma* Religion and its teachings.

(ii) Cosmological: The myth has cosmological origin.

(iii) Sociological: The myth has furnished *Yuma Samyo* or *Yuma* Religion to the *Limboo* society.

(iv) Pedagogical: The myth has interpreted the laws of life, ethical laws and other customary laws to the society.

(v) Mystery of afterlife: The myth elucidated the origin as well as destination of life. The soul comes to the life from the *Akashic* field "*Sangran Pedang Den*" and leaves to the origin after we die. The mystery of life is that the soul comes and enters into the physical body to play a life drama in this world. After the play is over the life shades its phycical body on earth and the soul returns to the place of origin in mental consciousness "*Sangram Pedang Den*" with the experiences gained during the play on earth. The mystery of life of origin and destination afterlife has been clearly explained in the myth.

Other Supernatural Powers and Spirituality

(a) *Him Sammangs* (Household Divinities)

Him Sammangs are worshipped mostly inside or at the household premises providing temporary *Lasso* (Altar) a sacred place to stay for them. The worship comprises of offering of flowers, fruits, millet beer, water, pine and Ghee incense, rice and many other food, fruit, vegetable and spice grown in the field.

Often blood sacrifices of fowl, pig, duck, and fish are also done in some places, but it should be avoided as far as possible. *Sammangs* are the sources of protection, power, energy, good luck, prosperity, reproduction, and guardian divinities. Example: *Yuma Sammang, Akwanama, Kappo Thungdang, Theba Sammang, Munama, Cherungma, Chanema, Phaksingdangma, Mephrama, Poyonglungma, Ka-amsama, Pitchchama, Yangphuma, Yumang or Payohangba, Kusong-Kuring, Khewaphukma, Lummayeppa, Maklangba, Nahangma, Mangenna* etc.

(i) Myth of *Kappo Thungdang*

Singarang Nugappoba, known as *Kappoba* (aged) *Sammang* or *Kappo Thungdang* is the divinity of health, happiness and prosperity. The myth divulges the accounts of the journey of the divinity from the land in the east to the land of *Yakthumbas* (*limboos*). In the course of his journey, he arrived at *Sinyuk Muden* (China-Tibet) and married a woman – *Lamudima.* The couple gave birth to various types of minor divinities there. He moved towards the south and reached *Minu Teljang Tembhe* where he met *Sekerengba Kengkerengba. Sekerengba Kengkerengba* assumed him just an old fellow and asked him to dance. They hold a kind of dance (*Pongpit Tanglang*) competition between them. *Kappoba* demonstrated wonderful skills of various dances including *Yasa lang* (dance of Himalayan chamois, *Nemorhaedus ghoral*), *Khire lang* (dance of samber , *Cervus unicolor*), *Takmi lang* (elephant dance, *Elephas maximus*), *Pengwa lang* (deer dance, *Muntiacus muntjak*), *Thakpu Kubu lang* (dance of various birds) etc. *Sekerengba Kenkerengba* was amazed by his performance and accepted his defeat. He humbly requested him that he had nothing except his beautiful sister *Tappeso Nawengma. Kappoba Sammang* married and embraced her with love. They brought several offspring forth. They also became divinities and on of them is serpent king or ophicephalous divinity (*Singdung Wasek*).

Singarang Nukappoba again went to visit several places. He married a woman in *Minu Kubhak Tembhe,* whose offspring became minor divinities of crossroads, rocks and hills etc. He again married another woman *Dokhu Yangkhama* in *Minu Siring Chopma* and they gave birth to various divinities such as *Ayaso Dokhu Hangma, Sasik Yangdang Sama* etc. He again went to *Laik Khambu Pangbhe* and married a graceful lady *Laik Khambu Hangma.* People of that country revered him very much and offered a pig to propitiate him. He came in contact with the local priest that he will take only the vital air of the sacrificial animals or fowls and the meat will be taken by offerers themselves. Various types of minor divinities appeared there as the progeny of *Kappoba* and *Khambu Hangma*. From that land, he went to *Samenja Pangbhe* (vegetarian food eater's village) where the local inhabitants propitiated him as a new powerful divinity (*Bhimsen*). After spending sometime in this land, he went down to the confluence of eight rivers (*Yetchiri Yetwado*) for purification. Then he returned back to the land of *Limboos*. While visiting *Susuwa Lilim Yakthung Pangbhe, Kappoba* met a *Kallere Kandangwa* on the way of hunting and found each other perfectly similar. They were introducing each other and *Kandangwa* told him to come some day in his house as an expression of his decorous gestures. After a gap of sometime, *Kappoba* came to the house of *Kandangwa*. Nobody knew him and nobody cared him. He caused illness, deformities and abnormalities to the family of *Kandangwa*. They did not know the reason and approached *Phungjiri Phungappo Phedangma*. The *Phedangma* identified the reason, recognized the old person (*Kappoba*) as *Singarang Nukappoba* who caused the sufferings and who was the source of pain and pleasure, ugliness and beauty, decadence and prosperity, defeat and victory. *Kappoba* was propitiated in his altar *Thilliphukma Karangphukma* by *Kandangwa* for the first time in *Susuwa Lilim Yakthung Pangbhe* and thus he became a guardian divinity. Today this *Sammang* has spread in all groups of *Limboos* through their sisters and daughters and thus has become a guardian divinity of all Limboos.

(b) *Tap Sammang* (Nature Divinities)

Tap Sammangs are the manifestations of *Mangs* (Deities) and are considered the owner of Nature. They form the group of nature divinities in spirit or soul form as gods and goddesses. *Tap Sammangs* are the nature divinities and worshipped away from the household premises often with animal sacrifices, millet beer, rice, flour, *namyoba* (*Artemisia vulgaris*) twigs, and other offerings. Example: *Tambhungma, Tenchama, Mudemba Sammang, Singbung or Thimennamma, Yobedangma, Thungdangba, Toksongba, Wagongma, Tahangma, Thema, Nangepma, Sakmurama, Singlaba, Misekpa, Khonjoma or Senghama, Worakma, Phakmurama Thungdangna, Nahen,* etc.

(i) Myth of *Mudemba Sammang*

Mudemba Sammang is supposed to have come from *Mangjiri Mangonjya*, a land of human settlement from where the ancestors of *Limboos* spread in all directions. He is invoked as a brother of *Satthding Pangen Hangma*, primeval female deity. The myth relates him to have visited *Sinyuk Muden* where he was invoked by *Kanden Hang, Yonchhen Hang* and other renowned leaders and finally by the leaders of the land of *Limboos*. While visiting, he arrieved at the village of *Lekwa Hangs*, but they did not care about him. He caused troubles to them. They went to *Phedangma Saplingek Warin* and the *Phedangma* propitiated the *Sammang* by constructing an altar at *Thilli Saptemphukma*. Thus he also became a guardian divinity of certain groups of *Limboos*. Today this *Sammang* has also spread almost in all groups of *Limboos*.

(c) *Thokley Sammang*

Thokley Sammangs are manifestations of *Mangs* related with particular groups of *Limboo* clans and only the *Phedangmas* of the particular clan are competent to deal the particular myth. The most popular once are *Chokhoba, Saba Sammang* or *Yetchhama, Dungdunge*, etc.

(i) Myth of *Saba Sammang (Yechchhama Sammang)*

Soba (monkey) *Sammang* is also one of the popular divinities of *Limboos*. He is also known as *Yechchhama* or *Yechchhawa*. Myths vary about the origin of *Saba Sammang*. The myth of creation says that *Saba Sammang* was originated from *Chijiklung Makmaklung* rocks during the process of creation. Others say that *Saba Sammang* was born as a son of *Sodhung Lepmuhang*. He was neither in a form of god, nor human or animal. So, *Sodhung Lepmuhang* threw him into the cloud. But *Saba*'s shrill cries greatly annoyed him and he threw him again in the steep slope and precipice covered with forests. He again yelled and screamed in the precipice without food and water which caused the heart of his father fill with pity. *Sodhung Lepmuhang* visited him and told him to go to the village of *Sawa Yethang* where there are abundant foods. Following the instructions of his father he came down along the course of the river *Tashi, Yangsi, Aptangwa, Tidangwa* crossing the lands of *Parung Marung Tembhe* and the mountains of *Phoktanglungma*, finally entered into the land of progeny of *Sawa Yethang*.

In some myth, it is narrated that *Saba Sammang* accompanied *Yuma Sammang* in her journey. *Yuma* told him to break a lake on her way but he could not. Finally *Yuma* had to rethink to break the lake and form a better team for her retinue for her mission. After breaking the lake, they continued to travel from place to place and eventually reached the land of *Sawa Yethang*. *Yuma* tried to spread her loom in various places there. But most of the places could not accommodate her warp and woof and shuttle. After trying in *Hangchum Hangwa Pangbhe, Mino Lakhu Pangbhe,* she reached *Kesalung Namsalung Kokma* and disperses her retinue. One of them was *Saba Sammang* who was told to go to the mountain laps and meet again when crops would be ready for food and people would offer them before taking it.

One day when *Saba* was roaming around *Sawa Yethang Pangbhe, Hanglere Hangmukhang* of *Hembhya* clan of *Limboo* met him in the way of his hunting. They got acquainted with each other exchanged some small things as tokens of friendship. *Hembhya* told him to come to his house when crops get ready. At the harvesting season, Saba came to the house of *Hembhya,* but he could not recognize *Saba Sammang*. So he had to roam in the field of *Hembhya* for quite a few days. One day he was hungry and entered the house of *Hembhya* and ate the fermented millet kept in a big pot. *Hembhya*'s family were in the field and they found the big pot of fermented millet empty when they returned back and examined the various items of the house. So, they prepared a trapping net to ensnare those who attempted to eat the rest of the fermented millet from the big pot. One day *Saba* was entrapped and beaten to death by all of the family members of *Hembhya* and others who were assembled there. They threw him into the *Kangwa* river. The river carried him away and he floated aside on the bank at the confluence of seven rivers, where the divinities of the confluence (*Yetwado Mang*) including the boar divinity (*Phakmura)* saw him almost in rotten stage. They made him alive and asked about how he was carried away by the river. He told the whole story to the divinities. The divinities deemed that it was the fault of *Hembhya* to call him to visit and not to recognize and respect the invitee. So they made him immortal and sent back to the village of *Hembhya* and cause pains and throes to them similar to the pangs he felt while he was beaten mercilessly. He then visited southern plain lands, western hills and valleys and finally entered into the zone of seven rivers. He came back to the village of *Hembhya. Hembhya* began to feel severe pains and aches and consulted an old *Phedangma Singdung Ing Phekwa Ing* of *Yungwa* clan. The *Phedangma* told them the cause of their sufferings. They propitiated him by offering fruits and crops. Thus, *Saba* became one of the active *Sammang* of some group of *Limboos* which eventually spread in all groups.

(ii) Myth of *Chakhoba Sammang*

Chakhoba Sammang is divinity of water. The myth of *Chakhoba* relates the tragic story of two brothers – *Kuget Nam Ingwaba* (*Kugetnamba*) and *Kutha Nam Ingwaba* (*Kuthanamba*). They were involved in trading. They were the inhabitants of *Miklung*. They used to go the west with their small knives made of iron and flint – stones to collect caps and various garments. They used to exchange those things with calves (*Karangpit*) in the south. Again they used to go to Tibet to barter their calves with various commodities including *Namja* (bags). Once when they were going to Tibet, they came to the side of seven lakes and cooked their foods. They threw the dirty water into the lake, which made the lake filthy. The goddess of the lake got enraged and caused storm, torrents of rain and shower of hailstones. They invoked the water goddess and promised to offer something when they return back from Tibet.

They exchanged a lot of goods in Tibet. The possession of lots of goods made them greedier. While coming back from Tibet, they thought to come down through another way to avoid the water goddesses, so that they do not need to offer anything. But the storms and heavy rain made them to follow the same path and reached the lakes where they were drowned and died. Their spirits became *Sogha* and began to stray in the villages. People were in trouble and consulted an old *Phedangma – Abaso Changbhahang*. Through hi art of necromancy, he related the story to the common people there. On behalf of the laymen, *Phedangma* began to propitiate the water goddess *Chakhoba* with grown up white chicken. The altar to propitiate her was constructed at *Lokten Kokma* of *Choubish* for the first time. It is believed that this divinity causes various kinds of ailments – cooling of the body, swelling of stomach, vomiting just like the symptoms of drowned person. This divinity has become popular amongst all groups of *Limboos*.

(iii) Myth of *Dungdunge*

Dungdunge is considered protector, boon bestower and destroyer divinity. According to the myth *of Dungdunge*, he was visiting the various places on the mountainous areas. He was extremely powerful and giant figure. There were none to challenge him. He was searching for wicked persons to slay and looking for amiable, immaculate persons to establish relation. Once he was walking on the hill and mountain side by making heavy sounds and heavily stomping the earth surface. On the way he met *Phago, Chongbang, Thopra, Thallang*, but no one responded him. Eventually he met *Mikkendang Samba*, who revered him much by making an altar at *Phangphang Demma* as he knew his miraculous power and found liberality. He is worshipped by making statues of cooked millet or rice powder on the altar and offering the heart of a well grown-up un-castrated living male goat and a fat male chicken. The sacrificial ritual is terrifying. Red and white piece of clothes are also offered. Various types of weapons are also presented at the altar. Even the guns are boomed while performing the ritual. *Thimendhung Payonama, Wandalgekpa, Namyuk, Padak* etc. are his brood (*chyangs*) and *Tambhungna* is his wife. If he is pleased, he provides power, life, vigor and success and if offended, causes mental illness, unconsciousness, dumbness, deformities and barrenness.

Mythological Functions

(v) Mystical: The myth describes the mystery of the origin of *Sammangs* (Divinities) and *Sammang Chyangs* (retinue of divinities. It also elucidates the mystery of who identified the benevolent and malevolent Divinities and retinue of divinities and tells us how to get benefit from them or to propitiate to avoid their harmful affects.

(vi) Cosmological: The myth explains that most of the Divinities and retinue of divinities have cosmological origin.

(vii) Sociological: The myth has furnished a number of rituals to be performed in household (for *Him-Sammangs*) and also away from household for nature divinities (*Tap-Sammangs*) and clan-divinities (*Thokley-Sammangs*), and are related to both nature (nature divinities) and clan of the society. Many divinities are affiliated to a particular clan and disseminated through matrimonial relationships.

(viii) Pedagogical: The myth also interprets customary laws as some of the divinities are disseminated through married daughters.

Myth of Soul (*Sam*)

Yumaism recognizes *Yetcham Thim* (eight soul tradition) of an individual. These are two perceptive, three conceptive and three vital souls. The two perceptive souls are *Ni-Sam* (the soul of sight) and *Khem-sam* (the soul of hearing); the three conceptive souls are *Sikkum-Sam* (the soul of intuition), *Ningwa-Sam* (the soul of mind) and *Thona-Sam* (the soul of wisdom/consciousness); and the three vital souls are *Si-Sam* (the graveyard soul), *Pung-Sam* (wandering soul) and *Kunu-Sam* or *Hang-Sam* (the great soul). These souls are briefly described as follows:

(i) *Ni-Sam* (the soul of sight)

This is the perceptive soul symbolized by the light and the fire. The development of this soul is initiated on the day of *Yangdangphongma* (child naming) ceremony, when the child is taken out to see light for the first time at the door preferably by his or her father. *Tagera Ningwaphuma* is a light, a source of power or energy and a source of creation. Showing the child to light at the child naming ceremony is also for the blessing of the Almighty Goddess. The ritual of *Yangdangphongma* is performed on the third day for female child and fourth day for male child after birth, when the newly born child is brought to the door for sowing to the light three times doing inside and outside of the main door.

(ii) *Khem-Sam* (the soul of hearing)

This is the second perceptive soul for hearing symbolized by the sound *'Ke"*, *"Negra"* and *"Sirpong"* etc. At the time of child naming ceremony while doing in and out of the door, the child is also said *"Khiriktya"* (wherever you go come soon) three times at the door preferably by his or her father. This is for initiation of *Khem-Sam* soul of the child.

(iii) *Sikkum-sam* (the soul of intuition)

This is the soul of knowledge (*Gyan*) discerned directly by the mind without reasoning or analysis or a truth or revelation arrived at by insight; or the power or capacity to perceive truth without apparent reasoning or concentration. It contains the moral virtues and the ability to distinguish between good and evil. It equates to psyche or ego-personality and starts development in the later part of life.

(iv) *Ningwa-Sam* (the soul of mind)

This is the soul of superior intellectual power, compassion; the cognitive and intellectual faculty (*Budhi*). The soul of unsullied mind are overcoming hankering lust, anger, and dejection; the soul of self-control, austerity, purity, uprightness, forbearance, generosity, vigour and heroism. This distinguishes man from all other life forms. It related to the intellect, and allows man to enjoy and benefit from the afterlife. It also allows one to have some awareness of the existence and presence of God. It is comparable to *Ruach* soul of Jewish. It also starts development in the later part of life.

(v) *Thona-Sam* (the soul of wisdom/consciousness)

This is the soul of the upper level of mental life marked by awareness consciously – wisdom (*Chetna/Vivek*); the soul of good conscience. This is the higher soul, higher self or super-soul and allows one to have some awareness of the existence and presence of God. This distinguishes man from all other fife forms. It relates to the intellect, and allows man to enjoy and benefit from the afterlife. It is comparable to *Neshamah* soul of Jewish.

(vi) *Si-Sam* (the graveyard soul)

The soul finds it difficult to accept his or her death. It escapes from the body before the actual death of the individual. The adherents believe that many laymen may see the vital soul *Si-sam* when it leaves the dead body immediately after an individual's death and is known to visit the neighbors, often with a white shawl. The *Phedangma* cannot retrieve the soul and reach to the ancestor deity during *Samsama* ritual. The mourners mostly the deceased sons and other family members offer foods and drinks (*Cha-Thi*) to this soul during the pollution period. It is believed that, the soul often visits the house during the pollution period in search of the physical body. However, after the death pollution is over the soul returns to the burial place and believe to remain there till the day of final death ritual when the soul is invited for the final feast offered by the close family members at cemetery ceremony. The construction of cemetery at the graveyard is mainly for this purpose. The soul is then, finally retrieved during the *Sam-Chomma* ritual performed during the final death ritual and handed over to the ancestor deity.

(vii) *Pung-Sam* (the wandering soul)

This is a wandering soul of the individual. The soul leaves the body at the time of sleep and thus gets a variety of dreams while sleeping during his or her lifetime. When you dream returning home, you are awakening. At the time of death, the soul escapes from the body before the person is actually dead. The *Phedangma* cannot retrieve and hand over this soul to the ancestor deities at the time of *Samsama* ritual, as the soul finds difficult to part with this world at the time of the individual's death. The mourners mostly the deceased sons and other family members offer foods and drinks (*Cha-Thi*) to this soul also during the pollution period. It is believed that, the soul often visits the house during the pollution period in search of the physical body. The construction of a platform known as *Lagaklung Kaklung Tembhe Namkaklung Kaklung Tembhe* is mainly for this soul where the soul is invited for food and drinks one day before the final death ritual. The soul after the day of judgment at *Mundhang Khara Den* on the eighth (for female) or ninth (for male) day after burial (not after death) realizes that he or she has to obey the judgment of the god. After that the *Phedangma* retrieves the soul during *Sam-Chomma* ritual and hand over it to the ancestor deity. The process of separating the souls of the dead person from the living souls of the family members takes place during *Sitongsing Khema* and finally the handing over of the souls of the dead person to the ancestor deity is repeated once again.

(viii) *Kunu-Sam* or *Hang-Sam* (the great vital soul)

This is the main soul of the individual and is considered as a guardian soul of ancestors. For this soul *Samlopma* and *Samsama* rituals are performed during the day of burial, for handing over the soul to the ancestor deity. The soul of the dead person as well as the ancestor deity (the soul of the forefather) speaks through the mouth of the *Phedangma* during *Samsama* ritual, thus proving that the soul of the dead person never dies and also maintain individuality even at *Sangram Pedang Den* (Subba, J.R. 1999: 379-382; 2005a: 111-130; 2005b: 55-137).

Mythological Functions

(i) Mystical: The myth describes the mystery of origin of multiple souls in *Yumaism* so that one is aware of souls everywhere. Soul is equated with the vital air of the human beings. When the creator god designed the human body with abiotic materials (law of abiogenesis) he could not make the idols alive. Finally, he designed human body with biotic materials (law of biogenesis) he could succeed in making the human idols alive. In disgust, when he spat on them the humans died. Then with the advice of Almighty Goddess he performed the *Mangenna* ritual to make them alive again. The myth unfolds the mystery that a normal individual has eight souls while the incarnate Shaman priest – *Phedangmas* have nine or more souls. The shaman with his additional souls performs the shamanic functions in the society.

(ii) Cosmological: The myth elucidates that the souls have cosmological origin, as it deals with creation of human beings in the cosmic world. After death the soul of the individual has to join the ancestors or return to the origin - to the cosmic or *Akashic* field known as *Samyukna Den*. It unfolds that the soul of the individual enters into the physical body for a lifetime with physical consciousness temporarily. It has to return to its origin, transcending to mental consciousness once again, to the cosmic or *Akashic* field to the ancestors at the *Samyukna Den* ultimately.

(iii) Sociological: The myth described the multiple souls of an individual, and it has to discharge multiple functions of the individual in this physical body of our life. A normal individual has eight souls and hence known as "*Yetchham Thim*" (eight soul tradition) in *Yumaism*. The Shaman priests (*Phedangmas*) usually have nine or more souls (one soul as their incarnate deity or soul of the departed person). He functions as shaman priest with this incarnate soul of the departed individual and master spirits. The myth has provided a number of rituals in the society based on these multiple souls.

(iv) Pedagogical: The myth has interpreted customary laws of constructing cemetery, *Lakaklung Kaklung Namkaklung Kaklung Tembhe*, etc.

(v) Mystery of afterlife: The myth explains the dimension of afterlife such as inward journey, soul journey to the ancestors, physical consciousness transcending to mental consciousness, journey to *Sangram Pedang Den* (heaven) and *Khema Yongsong Den* (hell) etc.

Myth of Eighteen Dens (Underworlds and *Akashic* fields)

Yumaism believes that there are Eight Dens (*Akashic* fields) above the earth surface and Nine Dens (underworlds) below the fertile layer of the earth surface, thus making Eighteen Dens (Eighteen worlds) with the fertile layer of the earth surface. In *Yumaism* myth these are known as *Dens* (*Loks*/worlds), and without these *Dens* existence and survival of life was not possible as in the case of the scientific reasoning. Scientifically, the earth's atmosphere has been divided into five layers (troposphere, stratosphere, mesosphere, thermosphere and exosphere) above the earth surface and six layers inside the earth surface (crust 0-30/35 km, lithosphere 0-60 km, mantle 30/35-2,900 km, asthenosphere 100-700 km, outer core 92,900-5,100 km, and inner core 5,100-6,375 km) excluding the living layer of the earth. *Yumaism* believes that these eighteen Dens are governed by different *Mangs* (Deities), *Sammang* (Divinities) and *Sammang Chyangs* (retinue of divinities), and enlightened spirituals. They are briefly described as under:

(i) Sangram Pedang Den (topmost layer of the atmosphere)

This is the topmost part of the earth's atmosphere. This is the sacred, bright and cheerful place where the primordial Goddess *Tagera Ningwaphuma* (*Yuma*/Goddess grandmother) stays. The myth relates that the Almighty Goddess (*Yum*) is the Omniscient (all knowing), Omnipresent (in all places at all times), Omnipotent (all powerful), Infinite (without beginning or end), and Eternal force, Light or Power of existence which has none of the attributes, stays in this atmospheric layer. This is equivalent to heaven or *swarga/baikuntha* and is the ultimate destination of lives on earth for staying with the Almighty Goddess to learn more lessons and wisdom. Only the souls of the lives on earth with righteous deeds (*nu yambok*/good action) and having good relation with the Goddess can go to this place. The souls of the dead persons have to face a trial in "*Mundhang Khara Den*" (*nyaya loka*/world of judgment), where judgment (*Suyo Kheyo*) on the actions of virtue and vice takes place. Till the day of judgment of 8 (for female) or 9 (for male) days, they have to stay in "*Samyukna Den*" (*Atma lok*/world of ancestors). The *Phedangma* can accompany soul journey and reach the souls of the dead person only up to this place. Once the judgment is passed, the souls of the dead persons have to follow the judgment either to "*Sangram Pedang Den*" to stay with the Goddess or to the "*Khema Yongsong Den*" for retribution of the evil deeds or to the "*Iksa Khambek Den*" to repeat the *Karmic* life cycle.

(ii) *Sang Sang Den* (Sacred world/*Pabitra loka*)

This is a second layer next to *Sangram Pedang Den* and is a sacred place, where the most powerful creator god "*Sigera Yabhundin Mang Porokmi Wambhami Mang*" stays. The creator god created the Earth, the Water, the Air, all living beings inclusive of Man with the guidance of the Almighty Goddess. Hence, he stays praying and meditating Her for Her blessings of power, intelligence, knowledge, wisdom, and for the success of universal management.

(iii) *Mangkhoma Den* (*Top Loka*/Meditation world)

This is the third atmospheric layer next to "*Sang Sang Den*". At this world all the *Mangs* (Deities), *Sammangs* (Divinities), *Sammangchyangs* (retinue of divinities), *Sam Sires* (master spirits) and Phedangmas meditate; sing devotional songs for management of the universal creation and blessings of the Almighty Goddess for power, knowledge, intelligence, wisdom etc.

(iv) *Sey Seywa Den* (*Dev Loka*/World of Deities, Divinities, *Sammang Chyangs* and *Sam Sires*)

This is the fourth layer of the atmosphere from the top, a sacred world for powerful *Mangs* (Deities), *Sammangs* (Divinities), *Sammangchyangs* (retinue of divinities) and *Sam Sires* (Master spirits). The gods and goddesses both benevolent and malevolent stay here. They are indefinable absolutes. *Mangs* (Deities) are prayed only in the context of propitiating *Sammangs* (divinities), worship ceremonies and rituals for specific purpose, and it is believed that they too discharge their responsibilities in specific times. *Sammangs* (divinities) are spiritual or soul manifestations of *Mangs* (Deities) and are considered to have both benevolent as well as malevolent powers. *Sammang chyangs* are retinues of divinities. All these categories of gods, goddesses and master spirits stay in this atmospheric layer.

(v) Sunaingtong Den (*Satya Loka*/world of truth)

This is the fifth layer of the atmosphere from the top, where *Sandige Pekesappa Mang* (god of destiny/ *Bhavi*) stays and maintains the records of all activities of the living beings and submit to *Pasti Mang* for final judgment. The activities of all the living being of the universe are recorded and maintained here by seven wise *Mangs*.

(vi) Mundhang Khara Den (*Nyaya Loka*/world of judgment)

This is the sixth layer of the atmosphere from the top, and is called *Mundhang Khara Den* (*Nyaya Loka*/world of judgment) where *Paoti Mang* makes the decision, *Tunghike Mang* supervise the process to make the judgment rightful and accurate based on records of activities maintained in *Sunaingtong Den* by the seven wise *Mangs* and submitted by *Sendige Pekesappa Mang*. Whatever we do, with our body, speech, or mind, will have corresponding result. It is only merit or an equal amount of good *karma*, which can neutralize the same amount of evil *karma*. All bad actions performed intentionally by action, speech or mind is bad *karma*.

(vii) Torongding Tangsang Den (*Akash loka*/the world of sky or ether)

This is the seventh atmospheric layer from the top, where the malevolent gods, the destructive forms of gods and goddesses *Haha Mang* (god of laughter), *Habe Mang* (god of crying), *Hadok Mang* (god of sadness) and *Hasu Mang* (god of greed and love removing) stay. When the souls come in contact with these gods, they attract the human souls and make them forget everything. The souls of perpetrators of heinous acts and crimes are captured by these brutal and cruel gods and taken to the *Kema Yongsong Den* for punishment and torture.

***(viii) Samyukna Den (Atma Loka*/Ancestor world)**

This is the atmospheric layer next to the earth, and is the land of ancestors (*Atma Loka*). The souls of the dead persons are reached here by the *Phedangmas*. The souls have to stay here till their day of judgment. The judgment normally takes 8 days for female and 9 days for male. Once the judgment is passed, the soul is either allowed to go to *Sangram Pedang Den* or has to take rebirth depending on the karma and relation to the Almighty Goddess of the individual,

***(ix) Iksading Khambek Den* (the earth surface)**

This is the living layer of the earth's surface, represented by the fertile layer of the earth. This is the world of all living beings. The gods and goddesses are propitiated here with flowers, rice, fermented beer, cooked rice, sacrifices, etc. This is the place where every living being has to come and improve his or her karma as well as improve the relationship with the Almighty Goddess for securing a place at *Sangram Pedang Den.*

***(x) Khambongba Lungbongba Yukna Den* (the land of the aborigines)**

This is just below the fertile layer of the earth surface, where the owners of the earth "*Khambongba Lungbongba*" gods and goddesses stay. This underground layer of the earth consists of *Sipukhamma, Simakkhamma* and *Themakkhamma* soils. *Yumaism* believes that the corpse of the dead person should be buried within this layer of the earth by purchasing the graveyard from these gods and goddesses.

(xi) Muroplung Kheroplung Den

This is the second inner layer of the earth inside, and is ruled by the gods known as *Muroplungma, Kheroplungma, Makkalungma* etc.. They are the gods of stones and rocks and propitiated to avoid landslides and landslips.

(xii) Muguplung Theguplung Den

This is the third layer of the earth inside, and is the world of metals and ruled by *Muguplung Theguplung Mangs* (metal gods). Heavier metals like iron, gold, silver, lead and nickel are available in this layer.

(xiii) *Murupli Kherupli Den*

This is the fourth layer of the earth inside, and is the world of *Seakkum Akwanama Mang*, a household divinity propitiated at the main pillar of every household of the adherents. It is a god of thunderbolt and earthquake and causes a tremendous loss of lives on earth if not propitiated.

(xiv) *Mujikna Kheyongna Den*

This is the fifth layer of the earth inside, and is full of inner locked earth water. *Mujikna Kheyongna Mang* the goddess of underground water stays here in the form of a big fish.

(xv) *Musekhu Sekhana Den*

This is the sixth inner layer of the earth, and is the world of warak (lakes), where the lake god *Warakma Mang* stays.

(xvi) *Tungutlung Haralung Den*

This is the seventh layer of the earth inside and ruled by the ocean god *Tungutlungma Haralungma Mang* who stays here.

(xvii) *Sumbodona Lekwadona Den*

This is the eighth inner layer of the earth and is ruled by *Sumbodona Lekwadona Mang* who stays here.

(xviii) *Khemading Yongsong Den*

This is the innermost heaviest core of the earth and is comparable to hell or *Narak Kunda*, surrounded by flames of fire. *Siyasam Jemahang* (*Damuhang*) rules this (Subba, J.R. 1998: 1- 18; 1999: 303-338; 2005a: 40-64; 2005b: 1-54).

Mythological Functions

(i) Mystical: The myth describes the mystery of experience or understanding the *Akashic* field/*Lokas*/*Dens*/spiritual worlds that requires an expanded state of awareness. Contracted awareness keeps us anchored in daily affairs. The critical thing is to have a life of the soul, and that comes about only through expansion. *Akasha*/*Den*/*Loka*/spiritual world is the home of the soul and therefore cannot be limited in any way. The mystery, strangely enough, is how we manage to restrict the undoubted potential of our own minds. We have variety of choices depending on the qualities of your own mind, which expands and contracts depending on many factors. In *Yumaism*, the mystery of *Akashic* fields/*Dens/Lokas*/spiritual worlds as well as underworlds/*Dens/ Patal Lokas* has been divided in several layers of atmospheric worlds and underworlds. Different gods and goddesses rule these worlds/*Dens/Lokas*; and they discharge different functions in the expanded state of awareness of human mind. Consciousness is consciousness no matter who is interpreting it on the basis of what religion. *Akasha* field/*Lokas/Dens* exist beyond choice, beyond mind.

(ii) Cosmological: The myth describes the mystery of eight cosmological *Akashic* field/*Dens/Lokas* in the atmosphere above the earth and nine inner underground fields/*Dens/Lokas* in the expanded state of mind of awareness in the universe.

(iii) Sociological: The myth provided how the entire natural mythology and social mythology of *Yumaism* depends on supporting and validating different social order in the *Yumaism*. The belief system of the society of *Yumaism* is entirely based on these eighteen *Dens/Lokas*/worlds.

(iv) Pedagogical: The myth interprets the laws of life, ethical laws and other customary laws in the society. The myth strongly believes on *Karma/Suyo-Kheyo*, providing all ethical and social laws to its adherents.

(v) Mystery of afterlife: The myth explains the dimension of journey inward, soul journey to *Samyukna Den* (Ancestor's land), *Sangram Pedang Den* (heaven), *Khema Yongsong Den* (hell) etc. and try to link with the origin of soul. It explains the mystery of both life and afterlife of human beings.

Myths of spirit possession in *Limboo Shamanism*

Spirit possession: is an altered state of consciousness on the part of an individual as a result of what is perceived or believed to be the incorporation of an alien form with vital and spiritual attributes. The spirit may be a soul of the departed individual (incarnate soul- *Sam Sire*) or god and goddess or a natural divinity or household divinity or clan divinity or a master spirit (*Sam Sire*) (Jones, R.L.1994: 1-11).

Types of Spirit Possession: Spirit possession could be distinguished into two types:

(a) Peripheral spirit possession: is seemingly spontaneous. It might happen only once in a life time or on a number of occasions, but seldom able to predict its occurrence by him or society. It is uncontrollable – both time and space undesignated. It has the social function of an oblique aggressive strategy. The possessed individual is able to manipulate his superiors without openly questioning their superiority. This type of possession most often afflicts women who use it as a way in which they manipulate men and thus achieve a balance of power between men and women in societies where women are denied positions of power and authority. It also afflicts men in circumstances where they are unable to advance to positions of power as a result of economic or caste system or other historic conditions. For example – individuals possessed by deity *Yuma Sam, Theba Sam, Chokhoba, Poyonglungma* etc.

(b) Central spirit possession: has the function of holding and sustaining public morality. Unlike peripheral possession cults, central possession cults are openly used to uphold power and authority rather than subvert it. On the basis of time and space spirit possession could be classified into four types (Jones, R.L 1976: 29-55).

(i) Reincarnate possession; is for life and therefore time is undesignated. An individual reincarnates the spirit of a deceased individual and then takes up residence in a Monastery or *Mangkhim* or temple or religious center. He becomes, as a result of his reincarnate status, a focus of power in divination, ritual, curing, healing and predicting and allaying misfortune. He is a fulltime religious practitioner, centered in a religious institution or designated sacred space. For example – Buddhist *Rimbuchis* (*Tulkus*).

(ii) Tutelary possession: is for life and therefore time is undesignated but space is not. An individual calls upon a tutelary spirit during a séance or ritual to possess him or take over his body for the duration of the ritual or ceremony. The individual, however, is not relegated to an institution such as a *Monastery* or *Mangkhim* or *Samkhalung*. His possession is periodic and specific, but the place in which he conducts his activities as a result of possession is sporadic and unspecified and is determined solely by individual choice or situational demands. It might be in someone's home, in the forest, or field, or at a cemetery or *Lakaklung Kaklung Namkaklung Kaklung Tembhe* or a place of burial. For example - *Limboo Ongsi, Phedangma, Samba, Yeba, Yema, Yuma; Khambu-Rai Mangbas, Bijuwas, Nakchhong, Mabini, Kubini, Dowang; Lepcha Bongthings, Muns; etc.*

(iii) Oracular possession: In this both time and space are designated. A spirit, a god or goddess possesses an individual on designated occasions such as a village ceremony, a curing séance or a ceremony of divination. His possession invariably takes place in a designated sacred space such as a temple, a church or a monastery. For example – *Dhami, Jhankri, Poibo, Natso, Ngyami; Bhusal* or *Wapa* etc. These four types of spirit possession are structural classifications based on time and space (Jones, R.L.1976: 1-11).

Functions of Spirit Possession

Spirit possession has two social functions of human behavior and institutions. They are "manifest" function and "latent" function. Manifest function has to do with intent while latent function is frequently unintended.

(a) **Manifest or "Emic" function**: In anthropology manifest function is "emic" explanation of the causes and effects of illness and misfortune. Illness and misfortune are attributed to a variety of supernatural forces such as attacks by witches, sorcerers, forest divinities, spirits of deceased individuals and angry gods and goddesses. People of this Himalayan region frequently recognize that human neglect is usually the cause of supernatural discontent. For example, the failure to propitiate household or nature divinities or clan divinities is frequently cited as the source of anger. In Limboo, human envy and jealousy leaves the individual or family open to attacks by witches or evil spirits. Through human failure and neglect supernatural forces are unlashed and bring chaos, disorder and disaster. These forces are combated, held in check or defeated by individuals, who are capable of seeing and identifying them. Such individuals receive their primarily through successful encounters with supernatural forces in the past. They become living metaphors through controlled spirit possession, or contact with supernatural power. The system of cause, effect and cure, is thus a circular and enclosed system of knowledge. The cause is a spirit, the effect is spirit possession, and the cure is controlled spirit possession. This system of knowledge provides the manifest function of explanation and control disorder, chaos and inexplicable circumstances. The social function here described is adaptive and spirit possession is the basis of social stability in potentially unstable and disruptive social circumstances.

(b) Latent or "Etic" function: Peripheral spirit possession provides a means for status achievement that is otherwise inaccessible to many people, especially women. In other words, the system of spirit possession not only functions as a system of explanation for misfortune and disaster, but it also functions as a means by which individuals are capable of achieving social functions related to the society.

Shamanism

The term shaman originated from Siberian Thungus after studying and comparing the phenomena in North Asia that Oesterreich and Eliade in 1921, and 1964. Thereafter, the various anthropological experts have defined shamanism from time to time based on their studies as under:

Eliade defined that "the shaman specializes in a trance during which his soul is believed to leave his body and ascend to the sky or descend to the underworld. The shamanistic phenomena are known as shamanism."

Shirokogoroff defined "shaman as a person of both sexes who have mastered spirits, who at their will can introduce these spirits into themselves and use their power over the spirits in their own interests particularly helping other people, who suffer from the spirits".

Johan Reinhard summarized the definitions and defined a shaman as "a person who at his will can enter into a non-ordinary psychic state (in which he either has his soul undertake a journey to the spirit world or he become possessed by a spirit) in order to make contact with the spirit world on behalf of members of his community." (Jones, R.L.1994: 1-11; Subba, J.R. 1999:383-390).

Mythological Functions

(i) Mystical: The myth describes the mystery of spirit possession, various types of spirit possession and their functions both manifest (*emic*) and latent (*etic*) in the society.

(ii) Cosmological: The myth elucidates the cosmological origin, as it involves both *Akashic* fields and underworlds spiritual journey of souls, spirits and master spirits

(iii) Sociological: The myth furnished how the spirit possession in the individual performs two functions (a) manifest or "*emic*" and (b) latent or "*etic*" functions in the society.

(iv) Pedagogical: It has interpreted laws of life, ethical laws and other customary laws in the society.

(v) Mystery of afterlife: The myth explains how the spirit possession involves the dimension of inward journey, journey of the souls of the living, dead persons and master spirits to heaven and hell are performed.

Myths of *Limboo* Shaman Priests

The *Limboo* religious priests are defined as part time tutelary spirit possession shamans who perform both shamanic as well as non-shamanic social ceremonies in the *Limboo* society, and hence known as shamanic priests. They perform shamanic rituals through controlled state of ecstasy, trance or possession to gain intimate knowledge of supernatural beings, their where-about, their mannerisms, their desires, likes, dislikes, needs and requirements. They are specialist in human soul and therefore perform manifest functions in the society. They are part time professionals of curers and healers and limit their activities to prayer, worship and religious offerings to supernatural beings.

The *Yuma* religious practitioners are collectively known as *Phedangmas*. It is a general term for all types of *Limboo* religious practitioners.

They officiate and perform all the life rituals and worships such as pre-natal womb worship, birth rituals, new born child naming to initiate the perceptive souls of the child, purify the new born pollution, solemnize marriage weddings, conduct death rituals, offerings of household divinities, harvest ceremonies etc. besides curing and healing of the sick.

Types of Limboo Religious Priest - *Phedangmas*

Historically, the *Limboo* society recognizes nine types of *Phedangmas*. They differ in their gear or costumes known as *Sama*, their role in the religious functions in the society, worship methodology as curers, healers, and offerings to supernatural beings. They are briefly described as follows:

(a) *Muhikkum Ongshi*

They are wise incarnate male religious shaman priests with great erudition. They usually lead a mundane life, abandining the worldly things, ascetic, mostly involved in preaching and devotion. The most revered ongshis are *Sunamal, Chounabal, Kounabal, Tiruabal* and *Sahalman*. The *Limboos* believe that *Teyongshi Sirijunga Singthebe* (1701-41) was also an *Ongshi,* and hence known as *Teyongshi*. The essential gear of this category of religious shaman priest is *Phengbo* - garland of seeds of *Rudraksha* seeds of one hundred and eight in numbers with two to four numbers of *Sirpong* (small brass bells) hung at the lower ends. He also uses *Mudenphe* or *Laphija* (long sword) and *Yethala* (brass plate). In some cases, tiger nail, wild pig tusks etc. may also find the place along with the brass bells. They perform most of the rituals performed by the *Phedangmas* and *Sambas*. *Sunamal Ongsi* of *Kedemba* group (clan) of *Limboo* recognized *Warakma* divinity for the first time and propitiated.

(b) *Phedangmas*

They are male incarnate religious shaman priests with a simple gear of *Phengbo* as in the case of *Muhikkum Ongshi*. He also uses *Mudenphe* or *Laphija* (long sword) and *Yethala* (brass plate). They perform harvest rituals, worship household divinities, rituals of birth and death pollutions/impurities, wedlock, offerings of benevolent *Mangs, Sammangs,* and *Sammang Chyangs*. Their vocation is considered more abstemious, sober, neat and clean, and non-violent in comparison to other shaman priests. *Phungjiri Phungappo Phedangma* was the first *Phedangma* incarnated in the community to perform household rituals, cure illness and prevent natural calamities.

The *Sawa Yethangs* did not know to offer foods to their Tutelary deities. They began to suffer from various illnesses. They consulted their father and brought *Phungjiri Phungappo Phedangma* who officiated harvest rituals and they became well. To over come the day-to-day problems of life and to help them to worship nature and ancestors, they brought *Nenjirima Nembothangba, Tetlara Laphungyangba* and *Miktikke Samsui Phedangmas* in the land of *Sawa Yethang* from the ancestor's world.

Saplingek Warin Phedangma propitiated the *Mudemba Sammang* for the first time for curing and healing the sick. *Soba Sammang* was propitiated for the first time by *Phedangma Singdung Ing Phekwa Ing* of *Yungwa* clan. *Abaso Changbhahang Phedangma* began to propitiate the water goddess *Chakhoba* for the first time to cure the sick. *Tanghangba Phedangma* was the first to propitiate *Misekpa* divinity. *Samdangwa Karangwa Phedangma* identified *Tambhungna –Yobadangma* (mistress of the earth), *Senjekum Semmethumma* (mistress of the day) - *Yakwadangma-Hangwadangma* (mistress of agriculture and good luck or power), *Mangwadangma* (protector goddess); *Phatrahang Phedangma* identified *Khonjoma* or *Senghama* as divinity coming from the low land to the hill regions to cause illnesses to those who do not propitiate her. *Tanghang Penkhang Phedangma* met *Toksongba* for the first time and propitiated him and began to worship.

(c) *Sambokko Samba*

Sambokko Sambas are also male incarnate religious shaman priests with immense erudition in myths and rituals. The essential gears are *Phengbo, Laphija, Yethala, Paga* without *cowries* (head gear consists of red and white cotton cloth where *wasangs* are sewn), *Aplak* without *cowries* (consists of two necklaces worn as bandoleers), *Pangphoyee* (wide belt of red cotton), *wasang* (pointed hollow cone with feathers inserted), *Yesim* (long plated robe), *Hongsing Ke* (two feet long hollow drum) etc. They usually perform the ritual of *Tongsing*; driving of *Sogha, Sugut, Sasik*; conducting funeral rites, etc. Their vocation mostly concerns with impending trepidation, tribulations and implications, believed to have originated from incest, envy and jealousy, curse and other social anarchy and absence of ethic. *Sajuwet Mundhangwet Samba* was the first *Samba* who incarnated in the community to save from disorder, distress, disaster and illness. Next was *Sigonda Thegonda Samba* incarnated for avoiding death among the descendants of

Sawa Yethangs. Following this, *Thappura Thyonge Samba* incarnated to drive away the evil spirits of jealousy and envy (*Nahen*) and blocking the path of death (*Silan sakma*); *Thangseri Musedi Teannang Samba* incarnated for blocking thunderbolt and earthquake; *Sikiling Kambokling Samba* incarnated for identifying and tracing the wandering human souls, saving them from malignant supernatural beings, bringing them back safely in their own bodies and so on. A number of *Sambas* incarnated in the community for curing, healing, and protecting various illness in due course of time.

Mugoplung Khegoplung Samba was brought from the ancestor world by *Suwa Yethangs* to extinguish the fire brought from cosmological world. Then they brought *Suketling Tangetling Samba* from the ancestor world to find out the fire for their livelihood on earth. He discovered the fire for livelihood in *Isewasing* and gave it to *Sawa Yethangs*. Then onwards, they began to eat cooked food. *Sawa Yethangs* could not get rid of the evils of incest, envy and jealousy, curse, diseases and sin. So, they brought *Sajuwet Mundangwet Samba* from the ancestor world, to get rid of such evils. *Mikkendang Samba* propitiated *Thokley Sammang Dungdunge* for the first time to cure the sick. Supreme Goddess *Tagera Ningwaphuma* sent *Sigonda Thegonda Samba* to the earth to cure illness and avoid untimely deaths. *Sawa Yethangs* brought *Sajuwet Mudangwet Samba* and *Thappura Theyonge Samba* to perform the ritual of blocking the paths of death by using a special instrument made of tasseled sticks of *Muktubung* (*Neyraudia madacascarensis*) placed in crossed position and tied by thread and a net weaved around it. *Mikhappu Chama Thekong Samba* and *Namdhingo Suyekten Samba* performed rituals for protection of *Sawa Yethangs* from evil spirits.

(d) *Yabokko Yeba*

The next to incarnate in sequence was *Yabokko Yeba*, a male religious shaman priest with gears consisting *Phengbo, Yethala, Laphija, Yesim, Yejephe, Yephoyee, Wasang, Yeburko, Aplak* with cowries, *Paga* with cowries, *Yehang-pongey, Hongsing Ke* etc. They are specialized in diseases, which are thought to have their origin in *Nahen*, the spirit of envy and jealousy. The *Yebas* effectively worship *Nahen, Yeepley Songdok, Sugut, Sogha, Sasik Yangdang, Lungdhung Kai*, and other malevolent divinities and evil spirits.

Yebhung Yeba was the first to incarnate to drive away *Sogha, Sugut* and *Sasik Yangdang* in the community.

(e) *Yabokko Yema*

The next incarnate religious shaman priest is the *Yabokko Yema*. It has the same essential gears as that of the *Yabokko Yeba*. Their specialization is same as that of *Yabokko Yeba*. *Yebhung Yema* was the first incarnate *Yema* in the community. The collective term used for both *Yeba* and *Yema* is the *Ya* or *Yea*.

Sawa Yethang brought *Tetlara Tenchiyeppa Yea* from their ancestor land to perform the ritual of destroying *Chellung Khaklung* (symbolic representation of incest) and killing or propitiation of several evil spirits, divinities, devils, ghosts and witches of incest origin. *Sodhung Lepmuhang* instructed *Chillima Pesumma Yea* and *Nenjiri Nemmethuk Yea* to kill (*Idhuk Setchhene, Sogha Setchhene*), to eat (*Idhuk Chaseni Sagha Chaseni*), and to drive away *Sogha* (*Idhuk Nachchhene, Sogha Nachchhene*) from Saw Yahangs pangbhe. They danced and searched the *Sogha* in the house, around the poles, at the doors and called the female *Sogha "Pari Nu Kheknu Nu Khemyangma"* and male *Sogha "Tumbariba Wangdung Kemba"*, earliest among male *Sogha* to come to the door showing them their tasty foods, coaxing them by producing typical sounds, uttering series of puns etc. *Sawa Yethangs* brought *Sajara Yea Lungdongba Yea* who licked and ate away *Tingding Nahen* of various types such as *Tingding Nahen* of diamond, pearl, precious minerals, land, plants, youth, water, soil, divinities, etc. from the descendants of *Sawa Yethang* and thus they were made free from *Tingding Nahen*. They brought *Telete Tenchhammuk Yea* and *Telele Tenjiyep Yea* to destroy and control evil spirits such as *Sogha, Sugut* and *Sasik Yangdang*. *Chillima Pesumma Yea*, also known as *Yetchillek Phangchillek Yea* – a *Yema* having a weird power of turning into eight-nine forms or entering into the bodies of various animals, had to persuade them and drive away *Sogha, Sugut* and *Sasik* evil spirits from the land of Sawa Yethangs.

(f) *Yuma Sam*

Yuma Sams are male or female devotees of *Yuma*, the divine soul of *Tagera Ningwaphuma*. The gears are *Khurmi* (sickle), white colour Yak's tail, *Yelumbhu* (*thunchey*) and *Soyang* (cymbals). *Yuma Sam* is not an incarnate shaman religious priest and usually do not conduct any prayer, worship as a curer or healer. *Yuma Sam* is possessed by *Yuma Sammang* divinity and a devotee of *Yuma*.

(g) *Sammundhumms*

They are male or female singers of myths (*Mundhumma*). They are not incarnate shaman religious priests. They do not have any gear and do not perform any prayer, worship rituals but assist the incarnate shaman priests in their myth recitation/chanting and singing.

(h) *Yepmundhums*

They are also of both sexes without gears and not incarnate religious priests. They do not perform any shamanic rituals independently but assist the incarnate shamans by dancing (*Ya-yeppma*) while performing the rituals.

(i) *Sada-Samba/Samma*

They are both male and female herbalists without any gear. They are not incarnates but they practice as disease curers and healers in the society. They use medicinal herbs, animal products, talisman or amulets to cure and heal their clients in the community (Subba, C. 1995: 72-92; Subba, J.R. 1998: 19-57; 1999: 339-378; 2005b: 32-41)

Mythological Functions

(i) Mystical: The myth describes the mystery of origin of *Limboo* religious shaman priests.

(ii) Cosmological: The myth explains the cosmological origin of all the incarnate *Limboo* religious shaman priests.

(iii) Sociological: The myth explains how the Limboo religious shaman priests discharge "manifest" or "Emic" function. They not only function as curers and healers but also as priests in the society.

11

RELIGION AND MYTHOLOGY OF *NINNAMMISM* ⌒ANIMISM⌣ OF THE KIRANT KHAMBU-RAIS

The *Kirant Khambu-Rais* and some *Yakhas* are the believers of *Ninnammism* (Animism) belief system. The belief system of this group of people is still in oral tradition. The rituals are conducted by a number of their own tutelary shaman priests known as *Mangpas* or *Bijuwas, Nakchhong, Mabimi, Kubimi* and *Dawang*. The belief system is almost similar to *Yumaism* of the *Limboo* tribes - the closest tribe to *Khambu-Rais*. Westerners often used the term "Shaman" for such type of persons, after the term used for such religious specialists for *Thungus* of Siberia. Further, "Animism" is also termed by the Westerners, as all the *Karma* based oriental religions of the Eastern world are nature worshipers (Natural mythology) in their early developing stages. These nature worship rituals are intricately interwoven with Social Mythology in these religions or belief systems. There is no religion without nature worship (Natural Mythology) originated from the eastern world. Hence, it is not appropriate to term such belief systems or religion of the races as "Animism". The Western religions are devoid of nature worship (Nature Mythology). The developed religions of Western world of today consider nature only a congregation of matter. The religions are non-*karma* based and have only Social Mythology in their religion (e.g. Christianity, Islam etc.).

The dictionary meaning of the word "Animism" refers to the worship of nature and natural phenomena, such as rocks, mountains, rivers, streams, thunder and lightening, to ascribing inanimate things as having a soul. The Eastern belief systems, however, do not outrightly worship these phenomena. They respect their natural surroundings but do not ascribe souls to them. They think that these places are where the spirits dwell. The spirits as such are not identified with the rocks or trees themselves, but are seen as separate from them. As such, the belief system of *Khambu-Rai* is inappropriate to be named as "Animism". Thus, it is appropriate to name the belief system as ***"Ninnammism"*** *or* ***"Mangchhamism"***, as the *Khambu-Rais* refer their Almighty Goddess as *Ninnamma* or *Mangchhamma* in their ritual recitation. *Ninnamma* is referred to be an attributeless, formless, Almighty Goddess.

The *Khambu-Rais* mainly worship their ancestors, known as *Mangs* (*Ptri Puja*). They believe that their most venerated deities (*Mangs*) *Paruhang* and *Sumnima* are their progenitors and ancestors. They do not believe in heaven and hell. The deities are the creator, preserver and sustainer god and goddess of the *Khambu-Rais*. Hence, it is not appropriate to equate these venerated god and goddess with the *Shiva* (a destroyer god of Hinduism) and *Parvati* (concert of *Shiva*), as it is often equated in many *Khambu-Rai* literature these days. This is simply *Hinduisation* of the lesser-known *Khambu-Rai* belief system.

In the *Mundhum* (myth) of *Paruhang* and *Sumnima,* their daughter *"Phengma"*, *"Nakchong Susuli"* and young man *"Lekpa"* were turned into stones in the power testing competition of *Paruhang* and *Sumnima*. These stones became the Deities of *Khambu-Rai* belief system as *Samkhalung*. The *Khambu-Rais* worship the three stones of the sacred fireplace *Samkhalung,* as they believe that the souls of these ancestor deities dwell on these stones. This has led to the tradition of worship of their ancestors at *Samkhalung* and three stones worship tradition. These stones have now been Hindusized to *Linga* worship of Hinduism in many Khambu-Rai literatures, which is incorrect. *Toshlung* or *Yokolung* worship of *Assam-Lingzey* – the natural occurring three stones representing *Samkhalung* or *Sakalung, Situlung* or *Deepalung* and *Sutulung* or *Thankalung* are the representative stones of *Pheng-ma, Lekpa* and *Nakchong Susuli.* These stones are not the fertility symbol of *Shiva-Linga* of Hinduism (*Paruhang Sawanam: Visesank: Sakewa Parwa: Ninnamma ra Henkhammaq ko utpatti* 2008: 33-41).

Development Stages of *Khambu-Rai* Belief system - *Ninnammism*

The *Khambu-Rais* prefer to denote their belief system and practice as "Animism" rather than any other name is incorrect. Oswald Spangler (1937) in his book "Decline of the West" enumerated four different developmental stages of a religion.

(i) In its infancy religion was mythological.

(ii) In its youth religion took to nature's worship;

(iii) In its middle ages religion consisted of worshipping of gods and goddesses and its form was theological; however,

(iv) In its matured age religion searches for the essential elements and tends to be philosophical.

The mythological stage of *Ninnammism* is amply represented by its myths – *Mundhum*. There exists an elaborate tradition of reciting Oral *Mundhums* (oral myths) while performing the rituals by the incarnate shamans of the community – *Mangpas* or *Bijuwas* and other shaman priests. These oral traditions are the most important means of cultural continuity in a non-literate society, and are inherited and past down from generation to generation through their shamanic priesthood system – *Mangpas* or *Bijuwas*. *Mundhums* are the power of the great strength and believed to be true holy and powerful scripture. They live on more independently and steadfastly in the oral tradition, than in any other domain. The total corpus of the performed texts of *Mundhums* is myths - sacred, legend, mythological or spiritual instructions, ritual songs and ceremonial dialogues. It generally refers to inherited knowledge concerning the universe creation, creation of living beings, human beings, ancestor etc. It mainly comprises:

(i) Universe, gods and goddesses creation.

(ii) Creation of living beings and non-living.

(iii) Creation of human beings, origin of the ancestors and their worship.

(iv) The emergence of natural and cultural orders.

(v) The Means of communicating through *Mangbas* with gods, goddesses and ancestors and ritually maintaining the order they have established.

(vi) Continuing to the settlement of the ancestral territory.

(vii) It evokes a way of life predefined by the ancestors, a self-enclosed world, rooted in the past, and;

(viii) It is the very essence of their culture, the foundation of their identity.

There is no written religious book of the *Khambu-Rais* so far. Now they have started documenting the myths (*Mundhum*) in written form. They solely depended on the spoken verses of religious rites by *Mangpas* (Allen, N.J.1976a:258; Martin Gaenszle, 1991: 223-224; Chemjong, I.S. 1961:21; Rai, S. K.2005: 73; *Paruhang Sawanam: Visesank: Sakewa Parwa: Ninnamma ra Henkhammaq ko utpatti* 2008: 33-41; 61-62; 70-78).

The second stage of the *Khambu-Rai*'s belief system is Animism – the nature's worship. The *Khambu-Rais* believe in various divinities such as *Aitabarey, Sikari, Aathaney, Naya, Buddheni* and *Yowa*. These are all natural divinities and are worshipped to, for better health, good cultivation (free of diseases and pests), better harvest of the crop, good rain, prosperity and well being of the adherents of the belief system. The incarnate *Khambu-Rai Mangpa* or *Bijuwa* or *Nakchong* perform these nature worship religious rituals.

The third stage of the *Khambu-Rai*'s belief system is theological. This comprises worship of gods and goddesses constructing a temporary altar or *Mangkhim*, following a set of rules. The most important Deities (*Mangs*) of *Khamu-Rai* are their Almighty Goddess *Ninnamma*, creator god *Tayaripchi*, and their Progenitors – *Paruhang* and *Sumnima*. Then comes the three ancestor divinities *Nakchong Susuli, Pheng-ma*, and *Lekpa*, (which turned into three stones as previously mentioned) namely *Samkhalung* or *Sakalung, Situlung* or *Deepalung* and *Sutulung* or *Thankalung*. The other divinities of *Khambu-Rai* are their forefathers – ancestors *Raipas, Raimas*, who dwell at *Samkhalung* area of their sacred Kitchen.

The fourth stage of the religion of *Khamu-Rai* is philosophical. The *Khambu-Rais* believe that the souls of the *Raipas* and *Raimas* dwell at *Samkhalung*. At death, their incarnate shaman priest known as *Mabimi* accompanies the soul of the deceased and the soul is then persuaded to live in the *Samkhalung* as a venerated ancestors. The deceased souls of the unmarried man and woman are accompanied in their soul journey by *Mabimi* and persuaded to live in *rongeli* (i.e. *Akashic* field or atmosphere of outside the main door of the house). The young or immature married or adopted person's departed soul is accompanied in their soul journey by *Mabimi* and persuaded to stay in *Namelung* (i.e. ever sunny stone on the lap of highest mountain). The soul of the person who dies an unnatural death (such as an accidental or suicidal death), is accompanied in their soul journey by *Mabimi* and persuaded to live in *hillaten* (i.e. blood shaded rocky place). Further, a woman who dies during delivery, has her soul accompanied in her soul journey and persuaded to dwell in *Manmangten* (i,e. gloomy and steep rock). Thus, *Khambu-Rais* also recognize different (five) types of death and the souls of the dead are accompanied in their soul journey by the *Mabinis*, and their souls are persuaded to stay at different places (like the *Limboo* tribes).

The belief system of *Khambu-Rais* is not developed well in all the four aspects of the religion, but it has all the four components of a good religion, which need to be explored, recorded and streamlined properly (*Paruhang Sawanam: Visesank: Sakewa Parwa: Ninnamma ra Henkhammaq ko utpatti* 2008: 33-41).

Deities and Divinities

The main shrine of *Khambu-Rai* is called *Samkhalung* (sacred kitchen) having three stones where all the important religious rites are conducted. They also believe that all souls of the dead *Raipas* and *Raimas* (forefather and foremother ancestors) dwell here, where the ancestors are worshipped. *Samkhalung* forms the sanctumsanctorium and only clan members are allowed to go near it. Even married daughters have no right to go near it. It consists of a fireplace (*Chula*) made of three stones – *Samkhalung, Situlung* and *Sutulung*. Above the *Samkhalung* a small platform like structure is made which is supposed to be the seat for the spirits of ancestors being worshipped. Every item produced from the land has to be ceremoniously offered to the ancestors at *Samkhalung*. Only after such offering one is entitled to eat and drink the items. The worship ritual of ancestors is performed once in May-June (High season – *Ubhauli*) and another in November-December (Low season – *Udhauli*). The *Khambu-Rais* also believe in various other divinities such as *Aitabarey, Sikari, Aathaney, Naya, Buddheni* and *Yowa*. (Rai, S.K 2005:40-44; *Paruhang Sawanam: Visesank: Sakewa Parwa: Ninnamma ra Henkhammaq ko utpatti* 2008: 33-41).

Concept of Gods and Goddess

The *Kirant Khambu-Rai* have the concept of Almighty knowledgeable, conscious, attributeless Eternal, Infinite Goddess, which is known as *Ninnamma*. The Goddess appears suddenly in the void with the light, and starts the creation. The Almighty Goddess manifests Herself to creator god *Tayaripchi* to complete the creation. Thus the Almighty Goddess is the creator, preserver and sustainer of the universe as in the case of *Tagera Ninwaphuma* of *Yumaism* (*Paruhang Sawanam: Visesank: Sakewa Parwa: Ninnamma ra Henkhammaq ko utpatti* 2008: 33-41).

They also worship a hunting god known as "*Deebung Sikari*". For this they sacrifice a pair of pigeon or a pair of fowl, a thigh of deer, *Rawa* or *Mustey Charo*, a pair of *Kharawa* (quill of porcupine), etc.

Concept of Creation of the Universe

Ninnamma created the planets, the stars, the sky, the sun, the moon, water, air, windstorm, rain, ocean and the earth (*Henkhamma*). The Goddess created attributeless god "*Tayaripchi*" with intelligence to create the earth, but "*Kukurmi*" (evil god) blocked the rays of the light and thus created the darkness from that day on the earth. *Tayaripchi* was also attributeless like *Ninnamma*, but *Ninnamma* asked *Tayaripchi* to appear in physical form. The god acquired a form – half male and half female. *Tayaripchi* then, manifested himself and created the male creator Deity *Paruhang* in the sky and female creator Deity *Sumnima* on the earth. As desired by *Tayaripchi, Sumnima* lit the lamp and *Paruhang* started putting stones and earth in the ocean. Whenever *Paruhang* puts stones and earth in the ocean, *Kukurmi* stir the water causing immersing of the stones and earth dumped by *Paruhang* from the site while creating the Earth. Now, *Paruhang* created *Wayuhangma* from the water and then he planted a *Khapchtyang Khanue* (a plant) in the ocean. On the roots of the plant he placed a thin stone plate. Thereafter, he poured earth on it. Then only the soil poured by *Paruhang* settled to form the earth. *Paruhang* continuously poured the soil till the soil dumped appeared above the ocean to become the earth. Now, *Tayaripchi* created other living creatures and non-living objects on earth. *Sumnima* started to live on earth with these living beings and non-living objects then onwards. She used to spend most of her time with these living beings weaving clothes, as there was no man on earth (*Paruhang Sawanam: Visesank: Sakewa Parwa: Ninnamma ra Henkhammaq ko utpatti* 2008: 33-41).

Concept of Afterlife

The *Khambu-Rais* believe in afterlife, which is clearly indicated by the incarnate shaman *Mabimi's* accompaniment of deceased soul journey, and persuading the souls to stay at different places depending on the type of death of the individual described at the fourth stage of the religion above.

Myths and Mythological Functions

(a) Myth of creation of the universe

In the beginning there was no universe, no earth, no Moon, no Sun, no planets, and no stars. Everywhere there was idiocy of darkness, night and repose. Spontaneously motion was created; wisdom was created in the void. Along with motion and wisdom, knowledge was created. Along with motion, wisdom and knowledge the Almighty Goddess *Ninnamma* spontaneously appeared in the void with light. The light was full of motion and lighted the entire universe. There was no darkness in the universe. The Almighty Goddess added more wisdom to light. Along with wisdom the light started moving in a definite direction. The Almighty Goddess did not like the light to move in a single direction, as it may annihilate itself due to its own power, motion and heat. She divided the light into several crore pieces with their own wisdom, knowledge and light. All these pieces became planets, the Sun, the Moon, the Stars scattered in the sky. In a similar motion one piece of light was moving around. It was very hot. Due to its own heat and fast motion, the piece of light was congested itself. The Goddess was looking at it. She felt that She should sow the seeds of knowledge in it. She reduced the motion of that light piece. With the reduction of motion the heat of the light slowly transformed into steam, which vapoured off from the piece. With further reduction of motion, the vapour created the wind and windstorm and rain. It started moving along with the light piece. When the rainwater dropped on the light-piece, it created the Earth (*Henkhamma*) full of sweat. It was full of sweat and rainwater and was suffering greatly. The Almighty Goddess *Ninnamma* understood the suffering of the earth, and to help her She transformed herself into wisdom (*Tayaripchi*) and descended down to create the Earth. Before descending *Tayaripchi* to earth, *Kukurmi* (*Asatti*) blocked the Sunlight and made it dark. It is said that from that day onwards the darkness was created in the world (*Paruhang Sawanam: Visesank: Sakewa Parwa: Ninnamma ra Henkhammaq ko utpatti* 2008: 33-41).

Mythological Functions

(i) Mystical: The myth elucidates the mystery of the universe creation in *Ninnammism* in its own archaic way of creation of the wonderful universe. Although the myth is in very brief and perhaps lost various components of myths related to the creation of universe, it has its originality. The myth has lost the creation components of plants, crops, animals, human beings etc. The myth opens up the world to the dimension of mystery, to the realization of the mystery that underlies all forms of life. There is an urgent need of recording, compiling and understanding the myths relating to the creation of the universe from the oral traditions of the learned religious *Khambu –Rai* shaman priests who are the learned myth chanters/reciters as being done by the Limboo community for *Yumaism*. If you loose that, you do not have your mythology. If mystery manifest through all things, the universe becomes, as it were, a holy picture. You are always addressing the transcendent mystery through the conditions of your actual world. To do this one must have a deep understanding of *Khamu-Rai* language, religious and cultural traditions. You have to remain linked with your forefathers and the religious traditions provided by your ancestors. You must awake now and work before you loose any more myths. Do not listen to others; follow your own path blessed by your ancestors.

(ii) Cosmological: The myth has a cosmological dimension, not well understood even by science today. It describes in brief about void, the creation of planets, the Sun, the Moon, the earth, the stars, the sky, attributeless Almighty Goddess and the creator god etc. in the *Akashic* field or void.

(b) Myth of Creation of *Paruhang, Sumnima, Wayuhangma* and the Earth

Once the Earth appeared with wisdom, the Almighty Goddess *Ninnamma* asked *Tayaripchi* to appear in physical form. Before that *Tayaripchi* was also attributeless, formless, genderless god or goddess like *Ninnamma*. *Tayaripchi* appeared in form half male and half female. Then, *Tayaripchi* imagined creating self-sustaining life on earth. To fulfill its desire, *Tayaripchi* imagined a male form and a female form. According to *Tayaripchi*'s imagination lightening occurred and one light went to the sky while other to the earth. With this lightening, thunderbolt and thunderstorm occurred in the sky and rainfall occurred on the earth. Thus, the almighty God *Paruhang* appeared in the sky and Goddess *Sumnima* appeared on the earth. *Kukurmi* created the darkness by blocking the light rays. To over come this problem, *Tayaripchi* had to be manifested its male-hood and female-hood creating *Paruhang* in the sky and *Sumnima* on earth.

As desired by *Tayaripchi, Sumnima* lighted a candle and *Paruhang* started pouring stones and soil on earth. As and when *Paruhang* put stones and soils on earth's sweaty-water, *Kukurmi* used to stir the sweaty-water, which sunk the stones, and soils deposited on earth. *Paruhang* created *Wayuhangma* in the middle of the sweaty-water. *Wayuhangma* appeared with full of water in its body. *Wayuhangma* shook its body before *Kukurmi* to frighten it. Thereafter, *Paruhang* planted a tree (*Khapchitang Khanue*) in the sweaty-water. On the root of *Khapchitang* plant he placed thin stone plates (*Choyilungma*). Then he put the soil on the stone plates and roots of *Khapchitang* plant. The soils settled on the earth then onwards. He added more and more soils. Thereafter, the earth (*Henkhamma*) immersed in sweaty-water started appearing out. Thus *Paruhang* and *Sumnima* created the earth. They are the creator god and goddess in *Ninnammism* belief system and are not comparable with destroyer god and goddess of Hinduism – *Shiva* and *Parvati*. The comparison is simply Hinduisation of the tribal belief system of the *Khambu-Rais*.

Paruhang and *Sumnima* were of the same age but they had no contact for a long period as they dwell on the sky and the earth respectively. *Paruhang* used to see *Sumnima* on earth from the sky.

Tayaripchi created other living beings on earth. *Sumnima* used to spend her time with these other living beings. She used to weave looms and spend most of her time on weaving looms, and sometimes wandering on earth. There were only birds and animals, but no man-like creatures on earth (*Paruhang Sawanam: Visesank: Sakewa Parwa: Ninnamma ra Henkhammaq ko utpatti* 2008: 33-41).

Mythological Functions

(i) Mystical: The myth briefly describes the mystery of creation of the creator god, manifestation of male-hood – *Paruhang*, and female–hood - *Sumnima*; the progenitors of *Khambu-Rais*; creation of wind/air – *Wayuhangma*; creation of darkness and its divinity – *Kukurmi*. It also illustrates how *Paruhang* and *Sumnima* created the earth and how *Wayuhangma* helped them in the earth creation. It also explains that in the early evolution of life there were no sexual differences as in the case of a unicellular life. Manifestation of male and female took place at the later part of evolution of life.

(ii) Cosmological: The myth is a cosmological in origin.

(iii) Sociological: The myth explains how cooperation of each other is helpful to overcome difficulties. The creation of the earth could be possible only with the cooperation of *Paruhang, Sumnima* and *Wayuhangma*. It also expounds that difficulties and problems are a part and parcel of life. One can achieve success only through dedication of work and cooperation.

(iv) Pedagogical: The myth interprets how a human lifetime should be lived, through facing the difficulties of life and through cooperation with others.

(c) Myth of origin of *Samkhalung*

Both *Paruhang* and *Sumnima* attained a youthful stage. *Paruhang* used to gaze at *Sumnima* from the sky. One day *Paruhang,* mesmerised by the beauty of *Sumnima,* dropped a golden comb (*Sukhup*) for her while she was weaving the loom. She liked the golden comb and imagined how handsome the man who made such a lovely comb would be. She pledged herself to get married to him. *Paruhang* was looking at this from the sky and wanted to know the honest intention of *Sumnima.* He thought of testing her desire. He manifested himself into an ugly man. Thereafter he thought of sending the birds to *Sumnima* for marriage proposal, but assuming that birds may take many days to reach earth, he dismissed the idea. Then he asked the wind to go to *Sumnima* with his marriage proposal. The wind immediately came down to earth from the sky and delivered the proposal. Sumnima felt extremely happy with the proposal and asked nothing about him but agreed to the proposal. The wind returned to the sky and told *Paruhang* about the agreement. *Paruhang* did not believe it. The wind was ready to face any punishment if it had lied. *Paruhang* warned him that he would be punished if *Sumnima* did not agree for the marriage. The wind agreed the pledge. Then, *Paruhang* made the wind his mediator (*Kaliya*) for the marriage. The wind took *Paruhang* along with the birds to the earth and reached at the place where *Sumnima* was staying. The wind approached *Sumnima* showing *Paruhang*. When *Sumnima* saw *Paruhang* she refused, as he was a dwarf and externally ugly (opposite to what *Sumnima* imagined when she had received the golden comb). In anger *Paruhang* cut away the wings of the wind. It is said that from that day the wind has no wings but flees without wings. After punishing the wind, *Paruhang* went to *Sumnima* and told her "you wanted to love me in body not in soul. You insulted me. For that you will face the consequences." After that *Paruhang* manifested back to his original body in front of *Sumnima* and went back to the sky. *Sumnima* repented for her bleak decision and craved for getting married to *Paruhang*. On the other hand *Paruhang* started thinking about how he could take revenge of this insult to *Sumnima*.

Thereafter, the earth faced a severe drought not only for one or two years but for many years. Due to absence of rain the rivers also started drying. All the animals, birds and even *Sumnima* felt extremely thirsty for want of water. There was no water to drink. *Sumnima* sent the birds in search of water. A bird known as *Balakenwa* got some water on a tree-hole but drank all the water itself. Other birds found out and they dragged away its tongue. It is said that from that day onwards, the tongue of *Balakenwa* (*Katero, Pericrocotus brevirostris*) bird has a curve tongue. *Sumnima* and the birds were in search of water to drink. Even the greenery of the earth was drying due to drought. *Paruhang* thought that this was the right time for taking revenge to *Sumnima,* and he left *Parulep* (semen) on the leaves of *Karkala* (?) plant. The birds discovered it and told *Sumnima* about the watery substance. She drank it thinking it was water. Thereafter, it started raining on the earth and once again the earth became vibrant with greenery.

Sumnima gradually felt sick and felt blue day by day. *Paruhang* sent *Nakchhong Susuli* the religious shaman priest for looking after her on the earth. *Nakchhong Susuli* examined *Sumnima* and told her that she is pregnant. That is why she was sick. *Sumnima* became angry after hearing this and told *Susuli* that she was not married, how she could be pregnant? She also asked *Susuli* if she was pregnant, what was the gender of the child developing in her womb. *Susuli* told her that a female foetus was being developed in her womb. In utter disbelief, she told him that if it were so, the baby would be married to *Susuli.* Later on *Sumnima* gave birth to a girl child. She named her *Phengma.* The girl child started growing day by day to a teenage and then entered a youthful age while *Susuli* started growing older and older.

Phengma at her youthful age fell in love with a gentleman *Lekpa*. Both *Sumnima* and *Susuli* knew this. *Sumnima* told *Phengma* that she has already given her hand to *Susuli* for marriage. On this *Phengma* told her mother that it was better to commit suicide than to marry a man of the age of her father. Hearing this *Sumnima* recollected the ugly days of her when she met *Paruhang* for the first time. She also wanted her daughter to get married with *Lekpa.* When *Susuli* saw that *Phengma* had entered a youthful age, he went to *Sumnima* and asked to fulfill her pledge. Disregarding her pledge *Sumnima* told him that he should have a bow-arrow and a sword fight with *Lekpa,* and whosever wins, she will give her daughter for marriage. *Susuli* did not like this but he agreed her proposal.

Lekpa was a sturdy young man. *Sumnima* taught *Lekpa* the art of fighting with the bow-arrow and the sword. *Paruhang* knew this art. He taught *Susuli* all the eight powerful arts of fighting with the bow-arrow and the sword. *Sumnima* and *Phengma* were confident that *Lekpa* would be victorious while *Paruhang* was confident for the victory of *Susuli.* The day of fighting came and *Lekpa* and *Susuli* started fighting with bow and arrow for the first few days. Then, they started fighting with the sword. While fighting with the sword *Lekpa* was killed. Now, *Susuli* was ready to take *Phengma* for marriage. However *Phengma* committed suicide with the sword of *Susuli*. Upon this sight *Susuli* turned into a stone. It is said that all the three – *Susuli, Phengma* and *Lekpa* manifested as three stones and the souls of all the three started to dwell at one place on the three stones. Since then, they were regarded as *Samkhalung* (*Sam* = soul, *Khalung* = sacred stones). Thus, the soul of the three persons dwelling at the three stones at one place *Samkhalung* became the ancestor divinities of *Khambu-Rais* since then.

To represent the symbol of these ancestor souls, *Samkhalung* or *Samkha Dabbey* – the three stones of the fireplace is considered the most sacred place of *Khambu-Rais*. All the deities and divinities of *Khambu-Rai* pantheon such as *Mangchhami, Paruhang, Sumnima, Nawangma* (new god), *Belechhi Mang* (the god of wealth migrating with the daughters), *Hangkumang* (god of streams) etc. are worshipped and offered offerings atleast twice in a year at this place.

Samkhalung is made of three stones. The first stone is known "*Sakalung*" which is the symbol of the stone where the soul of *Phengma* dwells, and is considered to be the symbol of attributeless "*Mangchhami*". The second stone is known as "*Deepalung*" which is the symbol of the stone where the soul of *Lekpa* dwells. It is considered to be the symbol of ancestors. The third stone is known as "*Thankalung*", which is the symbol of the stone where the soul of *Nakchhong Susuli* dwells, and is considered to be the symbol of the protector deity of the ancestors and the descendants of *Paruhang* and *Sumnima*. The stones kept around the fireplace are known with various names as *Michaklung, Paralung, Diwalung, Ringrilung, Sawalung, Tayalung, Khawayeelung, Chasumlung, Ruthulung, Chhekulung, Rumilung* etc. The various items required for worship and offering at *Samkhalung* are: *Chhenbi* (one rupee coin), *Arawa* (dehusk rice), *Wabuk* (bottle gourd containing water or fermented beer), *Subi* (sliced ginger), *Tupla* and *Bedle* (banana leaves), *Waibak* (twigs of *Katus, Castanopsis indica*), *Bhakuna (Lohota* decorated with *Artemisia vulgaris*), etc. (*Paruhang Sawanam: Visesank: Sakewa Parwa: Ninnamma ra Henkhammaq ko utpatti* 2008: 33-41; 61-62; 70-78).

Mythological Functions

(i) Mystical: The myth has described the mystery of origin of the most important worship place of *Khambu-Rais* - *Samkhalung*. This is the place where the *Khambu-Rais* are linked with their ancestor Deities, Divinities and retinue of divinities. However, the myth has been Hindusized and confused with *Shivalinghum*. The three stones of *Samkhalung* are the dwelling sacred places of the soul of *Phengma* (*Sakalung*), the first daughter of the Deities *Paruhang* and *Sumnima*; and are considered to be the symbol of *Mangchhami, Lekpa* – the youth that *Phengma* wanted for the marriage (*Deepalung*), and *Susuli* the first *Nakchhong* religious priest of *Khambu-Rais* who was sent by *Paruhang* to earth for looking after the pregnant *Sumnima* (*Thankalung*). It will be incorrect to compare with the fertility symbol – *Lingum* of *Shiva*.

(ii) Cosmological: As in all archaic mythologies, the myth has cosmological origin. The father is always somewhere in the *Akashic* field (in the sky) while the mother is always on earth or is always comparable with the earth, reproducing children, taking care of and nourishing them, sustaining in their suitable environment. Whenever the mother and descendants face any problem they look towards the sky for problem solving and in most of the cases the father who is in the sky sends the religious priests *Bijuwa* or *Mangpa, Nakchhong, Mabimi* etc. for problem solving. In the myth *Nakchong Susuli* was the first religious priest sent by the father to look after *Sumnima*. And whenever the mother or descendants do good work or are blessed with good fortune, they look up to the sky for thanking the father or the God.

(iii) Sociological: The myth has furnished a worship place for the ancestor Deities, Natural divinities, household Divinities – *Samkhalung*. The myth has linked them with *Paruhang* and *Sumnima* as their progenitors. They believe that they are the descendants of *Paruhang* and *Sumnima*. The myth provides the linkage to the ancestors.

(iv) Pedagogical: The myth has interpreted the laws of life, ethical laws and other customary laws of day-to-day activities. Worship of gods and goddess, nature divinities, protection of the environments etc.

(v) Mystery of afterlife: The myth has furnished a sacred place – *Samkhalung* for the souls of dead persons. The souls of the dead persons are accompanied soul journey and reached here in *Samkhalung* by *Mabimi* religious shaman priests. The soul of the *Raipas* and *Raimas* dwell at *Samkhalung*. At death, their incarnate shaman priest known as *Mabimi* accompanies the soul of the deceased and the departed soul is persuaded to live in the *Samkhalung* as a venerated ancestors.

(d) Myth of Marriage of *Paruhang* and *Sumnima* and their descendants

Now *Sumnima* realized the power and intelligence of *Paruhang*. She also realized that she was facing problems because of her ignorance in understanding *Paruhang* from her heart. Then, she started to meditate to get *Paruhang*. *Paruhang* found out it and finally they compromised. But due to the law of creation of the creator god *Tayaripchi* they were not allowed to reside at one place. The place of *Paruhang* was the sky while that of *Sumnima* was the earth. It is said that *Tayaripchi* then created the horizon, as a meeting place for *Paruhang* and *Sumnima*.

Marriage between *Paruhang* and *Sumnima* was essential as per the creation of *Tayaripchi*, as there was no other man or woman on earth. They were proud of their own power and intelligence but they had no alternative for further creation unless they would get married. Thus, the wind once again went to *Paruhang* and requested him for another chance. He asked the wind to go to *Sumnima* and find out about her desire for marriage. The wind came down to the earth and found out her desire and return to report it to *Paruhang*. *Sumnima* had realized her fault and she agreed to the marriage proposal of *Paruhang*. *Learning* this, *Paruhang* asked the wind to invite the birds for the marriage procession. The wind brought all the marriage procession along with *Paruhang* to the earth. Finally the marriage was accomplished.

After marriage they spent some time on earth. As desired by *Tayaripchi* they had to create different living beings required for the survival of the human beings. They started creating the various living being on earth. Their first son was the tiger, the second son was the bear, the third son was the monkey, and the last son was the man (*Hangchhpok*). They blessed the youngest son with intelligence, wisdom and their own image and named him "*Henkubung*". *Khambu-Rais* believed that man is the descendant of *Paruhang* and *Sumnima*, and he is considered as the progenitor of human beings. The eldest son – Tiger was an angry animal. He used to frighten all the animals in the forests and at home he used to fight with everybody. The bear and the monkey were afraid of him but the man was not. The man had received knowledge, intelligence, wisdom and power from his farther *Paruhang*. The bear was very lazy. He wanted to eat good food but he did not like to work. Thus, most of the time, he used to stay at home. The monkey (*Helawamangla*) was very naughty. He used to drive away the prey while hunting. Thus, the tiger and man used to avoid taking him for hunting (*Paruhang Sawanam: Visesank: Sakewa Parwa: Ninnamma ra Henkhammaq ko utpatti* 2008: 33-41).

Mythological Functions

(i) Mystical: The myth elucidates the mystery of marriage of *Paruhang* and *Sumnima*. *Wayuhangma* mediates for the marriage. They stay for sometime on earth and create more living beings. However, the details of living beings created by them is missing in the myth. There is again a big gap of creation history in the myth. It is hoped that the gap will be filled by more research in due course of time. It also describes about the progenies – the tiger, the bear, the monkey and the man. The parents blessed the man with knowledge, intelligence and wisdom.

(ii) Cosmological: The myth has cosmological origin, when *Wayuhangma* flies up to the sky and down to the earth with *Paruhang* and the birds.

(iii) Sociological: The myth furnishes not only to look at the external beauty of the body but also at the internal beauty, strength, knowledge, intelligence and wisdom which are essential for a successful marriage. For that, an effective mediator is also beneficial.

(iv) Pedagogical: The myth interprets how to proceed for a marriage proposal.

(e) Myth of Origin of Human Ancestor

The sons of *Paruhang* and *Sumnima* – the tiger, the bear, the monkey and the man (*henkubung*) always used to fight amongst themselves. The tiger was strong and angry and wanted to eat everybody. But he was also afraid of *henkubung*. *Henkubung* knew this. *Henkubung* used to tell his mother "I may kill the tiger one day. I will not say he is my brother. He always gives us trouble. Why he is always jealous of my works." His mother used to advice him and say " O my son *henkubung* ! you are the only son who has the knowledge, intelligence and wisdom. You should not do that. You are the only son who has to sustain the creation."

One day, the tiger and *henkubung* went for hunting leaving the lazy bear and the naughty monkey at home. That day also the tiger wanted to eat *henkubung* whereas *henkubung* wanted to take his revenge. Usually they used to keep their tiffin at one place and after hunting was over they used to come together to eat from their tiffin. That day *henkubung* ate up the entire contents of the tiffin; he took out his clothes and put the clothes to a wooden log, and climbed on a nearby tree. At the meal time the tiger came to that place but could not find his tiffin and he got angry. In anger he attacked the wooden log with *henkubung*'s cloth to kill his brother. He tore away the clothes. Finally he found out that it was just a wooden log and not his brother. He lay down flat with hunger and tiredness. While lying flat on the ground he saw his brother *henkubung* on the tree pointing an arrow at him. By then, the tiger could not escape. *Henkubung* asked the tiger to open his mouth. The tiger opened his mouth. *Henkubung* shot the arrow, which killed the tiger instantly piercing through his heart. Thereafter, *henkubung* crossed over the tiger's body three times and said that "Now onwards I am the eldest amongst the brothers". Their mother was worried, as they did not return home in time. *Sumnima* doubting the worse meditated and saw that *henkubung* had killed his tiger brother and was crossing over its body. She immediately went to that place and sent *henkubung* home. *Sumnima* took leaf blades of thatch grass (*siru*), fire and water and chanted "*Dhaidhai Chhubik dhai*", which made the tiger alive again. When the tiger was brought to life, he told his mother "I was in deep sleep". His mother told him that he was not in deep sleep but he was killed by *henkubung*. When the tiger came to know that he was killed by *henkubung* and that he had become the elder brother (now onwards), the tiger refused to go to home. *Sumnima* was anxious to know whose fault it was. So she also wanted to go with the tiger into the forest. The tiger requested her not to go with him but she turned down his request. While walking in the forest, the tiger thought of a trick. He told his mother that there was a blood sucking mite parasite on her throat and he wanted to take it out. His mother knew his trick however she agreed to it. Taking this chance, he killed his mother and went to the forest alone. Since then, no animals considered as powerful as the tiger was in the forest. *Sumnima* also disappeared for some time from the earth.

When *henkubung* arrived home after killing his tiger brother, the bear and the monkey were sitting together idle. Usually the food used to be ready when the bear started dancing. That day, the monkey wanted to compete with the bear and as a result there was no food. When the bear came to know that *henkubung* got angry without food, he told *henkubung* that it was because of the monkey. When *henkubung* went to ask the monkey about it the monkey ran away into the forest fearing *henkubung*'s anger. Now, only *henkubung* and the bear were there at home. The lazy bear was afraid of *henkubung*. He used to dance and the food used to get ready every day. *Henkubung* wanted to know why his mother did not return home. Both the bear and *henkubung* went to visit the place where he had left his mother with the corpse of his tiger brother. When they reached on the spot they could not found the corpse of the tiger, but they found the corpse of their mother. They thought of burring the corpse of their mother. He asked the bear to dig out the soil and burry the corpse. But the bear was hungry and he ate away the corpse of their mother. When *henkubung* came to the burial place the bear said that he had already finished burying the corpse. *Henkubung* doubted the bear, but he did not say anything. After the burial *henkubung* asked his bear brother not to mourn anymore. "Let us enjoy". Meanwhile the bear laughed exposing his front teeth. *Henkubung* saw a piece of their mother's hair on the teeth of the bear. *Henkubung* got angry and hit him on his head. The brain of the bear came out from its head and it fainted. *Henkubung* thought that the bear was also dead. He returned home. The half dead bear slowly went to the pond and asked his *Mit*-brother the frog to put his brain (as his brother had taken out his brain) on the bear's head. Hearing this frog jumped inside the pond. The bear also followed, caught the frog and put the frog's brain in his head. It is said that from that day onwards the frogs have no brain and the bears have very little brain. Once, the bear put the frog's brain he also did not return home. He also went into the forest. Leaving *henkubung* at home all his brothers – the tiger, the bear and the monkey went into the forest. Thus, it is believed that *henkubung* ultimately became the ancestor of the human beings (*Paruhang Sawanam: Visesank: Sakewa Parwa: Ninnamma ra Henkhammaq ko utpatti* 2008: 33-41; Chemjong, I.S. 1965: 7-9).

Mythological Function

(i) Mystical: A similar type of myth of the mystery has also been found in the myth of *Ipnana Sarengdhangma* of *Yumaism,* where the two brothers *Kesami* (tiger) and *Namsami* (man) fought each other, and the *Namsami* killed the tiger. The myth has furnished the rituals of *Yumchama* (restrict eating of pungent spices – garlic, ginger, oil, pepper, meat, etc. during mourning period). However, in this case no such out come is deducible. It appears that the myth needs further research to be understood fully redarding its functions in the society. Further, the myth do not reveal about the woman partner of *Henkubung* (man) essential for reproduction of the progenies.

(ii) Sociological: The myth unfolds that there are a variety of living being with different characters. But tolerance to each other and establishing an optimum relation amongst all the living being on earth is essential for our existence.

(iii) Pedagogical: The myth interprets the ethical laws.

(f) Myth of Shamanic Religious Priest

All the shamanic religious priests have been sent by the father *Paruhang* from the sky (*Akashic* field), as in *Yumaism* to look after his progenies on earth. The first shaman religious priest *Nakchhong* sent by Him on earth was *Nakchhong Susuli* who looked after *Sumnima* during her pregnancy and *Phengma* the first daughter of *Paruhang* and *Sumnima*. He also performed birth rituals of *Phengma* and took care of her after the birth. All the religious functions of *Khambu-Rais* are performed by a group of shamanic priests known as *Mangbas* or *Bijuwas*. It is a general term used for the *Khambu-Rai* shaman priests (as in the case of *Phedangmas* of the *Limboo* tribes who functions both as shaman and priest in the community).

There are five categories of such shaman priests in *Khambu-Rai's* society. But unlike *Yumaism,* myths for their coming to earth for the protection of the progenies of *Khambu-Rai* is lacking. They are:

***(i) Mangpas* or *Bijuwas*:** are the main shamanic priests of *Khambu-Rais.* They conduct the *Samkhalung* ritual ceremony as well as other religious rites of household divinities, nature divinities and clan divinities. They perform *Thomwa* (*Chinta*) for the well being of the family members and also prophecy the future happenings for the family and the society.

***(ii) Nakchhong*:** mainly conducts the *Sakewa* (worship of nature) ritual ceremony, which takes place twice in a year. *Dongwangna* worship is performed to appease the natural power of cultivation and *Donglasha* worship is performed to appease the natural power of harvesting. They represent the shamanic priests of nature mythology in *Khambu-Rai* community.

***(iii) Mabimi*:** performs the last rite of the deceased individuals. They are the soul specialists, and perform soul journies and handover the souls of the deceased person to the ancestors.

***(iv) Kubimi*:** conducts the last rite of the deceased in the absence of *Mabimi.*

***(v) Dowang*:** performs only minor religious rites and cures the sick. He chants the spell to ward off the affected evil spirits or the diseases of the sick person and uses wild herbs as medicines. Senior or experience *Raipas* may also conduct some of the minor religious rites in absence of *Mangpa* (Rai, S,K, 2005:4—44).

The shamanic *Khambu Rai* priests *Mangpas* or *Bijuwas* are tutelary incarnate shaman priests, as that of *Phedangmas* of *Limboo* tribes. Tutelary shamans of *Khambu-Rai* possess the spirit of a deceased individual and then the deity remains with them in the entire lifetime as in the case of *Yumaism* or *Mahayana* Buddhist *Rinpuche/Tulku.* But they differ in structural classification by space with the *Tulku.* In a developed and institutionalized religion like Buddhism it take residence in Monastery or *Gumpa;* while in the case of *Yumaism* and *Ninnammism,* the religion is yet to be institutionalized in *Mangkhims,* and thus spirit possession differs structurally in space but not in time (Hitchcock, J.T & Jones, R.L. 1994:1-11).

Mythological Functions

(i) Mystical: The myth describes the mystery of religious shaman priest system in *Khambu-Rai* community. As in the case of *Yumaism* all the religious shaman priests of *Khambu-Rais* are tutelary spirit possessions sent by the father (*Paruhang*) from the sky (*Akashic* field) for protection, curing and healing of his progenies. They are Tutelary possession of the departed souls of their ancestors for life but structurally their space is not designated like that of Buddhist *Tulku*. Hence, they are part-time shaman priests. They discharge two functions in the society as in the case of *Yumaism*. They are manifest or *emic* and latent *etic* functions in the *Khambu-Rai* community also.

(ii) Cosmological: The myth relates the religious shaman priests with the cosmology. All of them possess the departed soul of one of their ancestor as their Tutelary spirit sent by their father ancestor *Paruhang* from the sky (*Akashic* field). Through it he functions as shaman priests in the society.

(iii) Sociological: The myth furnishes the religious shaman priest system in the society. They are the curer, healer and guide of the society working through manifest or *emic* functions. They discharge all the life rituals of womb worship, birth and death worship in the society.

(iv) Pedagogical: The myth interprets the laws of life, ethical laws and customary laws and unfolds how to live in the *Khambu-Rai* society.

(v) Mystery of afterlife: The myth linked the livings with the ancestors by performing journey inward, soul journey and persuading the souls of the dead persons by *Mabimi* or *Kubimi* to stay at the appropriate place with the ancestors at *Samkhalung*. The mystery of afterlife is wonderfully illustrated.

(g) Myth of *Sakewa* and *Sakela* Festival Celebrations

It is a worship ceremony of high season (*Ubhauli/Bungbanwa/Dongwanga*) celebrated during May-June (*Baisakh Purnima*) by the *Khambu Rai* communities in the entire Himalayan region. This is also sometimes known as *Bhumi Puja* or *Chandi Puja* and is an agricultural festival. *Dongwangna* worship is performed to appease the natural power of cultivation in *Sakewa* while *Donglasha* worship is performed to appease the natural power of harvesting in *Sakela*.

Worship of Nature Divinities

The religious shaman priest mainly *Nakchhong* with his assistant *Mahengkulu* perform the worship on the hilltop of the village. On the way to the hilltop the *Nakchhong* performs "*Akhat Swang Sengma*" (worship of nature divinities of fresh water). The altar of *Sakewa* consists of a stone known as *Narilung Pawo* representing *Samkhalung*. The items of offerings are: *Wabuk* (Bottlegourd) containing foodgrains, sliced ginger, and fermented beer. *Nakchhong* holds the *wabuk*. Other devotees hold a container filled with foodgrains of all types produced in their agricultural fields and water. Traditionally the *Nakchhong* blood sacrifices a fat cock or a pig or both on the altar. *Nakchhong* recites the myths and offer the foodgrains, fermented beer, and sliced ginger on the altar. In the prayer *Nakchhong* request the nature divinities for protection of the people from epidemic diseases, famine, etc. and to provide good rainfall, sunshine and bumper harvest of the crops. Thereafter, they return to a wide spacious ground where *Nakchhong* pegs a big bamboo pole. Then, *Nakchhong* enters into a house where *Samkhalung* is located. There he performs the *Samkhalung* rituals. There he performs worship offering sliced ginger, *manghulu* or sacrifice of chicken, fermented beer etc. as described in *Samkhalung* origin. There after, the owner of the house enter into the *Samkhalung* altar and offers foodgrains, sliced ginger and blood of the chicken in his tern and dance around the *Samkhalung*.

Silidance

After the worship ceremony is over, the *Khambu-Rais* assemble in a big ground and perform the *Silidance*. They fall in line and follow the dance steps of *Silimangpa* and *Silimangma* waving their hands. The musical instruments used for *Silidance* are *Dhol* (*Baraken-Chhamchhon ken*) and *Jhyamta* (*Sumniken-maniken, chamukhi*). Some *Nakchhongs* weave yak-tails. They imitate various agricultural operations, one of which is "*Chasum Sili*" which is popular. This is the imitation of paddy transplanting, paddy harvest, grain collection, rice cooking and eating while dancing. *Paklekwa Sili* is another dance where there is no movement of legs and hands. In some *Silidance*, they imitate various kinds of birds and animals. "*Narowa Silidance*" is the imitation of flamingoes (*Kawangkurung*). Thus there are numerous nature dances performed by the *Khambu-Rais* during this festival. Finally, they disperse weaving with the twigs of *Wahing Tang* (*Kattus*) to each other.

(h) Myth of *Sakela* Festival Ceremony

This is a low season (*Udhauli/Dong/Dawa/Donglasa*) festival celebration held in *Mangsir Purnima* (November-December). It is also an agricultural celebration (harvest festival). During this festival newly harvested foodgrains are offered to *Samkhalung* as in the case of high season worship festival. During this festival also *Silidances* are performed as in the case of high season festival (*Paruhang Sawanam: Visesank: Sakewa Parwa: Ninnamma ra Henkhammaq ko utpatti* 2008: 33-41).

Mythological Functions

(i) Mystical: The myths of mystery of *Sakewa* and *Sakela* describes a collective celebration of these two festivals with worship of ancestor deities, household divinities, clan divinities and nature divinities followed by *Silidance* participation to expresses happiness in the community. *Sakewa* is a high-season worship and festival while *Sakela* is low-season worship and festival. The former is a worship of nature divinities and ancestor Deities for blessing, good crop protection, good sunshine, good rainfall, protection from epidemic diseases etc for better crop production in the commencing season. While *Sakela* is also a worship ceremony of thanks giving for good harvest to the ancestor deities and nature divinities duly offering the newly harvested crops from their agricultural fields. These worship ceremonies are always fallowed by group dances and merry making in the *Khambu-Rai* society.

(ii) Cosmological: The myth has the cosmological origin, as worship and offerings are conducted at *Samkhalung*.

(iii) Sociological: The myth has furnished the *Sakewa* and *Sakela* worship and festival to the *Khambu-Rai* community.

(iv) Pedagogical: The myth interprets the laws of life, ethical laws and other customary laws, as to how to live a life in the society protecting the different components of nature.

(i) Myths of rites of passage

Rites of passage for birth, marriage and death are available within the society and are being duly followed in the community. However, the myths related to these rites have been forgotten. There is an urgent need of research on the myths to support these rites in the community.

12

RELIGION AND MYTHOLOGY OF ANIMISM ⌢MUNISM OR BONGTHINGISM⌣ OF THE LEPCHA TRIBES

The *Lepcha* aboriginal tribes of Sikkim consider themselves as the children of the Himalayas. They believe that the first man and woman were created by *Rum* (God) from a handful of pure, virgin snow from the top of Mount Pandim (*Pundim*), one of the Mountain peaks of Kanchenjunga. They also believe that their progenitors were *Fodong Theeng* (or *Komsithing*) and *Na-jong-nue* (or *Nazong-nyou*). They believe that their Lord *Tamsang Theeng* arrived at *Tarkaol Tam-E-Tam* from *Pundim Cho*, liberated out the *Lepchas* from the clutches of the demon king - *Lasho Moong Pano*, and rejuvenated their moral strength, gave supernatural powers to a chaste man and a chaste woman and gave them moral philosophy. It was Lord *Tamsangtheeng* who had first founded the ancient *Lepcha* religion – *Munism* and *Bongthingism*. The first consecrated *Bongthing* was *Thikoong Azor Bongthing* and the first *Mun* was *Nyookoong Nyoolik Mun*. The *Bongthings* and *Muns* are the *Lepcha* shaman religious priests, and are mediators between the God - "*Rum*", spirits, souls, and the sole liberators of the *Lepcha* souls after death. They also disclose divine revelations that one can attain desired objects by the efficacy of prayers, supplications and invocations. The *Lepchas* have the abiding faith in prayers, offerings and sacrifices, which they offer through spiritual shamans – *Bongthings* and *Muns*. It is *Lepcha*'s firm conviction that God could not but listen to the prayers fervently offered by them. In the beginning also, when they were suffering under the untold oppression of the demons, they prayed to God to have mercy on them and saved them from the demons by sending their Lord *Tamsang Theeng*. Also, when the whole of Sikkim and Darjeeling was being drowned by flood, the *Lepchas* climbed up on the top of Mount *Tunrong*, now known as *Tendong* and prayed to God – "*Rum*" to save them from being drowned and there "*Rum*" appeared in the form of a "*Kohome Fo*", a partridge bird and sprinkled *Chi* (millet beer) towards *Rumlyang* (heaven) and requested "*Rum*" to subside the flood and thus the *Lepchas* were saved from drowning (Tamsang, K.P. 1983:46-59).

The *Lepcha Muns* are classified into seven classes Viz: (a) *Avor Mun*, (b) *Pildon Mun*, (c) *Angan Mun*, (d) *Tungli Mun*, (e) *Munjyum Mun*, (f) *Mun Mook Mun* and (g) *Lyang-Eet Mun*. *Avor Mun* possesses the equal supernatural power as that of the ancient *Nyoolik Mun*. They are capable of fall of lightening and thunderbolt and conduct all shamanic rituals of the *Lepcha* tribes. *Pildon Muns* perform from ordinary ceremonies to the delivering up of the soul of a dead person to *Rumlyang* (heaven). As the *Lepchas* are the lover of nature, these *Muns* chant their oral hymns, invocations and prayers in the tune of birds, in the sounds of wind, falls, rivers etc. which are very melodious and very pleasing to the ear, very soothing to the soul, and very gladdening to the heart. Thus, the *Muns* are the liberator of souls of the dead persons to heaven (Tamsang, K.P. 1983:46-59).

The Lepcha shaman priests (*Bongthings* and *Muns*) have no written texts for prayer or worship of nature. They entirely depend on oral traditions - *Munthem*. The *Bongthings* and *Muns*, who both function as shamans, traditionally occupy the central religious roles in the *Lepcha* community. The *Bongthing* is traditionally a male shaman who presides at recurring religious ceremonies and seasonal festivals and may heal acute illness. The *Mun*, often but not necessarily a female shaman, is a healer who exorcises demons, helps to heal illness and guides souls to the afterlife. They discharge both manifest or "*emic*" and latent or "*etic*" functions in the *Lepcha* community as in the case of *Yumaism*. They are tutelary spirit possessions of their departed ancestor's souls (ancestor divinities). They also use many master spirits to perform the spiritual works during their manifest functions in the society.

Many western anthropologists term the *Lepcha*'s belief system as "Animism", after E.B. Tylor, but Jeffrey, S. and his group

(2000:35-36) do not accept it. In their view, "Animism" refers to the worship of nature and natural phenomena, such as rocks, mountains, rivers, streams, thunder and lightening, to ascribing inanimate things as having a soul. The *Lepcha,* however, do not outright worship these phenomena; they respect their natural surroundings but do not ascribe souls to them. Rather, they think that these places are where spirits dwell. The spirits as such are not identified with the rocks or trees themselves, but are seen as separate from them. Religious specialists are called shamans, in the west, after a word used by the *Thungus* of Siberia to denote such a person". Their view is to refer shamanism for such a belief system. However, both the terms animism and shamanism were strongly refuted by Tamsang, K.P. (1983: 46-59). He preferred to term the *Lepcha* belief system as *Bongthingism* and *Munism.*

Now, the *Lepchas* of Sikkim accept the term "Animism", and called themselves animist. The *Lepchas* of Sikkim today are divided into three religions, Viz: Animist, Buddhist and Christianity. In the last half of 17th and early half of19th century, the *Lepchas* were converted by the Chiefdoms (*Chogyals*) to Buddhism, although indigenous *Lepcha* shamans managed to coexist with Buddhist customs and beliefs. Both Buddhist *Lamas* and *Lepcha* shamans preside at many important ceremonies in *Lepcha* life, each to perform their own rituals even today. Since, the middle of the 19th century, a significant number of *Lepchas* have converted to Christianity by the Missionaries. Many Christian *Lepchas* have lost their language and have distanced themselves from the old shamanic rituals and beliefs (Gurung and Lama, 2004:124; Plaisier, 2005: 7-9; Subba, J.R. 2008a: 259-261).

The *Lepchas* of Sikkim believe in two types of spirits, the good, which brings good things to the people and the bad, which do harm to them. They perform religious ceremonies to ward off evil spirits from doing harm to them. The *Lepcha* shamans perform all the ceremonies from birth to death for the *Lepcha* society as a whole. They perform birth pollution purification and child naming ritual (*Tungbaong Faat*), cleansing ceremony (*Hitsa* ritual), marriage ceremony (*Moongkoong Mungla Faat* and *Nungnyoo Nunglyon Faat*), for the longevity, happiness and prosperity of the bride and the groom. At death, the shamans perform the funeral ceremony by burying the dead body into his or her final resting place. They do not only possess supernatural powers but are also able medicine men. They cure the patients by *mantras*, and medicinal herbs about which they have deep knowledge (Das and Banerjee, 1962: 105-119).

Concept of God

The *Lepchas* believe in existence of a God known as "*Rum*" (or *Itpomu*). The God is believed to be attributeless, and the *Lepchas* offer thanksgiving prayers with seasonal first fruits, crops, *Chi* (millet beer) etc. The first fruit and crops of the season are always offered to God. They also believe in evil spirits, demons etc. who cause illness and misfortune, and to them also they offer offerings.

Concept of creation of Universe

The oral tradition of the *Lepcha* shamans has elaborate oral tradition of universe creation. Formerly, *Lepchas* believed that they have only one heaven called *Rumlyang*, and nothing else, but since the advent of Buddhism into Sikkim, they now believe in more mythical world besides their own ancestral belief of *Rumlyang*. Now, due to Buddhist influence, they also believe in *Rumlyang* (heaven), *Nyolyang* (hell), *Numsyim-Nyolyang* (human world), *Moonglyang* (evil spirit world), *Thamchyanglyang* (animal world) and *Muknyamlyang* (demon world). These are the belief systems of Buddhism only. They believe that as this world is the very living house of all human beings, so is the heart of every man is the temple of God, and therefore, God according to *Lepchas*, resides in every one of our own very heart.

Concept of Life and destiny

The *Lepchas* believe that the first man and woman were created by *Rum* (God) out of the snows of the untrodden peak of Mt. *Pundim* (Mount Pandim) one of the peaks of Mount Kanchenjunga. Their progenitors were *Komsithing* or *Fodongtheeng* (male) and *Nazong-nyou* or *Na-Jong-nue* (female), and they offer prayers with the first harvest fruits and crops every year. At death the dead body is buried in a sitting position, facing to Mt. Kanchanjonga. *Pildon Mun* performs the death rituals to deliver up of the soul of the dead person to *Rumlyang* (heaven). By her supernatural power, she finds out the wondering soul of the dead person, which is believed to be wondering in the atmosphere and then take it back to heaven. Also, she has the power to call back the spirit of the dead person on her own body and speaks out in the very voice of the dead person and tells the good and bed happenings of the future of the family members. The soul of the dead then, bids goodbye to all saying not to be grieved for him or her for he or she is going to the heavenly home to join the ancestors.

Concept of Soul

The Lepchas believe that there is only one soul, in a body, either in male or female or child and after death that soul, which is believed to be wondering in the atmosphere is taken back to heaven by the *Muns* by performing *Songlion* that is the death rite. The shamans can retrieve the souls of the living as well as of the deceased. They believe that the ultimate substance or principle, as mind or soul or something that is neither mind nor matter, but are ground of both, the position that reality is one.

Concept of Afterlife

They believe in afterlife. At death, the soul of the deceased is retrieved, accompany soul journey and reach to *Rumlyang* (heaven) through the sacred path of "*Lep*" by crossing first a lake called "*Long-Nyoo da*" and then again crossing over a secret tunnel passage through the Himalayas by the *Lepcha Muns*.

Myths and Mythological functions

(a) Myth of creation

The *Munism* and *Bongthingism* religion of the *Lepchas* has a very copious validating mythology and theology. The origin of everything in the world, visible and invisible, animate and inanimate, and the changes they have undergone to bring them to their present state are told in a great number of stories of varying emotional importance. Some of the simplest of the origin stories are known and told by everyone; the more important ones require *loong* (qualification to perform the *Mun* ceremony by the pupils of *Lepcha* shaman) before they can be told; and the most important of all, the *Mun,* only knows the story of creation, in its full details. One of the chief parts of their training is the learning of this story, which it is said takes seven whole days in its telling, by heart. By far the greater part of it consists of lists of pairs of supernaturals who produce the phenomena, which greet our eyes today. However, it is sorry to know that there is no recorded and documented *munthem* (myth) told by the learned *Muns* so far in the society.

"Under this world is an ocean. Under that ocean are another earth of twelve super-imposed stores, and under that there lives *Itpomu*, the Creator Mother, and her husband *Debu*. Their first children were *Tak-seu* and *Tak-from*, who are also called *Nar-zong-nyou* (*Na-Jong-Nue*) and *Komsithing* (*Fodong Theeng*) . After them were born *Mlum Mukyam, Sakyeun-faat-it, Saba-faat-chaum, Suk-dum-lung-ming* and *Chi-lel*, all of whom are the present earth; *Palyou* and *Pakyam* who are gladness and joy; then *Ta-lyang, Ta-kook* and *Ta-kok* who are the blue sky without ornament; then *Bru-nong*, and *Jil-vong, Long-mu* and *Tso-kor* who are the forest in the sky where the stars live; then *Tak-bru-num* and *Jit-it* who are the stars. The ocean between the two worlds is called *Lyang-tak-yoor-oong, tagum-lyang-shin-mu oong* and is the home of *Tal-i-nau* and her husband *San-go*. Under the second earth are two huge copper vessels beside *Itpomu*, full of water, and under them is a fire; this is the reason why the earth becomes warm and wet. Then was born *Panjer-roong* and *Pan-tsong-roong* which is the *Rungit* river; then *Kum-zer roong* which is the origin of hot streams which cure all ills... then were born *Num-ri* and *Num-ra* who begot the thunder-bird, *Sadher....*" The greater part of the myth continues in this vein. Later on in the same myth the origin of devils and the creation of the *Mun* spirit is recounted. This is also a very long myth but is far better known than the Genesis. It is just an outline of it.

The first children of *Itpomu* and *Debu* were *Komsithing* (*Fodong Theeng*) and *Narzong-nyou* (*Na-Jong-Nue*) (Note: contrary to some other myths; they were produced from the untrodden snows of *Kinchenjunga* by *Rum*). Although they were brother and sister they married, and as a consequence all their children were incestuous progenies manifested into devils/evil spirits, snakes and lizards. As soon as they were born their mother cast them aside without giving them milk. Finally she produced a normal child called *Rilbu Shingbu* whom she nursed; but when the devils/evil spirits saw this child getting the milk that been denied them they were jealous and they took counsel and killed the child. The dog that guarded the door betrayed their incest. When the parents were shamed and the child killed they buried the child in the black rock on the right of the *Talung* valley, which can be seen to this day, and thereafter in disgust they divided their property and separated. *Komsithing* went to north (?Tibet) and he took with him all the riches and jewels and animals which the Tibetans have till this day. *Narzong-nyou* turned towards this country is so poor. After that *Komsithing* summoned all the devils to him and all came except *Doam moong* who is the devil of leprosy, and he counseled the devils and said to them :You are devils and you must act according to your nature; but you must take an oath that when men are born you will accept them if they give you pigs, oxen, rice and other things to eat. If you are looked after you must go away, you must obey the *Mun* and *Padem* (*Bongthing*) and the sacrifice. They all took this oath except *Doam moong* who was not present and that is the reason why you can never drive him away and leprosy cannot be cured.

"But still there was no *Mun*. *Itpomu* had placed all the devils in the big plain *Azum Patham*; but there they had nothing to eat. So then *Itpomu* created the *Mun* spirit and sent her to feed them. When the *Mun* arrived at *Azum Patham* she said to the devils "You are older than I am and I am helpless; I will return to *Itpomu*." But the devils begged her to stay, saying that if she went away they would always be hungry; if she stayed they would promise to obey her. They swore this by three great oaths; first they cut their fingernails and swore on them: then secondly, they spat on the *Kashou* tree (Chestnut tree) and the tree withered, and finally they spat in the sea and the sea dried up. Since that time the *Mun* must find out what sacrifices are needed and give them to the devils and the devils will always obey them."

The chief supernaturals of the *Mun* are the two feminine deities *Itpomu* and *Nazong-nyou*. *Itmopu* herself is never directly invoked; it is always her creations that are sacrificed and prayed to. *Nazong-nyou* is really the chief *Lepcha* goddess; she is as it were the local God of the *Lepchas*. She lived in the country and is responsible for its geography, flora, and especially fauna. She is also responsible for a great number of institutions. Her elder brother and husband *Komsithing* is also responsible for a number of habits and institutions, but he was away; after he and his wife separated he took himself to somewhere north (? Tibet) or in the *Akashic* field in the sky. Except in the harvest rites the two of them are always mentioned in prayers and sacrifices, together with all the other supernaturals involved. The invocation usually takes hours, for all the relevant gods in all their manifestations, with their wives and their children must be mentioned by name; in private sacrifices all the personal and *ptso* gods of the sufferer and his family must also be included (Gorer, G. 1938, Reprint in India 1996: 223-226).

Mythological Function

(i) Mystical: The myth unfolds the mystery of universe creation by the creator goddess *Itpomu*, creation of *Lepcha* progenitors, origin of evil spirits or devils, why *Itpomu* sent *Muns*, what are the important supernaturals in the *Lepcha* community etc. in their archaic way, as in the case of *Yumaism*.

(ii) Cosmological: The myth describes the mystery of creation of the cosmological planets, the earth, ocean, stars etc.

(iii)Sociological: The myth furnished the rituals of praying and worshipping various supernatural gods and goddesses, devils and evil spirits for protection of *Lepcha* community by the *Muns* and *Padems* or *Bongthings*.

(iv) Pedagogical: It interprets the laws of life, ethical laws and other customary laws in the society.

(b) Myth of *Muns* and *Padems* (*Bongthings*)

The *Muns* and *Padems* (*Bongthings*) are Tutelary spirit possessions. They are part-time religious incarnate shaman priests. They function through their lifetime spirit possession by a spirit, having certain gifts and duties in the society. The *Mun* spirit is a female spirit of a departed individual; attached to family lines and is hereditary – patrilineal or matrilineal; but there is no regularity about this. A man may inherit a possessing spirit from a woman, and *vice versa*. Once the vehicle dies the spirit returns to *Rumlyang* or *Mayel Lyang*, the ancestor's village and the manifestation of the spirit may choose another for its vehicle on the will of *Itpomu*. Both men and women can be *Mun*, but only men can be *Padem* (or *Bongthing*), and are far less powerful, and that instruction by an already qualified *Padem* is optional, whereas for *Mun* a three-year course of instruction is obligatory. *Padems* are weaker than *Muns* and capable of exorcising far fewer devils. They cannot prophesy nor perform the death ceremony. For many men *Pedem* is the first step to becoming *Mun.*

It is believed that there are two sorts of *Mun,* a good group called *Tungli Mun* and a bad group called *Mun-mook Mun.* The difference is that of similar to the traditional difference between white and black magicians. *Mun-mook Mun* deal with evil spirits and are possessed by devils which they employ for their own selfish ends. *Tungli Mun* deal with benevolence in their heart towards the people and houses to which they are summoned. The *Mun* takes full possession of spirit twice a year, once in the hot season and once in the wet season (Gorer, G. 1938, Reprint in India 1996: 215-222).

Mythological Functions

(i) Mystical: It describes the mystery of religious shaman priests *Mun* and *Padem* (*Bongthing*) sent by *Itpomu.*

(ii) Cosmological: It has cosmological origin.

(iii) Sociological: The *Muns* and *Padems* (*Bongthings*) function as manifest or *"emic"* as well as latent or *"Etic"* functions in the *Lepcha* society as described under *Yumaism.* They are the curers, healers, priests for life rituals, and are the philosophers and guides of the Lepcha society.

(iv) Pedagogical: It interprets the laws of life, ethical laws and customary laws in the society.

(v) Mystery of afterlife: The *Muns* deal with soul journey, journey inward, and reach the soul of the deceased individuals to the land of their ancestors – *Rumlyang.*

(c) Myth of *Naam Soong* or *Namboon*

This is the *Lepcha* New Year, falls every year in the month of *Lepcha* calendar *Kurnyit Lavo* during the last week of December to the first week of January which is celebrated for a week in Sikkim, Kalimpong and Darjeeling. This is one of most important festival of the *Lepcha* and is connected with the legend when truth triumphed over evil and brought ever-lasting peace in the land of the Kanchenjunga. *Rum* (God) created the earth, the hills, dales and the mountains, the sun, the moon and the stars. He also created the air and the water, the trees and vegetation, animals, birds, insects and many other things of the earth. God also created day and night. At last he picked up two fistful of snow in both hands from the top of the sacred Kanchenjunga, from the right hand he created "man" whom he called "*Fodong-Theeng*" or "*Komsithing*" which means most powerful and from the left hand he created "*Na-Jong-Nue*" or "*Nazong-nyou*" the woman which means full of everlasting bliss (contradictory to Gorer's description above; in many myths there are two or more stories which may contradict each other). The *Lepcha* (*Rongkup*) believe that these two were their first ancestors. As God had created them from the same snows of the sacred Kanchenjunga with his own hands their relationship was that of a brother and a sister. As the progenitors of the *Lepchas* grew up together and their youth began to bloom they got attracted to each other by bodily desires. God knew this and commanded both of them not to meet each other very often. The command of God went futile. He took care to separate them from each other completely. He took away "*Fodong Theeng*" to a Himalayan peak called "*Tand-Seng-Narim-Chu.*" He also took "*Na-Jong-Nue*" at the foot of the Himalayan peak called "*Na-Ho-Na-Thar*" which was beside a lake. Time went by but the desire to meet "*Fodong Theeng*" grew stronger and stronger in *Na-Jong-Nue's* heart. She forgot the command of the lord. She built a ladder of gold in order to reach his brother's abode and at last she became successful in reaching there.

There they began to live as husband and wife throwing away the command of God to the winds. In course of time "*Na-Jong-Nue*" became pregnant and a son was born to them. "*Fodong Theeng*" did not allow the child to suck milk from his mother's breasts but carried him away to a dense forest and threw him there. Like wise seven sons were born to them and each year *Fodong-Theeng* threw them all in a dense forest without paying attention to the weeping and wailing of the mother. He believed that these were the outcome of their unholy union and the curse of God will be on them if they were allowed to live. As the eighth son was born *Na-Jong-Nue* pleaded that this son should not be taken away to the forest as they have already committed the sin and they belonged to this earth. The curse of God will be there no matter what they would do. Killing an innocent child is also a sin. God will be angry with this act also. It is better to face the consequences than to commit another sin. She snatched away the child from her husband's grip and began to fondle the child with great love and affection; the child responded to the mother's affection and love and started sucking milk peacefully from the breast of his mother. They then got reconciled.

Years rolled by and twenty more sons and twenty daughters were born to them. They had grand and great grand children and thus the *Rong* tribe increased and thrived. The seven sons who had thrown away into the dense forest had taken the forms of demons and evil spirits. They created lots of trouble to the *Lepcha* tribe regularly. The eldest had taken the form of a demon. He was the strongest among all brothers and was called *"Laso-Mung-Panu"*, which means the powerful one. He could create illusions by taking many forms and shapes. He intended to destroy the whole *Lepcha* tribe. He gathered around him all the demons and the evil spirits and started torturing the *Lepcha* tribe. Panic spread all over *Renjyong* the land of the *Rongs*. They also combined to meet the challenge of the powerful *Lasho-Mung-Panu* and his allies, but the *Lepchas* could not stand be for their powerful enemy. The demons could create illusions by changing themselves into different forms of animals. The *Rongs* fled with fear and hid themselves in caves of the deep forest. Having defeated the *Rongs* in battle *Lasho-Mung-Panu* ruled over *Renjyong* the land of the *Rongs*. All the *Rongs* gathered on hillock and prayed to God for his help to get deliverance from the clutches of their enemies. God then appeared in a dream to an old wise person who revealed to them the way of deliverance from the demons.

From the peak of the Himalayan mountain called *Pundim* (Mount Pandim) God picked up a fistful of snows and out of this created a person named *"Tamsang Theeng"* which means deliverer. He was endowed with super natural power. God then commanded him to go to *Renjyong* in order to destroy the demons forever from the sacred land. He arrived at a place called *"Tar-Kol-Tam-E-Tam"* which means the land of deliverance. Arriving at the place *Tamsang-Theeng* laughed, roared and thundered, and challenging voice echoed through the hills and the valley of *Renjyong*. The king of the demons then sent his men under the leadership of his minister for spying. They all got the shock of as they saw the body of *Tamsang Theeng* throwing a shining radiance all around. Fear gripped them all. He told the minister and his followers that he has come to deliver the *Rongs* from the clutches of their evil leader "*Lasho-Mung-Panu.*" He also told them bluntly to run away to the underworld if they wanted to save themselves. He would destroy every one who would dare to face him. The minister and his followers took the message to their leader. *Lasho-Mung-Panu* who came with an army of demons fought with *Tamsang-Theeng*. Both sides fought with swords and arrows. *Tamsang-Theeng-Panu* killed everyone who dared to face him.

Seeing this, *Lasho-Mung-Panu* began to create illusions by taking many forms of dangerous beasts and attacked *Tamsang-Theeng*. The demon king was badly injured in the battle and at last took the form of a *Garuda* and flew away from the battle field to an unknown destination. The *Rongs* followed him led by their leader. They found him hiding in an old tree. *Tamsang-Theeng* aimed his arrow at him. The arrow hit him in the heart and he fell down on the ground. As he was struggling to die, the *Lepchas* surrounded him and slowly cut him into pieces.

To this day *Rongs* celebrate this day a victory over the demon king "*Lasho-Mung-Panu*" every year. This is the festival of triumph of good over evil. The *Rongs* go door to door singing "*Lasho*". The happy tidings are thus conveyed to every house of the *Rongs*.

(Gurung, M.M. and Lama, R.P. 2004:117-120).

Mythological Functions

(i) Mystical: The myth describes the mystery of creation of the universe and the creation of the Lepcha progenitors and ancestors. It also illustrates the hardships encountered by their early ancestors for their survival in their own archaic way. It explains the origin of good, evil, curse, sin etc. in the society.

(ii) Cosmological: The myth has the cosmological origin elucidated in their own primitive way of perception.

(iii) Sociological: The myth furnishes the sociological functions of supporting and validating the rituals in the society. It explains how God has sent his messenger *Tamsang-Theeng* to rescue the *Lepcha* ancestors from sufferings caused by the demons. The myth has unfolded the cause of curse, sin, and evil ever present in the society and also unfolds how to overcome with such evil, curse and sin through prayer to God, and performing worship through the learned religious shaman priests in the society. The myth also unfolds the mystery of sexual desire in human beings. The sexual desire is uncontrollable and is beyond the boundary of human understanding. It further expounds that the girls are transformed by nature itself and need no assistance. The progenitor "*Na-Jong-Nue*" goes in search of manhood herself. Nature guides her for her transformation, as she has been blessed her with everlasting bliss. She knows how to nourish her progenies with the blessings of the creator God; takes care of her sons and provide guidance, while the boys need assistance for such transformation to manhood. The mother provides this. They have no automatic means of transformation to manhood in nature. The role of man – "*Fodong-Theeng*" is only to provide service to the woman in the society.

(iv) Pedagogical: The myth interprets the laws of life, ethical laws, and customary laws and explains how to live a human life in the society. We human beings cannot live animal life. During social evolution our ancestors have evolved certain social laws – such as pairing, monogamous marriage systems and other such life passages. We have to evaluate them in the present circumstances and observe them accordingly.

(d) Myth of *Tendong Lho Rum Faat*

This festival is celebrated with great pomp and splendor at Sikkim on the 8th August every year. Realizing its importance the Sikkim Government has declared state holiday since 1997. This festival is connected with a legend of deluge, which nearly swallowed Sikkim, which was ultimately stopped by *Rum* (God) and saved Sikkim from drowning.

Rongnue, which was later, called Teesta and Rangit were born at the sacred lap of the Himalayan Mountains. They grew up together happily and as their youth bloomed they began to love each other secretly. But some how some people got know about this and started taking all sorts of things about them. They then decided to leave the place of their birth and go far away down to the meeting place of the hill and the plains. This place was called "*Pazoak*" by the *Lepchas* (the present day *Peshok*) which means covered by dense forest near the *Teesta Bazar*. Both did not know the actual path leading to the place. So they decided to take guides with them separately. *Rongnue* (*Teesta*) the female caught hold of *Paril-Bu* a snake and *Rungit* the male caught hold of a bird called *Tut-Fu* (*Danfy, Lophophorus impejanus*). He at first hesitated but then agreed to be a guide. The snake leads *Rongnue* wriggling and running with all his strength. He did not feel the necessary of stopping where any on his way except at the top of a hillock to have a glance of *Pazoak* from there. He gave a smile to *Rongnue* and with his head held high started moving forward with all his strength.

The sun was yet to set in. The western horizon looked crimson with the rays of the setting sun. It was certainly a beautiful sight to behold for a lover. Reaching *Pazoak* in time *Rongnue* anxiously waited for her lover *Rungeet* to appear. Time tickled away and it was already dark but he was no where to be seen. She lost her patience and her heart was filled with grief. She waited there hour after hour through out the night. The first light of the dawn began to descend on earth and covered the hills beyond. Still there was not a trace of her lover. *Rungit* that had been guided by the bird *Tu-Fo* (*Danfy*) had taken a longer and steeper road through the rocky and difficult terrain. Being hungry he had stopped on the way to collect insects for his food. So at last he arrived at their destination seeing the *Rongnue* waiting for him he was surprised and from his mouth come out these words, *"Thi-Sthaal"* which means already arrived. *Rungnue* now is called *Teesta* which has come *Running* from the *Lepcha* words *"Thi-Sthaa"*. *Rungeet* the male got very much ashamed to be defeated by a female. So he decided to go back to his usual home in the Himalayas. As he started returning the water of the river began to rise up swallowing up the dales and the hill by the deluge. There were two high mountain peaks at *Renjyong* where the water of the river was still to reach. One was called *Maanom* and the other was *Tungrong* popularly called *Tendong*.

The people of *Renjyong* had gathered at the peak of *Tendong* to save themselves from the deluge. They saw the water of the river slowly touching the hill of *Maanom.* They began to pray to the Almighty God to save them from the deluge. They offered *"Chi"* to *"Itpomu-Debu-Rum-Daar"* the creator and destroyer. A hill partridge called *"Kohom Fo"* (*Puro or Syabon, Arborophila torqueola*) appeared on the hill and drank *"Chi"* (fermented millet beer) offered by the people. The water then began to subside slowly and that was the end of the deluge. Peace and happiness once again prevailed at the land of the *Rongs* (Gurung, M.M. and Lama, R.P. 2004:120-123; Chemjong, I.S. 1965: 5-6).

Mythological Functions

(i) Mystical: The myth describes the mystery of the legend of deluge, which nearly swallowed Sikkim, which was ultimately stopped by the creator and destroyer god *Itpomu* and saved Sikkim from drowning. It also illustrates the love-hate phenomena a common once in a lifetime but there is no need of taking it so seriously.

(ii) Cosmological: The myth explains that the creator and destroyer God is always there in the *Akashic* field and helps us in distress. Prayer is essential to connect one-self to it.

(iii) Sociological: The myth has furnished a worship festival to the *Lepcha* society. A prayer and thanks giving worship to the creator and destroyer God (*Rum*) is performed every year collectively in the community. During the ritual, "*Chi*" and other offerings are offered to the God.

(e) Myth of *Zikding Rum Faat*

This myth is connected with nature and its greenery. The *Lepchas* are lovers of nature and all things living as well as non-living are connected to each other. The festival is observed during the month of February every year. The *Lepchas* feel that a balanced ecology and environment is most necessary for the survival of the human beings as a whole. The word *Muk* means greenery, *Zikding* connotes sprouting of vegetation. It is a prayer to *Rum* the Almighty God. This is the season of sprouting of all vegetation, trees and shrubs and is also the mating season of all animals and birds. The *Bongthing* offers prayers to *Rum* for timely rains and sunshine, clean air and water and to save the world from the natural calamities of flood, land slide and famine.

The altar is decorated with all kinds of shrubs medicinal plants, cereals, fruits, flowers and a stone pillar called *Longchaok* is erected near the altar. The *Lepchas* do not offer prayers to any statue of any God. Love of nature is in the blood of every *Lepcha*. Offering to Mother Nature is one of the best ways in educating people on the problems of ecology and environment (Gurung, M.M. and Lama, R.P. 2004:123).

Mythological Functions

(i) Mystical: The myth describes the mystery of prayer and worship of God for greenery.

(ii) Cosmological: The myth has cosmological origin.

(iii) Sociological: The myth has furnished a worship festival to the community.

(iv) Pedagogical: The myth interprets the laws of nature and protection of greenery as all living and non-living organisms on the earth are connected to each other.

(f) Myth of *Sakyo-Rum-Faat*

The myth is about the origin and the propagation of the various agricultural crops in the land of *Renjyong* (Sikkim). The Lepchas observe it in the form of a Lepcha festival called *Sakyo-Rum-Faat*. In ancient time the *Lepchas* cultivated ten kinds of paddy, nine kinds of millet, four kinds of wheat, nine kinds of maize and other cereals. They also grew many kinds of vegetables. In the days of yore a *Lepcha* hunter called *Sheyraboo* went on hunting expedition. He searched for an animal the whole day but found nothing. Tired and thirsty he sat to rest, after quenching his thirst in a nearby stream. Suddenly his eyes fell on a big boar grazing beyond the stream. He forgot his thirst and tiredness on seeing the animal. He moved forward cautiously towards the boar and let fly the arrow from his bow aiming at the animal. The boar was only injured and started fleeing from the place. The hunter *Sheyraboo* also went after the boar following the blood of the injured boar. As darkness set on he could not follow the animal any more. So he went towards a bamboo grove for the nights rest. He woke up in the early dawn and started following the animal. He could not find the animal anywhere. Still he did not stop following. At last when the sun was about to disappear in the far away horizon he saw the boar moving forward slowly. He went after it and reached a village farmhouse. He was surprised to find the animal resting in the group of other pigs of the farmhouse. As the dogs started barking a very old man with gray hair came out of the house. This old man was also pleased to find the long lost pig resting with other pigs. He thanked the hunter for his help for finding out his lost pig. The hunter was taken inside the house and was offered food and strong "*Chi*". He was really tired and fell into sound sleep in the bed made for him.

He woke up from his bed as the sun had already come up in the sky. He looked for his host and his wife but they were not seen anywhere. He saw a girl and a boy playing in the courtyard. He was surprised to see the children as he had not seen them anywhere yesterday night. He went out for a while and came back to the house but still could not find out the old man and his wife. He just waited for them closing his eyes. He was feeling sleepy as he was still very tired. As he opened up his eyes he saw that the two children had grown to become man and woman. He was filled with fear as he now thought that the place was the abode of evil spirits. At midday the two had again grown into a young man and a young woman. The young man told the hunter not to be afraid of them, assuring him that they were not evil spirits but immortal people who never die. The two people offered delicious food. The young man then took the hunter to a hillock just above the house and pointing at the valley down below the hillock told him that the valley is situated between the two Himalayan Mountains "*Paki* and *Mendong*". It is most fertile valley of the land. The name of the valley is "*Mayel Kyong*" i.e. hidden village.

The hunter *Sheyraboo* saw trees of pears, apples and oranges and also other kind of trees laden with ripe fruits. The valley looked beautiful as it was full of all kinds of flowers. In the fertile land of the valley he also saw lush green wheat and maize plants. The heart of the hunter was filled with awe and happiness. There were cascading waterfall and the bubbling mountain streams which added fertility to the soil of the valley. It was certainly a paradise on earth. *Sheyraboo* learnt from the young man, his host that in this land of "*Mayel Kyong*" there lives seven couples since the beginning of the earth. They are immortal beings who never die. They have no children. They have the power to be invisible anytime as they wish. In the early dawn they are small children at midday they become young persons and in the evening they become old couples. The agricultural crops, vegetables, fruits and flowers and the beasts and birds of the world were first created in the land of "*Mayel Kyong*".

Hearing these words of the young man he knew that this young man too was the same person who was a child in the morning and an old person in the evening. He took him down in the valley and introduced him to the immortal old couples of "*Mayel Kyong*". The two wandered through the valley observing all the beautiful things there. As the evening came the young man had already turned into an old person. The old person returned home leaving behind the hunter to rest for the night there. *Sheyraboo* slept in one of the house of the old couple for the night after having a heavy meal. The next day at midday the seven couples of *Mayel Kyong* filled a basket with all kinds of seeds of vegetables, fruits and cereals and took him towards a very steep mountain ridge and told him to sow and propagate all these in the land of *Renjyong*. He was also told that birds would be sent to tell the people of *Renjyong* when to sow these seeds at different seasons. After some time the basket touched the ground with a thud. As he took out the cloth from his eyes he found himself at the same place where he had hit the boar with the arrow.

It is believed that every year in each season the seven immortal couples send *Mayel Fo* (the birds of *Mayel Kyong*), the bird to tell the exact time for sowing seeds. The *Lepchas* do believe that various kinds of agricultural crops vegetables, the fruits and the flowers are the gifts of the seven immortal couples of *Mayel Kyong*. So to show their gratefulness to them they offer all kinds of vegetables, fruits and cereals every year during the month of November. The *Lepchas* dance and sing to celebrate the occasion. It is called the festival of *Sakyo-Rum-Faat* (Gurung, M.M. and Lama, R.P. 2004:73-76).

Worship rituals of sowing of the dryland rice: The people of *Mayel* are worshipped exclusively in connection with the crops of dry rice, millet and maize; on all other occasions they are markedly excluded from the long lists of supernatural who are called on to partake of the sacrifices and give their blessings. Everybody must worship them on two occasions, after the completion of snowing and at the harvesting of the dryland rice; in those houses where there is a *Mun* or a knowledgeable old man they are also prayed to in the winter to keep away snow and hail, in the spring to protect young crops, and, after the sowing of each of their grains, they are offered *Sakyou faat* to ensure a good harvest. Only the three crops are connected with the people of *Mayel*; the others come from different supernaturals. Barley, wheat, buckwheat and wet rice come from *Kongsen-bu*, the god of *Kinchenjunga*, a Sikkimese deity; no important ceremonies are connected with these crops.

The spring offerings consists of the *lafet* (the *Mun* sacrifice made on a winnowing tray, on which is placed first banana leaves, then grain, ginger, dried bird, dried fish, etc.) sacrifice and *Sakyou faat* (the chief *Mun* sacrament, consisting of drinking strained *chi* out of a cup on the rim of which dabs of butter have been placed). The food on the *lafet* is divided into three lines of three heaps each; the centre line is for the people of *Mayel*, that on the right for all men's patron gods, and especially those of the house-father, that on the left for all women's patron gods, and especially those of the house-mother. The dried bird's flesh in the *lafet* must be a special very small bird, which has been killed by a virgin boy. Before the ceremony begins a song is sung in honour of the people of *Mayel* and then the *Mun* offers to them *Sakyou faat* and powdered portions of the objects on the *lafet*, calling on the people of *Mayel* to accept the offerings and throwing them before him or her on the floor. The cup is constantly re-filled with *chi* with a wooden ladle by a young virgin girl who is sitting beside the *Mun*. After that everybody except the *Mun* officiating has to drink some stained *chi* from the buttered cup and eat a part of the offerings and sing songs in honour of the people of *Mayel*. The grain, which is used in this sacrifice, has to be specially ripened in the sun in the same way as the grain for seed is ripened. This completes the ceremony of sowing and a feast in which meat is eaten always follows it (Gorer, G. 1938, Reprint in India 1996: 235-246).

Worship Rituals of Harvesting of the Dry Rice

The ceremony of harvesting is only employed for the dry rice. When the dry rice is ripe a little is picked to prepare *chi* and when the *chi* is ready the owner of the field summons all his friends and they go together to pick rice. Until the ceremony is completed nobody, not even children, may pick any grain or he would get ill. It is necessary to have ready beforehand the smoke-dried *tafoot* (some internal organ, spleen or gall-bladder) of a pig. On the day of reaping this *tafoot* is taken up to the field of dry rice together with two burning brands from the house-fire and also a *patyoot* (bamboo can) of *chi* made from the new rice. When the party arrives, a place in the centre of the field is chosen as the *zolam* (the place where the crops are heaped); some rice-plants in the centre of the *zolam* are tied together into a sheaf and then the two burning brands will be held above them and on these a piece of the *tafoot* will be put. Then an old man stands below on the *tafoot* and speaks. The old man will summon the gods and ancestors and will say "Come and see the smoke; burr – burr – burr – burr". Then all the people present will repeat, "burr-burr-burr". By this invocation it is hoped that the gods will come and bring back all the grain eaten by wild birds and animals.

Standing by the speaker is a woman not directly connected with the field owner, who has been chosen for the day to represent *Talyeu-mu*, one of the earth sisters. When *Mayel-mu* has finished his invocation the measuring basket is put on his back and *Talyeu-mu* cuts the tied grain and puts it in the basket. Then *Talyeu-mu* and *Mayel-mu*, who acts as her load carrier, go round the *zolam* cutting a basket of rice for *Talyeu-mu*; at the same time the others cut two baskets of rice for the people of *Mayel*. When the three baskets have been cut four or five reed mats are put down on the flattened ground and all dance on the rice to separate the grain from the chaff. After the dancing *Talyeu-mu* goes round the edge of the field cutting another basket while all other reapers work in a row to fill two more baskets which are heaped up like the first. After these have been put on the *zolam* the *nam-toak* (potential curse) is lifted and all can cut, as they like. *Mayel-mu* offers *patyoot* of new *chi* and other offerings and thus the ceremony is completed (Gorer, G. 1938, Reprint in India 1996: 235-246).

Mythological Functions

(i) Mystical: The myth describes the mystery of origin of crops, fruits, vegetables and flowers and how the Lepcha people learnt cultivation in *Renjyong*.

(ii) Cosmological: The myth explains belief system that varieties of crops, fruits, vegetables and flowers were brought to the *Lepcha* land *Renjyong* from the *Akashic* field "*Mayel Kyong*" the land of seven immortal couples. The myth has cosmological origin, and the *Lepchas* offer newly harvested cereals, fruits, vegetables and flowers to these seven immortal couples of the *Akashic* field - *Mayel Kyong* every year. They also believe that these seven couples also send birds to *Renjyong* to tell the *Lepchas* to sow these seeds at different seasons.

(iii) Sciological: The myth has furnished worship rituals of sowing the seeds and offering newly harvested cereals, fruits, vegetables, flowers, "*Chi*" (fermented millet beer) etc. every year in the society.

(iv) Pedagogical: The myth interpreted the ethical laws of offering the newly harvested crops, protecting these valuable crops for next season seeds, customary laws of respecting and offering the foods to elders first etc.

(g) Myth of *Zolosi* (transplanted wet rice) to *Renjyong*

In ancient time, *Lepchas* knew the present day district of Jalpaiguri as *Zolosi*. It was mostly inhabited by the *Koch* and *Mech* tribes and was ruled by a *Koch king Devachandra*. The land was very fertile. It was a land of transplanted paddy. The *Lepchas* called it *Zolosi* i.e. the land of paddy. The people were very happy and lived in peace and amity away from the touch of the modern civilization. *Devachandra* had a beautiful daughter. She was called "*Zolosi Pandimir*". The king loved his daughter very much. He wanted to give her hands to an able person. This man should be both able and wealthy. So one day the king made a proclamation stating that he would give the hands of his daughter to a man who would bring with him the most precious gem. He also declared that the person should be brave and handsome as well. Many princes and young kings from far away lands came to ask the hand of the princess bringing with them precious gems, gold and silver but the princess refused to accept any one among them. At that time in the far away Himalaya kingdoms of *Renjyong* ruled a young *Lepcha* king named "*Ronjyi-Panu*". He was very brave as well as wealthy and handsome. He had also heard about the beauty of the *Kochi* princess "*Zolosi-Pandimir*". He was bachelor. King "*Ranji-Panu*" marched from his mountain kingdom and finally reached the land of the *Koch* king. As he was entering the palace he saw the princess *Zolosi-Pandimir*. She also saw the king *Ronji-Panu*. She quickly ran towards her mother and expressed her feelings about the handsome king of *Renjyong*.

The king and the queen had to bow down before the wish of their daughter and gave away their daughter to the king of *Renjyong*. The king and the queen bade them farewell giving them many precious gifts. The newly married couple then started their journey towards their mountain home. As they reached *Teesta* it was already dark. They then decided to spend the night on the bank of the silently flowing *Teesta*. The king ordered his soldiers to clean the overgrowth for night halting. The jungle was cleaned in a short time. In the meantime, some of the princes and kings having heard the marriage of the *Koch* princess to the king of *Renjyong* and to snatch away the princess attacked them. A fierce fighting took place on the bank of the river *Teesta*. The enemy soldiers were greater in number. The king then swam with the queen to the other side of the river. The officers and the soldiers followed them after giving a good fight to the enemies. The enemies were very tired and they slept soundly, thinking that the king of *Renjyong* had fled away being defeated in the battle.

The night was dark and silent along the bank of river *Teesta*. The soldiers of the *Renjyong* took this chance and crossed back the river on the bamboo raft and banana trunks and attacked the sleeping enemy soldiers. The surprise attack of the soldiers of *Renjyong* made the enemies to run for life. Most of them were simply butchered on the bank of the *Teesta*. The next morning the king's party moved happily to *Renjyong*.

The queen *Zolosi-Pandimir* had learnt that paddy and other agricultural crops were not cultivated in *Renjyong*. She taught the people to cultivate these crops in *Renjyong*. The *Lepchas* believe that the art of cultivating transplanted paddy at *Renjyong* is brought by the *Koch* queen *Zolosi-Pandimir* from *Zolosi* (Gurung, M.M. and Lama, R.P. 2004:123).

Mythological Functions

(i) Mystical: The myth describes the mystery of adventure of marriage of *Zolosi-Pandimir* by the king of *Renjyong* from *Koch* country who brought cultivation of transplanted paddy in Sikkim.

(ii) Sociological: The myth furnishes the cultivation of transplanted paddy in Sikkim that was not known by the people of Sikkim during the early period of agricultural development.

(h) Myth of *Moot Rum Tseu (Pong Rum)*

Pong Rum together with his wife *Shing Rum* is the lord of all wild animals and the patron saint of hunters. Every year in October a joint sacrifice has to be made to him by all the hunters of the neighborhood. The sacrifice consists of popped corn prepared by a man or by a virgin girl, *chi,* dried fish and bird, ginger, arum root, some other tuber, sugarcane, banana and wormwood flowers. If possible a man should make all the prepared ingredients and no woman must witness the sacrifice or even know when it has been performed. *Pong rum,* it will be remembered, is the guardian of the road to *Mayel.* In the forest as soon as an animal has been killed and cut up a sacrifice must be made to *Pong rum.* Big leaves are cut and put on the ground and then the animal is divided up and the head is put in the front with a foreleg and hind leg on either side or singed intestines in the middle. This is all offered to *Pong rum,* and the hunter crouching behind and speaking very slowly and softly, gently throws the burnt intestines bit by bit over the animal's head. On his return to the village great care must be taken that no woman sees the animal's head; if she did the hunter would have no success in future.

To know how to sacrifice to *Pong rum* it is necessary to learn how to, and to receive *loong* (the ceremony by which a teacher acknowledges his pupil's efficiency). For this purpose the novice goes to anybody who knows – may be his father or some other relation or friend, taking with him *chi* and a ceremonial scarf and a rupee. Great care must be taken that no woman is present at this time. When the older man sees the gifts he enquires what they are for and is told it is to learn how to sacrifice. The older man then arranges the sacrifice and tells the neophyte to sit with his back to him. He must not look but must listen most attentively. After that the neophyte on the next suitable occasion will make the sacrifice; the instructor will be near him and if he makes a mistake will nudge him, whereat the sacrifice must be stopped short. Subsequently the neophyte will take another lesson, continuing until he is word perfect and has received his *loong* and can sacrifice on his own. A person who has once been to the communal sacrifice to *Pong rum* should continue to do so all his life; he may, however, give it up, in which case he is liable to be troubled with poltergeist manifestations by *Pong rum*, who anyhow if he is displeased with a hunter will pursue him whistling, and the thump of heavy stones falling will be heard, though no stones are seen to fall. It is even preferable for hunter's children to continue the ritual (Gorer, G. 1938, Reprint in India 1996: 244-246).

Mythological Functions

(i) Mystical: The description of ritual provides the mystery of worship of *Pong rum*, a hunter divinity. However, there is no recorded myth of the ritual *munthem* spoken by the worshiper during the ritual. In view of this it is very difficult to unfold what actually the myth is? But it is certain that the hunter divinity is offered the prey hunted before it is taken home for eating by the *Lepchas*.

(ii) Sociological: The description of *Pong rum* furnishes the ritual of *Pong rum* in the *Lepcha* society.

(i) Myth of foetus and womb worship

The early life of *Lepcha* starts at the moment of conception. When the two secretions of male and female mingle, the soul arrives from heaven - the place of the gods, the repository of unborn people. The first portion of the foetus to be formed is completed at the end of the first month. The fetus is completely human with all its organs, and even its hair, at the end of the fifth month. At the fifth month when the baby is considered fully formed the expectant parents must start observing the numerous prenatal precautions which have to be followed if the child is not to be born malformed, or if the mother is not to have a difficult delivery. Both parents are equally capable of influencing the child within the womb. Some of the common pre-natal precautions are:

- If engaged in making a fence the parents must do the whole work by themselves; otherwise the baby cannot be born properly.
- The father must not take any fish out of a trap in the river; otherwise the child will be born its nose stopped up.
- The parents must not lock up anything except their own box; or the child will not be able to be born until what is closed is opened.

- Neither parent may eat animals, which have met their death by accident or by being killed by a wild beast.
- The father must not touch the iron or rope of a horse's bridle; otherwise the child is liable to die.
- If weaving a mat or cloth must leave a little bit over.
- The mother must not eat any joint fruit such as a double banana or the child's toes will be webbed.
- Neither parent must stick poles into the ground or tie knots or drive in nails or put small stones into the cracks between bigger stones when building a wall; all of these prevent proper delivery.
- Expectant parents must not look at a solar or lunar eclipse or the child will be born dead or deformed.
- Should either parent eat rice, which has stuck to the bottom of the cooking-pot the placenta will not descend at child birth.

The second half of pregnancy is a period of constant watchfulness for both parents. Thus, a number of precautions are to be observed during this period.

Miscarrying is caused by an evil spirit "*Sor moong*" and is a hereditary sex-linked disability. As soon as a woman has miscarried unless she is seriously ill, and at all events her husband must carry the foetus down to the river accompanied by a *Mun* who will there pray for preventive and curative rites for the couple with a branch of elephant grass to which coloured threads, two rings, a rupee and a turquoise have been attached. On returning home the *Mun* will pray for preventive and curative rites for the couple again. Ordinarily after the sixth month of pregnancy the mother will be conducted preventive and curative worship by a *Mun* to avoid miscarriage as a routine precaution.

Womb worship: To procure easy delivery a *Mun* will offer two chickens to "*Sor moong*" in the seventh or eighth month of pregnancy. Unless the worship is performed the evil spirit "*Sor moong*" may cause stillbirth or difficulty in easy delivery of the child. If a stillborn infant is born, two or three friends of the parents immediately take it down to the river. A *Mun* will prepare a bunch of stinging and prickly plants and will wash for the carriers to return so that *Mun* can perform preventive or cleansing rites some way away from the house. It is believed that stillborn babies and infants manifest to evil spirits known as *"Ing-bong moong"*, and in this guise try to kill other children.

Child naming ceremony: For the first three days of life of a newly born baby is considered to be still in the womb of the mother and all the pre-natal precautions has to be observed. On the third day the baby is officially born and a special birth feast for child naming is held. The mother and the child are cleaned, washed. *Mun* offers the sacrifice with a prayer to the birth god *"Gek rum"*. He then weaves incense burning over all who are present, starting with the parents. The child is named. Then, all except the *Mun* eat the offerings. It is believed that as soon as a child is born, the fairy *"King-chum-darmit"* appears to scribble the fate or destiny on the forehead of the person just born; and throughout his or her lifespan, whatever is scribbled, he or she has to live such a life. *"Aking"* or *"King"* in short, means forehead; *Achum* or *chum* is filigree or design; *Dar-Mit* is a powerful fairy or goddess. This fairy *Kung-chum-darmit*, who shapes and scribbles designs on the forehead, among other things, is believe the one who categorizes or classifies females into four distinct types. These types are *Emu, Song-mu, Chay-mu* and *Su-mu*. The first type, i.e., *Emu*, is the ones who get the best of the blessings. They are nice and lovable people; whatever they do is sure to be appreciated by everybody that comes in contact with them. They bring good luck into the house. Then the second type, *Songmu*, by nature they are religious minded. They are very particular about worship and offerings, and they become excellent helpers when religious functions are held. They are ideally suited to be wives of *Bongthings*. The third types *Chay-mu*, possess strong and powerful *"Kathong Fee"*, the supernatural individual spirit of amour and sex. They are fickle and possess insatiable sex inclinations. The last is the *Su-mu* class is the worst blessed or cursed. Their very presence is supposed to bring bad luck to others. Associating or dealing with them is sure to put one into trouble and difficulties. When looking for a bride one should always try to find out which type is the one have set our eyes on; with a little scouting it is not difficult to find this out (Gorer, G. 1938, Reprint in India 1996:283-314; Foning, A. R. 2nd Edn. 2003: 236-246).

Mythological Functions

(i) Mystical: The myth describes the mystery of early *Lepcha* life, womb worship, birth ceremonies and early development of the child.

(ii) Cosmological: The myth establishes the linkage of life with the place of the gods, repository of unborn people called *Rumlyang*. They believe that the soul of the developing child in the womb comes from *Rumlyang* as soon as the seeds of the parents start mingling in the womb. *Rumlyang* is the *Lepchas* heaven and is located somewhere in the *Akashic* field.

(iii) Sociological: The myth has furnished rituals of womb worship and birth worship and rituals of worshipping gods and goddesses in the society.

(iv) Pedagogical: The myth interprets the laws if life, ethical laws and other customary laws of accepting parenthood of the newly developing child in the society.

(v) Mystery of afterlife: The myth unfolds the mystery of the source of the soul of the individual. This also indicated the destination of the soul after death of the individual.

(j) Myth of the Origin of marriage

When *Itpomu* had completed creation there were no husbands and wives. The last person she bore was a son called *Tarbong-bo* whom she nursed. When the child grew big enough to work he told his mother that he would like to travel and see the world. His mother said "No, you are too young" but he insisted, and so she cooked some rice for him and put it into his knapsack. So the next morning he traveled by the road called *Parhi Pageum* and came to the top of *Paki Chu*; from there he went down to *Palyang Chu*, which is a mountain above *Sakhyong* and can be seen on a clear day. From there he saw the *Palit Samper koong* (?) tree covered with fruits, and *pedong* (?), *taryong athyuk kanyoong* (?) and many other birds eating the fruit. When he saw that he sat down and ate his rice; then he returned home in the evening and climbed on to his mother's lap and sucked her milk. His mother then asked "What did you see?" He told her what he had seen. Then his mother said, "If you are my son you must go and get *yongming yong-song* (a kind of bamboo) and the thread *komok ki* to make traps." That night he slept at home and the next day he went and got what his mother had said. He cut down the bamboos and returned home. The day after that he went back to *Palyang Chu* and made snares with the threads and set them on the trees and returned and climbed on his mother's lap and told her what he had done. His mother told him that he must go back early in the morning. He did so and found all the different sorts of birds caught in the snares, so many that they made a full load. When he had collected the birds he reset the snares and then went home and said to his mother "Mother, if these birds are good to eat, eat them and take them as my repayment for your milk: if they are no good, throw them away." *Itpomu* replied "They are good to eat: and I accept them as a recompense for my milk." The next morning *Tarbong* returned to the tree, but instead of birds in the traps he found in every trap a penis, exactly like real life, made out of wood. *Tarbong* was angry at this, threw the penises away, and reset the traps. Then he went home and climbed on to his mother's lap and said "Mother, today I have nothing to bring you; there were no birds in the traps, just penises of wood." At this his mother said "If you are my son, you will go and hide yourself so carefully that even the birds cannot see you, and then in your hiding place you can stay and see who does this thing." The next morning he returned and found the snares again full of penises; he threw them away, and reset the snares and then hid himself so well that even the birds could not see him. After a time a beautiful girl dresses in *kaji lasong* (nettle cloth) arrived and started to make wooden penises. She was very beautiful; her name was *Na Rip Nom,* and mother was *Ta Im Ta Mit*. *Tarbong* was angry when he saw her doing this and he climbed up the tree to try to stop her, and they struggled and rolled hither and thither; and then he got exited and tried to rape her, but he could not do so and so they separated and he went home and climbed on his mother's lap and said to her "Mother, I have come home without any birds." "What did you see, my son?" "I found *Na Rip Nom* making penises of wood. She is very beautiful." Then *Itbomu* said "If you want to possess that girl you had better go to your elder brother *Komsithing* who lives at *Rungzing Patham*."

So *Tarbong* went to *Komsithing*, and when he saw his younger brother he asked him why he had come. So *Tarbong* told him: "This girl was putting penises in my traps, and I wanted to possess her but could not, and my mother advised me to come to you." Then *Komsithing* said "How can you expect to possess the girl unless you give the marriage price *nyomsa afaar* and make a sacrifice with *chi* and butter *sakyou tsok rum-faat*? Do you love this girl?" "Very much." "Then I advise you to go to your *ingzong* (trading friend) in the West and get from him the pig of the plains *Malu Mayeng* and buy a copper vessel." So *Tarbong* went to the low land and brought back a pig and a copper vessel. When he returned *Komsithing* said "I advise you to go to your *ingzong* in the East to get the cloth *Kamo*." So he went to East and returned with the cloth, and then he had the pig and copper pot and the cloth. From his *ingzong* of the North he got a rug *Nambo*. From *Mayel* near *Konchen* he got millet. From *Kanyong* he got an ox.

Now at this time there was no fire in the world; it was only in the land between earth and heaven called *Mashyok Matel* where the demons dwelt, in the houses of the *Deut moong* who were smiths and were called *Tangshyo Tangsong Karvo*. Now when *Komsithing* told *Tarbong* to go there to fetch fire to cook the millet he was frightened and said he would not go among the devils for then they would eat him. So *Komsithing* called on all human beings, animals, birds and insects to volunteer to go and fetch the fire, promising rewards of gold and jewels and rich cloths. When this offer was made the bird *Kahryyok Fo* (?) smiled and said "I will go for a reward." And the bird flew there and found the smith's house empty as all the people were out working elsewhere, so it took a brand in its beak from the fireplace and flew back. On its way back it came to the *Kasou* tree; there it fell hungry, and laid the brand on a branch while it looked for fruit. But the wind blew and the flames sprang up and a great fire raged over the world, and the bird was caught in it; that is the reason why till this day it has short feathers and a black face. It was ashamed and did not return to *Komsithing*. *Komsithing* waited for the bird but it did not come and he saw the fire, so he asked for another volunteer; and this time an insect - *taknyom nomyor nyom* (? firefly) volunteered to go for a reward. When it got to the smith's house all the *Deut moong* were away, so it lay on its back by the fireplace and looked at the house upside down; and the whole house turned upside down. When the *Deut moong* returned from the west it found its house upside down and searched and found the insect that had done it lying on its back; he tried to catch it, but it wriggled and flew away. The *Deut moong* said "Why have you upset my house in this way? I shall kill you for it." The insect said "If you do kill me, your house will never get straight again." "Please don't do that." "What have you come for?" "*Komsithing* has sent me to fetch fire." "I will give you some, if you promise to straighten my house; but you cannot carry fire in your mouth." "Yes, I can." They argued, and finally the insect took a brand in its mouth, and the *Deut moong* put a flint and tinder up its backside. On his return the insect rested by the *Mong Ing Pong* tree (?), and put down the brand at the foot of the tree; but the wind came and blew it to a blaze and the insect got there from a black face. But it flew back to *Komsithing* and gave him the flint and tinder from his backside, since he had lost the brand; and he told him all that the *Deut moong* had told him, and showed him how to make a fire with dry grass. So they made a fire and cooked the millet in the copper vessel, but when the millet was cooked they found they had no yeast.

The only person who possessed yeast was an old woman who lived in the plains called *Numli-nyou*; so *Komsithing* asked who would volunteer to go and fetch it, promising great rewards. The insect *takder thing* (?) said it would go and it went to live with the old woman for some days and helped her. One day she started to prepare *chi*, and cooked the millet; but when it came to the moment of putting in the yeast she covered *takder* with a close woven basket *tangar* (?). But when *takder* was inside he cried "Grandmother, in this basket I can see everything which is going on in the world; if you want to hide something from me you should cover me with a *tangjang* (?). The old woman believed what he said and covered him with a *tangjang* and so he could see all that she was doing, though he pretended he could not. He saw her take a pot from the back of her neck, and pour something from it into her hands. Then she rubbed her hands together and scattered the dust over the cooked millet; she replaced the pot; and put the millet in the basket. Then *takder* cried "Grandmother, please take me out of this basket; I am suffocating." So *Numli-nyou* removed the basket.

After two days the lovely smell of ferment rose from the millet, and then the old woman put it in an earthen pot and covered the pot well up, and stood it over the fire. *Takder* tried to get the pot with yeast in it, but he could not; at last he hit on a plan. He told *Numli-nyou* he could see a louse in her hair and asked her to let him remove it. She agreed so he jumped on her shoulders and started delousing her. While this operation was going on *Numli-nyou* became sleepy; and then *takder* removed the pot very slowly and very quietly and ran away. When he was half-way away she woke up and missed *takder*. Then she discovered the theft and saw him running away and shouted after him "I thought you were my grandson, but I see you are nothing but a thief. You have stolen my yeast and will give it to everybody all over the world. So I set my curse on it; may it make everything that drinks it drunk and quarrelsome." And so it has been; when people get drunk they quarrel.

When *takder* returned to *Komsithing* with the yeast, he asked him if he knew how to make *Chi*: *takder* said he did and they followed his instructions; but since they had no earthenware pots to put the fermented *chi* in they put it in baskets, well covered with leaves. Then *Komsithing* asked *Taknyom* what reward he desired for bringing the fire. *Taknyom* replied "Gold and jewels and clothes are no use to an animal; what I want is to be given the plants *mangder* (?) and *sanghlo* (?) which grow in the valley." He was given these. Similarly *Takder* was granted the leavings at the bottom of the spoons and plates and *patyoot*.

When the *chi* was ready all were afraid to be the first to drink. Eventually the snake *Putsong beu* was summoned and drank it; when it had drunk it dashed away like lightening. Seeing this all the gods and men were frightened to drink. After that the snake *Pamol beu* was summoned; but when it had drunk it ran about biting people and animals so that they all died. Next the snake *Poblyok beu* was summoned: when it had drunk it fell senseless. *Komsithing* gave that snake the ferns to live in; it is harmless. After this they thought that the *chi* was harmless; but then they found they had no butter for *Sakyou faat*. So *Komsithing* went to *Itpomu* and asked for butter so that they could *Sakyou faat* for the marriage of *Tarbong* and *Naripmu*. He said to his mother "We have the *chi*, but no butter." *Itpomu* said "Get a bamboo *yongtong*," and when he had got it she filled it with the butter which she had from her cows. Then on her instructions nine containers (*takner*) of *chi* were prepared, and their edges were smeared with butter.

Now all the gods and men gathered for the marriage of *Tarbong* and *Naripnom*. Everything was prepared in due order; all the gifts were placed on one side, and then *Komsithing rum faat* with *chi* and *sakyou*. This is the reason why today when a marriage is celebrated all gods are worshipped, and these gifts are given. Only when *Tarbong* and *Naripnom* were husband and wife was he able to possess her. This is the reason why today *Lepchas* still give the same gifts; this is *Bri-it,* the origin of marriage. The sacred myth of the origin of marriage has to be repeated in it's entirely by the officials at each marriage (Gorer, G. 1938, Reprint in India 1996: 315-343; 481-484; Foning, A. R. 2nd Edn. 2003: 236-246).

Mythological Functions

(i) Mystical: The myth describes the mystery of origin of marriage, origin of fire, origin and method of preparation of *Chi* and butter required for *Sakyou tsok rum-faat.*

(ii) Sociological: Although the *Lepchas* do not divide life into different periods the myth describes the training and guiding of male child to attain adulthood by his mother and brother or father as in other mythologies. The boys do not have natural means of transformation to adulthood unlike the girls. The myth furnishes the social rituals of worshipping gods and goddesses during the marriages in addition to other social rituals of *Sakyou tsok rum-faat.* Although they have no formulated notions of life, the majority consider that the happiest time of life was when people were at *fleng* (male) or *num-leng* (female) – youth and early married life. It has also provided the method of preparation of *chi* (fermented millet beer) and butter from the cow's milk to the society.

(ii) Pedagogical: The myth interprets the customary laws of marriage of the *Lepcha* tribes.

(k) Myth of Death and Death Rites

The *Lepchas* believe that death is the real enemy of *Lepcha* life. It is absolute and final and cannot be fought against. Some precautions can be taken against diseases, natural calamity, and preventable accidents but against death itself there is nothing to do. Once a person is dead there are two things to do in the *Lepcha* community. Firstly, the danger of the evil spirit that has caused his death finding another victim in the community must be averted. Secondly, the soul of the dead person needs to be retrieved, accompany soul journey and reached to the *Rumlyang* (heaven) so as to get rid of the dead person as thoroughly and completely as possible. The *Mun* conducts this. At the *Rumlyang* the soul of the dead person will born again as a tiny child, very often of a different sex to its former life. In the *Rumlyang* the child grows upto maturity and leads a happy and immortal life among all the other dead, a life similar to that here on earth except that there is no death or disease or want. The *Mun* will perform the *sanglion* (death ceremony) and any other benevolent people who know how to help the corpse on the road to the *Rumlyang* by meditation – *munthem*.

The corpse is carried in the basket to the burial place by one man; a near relation if possible; a husband must always carry his wife and a son his mother. A *Mun* accompanies the buriers. When the party arrive at the chosen site the corpse is placed on the ground and is washed and anointed with the mixture of butter, cloves, nutmeg and camphor, and wrapped in a new cloth which is arranged so as to cover the face. Then a circular grave about the height of a man is dug; a big stone is put at the bottom and the sides are lined with stones and four ropes are placed against the four corners. While these preparations are being made the surviving spouse or eldest son will stay by the corpse and talk to it saying; "We are preparing this new house for you." The body is put into the grave still sitting in the basket, oriented to face *Kinchenjunga;* then on the top of the grave and corpse is put a big flat stone and on the top of that four cooking stones supporting another flat stone. On the top of this is placed a little white stone which serves as an indication that the place is a grave and should not be touched. When all is in place the four ropes are pulled away simultaneously as in the case of Limboo tribes. The *Mun* then ceremoniously cleanses the hands of the buriers with a pot of strained *chi* and a bristle brush.

After the disposal of the corpse there are still two actions which must be performed: the getting rid of the evil spirit which has caused the death and the safe conducting of the dead man's soul well out of the physical world. The order in which these are performed depends on the types of death recognized by the *Muns* in the *Lepcha* society.

The present day *Lepchas* of Sikkim comprises of three religious groups, the ancient *Munism* and *Bongthism*, Buddhist *Lepchas* and Christian *Lepchas*. Thus, the life of passage – birth, marriage and death depends on the religious categories they belong. Under this work only the myths of *Munism* and *Bongthism* has been described ignoring the other religious groups. For instance, the Buddhist *Lepchas* recognizes the following types of death; Viz: (i) death caused by *Sande moong*; (ii) death caused by *Shdook moong*, and (iii) death caused by *Arot moong* (death by violence). And the death rites of the dead person differ accordingly to the Buddhist religion. Similarly, the Christian *Lepchas* conduct death rituals according to Christianity.

Death rites of the child before the age of about ten years

In the case of a child dying before the age of about ten years none of the death ceremonies are performed. Neither *sanglion* made for it. However, a *Mun* performs the ceremony of "*Dek Flee*" three days after death. For this ceremony a goat is required and also a tray covered with a black cloth on which is put samples of every sort of grain and a bundle of seven pieces of wood tied up with reed. Besides that a bundle of elephant grass and other prickly plants are needed. The ceremony is performed inside the house. The goat is tethered to a pole and a second rope made out of reed with three knots in it is tied round the goat's neck. This the *Mun* and all the members of the household in turn touch, and then the *Mun* throws the rope forward out of the house door three times. If by any chance the knot should point inwards there will be another death in the same household. After this a young boy takes some firebrands from the hearth some way away from the house; then the goat is led to the same place, stabbed to death and singed. After this the crops on the tray are *pek* (protective and curative measures) over the inhabitants of the house and set down by the goat. Then the *Mun* takes the bundles of leaves already prepared in his right hand and a live hen in his left and *peks* the members of the household. The hen is then given to some neighbour to kill and eat; for neither the *Mun* nor any members of the household may eat anything used in this sacrifice. Then the intestines of the goat are cooked and mixed with rice; the *Mun* throws *chi* from a buttered cup to the evil spirits, his assistant the chopped meat and rice. When this is finished a wooden phallus (*tiklyong-kup*) is set up between two stones on the way to the house; it is given hundreds of small cuts, each cut representing one year that the evil spirit cannot pass. It is anointed with blood and chi. All that night the *Mun* communes – *munthen,* but he does not go into a trance. No food is given to the soul of the child. If the child was young he did not eat in real life and even if he did eat solid food, he was fed in his lifetime.

Death rites of adult individuals

(i) Death rituals in the case of normal deaths:

It is considered desirable that the *Mun sanglion* should take place on the same day as the disposal of the corpse. Before the *Mun* comes out of his house to perform the ceremony he will spend the night communing and calling on the gods to help him conduct the soul to *Rumlyang* (heaven); in particular he will call on *Hit-rum* and *De-rum,* the ancestral gods, and such ancestors of the deceased as have died in the same way as the present man. A friend or assistant called *Mun-tyol* accompanies the *Mun*. After the funeral a pig is killed and one of its trotters is put aside on a wooden tray for the ceremony. The following articles, all very small are also prepared inside the house and put on the tray: on either side of a tiny log, two small torches, one dish of rice mixed with charcoal and pebbles, a comb and a bristle brush. There is also prepared separately a rope of bamboo bark about twelve feet long and also 40 kg of *chi,* 20 kg of rice, and stained *chi* in a filtering bag. When all is prepared everybody in the house goes outside into the yard. First of all the *Mun* takes the knife of the deceased (or her sickle in case of female) and starts cutting the weeds in the courtyard. If there are many weeds others will help after the *Mun* has started. When the space is cleared the mourners have a meal; the *Mun* sits aside and is merely given *chi* to drink. An animal, preferably an ox, is brought in and offered to the evil spirits who are plaguing the dead man's soul in order to induce them to desist; then the ox is killed by some unrelated layman and skinned and cut up. The intestines are boiled. While the ox is cooking a shed is made for the *Mun* out of bamboo mats suspended from a post; to this post the cooked intestines are tied. A little way in front of this is another post of a special sort of wood to which is attached the rope of bamboo bark; two knots are tied in it, the one nearer the post being for the evil spirits, the farther one for the gods. The other end of this rope is held during the whole ceremony by the *Mun* and is finally served with a pointed knife after the *Mun* has communicated with the dead. The household sends out to the *Mun* a dish of boiled rice and a portion of the ox's ribs cut in two, one part for the *Mun* and the other for the *Mun-tyol*, and also black and white sausages. Generally the *Mun* only eats the rice, the meat being taken away in the morning with the other presents. There is also prepared a dish of all the sorts of food, dried bird and fish, ginger, different sorts of grain and fruits and roots and chi for the deceased.

When everything is ready the *Mun* retires to the shed with his assistant. The rest of the people sit around but not so near that they can hear what is going on. Before retiring the *Mun* puts on a special headdress of white cloth arranged like a turban with in the centre porcupine quills and tigers' whiskers and at the side peacock's feathers. The *Mun* now starts to chant/recite *munthen* and calls on the dead man's soul, always holding the rope in the left hand. When he has got into communication with the dead man he starts giving him advice and help. When the *Mun* starts talking to the soul of the deceased the *Mun-tyol* sends for the tray, which was prepared in the house and these objects are given to the soul by means of throwing them out of the shed with instructions how to use them. First the soul is given the rice with the charcoal and pebbles in it; he is told to eat the rice and leave the charcoal and stones; the evil spirits, pursuing and hungry, will pick over the stones for food and give him time to escape. Then he is given the ladders and torches to help him. With their aid he will be able to climb over the log which will block the way of the evil spirits. He is also told to throw behind him the brush and comb which will grow into huge fences and block the evil spirits away.

Now the dead man's soul is coming near; when the *Mun-tyol* sees the signs that it is approaching he sends for the collection of food which has been prepared and this is offered to the dead man with the words: "All these foods which you used to eat when you were alive you can have now." Then suddenly the *Mun* become unconscious; he falls and his assistant catches him. The *Mun*'s soul has departed from his body and in its place is the soul of the dead man who speaks through the *Mun*'s lips: he speaks very slowly and in a very soft voice; it is not the voice of the *Mun* nor is it the voice of the dead man. The *Mun-tyol* will then question the dead man, saying: "Tell us what evil spirits are troubling you; tell us how you died." Then the dead man will say the cause of his death, whether it was caused directly by an evil spirit or whether it was through the intervention of some human enmity, either *mik-jit* (envy and cursing) or the direct sending of a devil.

When the dead man has said what was the cause of his death he leaves the body of the *Mun,* who recovers and cuts the rope between the two knots, so that the devil's knot is left attached to the post, with the pointed knife that he has held in his right hand all the time. He then conducts the soul to the *Rumlyang,* where all the dead live; he will find there a house prepared with bedding and all utensils; he will lead the soul into it and lock it in. This ends the *Mun sanglion* and in the morning the *Mun* goes home, taking with him his presents. They consists of the meat already mentioned, a leg of beef, Rs. 5/-, the dead man's knife, or sickle, and one complete set of his clothes. These he wears or gives to his wife. The rest of the dead man's clothes are divided up among the children six months after death; they are washed three times and fumigated with incense before wearing.

One year after the original *sanglion* the *Mun* will go into a trance again, though a lighter one this time, and visit the *Rumlyang* once more. Outside the house in which the soul of the dead man is enclosed *Hit-rum* will be standing on guard; for him will be offered presents of chi and butter and sugarcane and fruits and flowers and roots of many different sorts. After this the *Mun* unlocks the door of the house and finds a little baby inside; to this baby he presents a dress suitable to its sex. When the *Mun* has opened the door the baby comes outside and lives with the other people in the *Rumlyang* who are his ancestors; the baby will grow up as human beings do and when the *Mun* visits the *Rumlyang* in future years he will see the soul grown to be an adult. There is no death in the *Rumlyang*.

(ii) To get rid of *Sor moong* (Violent Death or *Apang moong* - genito-urinary diseases in the case of Violent deaths

A goat is tethered by a long rope which has three knots tied in its length. First of all, all the members of the affected household must touch the knots and then the *Mun*. Then the *Mun* will call on all the devils to be contended with the blood of the sacrifice and not to take the patient, after which he throws the rope into the air. If the rope falls end outwards it means the devils will be satisfied; if it falls towards the house the prognosis is bad. After this the animal is killed and the *gazook* (the head, one fore-leg and one hind-leg of the animal sacrificed by a *Mun*) and *sha-fot* (the heart, liver and lungs of the sacrificial animal in a *Mun* sacrifice) offered to the devil with a plate and a pot filled with rice, a rupee and a ceremonial scarf, together with some of the invalid's ornaments and clothing and also a cup of chi with different grains in it. Then the *Mun* constructs a phallus out of wood, which is called in its guardian functions *moong long tik*; this is set up between two stones leaning slightly forward, somewhere in the forest, and anointed with the blood of the slain animal and chi. This will keep the devil away, for no devil can pass this guardian.

(iii) To drive away the ghost of a dead child, called *Num-een moong*, which kills young children by infantile diarrhea

After an animal has been sacrificed the person who is troubled by the *moong* goes down to a narrow stream. The troubled person stands on the right of the stream and the *Mun* on the left of it. Then a gateway is made over the stream of two bundles of elephant grass and brambles. The *Mun* holds in each hand a bundle made out of wild raspberries, nettles and all other thorny and prickly plants. These bundles are dipped in water and *pek* over the sufferer several times. Then a bamboo chi holder filled with blood and *chi* and shut up at both ends, and a leaf filled with fried rice and meat and blood are *pek* over the patient and thrown through the gateway for the devil. Then the bundles of thorny plants are through the gateway and finally the gateway is filled up with thorny plants so that it looks like a tree. The *Mun* does this two other places some way apart on the stream. He must do these second two – one above and one below the original one alone, and after completing them he must return straight to his own house without meeting anybody. Should he meet people *Num-een moong* will start haunting them.

Num-een moong is the devil released by the death of young children under the age of about ten. This devil pursues living people and especially other children. Older people which die do not let loose a devil. The *Num-een moong* persists for about three years after the child's death. When there are bad storms the devil can be heard hooting "*Oo-oo-oo*". Children are particularly frightened of this devil and a great number of Lepchas claim to have heard it cry.

(iv) To get rid of *Chyom moong* (that is the devil who causes people to die by falling from a tree or cliff) or *Rot moong* (that is the devil who causes people to commit suicide)

This ritual is called *Moong Sot,* killing the devil, and should be performed by the surviving members of the family in which one member has either died violently or committed suicide. It should be performed every years, but it is sufficient if it is performed after the violent death and at the birth of each new member of the household. If the ritual is not performed the devil will return and claim another victim. A dead goat is skinned except for its legs below the joint and is laid on its back with its hind quarters towards the bowman. Beside it is a hole already dug and above it is made a small shelter of bamboos thatched with reeds. Beyond that is set up a red head of banana flower struck into the ground and against it a post on top of which is attached the goat's heart, in such a way that the blood drips on the banana flower. In a line with this stands a bowman with an arrow in his bow ready to shoot. The *Mun* is at one side not looking at the post. The other men who are present are all armed with knives.

After a time the *Mun* starts shivering uncontrollably and summons the devil in a loud voice. As he calls some insect or other will climb up the pole towards the heart, and the bowman must shoot it with his arrow before it reaches it. As soon as he has shot he must call to the *Mun* to say whether he has hit or missed the insect. If he has missed the Mun must recall it. When the insect is killed it and goat are chopped to pieces by the bystanders with their knives and buried in the prepared hole. Stones and earth are rammed on top of the sacrifice to fill up the hole, and then a second time to make a little mound (Gorer, G. 1938, Reprint in India 1996: 345-362; 232-234).

Mythological Functions

(i) Mystical: The ritual describes the mystery of death rites conducted both for children and the adult. What *munthem* reveals in the myth by the *Mun* is not recorded so far in the *Lepcha munthem*. Only the rituals performed in the death rites of the individuals are known or speculated. Actual myth illustrated by the *Mun* is not known so far. From the rituals it has been concluded that death occurs only at the influence of some evil spirits or devils. Hence, the death rites of a deceased involve two things: first knowing the actual cause of death from the soul of the deceased individual and worship of evil spirit or devil to let the soul be freed from it; and secondly, to conduct the soul of the dead to *Rumlyang* (heaven). For these two, the *Mun* performs the *Sanglion* rites for the deceased. It also unfolds the mystery of death caused by *Sor moong, Apang moong, Num-een moong, Chyom moong* and *Rot moong* and their remedies and death rites in the *Lepcha* society.

(ii) Cosmological: The rituals provide the evidence of cosmological origin. The soul of the deceased has to be reached to *Rumlyang* located somewhere in the *Akashic* field.

(iii) Sociological: The ritual has furnished several types of deaths and death rituals in the *Lepcha* society.

(iv) Pedagogical: It has interpreted the laws of life, ethical and cosmological laws of death in the society.

(v) Mystery of afterlife: The rituals have unfolded the belief system of afterlife. After death, the soul of the deceased has to go to the ancestor's place *Rumlyang* (heaven), which is the origin centre of the souls of the individuals.

(l) Myth of people of *Mayel Kyong*

The *Lepchas* believe that the people of *Mayel* consist of seven brothers each with their own name and each patron of some sort of grain. These seven brothers are considered to be the progenitors, ancestors and guardians of the *Lepchas*. *Itpomu* created them, and placed rice, millet and maize in their charge when she made these crops. The people of *Mayel* live in seven huts. They are immortal; each morning they are infants, at midday they are grown men and in the evening they are old. They all have huge goiters and it is from them that people know that big goiters are a sign of prosperity and a large harvest. They wear the traditional *Lepcha* costume of clothes made of nettle cloth and small basket-work hats. They are somewhere between the gods and ordinary human beings (*Demi*-gods). They are not gods because they live on the earth but they are not human because they do not die. The land of *Mayel* is far up the *Talung* valley, somewhere behind *Kinchenjunga*. At one time in the past the road thither was open but now it has been closed and is as un-passable as the cutting edge of a knife. On the road to *Maye*l are three guardian spirits called *Sok-po,* who is brothers; the eldest is called *Mayel Yook rum*. He is also called *Pong rum* when hunters sacrifice to him. His younger brothers *Mi-tik* and *Tom-tik* are cruel deities who kill and eat men and animals. *Tom-tik* is like a bear. They are the special guardians of the ibex and musk deer (*Moschus chrysopoter*) which come from *Mayel,* and that is the reason why these animals are so difficult to kill.

In the country of *Mayel* crops grow a hundred times as big as here and it is from that country that the seeds of our present crops originate. These crops are always ripe for harvesting. The migratory birds are called *Mayel fo,* birds of *Mayel,* and they are sent out by the people of *Mayel* to the *Lepcha*; to indicate the seasons and the times when the various agricultural acts should be performed. When the time comes for the migratory birds to return to *Mayel,* the parent birds die on the way and only the newly hatched ones survive the arduous journey to *Mayel* from whence they are sent the next year to act as indicators for the *Lepchas*. The people of *Mayel* have no wives living with them but the two oldest of the people, *Adoo Yook* and *Alau Yook,* have in a way as wives the two sisters called *Talyeu Nimu* and *Sangvo Nimu,* who are the spirits of the earth. These two women lie on their backs under the earth and on their bellies are the cultivable lands; into this *Adoo Yook* and *Alau Yook* send rice, millet and maize, just as if it were human seed from a husband, and the women are fertilized and bring fruitfulness.

In the old days the path to *Mayel* was open and sometimes the people of *Mayel* used to come into the other parts of the world and occasionally adventurous hunters found their way into the *Mayel* country. Once a hunter went across *Sakhyong* and over two distant peaks; there he saw floating in a stream a branch of a certain sort of tree which he realized must have been thrown there by the people of *Mayel* and he followed the stream up. He reached a path as narrow as a razor edge on which was the feathers of the *Mayel* birds that had died on the return journey. After passing this ridge the hunter followed the road for three days round the mountain and came to the village of *Mayel* and there saw seven houses and asked for shelter for the night. They had big pigs lying down and they killed a pig and gave him pork to eat, rice and *chi*. The hunter stayed there seven days and when he went away the people of *Mayel* asked him not to talk about them when he returned. They gave him as gifts rice seed which he sowed and the fruit of pumpkin and cucumber which turned into stones. Another hunter from *Sakhyong* also found his way there but he was not so fortunate. When he came to the village he found a child and asked him "Who are your father and mother?" The child said, "We are our own fathers and mothers, we are babies and young people and old people." The man picked and cooked some rice. When the people came near he threatened them with his knife. At this they said to him "Do not do that; cook and eat your rice and go away. If you do not we will drive you away with our dogs." When they said that he looked round and saw huge dogs like bears with enormous eyes. Then he was very frightened and ran away at once with some of the cooked rice in his hand. as he ran home there was a terrific thunderstorm, and he was pelted with snow and hail. Since the time of these adventurous travelers the road has been closed with enormous rocks (Gorer, G. 1938, Reprint in India 1996: 239-246).

Mythological Functions

(i) Mystical: The myth describes the mystery of the people of *Mayel*. The *Lepchas* consider that it is the land of their ancestors.

(ii) Cosmological: The myth has cosmological origin. *Mayel* is an *Akashic* field or a land existing in the mental construction somewhere behind the mount *Kanchanjunga.*

(iii) Sociological: The myth has furnished a number of worship rituals in the *Lepcha* societies. It is supposed to be a land of immortals - *Rumlyang,* and everybody in *Renjyong* would like to attain immortality by going there after death.

(v) Mystery of afterlife: Every *Lepcha* individual of *Renjyong* would like to go to *Rumlyang* or *Mayel Kyang* after his or her demise.

13

RELIGION AND MYTHOLOGY OF ANIMISM OF THE SUNUWARS

The *Sunuwars* of Sikkim are basically animists - worshippers of natural divinities and ancestors. They have no concept of God, universe creation, life and destiny, and heaven and hell in their animist belief system. However, Hinduism has heavily subjected the *Sunuwars* as early as 1760s, after the unification process of Nepal started by *Prithvi Narayan Shaha* since September 5, 1768 onwards (Stiller, L.F. 1968). Now, most of the *Sunuwars* of Sikkim have adopted Hinduism, some of them have adopted Buddhism, and now, their animist belief system, myths, folktales, folklores etc. are mostly affected by these two religions (Subba, J.R. 2008a:339-345). In spite of this, a few traits of their animist belief system could be traced from the study conducted by Pradhan, Budhiman (1999), *Sikkim Sunuwar (Mukhia) Koinchbu* (2003) and Subba J.R. (2008a: 342-343) as follows.

The *Sunuwars* believe to have been blessed by the goddess *Shandar* for their protection and food, and were granted the *mantras* of *Mukudum* – an oral tradition that are pronounced by their oracular *Poibo, Natso* and *Ngyami* shaman priests to this day on all life as well as afterlife rituals and ceremonies. These shamans are oracular possessions of the nature divinities and fall into a state of trance during which time voices speak through their person. In so far as they communicate with the world of spirits, they know the past, present and future, they can find lost or misplaced objects, discern the causes of evils inflicted by an angry spirit and then exorcise them. With the spirit aid of "*Lawa tung*", an embodiment of the rainbow (*washi*), the most important spirit, a shaman can confront the household spirit (*gu-muk-ki*), the most dangerous of all spirits. The other *tung*: *Dhali, Gungirwa* and *Kiabra,* are much weaker and their powers are no longer sufficient to enable the shaman to exorcise the household spirit. The shamans perform various types of rites: (i) the major public rites: *Tsandi, Ghil, Khas, Pol* etc. (ii) Seasonal rites: *Rikhitarpani* (*janaipurnima*), *Sri-panchami,* feasts of the full moon (*purne*) etc. (iii) domestic rites: birth, granting of a name, marriage, funeral etc. (iv) propitiatory rites: selection of a site for a dwelling house, and (v) curative rites for humans and livestock: *Iwa Tsinta, Mewal* etc. The shaman *Naso* knows the divinities of sunuwar pantheon and sacrifices buffaloes, pigs, goats or chicken during public or semi-public ceremonies

They observe and perform the following ceremonies and worships on different occasions by these shamans in Sikkim:

Sagoon : This is a minor worship done twice a year by *Naso* to propitiate their gods and souls of the deceased ancestors.

Chhengoo: This is ancestor worship performed by *Poibos* invoking deities and deceased souls of the ancestors twice a year for peace and prosperity of all.

Geel: It is a festival of blood sacrifice of birds and animals to fulfill their various wishes.

Kash* and *Shandar: these are also performed by the Shamans (Sinha et. al, 2005: 48; Subba, J.R. 2008a: 339-345).

However, myths to support these rituals are lost or lacking in the modern day sunuwar society in Sikkim.

14

RELIGION AND MYTHOLOGY OF ANIMISM OF THE MANGARS

The *Mangars* are essentially animists. They worship a host of nature divinities and spirits through their own shaman priests known as *"Bhusal"* or *"Wapa"*. Worship of ancestors is another critical element among them. They sacrifice animals for their gods and goddesses. The animist *Mangars* has no concept of God, universe creation, life and destiny, afterlife, and heaven and hell in their animist belief system. (Alle, S. 2003: 91-92; Subba, J.R. 2005a; 2008a: 352).

The Mangers are the first in Nepal to receive the influence of Hinduism, as their habitat was the first to be touched by the Hindu immigrants taking refuse there during the rise of Muslim power in India. Further, Hinduism has heavily subjected the animist Mangars as early as 1760s, after the unification process of Nepal started by *Prithvi Narayan Shaha* since September 5, 1768 onwards (Stiller, L.F. 1968). Now, most of the *Mangars* of Sikkim have adopted Hinduism. Their animist belief system, myths, folktales, folklores etc. are mostly affected by the Hindu religion. Although, the present day *Magars* perform various early belief system rituals, they have lost the myths to support it (Subba, J.R. 2005a; 2008a: 352).

15

RELIGION AND MYTHOLOGY OF ANIMISM OF THE THAMIS

The *Thamis* of Sikkim are essentially animist. They worship a number of nature divinities. They worship *Dolakha Bhimsen,* their main deity along with a number of other divinities such as *Bhumya, Nagey, Bisakarma, Gosai, Chirkun, Nepalya Devi, Chan Deva, Lakhin, Gatyako Deva, Shyakri Deva* and *Bahara Deva* by their Thami shaman priest known as *Khami*. The *Khami* shaman priest also conducts all life rituals and act as curer, healer, fortune teller etc. in their society. *Bhumya* is a god of agricultural crops and provides food to the people with good harvest. It is worshipped twice a year once before starting cultivation *Ubhauli* (February-March) for good cropping season; and other after the crop is harvested *Udhauli* (December) for thanks giving and offering newly harvested crops. *Nagey* is the god of nature and worshipped for protection of houses, agricultural farms and land from natural calamities. *Bisakarma* is a god worshipped for protection of the family from diseases, sickness and unhappiness. *Gosai* god is worshipped for protection of buffalo, as livestock rearing is an important activity of *Thamis*. *Chirkun* is another god worshipped for protection of other domestic animals such as cows, chicken, duck etc. They also worship *Narayaini* (*Vayu devta*), *Budaeni, Kholako mai, Kalingchoke mai, Gamalae devta, Shakari,* etc. The animist *Thamis* has no concept of God, universe creation, life and destiny, afterlife, and heaven and hell in their animist belief system. However, Hinduism has heavily subjected the *Thamis* as early as 1760s, after the unification process of Nepal started by *Prithvi Narayan Shaha* since September 5, 1768 onwards (Stiller, L.F. 1968). Now, most of the *Thamis* of

Sikkim have adopted Hinduism, and now, their animist belief system, myths, folktales, folklores etc. are mostly affected by the Hindu religions. Although, they continue to perform various animist rituals in the present day society also, they have lost or lack myths to support these rituals (Subba, J.R. 2008a:378).

GLOSSARY

A-akwanama phongma – the initiation ritual of god of the main pillar of the Limboo Newly constructed house.

Adhi Granth or *Guru Granth Sahib* - Sikh's holy religious scripture

Aitabarey, Sikari, Aathaney, Naya, Buddheni, Yowa – the gods and goddesses of Khambu-Rais.

Ajiva - non-living matter.

Akasha/Lokas/Tangsang Den - the sky

Anduk Saham Lose - body itching of the pregnant woman.

Arahat - living enlightened one.

Arun/Phakmasinyuk/Kudapma - the planet Uranus

Awakening - discovering that one's true nature is *Atman,* soul, Sam-complex, etc.

Baikuntha – the god Vishnu's heaven.

Bardo, delogs or *deloks* - intermediate stage of the moment of death

Barun/Tungdungtheba/Maksama - the planet Neptune

Bhakti Era (500 A. D. – the present) - *Upasana Kanda* Phase or age of worship in Hinduism

Bhimsen – the household god of *Khasas*

Bhusal, Wapa – the oracular shaman priests of Magars

Bodhisattva - a celestial being that postpones his own entrance into *Parinirvana* or final Extinction.

Brihaspati/Chamthima/Khawalumba - the planet Jupitar

Budha/Thungyaba, Keksuba - the planet Mercury

Chandrama/Laba/Singlaba/Okwama – the Moon

Chellung Khaklung - symbolic representation of incest in Limboos.

Chikhai Bardo - when, at the end of a process of sensory dissolution that presages physical death, a profound state of consciousness, called the "Clear Light", dawns.

Chokchokke mang yangyange mang – the creator and developer god.

Chonyid Bardo - the consciousness of the deceased person moves into the second *Bardo*, called the *Bardo* of reality

Chukchi khamba yoyong khamba, Sibring khamba thebring khamba, Khambo khamba yupling khamba, Henkham khamba makkham khamba, and Laha khamba rutaak khamba – various types of soils on earth formed during creation.

Chi - millet beer in Lepcha

Deebung Sikari – hunter god of Khambu-Rais

Dhami/Jhankri – the oracular Shaman priest of the *Khasas*

Faat – sacrifice of *Mun* Lepcha religious priest

Fodong Theeng (or *Komsithing*) – male Lepcha progenitor

Gazook - the head, one fore-leg and one hind-leg of the animal sacrificed by a *Mun*

Hangchhapok – man in Khambu-Rais

Hang Sam, Purkha, Pitri - the great ancestor Deity

Hangsitlang – main-pillar of the Limboo house

Henjiri Henbonge Chotlung - fortified place of the Children in Limboos

Henkhamma – the Earth in Khambu-Rai

Hilli – diamond in Limboo language.

Him Sammangs - household divinities

Hitsa ritual - cleansing ceremony

Idhuklung samsogha semi - the fire of evil spirits

Ijum Iwa Kak - a wasp

Iksakhambek Den – the Earth

Iksama/Prithivi - the Earth

Ing-zong – trading friend

Jiva - soul

Jiva-atma - the crumpled consciousness of the unenlightened, ignorant, ego-dominated *jiva*.

Kailasa – the god Shiva's heaven

Karma – the cosmic effect implies the eternal struggle between good and evil

Karma - personal effect good or bad of a person

Kejong Sammet – wind-storm in Limboo language

Kejong surit – the vital air

Kerung Kohim – felting blue of a pregnant woman.

Khaamet-thumbon – the cloud in Limboo language

Khambongba lungbongba sa – the gods and goddesses of the earth below the fertile layer of the soil.

Khambuling Picchamma - an agile lightening goddess emerged from the earth during creation of the universe

Khe-Bumsa - the Lhopo (Bhutia) Tribal Leader ancestor of Sikkim.

Khema Yongsong Den – underworld/hell – the place of retribution

Khemjong and *Najong* – the divorce agreement in Limboos

Khem-sam - the soul of hearing in Limboos

King-chum-darmit – goddess of fate and destiny in Lepchas

Kingna – copper in Limboo language

Kohome Fo - a partridge bird in Lepchas

Kukurmi – evil god of darkness of Khambu-Rais

Lafet - the *Mun* sacrifice made on a winnowing tray, on which is placed first banana leaves, then grain, ginger, dried bird, dried fish, etc.

Laikkumsa pheniangsa – the male human idol of creation

Lakejok kamala mang - the creator god of the Moon

Laotima mang phungphahangma mang – the goddess of flowers in Limboos

Laphinjongba and *Namphinjongba* – the gods of shot put game in Limboos

Lasang – the Moonlight

Lepmu Sikcha- a blue fly in Limboo language

Lho-Mon-Tsong Sum – the tripartite treaty signed between the Bhutias, Lepchas and

Limboos leaders accepting the Chiefdomship of Phuntso Namgyal in 1666 A.D. on Water Hare Year of Tibetan calendar at Denzong Phuntso Khangsar.

Loghe – a female-child dress in Limboos

Lonlenwahi - thin green layer of soil of marshy land in Limboo language

Loong – qualification to perform the *Mun* ceremony by the pupils of Lepcha shaman.

Mangal/Samyangmuden/ Pungmimi – the planet Mars

Mangenna - a boon bestowing prayer in Limboos

Manghup mangde – curse in Limboo language

Mangjirima manglondhama – the place of appearing gods and goddesses at Mt. Jannu.

Mangjum Mangwa Kak – the hornet in Limboo language

Mangpas, Bijuwas, Nakchhong, Mabimi, Kubimi,Dawang – Khambu-Rai shaman priests

Mangs – Deities in Limboos

Masta, Kul Devta – the ancestor deity of *Khasas*

Mayel Kyong - the hidden village in Lepchas

Menja - lead in Limboo language

Mik-jit - envy and cursing in Lepchas

Mikthama/Nam - the Sun

Moksha- the total freedom from the cycle of birth, life, pain, misery, and death and the final release.

Moong – devil or evil spirit inn Lepchas

Moongkoong Mungla Faat - marriage ceremony in Lepchas

Moonglyang - evil spirit world in Lepchas adopted from Buddhism.

Mudhing – pearl in Limboos

Muknyamlyang - demon world in Lepchas adopted from Buddhism

Mukudum – an oral tradition of Sunuwars

Mundhang Khara Den- nyaya loka/world of judgment in Limboos

Mundhang seri semi - the fire of lightening in Limboos

Mundhum – the Limboo oral myth

Muni – precious stones in Limboo language

Munthem – the Lepcha oral myth

Muringla Kharingla Tembhe – the *Akashic* field where the nine ancestors of Limboos left with their Father (progenitor) during separation with the Mother (progenitor)

Nag-Nageni - the serpent gods and goddesses of hill tribes

Na-jong-nue (or *Nazong-nyou*) – female Lepcha progenitor

Namkejok mamandin mang – the creator god of the Sun

Namsang - the Sunlight

Naraka or *Khema Youngong Den* – the place of retribution or hell

Narayana or *Param-atma* - the un-crumpled consciousness of God Vishnu.

Naso thapon pokhenne – origin of mental disorder in Limboos

Nawalung mang chosaplung mang – the god of fate and destiny in Limboos

Ngerere Nahangma - a boon-bestowing god in Limboos

Ninduli pasanga - weighing balance in Limboo language

Ningwa-sam - the soul of mind – intellectual power/*Buddhi*

Ninnamma – the Almighty Goddess of Khambu-Rais

Ninnammism/Mangchhamism – Religion of Khambu-Rais

Ni-sam - the soul of sight in Limboos

Nyolyang - hell in Lepchas adopted from Buddhism

Numsyim-Nyolyang - human world adopted from Buddhism

Nyookoong Nyoolik Mun – the first consecrated Lepcha *Mun* shaman priest

Om mani padme hum! - the mystic incantation of Eight-fold path transformed by the patron deity of Tibet – Cheresi

Padamlungma Thakedhak Chotlung (*Yaklasuhangma Chotlung*) - fortified place of Women in Limboos

Paoti Mang - an eternal judge in Yuma religion

Parinirvana - final extinction in Buddhism

Paruhang – the creator as well as progenitor god of Khambu-Rais

Patyoot - bamboo can of *chi* or millet beer in Lepchas

Pek - protective and curative measures in Lepchas

Phajiyeng Makchiyeng Pit - black and white bull gods in Limboos

Phanghangs –The great nine Ancestors of the Limboo tribes who left with the father (progenitor) in the *Akashic* field during separation.

Phengma, Susuli, Lekpa – ancestor gods and goddess dwelling around the *Samkhalung* of Khambu-Rais

Phangmuksam – a symbol of Pythagorean Tetrakys representing both Natural and Social Mythology of *Yumaism*

Phenje – iron in Limboo language

Phogiya puro magiya pu, Puringla puro kumaey puro, and *Pulingla puro puroti puro* – the mythological birds in Limboos

Phojiyeng pit makchiyeng pit – the cow goddess in Limboos

Phoktanglungma Pembenlungma –Mount Kumbhakarna or Jannu

Poibo, Natso, Ngyami – the oracular shaman priests of Sunuwars

Pong Rum - together with his wife *Shing Rum* is the lord of all wild animals and the patron saint of hunters in Lepchas.

Porokmi mang wambhami mang – the creator god in Limboos

Ptso – the patrilineal group in Lepchas

Pu pokheden pudhamlung den - origin of birds in Limboos

Pung-sam - the wandering soul in Limboos

Rahu-Ketu/Phagna - the Pluto

Rig-pa - pure consciousness equal to Buddha-nature

Rum or *Itpomu* – the Goddess in Lepchas

Rumlyang – place of the gods or heaven in Lepchas

Sakkong – bronze in Limboo language

Samadhi - calm meditation

Samkhalung – secret worshipping fireplace of Khambu-Rais

Samkhalung (*Sakalung*), *Situlung* (*Deepalung*), *Sutulung* (*Thankalung*) – the secret three stones of *Samkhalung* of Khambu-Rais

Sammang Chyangs - Retinue of Divinities in Limboos

Sammangs – Divinities in Limboos

Samsa-ma, Sam-chomma – ritual of soul journey to reach the soul of the deceased to the Ancestor Deity.

Samyang – gold in Limboo language

Samyo cheksingma lingyo cheksingma – the broom grass in Limboos

Samyukna Den - *Atma lok*/world of ancestors

Sangarek Nugarek Tembhe – the Earth where the eight Limboo ancestors lived with their Mother (progenitor)

Sangphiri Lingphiri Chotlung (*Thangben-Menchin Chotlung*) - fortified place of Limboo youth.

Sangram Pedang Den – The Almighty Goddess's world or heaven in Limboo

Sani/Pungsam/Thakrama - the planet Saturn

Sapchong tembhe – blacksmith's village

Sapokhe den Sadhamlung den - origin of mammals in Limboos

Sat-chitta-ananda - The aim of *yogi* is to unknot the mind, uncrumple the consciousness, and attain the triple state of unconditional truth, purified consciousness, and tranquil bliss.

Sawa Yethangs – The Great Eight Ancestors of the Limboo tribes who stayed back with the mother on earth.

Sawa Yukphung Ke-mba – The tall hunter ancestor of the Limboos

Sha-fot - the heart, liver and lungs of the sacrificial animal in a *Mun* sacrifice offered to the devil in Lepchas

Sidiphekkhanamle madiphekkhanamle – string made of cane

Sidiyangdang madiyangdang - a kind of child rearing basket or cradle

Singmanglung mang yayiklung mang – the god of earth, plants, water, soil and stones in limboo

Sisari phandari - maidservant

Siyakhamit mayakhamit - cloudy high mountains

Sor moong – evil spirit of hereditary sex-linked disability in Lepchas

Sugut or *Sugup* - spirit of causing death at parturition in Limboos

Sumnima - the creator as well as progenitor goddess of Khambu-Rais.

Senwalung Ngekwalung Chotlung (Phejiri Phedangma Chotlung) - fortified place of the Limboo shaman priests.

Shes-pa - the principle of consciousness.

Sidpa Bardo - the third *Bardo*, the *Bardo* of mundane existence dawns during which one must again take rebirth in one of the six realms of gods, demi-gods, humans, animals, hungry ghosts, or in hell.

Sijo Ingmi Sa - messenger gods and goddesses

Sikkum-sam - the soul of intuition – knowledge/*Gyan*

Simey-Bhumey - minor divinities of hill tribes

Si-sam - the graveyard soul in Limboos

Sitongsing Khema – ritual of separating the soul of the deceased from the living souls; and guiding, accompanying and handing over the deceased's soul to the ancestor deity.

Sodhung Lepmuhang (*Sutsuru Suhangpheba*) – the progenitor (father) of the Limboo tribes

Sukra/Sringma/Pyanglungma - the Venus

Suyo Kheyo - good or bad action (virtue and vice) in *Yuma* religion.

Swargha - in Hinduism it is very much part of *Samsara*, governed by rules of *karma*, – the god Indra's paradise.

Tafoot - some internal organ, spleen or gall-bladder of a pig for offering *Mun* sacrifice of Lepchas.

Taga – a male-child dress in Limboos.

Tagerama Ningwaphuma Mang – the Ultimate, Supreme, Omnipresent, Omniscient, Omnipotent, Infinite, and Eternal Goddess in *Yumaism*.

Tambhungna – goddess of the forest or darkness in Limboos

Tandi, Lungdhung kai choginne – a curse to get ruined from incest in Limboos

Tap Sammings – the gods and goddesses of nature.

Tayaripchi – creator goddess of Khambu-Rais

Terton or *gter ston* - revealer of hidden treasures

Tetlara Lahadongna (*Thillilung Thamdenlungma*) – Progenitor (mother) of the Limboo

Thamchyanglyang - animal world in Lapche

Thekong-Tek - the Lepcha leader

Thokley Sammangs – the clan divinities in Limboo

Thokley sammang semi - the fire of the divinities in Limboo

Thikoong Azor Bongthing – the first consecrated Lepcha *Padem* or *Bongthing* shaman priest

Thoklingma mang kugapma mang –Tiotti mang paotti mang – god of light in Limboos

Thona-sam - the soul of wisdom/consciousness/*Vivek*

Tingding Nahen - envy and jealousy in Limboos

Tiutti mang kautti mang, Kautti mang mautti mang – the goddess of flower

Transcendence - rejoining the sea of consciousness Transmigration - the eternal cycle of rebirth

Tulku – the incarnate possesses a continuity of personal identity in Mahayan Buddhism

Tungbaong Faat - child naming ritual in Lepcha

Tusroti Umroti – Brahmaputra River in Limboo

Tungutlisa simbumasa – female human idol of universe creation in Limboos.

Tuttu Tumyang Chotlung (*Khorung Maklung Chotlung or Sawa Yethang Chotlung*) – the sacred fortified place of gentlemen in Limboos.

Upanishadic era (500 B.C. – 500 A.D.) - *Gyan Kanda* Phase or Speculation age of Hinduism

Vaikuntha - Vishnu's heaven

Vedic era (1500 B.C. -500 B.C.) - *Karma Kanda* Phase or age of ritual of Hinduism

Vipassana - insight meditation in Buddhism

Wabholung sellobhung - a type of crystal stones in Limboo language

Wadumbokwa – the holy sacred rainwater collected on the stones or rock holes or tree trunk holes in Limboo language.

Wahichellekna/seningwahi – fowl's excreta in Limboos

Wayuhangma – god of wind and water in Khambu-Rais

Yagna - ritual in Vedic era of Hinduism

Yagrangsing – The Limboo shaman's Altar

Yama or *Thakede?ba* or *Sandey* – the god of death

Yeebung – graveyard of the Limboos

Yetchham thim – the eight soul tradition in *Yumaism*

Yoga-maya or Usha - the goddess with stimulating the senses

Yoga-nidra – the goddess with dormant senses

Yuppa – silver in Limboo language

SELECTED REFERENCES

Alle, Santosh (2003). *Magar Jatiko Itihas ani Sanskriti – Sikkim ko Sandarvama*. Gangtok, Sikkim.

Allen, N.J. (1976a). Studies in the Myths and Oral Traditions of the *Thulung Rai* of East Nepal. Ph.D. Thesis, Oxford University.

Blank, Jonah (2001). Mullahs on the Mainframe – Islam and Modernity among the Daudi Bohras.

Campbell, Joseph (1959). Primitive Mythology – The Masks of God. The Viking Press.

Campbell, Joseph (1962). Oriental Mythology – The Masks of God. Viking Penguin Inc.

Campbell, Joseph (1964). Occidental Mythology – The Masks of God, Viking Penguin Inc.

Campbell, Joseph (1968). Creative Mythology – The Masks of God. Viking Press.

Campbell, Joseph (1988). The Power of Myth with Bill Moyers. Pub. Doubleday, N. Y. Census (1981) of Government of India.

Chemjong, I. S. (1961). *Kirant Mundhum*. Champaran, Bihar: Rajendra Ram.

Chemjong, I.S. (1965). Reprint 1982. *Kirat Mundhum Khahun*. Darjeeling, West Bengal.

Chopra, Deepak. (2006). Life After Death, the book of answers. Pub. RIDER, London.

Das, A. K. and Banerjee, S. K. (1962). The Lepchas of Darjeeling District. Bull. of Cultural Institute, Sl. No. 2.

Diamond, J. (1997). Guns, Germs, and Steel – the fates of human societies. Pub. W.W. Norton & Co. N.Y.

Frazer, James (1996). The Golden Bough – a study in Magic and Religion. Penguin Books, London.

Fergus Fleming et. al. (1996). Heroes of the Dawn – Celtic Myth. Duncan Baird Publishers. London.

Ferguson, J. C. and Anesaki, Masaharu (1964). The Mythology of All Races – Chinese and Japanese. Cooper square Publishers Inc.

Foning, A. R. 2nd Edn. (2003). Lepcha my Vanishing Tribe. Chyu-Pandi Farm: Kalimpong.

Fung Yu-lan (1948). A short History of Chinese Philosophy. The Free Press. N.Y.

Gorer, G. 1938, Reprint in India (1996). The Lepchas of Sikkim. Pub. By Gyan Pub. House, New Delhi

Gurung, M.M. and Lama, R.P. (2004). Sikkim Study Series – Culture Vol. III. Pub. by Information and Public Relations Department, Govt. of Sikkim.

Hitchcock, J.T & Jones, R.L. (1994). Spirit Possession in the Nepal Himalayas. Pub. Vikas Pub. House Pvt. Ltd.

Hyde Maggie & McGuinness Michael (1999). Introducing Jung. ICON Books UK, TOTEM Books USA.

Jeffrey, S., Tuinstra, S. and Vaidya, J.P. (2000). The Lepcha of Nepal. Udaya Books, Kathmandu, Nepal.

Johnson, Paul (1972). The Civilization of Ancient Egypt. Harper Collins Publishers

Jones, R.L. (1976). Limboo Spirit Possession and Shamanism: 29-55pp

Kainla, Bairagi (1991) *Limboo Jatima Kakhpuja*; Nepal Academy

(1994) *Nahen Mundhum*; Kathmandu, Nepal.

(1994) *Samsogha Mundhum*; Kathmandu Nepal

(1995) *Sasik Mundhum*; Kathmandu Nepal

(1995) *Tongsing Tokma Mundhum*. Nepal Academy.

Mckay, Alex (2004) The indigenisation of Western Medicine in Sikkim. Bulletin of Tibetology: Vol. 40(2), Namgyal Institute of Tibetology, Gangtok, Sikkim.

Martin, Gaenszle (1991). Origins & Migrations of Mewahang Rai.

Moody, Raymmond (1976). Life after Life: the investigation of a phenomenan-survival of bodily death. NewYork.

Nunes, Antonio B. (1996). Statistics on religion. Internet.

Oswald Spangler (1937). Decline of the West. London: Allen & Unwin, Ltd.

Paruhang Sawanam: Visesank: Sakewa Parwa: Ninnamma ra Henkhammaq ko utpatti (2008).

Pattanaik, D. (2006). Myth = Mithya – A Handbook of Hindu Mythology. Pub. Penguin Books. India

Plaisier, Heleen (2005). A brief introduction to Lepcha orthography and literature. Bulletin of Tibetology: 41(1). Namgyal Institute of Tibetology, Gangtok Sikkim.

Pradhan, Budhiman (1999). *Kirantbangshi Sunuwar (Mukhia) Koinch.* Gangtok, Sikkim.

Rai, S. K. (2005). Kirat Khambu Rais of Sikkim and Eastern Himalayas. Shivika Enterprise, Deorali, Gangtok.

Shreng, Ranadhoj (1992). *Idhuk Sogha Pokma Mundhum. Kirat Sumyamba Yagrangsing.*

Pathari, Morang (1993). *Kubung Yakthung Thim. Kirant Yakthungba Mekhim Phungnawa Samlo.* Dharan Chadra Vir Nalbo.

Sinha, et al (2005). Ethnographic Report on Selected Communities of Sikkim. Submitted to the Govt. of Sikkim.

Sogyal, Rimpoche (2002). The Tibetan Book of Living and Dying. RIDER, London.

Stiller, Ludwig F. (1968) Reprint 1995. The Rise of the House of Gorkha. Modern Printing Press, Nepal.

Subba, C. (1995). The Culture and Religion of Limbu. Kathmandu, Nepal.

Subba, J. R. (1998). The Philosophy and Teachings of Yuma Samyo, Gangok, Sikkim.

(1998a) *Yakthung re Tendham Mekkhim Mundhum*; Gangtok, Sikkim

(1998b) *Yakthung re Phungsoktimma Mundhum*; Gangtok, Sikkim

(1999) The Limboos of the Eastern Himalayas with special reference to Sikkim, Gangtok, Sikkim.

(2001) *Sumsenba Tongsingtok Mundhum.* Gangtok, Sikkim

(2002) Biodiversity of the Sikkim Himalayas. Gangtok, Sikkim.

(2003) *Mujoklung Khejoklung Mundhum.* Gangtok, Sikkim.

(2004) *Simering Mundhum.* Gangtok, Sikkim.

(2005a) The Philosophy and concepts of Yuma Samyo Tradition. Gingtok, Sikkim.

(2005b) Concept of Life After Life and Funerary Practices in Yuma Samyo Tradition. Gangtok, Sikkim.

(2008a) History, Culture and Customs of Sikkim. Gyan Publishing House, New Delhi.

(2008b) The Evolution of Man and the Modern Society in Mountainous Sikkim. Gyan Publishing House, New Delhi.

Tamsang, K.P. (1983). The Unknown and Untold Reality about The Lepchas. Kalimpong, West Bengal.

Zimmer, Heinrich (1969). Philosophies of India. Edited by Joseph Campbell. Pub. By Princeton Univ. Press. New Jersey.

INDEX

Y